LEFTOVER SALMON

LEFTOVER SALMON

Thirty Years of Festival!

Tim Newby

ROWMAN & LITTLEFIELD
Lanham • Boulder • New York • London

Published by Rowman & Littlefield
An imprint of The Rowman & Littlefield Publishing Group, Inc.
4501 Forbes Boulevard, Suite 200, Lanham, Maryland 20706
www.rowman.com

Unit A, Whitacre Mews, 26-34 Stannary Street, London SE11 4AB

British Library Cataloguing in Publication Information Available

Library of Congress Cataloging-in-Publication Data

Newby, Tim, 1974– author.
Title: Leftover Salmon : thirty years of festival! / Tim Newby.
Description: Lanham, Maryland : Rowman & Littlefield, [2019] | Includes bibliographical refer-
ences and index.
Identifiers: LCCN 2018032300 (print) | LCCN 2018035038 (ebook) | ISBN 9781538113301 (elec-
tronic) | ISBN 9781538113295 (cloth : alk. paper)
Subjects: LCSH: Leftover Salmon (Musical group) | Jam bands—United States. | Bluegrass musi-
cians—United States—Biography.
Classification: LCC ML421.L415 (ebook) | LCC ML421.L415 N38 2018 (print) | DDC 781.64092/
2 [B]—dc23
LC record available at https://lccn.loc.gov/2018032300

∞™ The paper used in this publication meets the minimum requirements of
American National Standard for Information Sciences Permanence of Paper
for Printed Library Materials, ANSI/NISO Z39.48-1992.

Printed in the United States of America

CONTENTS

PREFACE

Vince Herman's unrestrained laughter echoed around his house. I had just told him that his good friend and mentor, Bruce Hampton, once said to me, "Leftover Salmon was the only band to make state birds evaporate and get healthier." Herman's laughter was infectious and built every time he thought again about Hampton's seemingly nonsensical quote. It was a classic Hampton quote, that on the surface may seem to make no sense, but upon deeper thought makes perfect sense. It spoke to the absurdity Leftover Salmon has embraced since first coming together three decades ago when they added drums to bluegrass and turned the staid, traditional style on its head.

As I sat in Herman's living room flipping through old notebooks and digging through boxes of memorabilia, you could smell thirty years of history. Thirty years of Polyethnic Cajun slamgrass. Or maybe it was just the musty smell of old newspapers that is so distinct; or perhaps it was simply the smell of Herman's joint as he stood over my shoulder pointing things out as I dug through box after box. I was in Herman's living room continuing a journey that had begun when I first approached Leftover Salmon's manager John Joy about writing a book on the band. They were about to celebrate thirty years together, no small feat, but more importantly, they are a band who, while not always getting the mainstream recognition and wider acclaim they deserve, are massively influential. Their presence and influence are felt and seen in countless bands they have mentored and inspired over those thirty years, and it was that story that needed to be told. Through the course of my research I have lost count of the number of times someone told me, "I would not be doing what I am doing now if it was not for Leftover Salmon," or, "They are the most important band in my life," or some similar statement acknowledging their importance. Each of those interviews made it clear how necessary Leftover Salmon's story was to tell.

I was in college when I first discovered Salmon's music tacked as a filler to the end of a live Phish show tape a friend passed onto me. I wish I could I say exactly what show and song were on that tape, as it would make this story much cooler, but I can't. As a twenty-year-old then, I had no idea I would be writing a book about that music as a forty-three-year-old now. That first exposure did what Salmon's music always does—it inspired me, made me smile, and made me want to have a really good time.

A few years after that initial discovery, on a weekend when we packed way too many people into a 1990 Chevy Corsica and sacrificed necessary supplies we would need for the weekend to make more room for beer, I saw Leftover Salmon for the first time in the mountains of West Virginia at the AllGood Festival. On a chilly, wet night, with a head full of good times and some of my best friends (Ben, Pat, Russ, and Skuz), Salmon showed there is nothing better than having a good time with good friends, while listening to good music. That night Salmon led a large contingent of fans in parade formation across the stage in full costume. My friends and I shared their energy and excitement in the audience. Since that show, as Herman so accurately stated from stage that night, "In no way, shape or form, has the party ended." For Leftover Salmon, the party has not ended, as few bands have been able to stick around for thirty years as they have done. Even fewer bands leave a legacy that establishes them as a truly special, once-in-a-lifetime band. And no band has done all that and had as much fun as Leftover Salmon.

Since their earliest days as a forward-thinking, progressive bluegrass band who had the balls to add drums to the mix and was unafraid to stir in any number of highly combustible styles into their ever-evolving sound, to their role as a key player in the jamband scene that emerged in the nineties, to being pioneers of the modern jamgrass scene, through days of tragedy and rebirth, to their current status as elder statesmen, they have cast a huge, influential shadow over every festival they play. Leftover Salmon has been a crucial link in keeping alive the traditional music of the past while at the same time pushing the music forward with their own weirdly unique style. When listening to Leftover Salmon it is easy to draw a line that runs straight from Bill Monroe to John Hartford to the Grateful Dead to Hot Rize to Little Feat to New Grass Revival to Col. Bruce Hampton and end with Leftover Salmon. Connecting all those disparate sounds is no easy feat, but Salmon pulls it off with acrobatic ease. It is simply what they have done since first forming thirty years ago in Boulder, Colorado.

Their story starts in Boulder, with a chance encounter between two young musicians in the Walrus Saloon on a late October evening in 1985. Emmitt was there playing a show with his Left Hand String Band and Herman, who had just arrived in Boulder early that day after a cross-country drive from West Virginia, stopped in looking for a beer, a burger, and some bluegrass music to listen to. The two become friends. They began playing music together whenever the opportunity arose, at house parties, in the Left Hand String Band, and in the campgrounds of the bluegrass festivals they frequented around Colorado. At one of those festivals in Telluride in 1989, they met a banjo picker, Mark Vann, from Virginia, whom they recognized as a similar musically mischievous soul. After a couple of campground jams and a late-night show at the Roma during that Telluride Bluegrass Festival, a new band—Leftover Salmon—was formed. Emmitt, Herman, and Vann would affectionately come to be known as the "The Big Three," and form the nucleus of Salmon for the next decade.

In their thirty years together as a band, Leftover Salmon has lived at the edge of the music world, blazing their own path and avoiding easy description. During that time, they have released eight studio albums, three live albums, played over four thousand shows, and been at the forefront of the jamband and progressive bluegrass scenes. Through those years the band has experienced turnover in their ranks. Each of those lineups defined an era and the sound of the band and furthered the story. Each chapter in this book reflects the change in personnel as they are named for various members of the band. Salmon's story is told chronologically with those different band members serving as guide-posts for the journey.

Since the band's humble beginnings born from Drew Emmitt's bluegrass outfit, the Left Hand String Band, and Herman's Cajun-jug band the Salmon Heads, Leftover Salmon has always tiptoed the line between genres with their musically diverse approach of effortlessly bouncing from one style to another. They found their own piece of musical real estate existing somewhere between bluegrass and rock 'n' roll. It is musical real estate not settled before Leftover Salmon slam-grassed their way onto it, planted their freak flag, and created something entirely new. It is a sound uncomfortable to some. As bluegrass icon Sam Bush says, "When the bluegrass people think you're playing rock and the rock people think you're playing bluegrass, you're on the right track."[1] Leftover Salmon was on the right track.

There have been other attempts at this fusion of bluegrass and rock 'n' roll. The Earl Scruggs Revue, John Hartford's *Aereo-Plain*, David Bromberg, and New Grass Revival immediately come to mind, but no one has done it quite like Leftover Salmon. "It was like Sam Bush was thrown into a Vitamix with Robert Hunter and Hunter S. Thompson," says famed festival MC, musician, and educator Joe Craven of Salmon's music. "They have since been heaving themselves and their fans—in Evel Knievel style—across a Grand Canyon of the American vernacular. Their music is filled with delicious desperation, debauchery, deliverance (as in the movie, or maybe not), and some lovely tropical coconuts."

Over the years, Salmon has never had a hit song or mega-selling album, never crossed over into the mainstream (beyond a brief flirtation in the nineties), but they have amassed a passionate legion of fans, including many legendary musical icons who sing their praises every chance they get. "They should be ten times the size they are," says Col. Bruce Hampton.

"We are not a commercial band," explains Emmitt with a sense of pride in his voice. "We are ever the underdog band. We are the band that clawed our way out. We toured in a school bus for years and did everything grassroots style from scratch. We are the band that never got radio help or financial backing. None of that. Everything this band has gotten is purely from the love of music and touring and I am proud of that. Sometimes I wonder what would have happened had we gotten some of those breaks other bands got, but historically in the music business the bands that set trends, the bands that come before, or start movements are not necessarily the bands that get huge."

Leftover Salmon came first and did help start many movements. They were part of the first wave of jambands originally lumped together on the H.O.R.D.E. Festival and helped spawn a new sound and style, often referred to as jamgrass, that has seen bands including The String Cheese Incident, Yonder Mountain String Band, Railroad Earth, Greensky Bluegrass, the Infamous Stringdusters, and many others follow in their footsteps. Their lasting impact and legacy is not only in the music they have created, but also the countless bands and musicians they have influenced.

Along the way, Leftover Salmon has established themselves as one of the foremost stewards of Americana music, comfortably traveling down the highway of American music and making all of it their own. They belong in the long lineage of bands defying simple categorization, who instead set their own musical agenda. Like their musical forefathers Hot Rize, New Grass Revival, and Little Feat, they have achieved greatness, suffered loss, and found rebirth. Like so many bands who experienced tragedy and hard times, Leftover Salmon could have easily faded away and become a footnote in the long history of American music, but much like their namesake, they persevered, swimming upstream through obstacles and struggles, and in year thirty are still standing and playing some of the best music of their career.

They are Leftover Salmon. This is their story.

ACKNOWLEDGMENTS

The most important thing to be acknowledged is the music of Leftover Salmon; without it there is no story. No matter how compelling the band's history is, it is because of the music that we pay attention. Music is meant to remind us of the good times and help get us through the bad times, and that is what Leftover Salmon's music has always done

Leftover Salmon's story is one of friendship, triumph, tragedy, rebirth, and is best told through the voices of the band, their friends, their heroes, and all those they influenced over the years. This book is built on those voices and includes bands who have known Leftover Salmon since their earliest days, to bands who they played with at the beginning of the jamband scene, to bands they mentored along the way. This includes members of groups such as Hot Rize, New Grass Revival, Widespread Panic, Los Lobos, the Infamous Stringdusters, Aquarium Rescue Unit, Yonder Mountain String Band, The String Cheese Incident, moe., the Samples, Acoustic Junction, and many others.

The outpouring of love for Leftover Salmon that shone through in every interview over the last three years as I researched this book served as a reminder of how much Salmon has shared over their thirty years and the massive influence they have wielded. Every conversation reinforced the importance of telling their story. A huge thank-you to everyone who was kind enough to take some time to meet with me, chat on the phone, or share some thoughts by email. Many new friendships were born from those conversations and were an unintended, special bonus to this project. Quotes not cited directly in the text are taken from those interviews I conducted between April 2015 and April 2018. The full list of interviewees is too lengthy to thank here, but is fully acknowledged in the bibliography. I do need to recognize Adam Aijala and Jeff Sipe for their immense help and going above and beyond what was required by always being there with an answer.

Thank you to Leftover Salmon archivist Chris Mrachek and former tour manager Johnny Pfarr. Chris answered countless emails clarifying show dates and sent me stacks of CDs to help with my research. Johnny was always there to answer a question or email and was a huge help through this process.

An extra special thank-you goes to manager John Joy. Col. Bruce Hampton once told me, "There is no nicer human being than John Joy." He could have not been more right. This project started with an email pitch to publicist Perry Serpa, who was working with Salmon at the time. Perry liked what he read and passed it along to John and helped us connect (Thanks, Perry!). Over a lengthy conversation, John and I both agreed this was a story needing to be told. Throughout this process, John and I spoke often and at great length. Without his help and guidance, you would not be holding this book in your hands now. Thank you, John!

Thank you is not a big enough phrase for all of Leftover Salmon past and present and their immense help. I especially need to recognize Drew Emmitt, Vince Herman, Greg Garrison, Andy Thorn, Alwyn Robinson, and Erik Deutsch, for their time, thoughts, never-ending help, and willingness to let me tell their story. Without them and their openness to answer yet another question, email, or text from me, there would be no book.

The first interview I did was with Drew, who opened himself up with a series of interviews each lasting nearly two hours. His thoughtful insight provided the building blocks for the rest of my research. A later visit to Vince's house in Oregon, and a couple days spent going through boxes, crates, and footlockers unlocked many long-forgotten stories, dates, and facts and helped to crystallize those first interviews with Drew. Thank you both for all the times you have spent sharing your thoughts, memories, and stories with me. This project could not have happened without those many conversations.

Finally, a huge thank-you to my wife, Melissa, who has put up with me as I have obsessed over this project, as I continually fill dinner conversations and road trips with talk of Leftover Salmon and the latest thing I discovered. She has read drafts, made suggestions, and listened to ideas. She is the quite simply the best and makes it possible for me to do this. I could not have done it without her.

Chapter 1

DREW EMMITT

He doesn't play like anyone else. I have never met anyone who can play like Drew. He can play faster than anyone I have ever played with, but the speed is not the main feature of his playing, because he knows the rules of bluegrass. He knows when it is time to play the melody and when it is not time to. I can literally stand right beside him and not be able to figure out what he is doing and that is always a sign of my favorite players.—*Sam Bush*

"**I** don't know if it was the first time I saw Hot Rize, but it was at the Bandshell out in the park in Boulder," recalls Drew Emmitt. "I ended up picking with a bunch of people after the show including Tim [O'Brien]. I asked him if he would give me mandolin lessons. It was 1980 and he was still teaching. He said, 'Yes,' and I started taking lessons from him, which was a really wonderful thing."

At the time, Emmitt was just out of high school, working odd jobs and playing music locally with friends. The chance to learn from bluegrass legend and Hot Rize founder Tim O'Brien was a defining moment in the young musician's life. Since its founding in 1978 in his hometown of Boulder, Colorado, Hot Rize had a profound impact on Emmitt. "There was just something about the Hot Rize crew. The way they sang. Pete Wernick on the banjo, Nick Forster was such a great bass player, Charles Sawtelle on guitar, and Tim O'Brien. They just put it all together for me. They were the be-all and end-all for me." Hot Rize's forward-thinking, modern form of bluegrass, which incorporated elements of rock, jazz, Gypsy, and country, broke free of the bonds of traditional bluegrass and helped validate Emmitt's yearning and desire to find a way to combine both the traditional bluegrass he loved and the rock 'n' roll tugging at his soul. O'Brien is a multitalented performer, and while it is his vocal skills often garnering the most attention, it was his mandolin playing that spoke directly to the young Emmitt. "He is such an innovator," says Emmitt. "He was the first player I saw bend strings on a mandolin like in rock 'n' roll. That grabbed me because I was way into electric guitar and anything putting the two genres together was influential for me."

Emmitt took a handful of lessons from O'Brien, following the show at the Bandshell, over the course of a couple of weeks at O'Brien's house on 19th and Grove in downtown Boulder. He calls those lessons his "big introduction to bluegrass." The handful of lessons left an indelible mark on Emmitt, who was still trying to discover his style, saying, "Those lessons helped get me going on my way as a mandolin player. Tim has so much knowledge it was almost too much for me." O'Brien remembers those lessons as well, but he recalls a much more developed musician than the always-humble Emmitt recalls of himself at the time. He says he often joked with Emmitt, saying, "You don't need any lessons from me, but let's just hang out and drink coffee for an hour."[1] While they did drink coffee and hang out plenty during these lessons, O'Brien also imparted much knowledge to Emmitt. He was a willing student, and his eagerness to learn and infectious energy inspired O'Brien to extend their normal hour-long lesson time. "Drew could make a pretty good sound," says O'Brien, "but in a lot of ways he was already onto a style of his own, a style he still plays. He was into double-stops and fast chords. He had no problem with tempo. He could play as fast as you wanted him to play."

The sheer talent existing between Emmitt and O'Brien is mind-boggling. To be able to witness two masters of their instruments at the beginning of their careers would be a fly-on-the-wall moment, as them working to develop their craft is a humbling perspective rarely seen. Thinking of the pair casually sitting in O'Brien's living room trading licks back and forth and practicing scales, imagine forty years later if you were to assemble the Mount Rushmore of progressive bluegrass mandolin players—you must make space for both the student and his idol-teacher on that monument. Years later, O'Brien likened those afternoon lessons with Emmitt to taking a nice drive in a beautiful part of the country. "You just look out the window and say, 'Look over there, that would be a nice place to go.' I was just showing him things, pointing out places that might be nice to go to. It was already in front of him, he just needed to take a longer look at it. I was just there while he was learning. Maybe I helped him find a few more doors to open sooner than he would have, but he was already well on his way."

Emmitt was born in Tucson, Arizona, May 24, 1961. When he was three, his family moved to Nashville, Tennessee, after his father took a job as the managing editor at Vanderbilt University Press. According to local lore, the house the Emmitts lived in was once Hank Williams's summer house. It was an idyllic place to grow up. It had an expansive yard that backed up to the woods, providing plenty of room for Emmitt and his siblings—an older brother, older sister, and younger sister—to explore and play. Emmitt says, "We lived on a farm and we grew our own food and raised chickens." One evening, when Emmitt was eight, his dad was preparing to go out back to kill a chicken for dinner. Emmitt was standing on the patio with his dad as he prepared his gun to shoot the chicken. "He cocked it," says Emmitt, "which in retrospect was a really bad idea to do right there with people around. He was trying to hit the safety and accidentally hit the trigger. It was a real hair trigger and it went off." Emmitt's dad had the gun pointed down. When it went off the bullet ricocheted off the patio and broke into two fragments that ended up in both of Emmitt's legs. "It was pretty traumatic," says Emmitt. "The doctor could only get the fragments out of my right leg. They went deeper into the left leg and they couldn't get it out as they were worried it would cripple me." Despite the worry, Emmitt would make a full recovery and suffer no lasting effects besides a pair of nasty scars, one on each leg.

For Emmitt, his musical journey began as a young child. The family was an extremely creative one, as both of Emmitt's parents were writers and musically inclined. His mother played the piano, while his father played the autoharp and was a powerful singer. Music was omnipresent around the house growing up. "My parents played a lot of music. My mom played a lot of classical music and folk music," reminisces Emmitt. "They played Gordon Lightfoot, Kris Kristofferson, Josh White, Peter, Paul, & Mary, and that kind of stuff. My older brother and sister started getting me into stuff like Yes, Elton John, Black Sabbath, and later Led

Zeppelin. I had a lot of different influences growing up." Despite those influences as a child, the first album he bought himself in middle school, *Earl Scruggs: Performing with his Family & Friends*, was closer to the musical path he followed later in life than what he was hearing around the house growing up. Emmitt admits while he had a passing interest in bluegrass music growing up, he did not get deep into the genre until his teenage years. His older brother played harmonica, guitar, and saxophone and helped start Emmitt playing the guitar when he was five. Emmitt says at first, he learned to play mostly folk songs, but shortly after picking up the instrument, his dad bought him a John Denver songbook, and he began learning those tunes. He says he gradually moved on from Denver and began getting into more country and folk-rock type bands including the Eagles, Jim Croce, and Crosby, Stills, & Nash.

When Emmitt was twelve his father got a job at *The Denver Post* and the family moved to Boulder, Colorado, thirty miles north of Denver. It was a move that almost did not take place as the night before the family was to move, they barely avoided tragedy. It was a hot, August night, and Emmitt's dad left the door to the garden open. "I was twelve and told him it's a bad idea," Emmitt says. "I told him, 'It's summertime—something may come in.' My dad was pretty stubborn. He didn't want to listen to a twelve-year-old." The phone rang in the middle of the night, and Emmitt's mom got up to answer it. A copperhead snake that slithered in through the open door was coiled in the hallway and struck her three times. His dad heard her yell and went to help and was struck twice. The twelve-year-old Emmitt called an ambulance but knew it would be some time before it arrived. He had grown up in the outdoors and did what he learned at the time was the way to handle snake bites. He says, "All I knew was to put a tourniquet on and try to make a razor cut into an X and suck the poison out. Now they say that is not what you are supposed to do, but at the time all I knew. I was raised in areas with poisonous snakes and did what I had been taught to do." The ambulance arrived shortly after Emmitt administered first aid. His mom, who had gotten the brunt of the attack, almost died because of the amount of venom she had taken in. Despite her legs swelling up to nearly twice their normal size, both she and Emmitt's dad made full recoveries. "It was pretty damn scary," says Emmitt. "It was almost like there was a force to keep us there and it almost kept us there completely. It was crazy. My parents could have died." Emmitt's dad was released from the hospital first and flew out to start his new job in Denver. The rest of the family joined him a few days later after Emmitt's mom was released.

The move to Colorado would come to greatly shape the young Emmitt's personality and interests. "This was before Boulder was so cosmopolitan and trendy," he says. "It was just a college town. It was before the mall and all that. It was a great place to be growing up in the seventies. I was exposed to a lot of music. The festivals at the college are what got me into the bluegrass thing." Boulder and the surrounding area came to define Emmitt, with his love for skiing, the Rocky Mountains infusing his music and draping his lyrics with tales of mountains, willow trees near bends in the river, and full-moon valleys where dreams do come true. "There is something unexplainable about Colorado which permeates everything you do," Emmitt explains, "and I guess I can't avoid writing about it."[2]

During high school Emmitt would play his first paying music gig. "I had an acoustic duo with a guy named Chuck Hirshberg who played banjo," says Emmitt. "We were both fourteen and played at a backyard party. We had a bluegrass songbook and we learned all these traditional songs." The pair made twenty dollars apiece at that first gig. The excitement of playing live music for a crowd for the first time struck Hirshberg: "Man, I was so enthusiastic about it. I got the feeling we were both in the same place. We didn't play with anybody else and we both loved music. It was so exciting for me, and I assume him as well, to be just playing with someone else. You both got the same tune in your head. You are both excited about the sounds coming out. It was exciting for the first time to have a musical conversation."

Their musical conversation continued over the next couple of years at other parties and open mics around town. They landed their first big gig when they got hired to play at a local restaurant, the Colorado Coal Company. For the inexperienced Emmitt and Hirshberg, the evening was a rousing success when one of the patrons of the restaurant got up during their set, doing an exuberant traditional buck-and-wing dance. This got the rest of the crowd riled up as they began clapping and dancing along with him, creating a truly thrilling atmosphere for the two teenage musicians. "It was exhilarating," says Hirshberg. This led to them scoring a few more paying gigs at some of the local bars. These gigs came with the bonus for the underage pair of being able to, through their connections at the bars, attend other shows despite not being old enough to enter the establishments otherwise.

The Emmitt–Hirshberg set at the time was filled largely with bluegrass standards including "Dueling Banjos," "Foggy Mountain Breakdown," and "Little Maggie." It also featured an Emmitt-sung version of the Beatles "I've Just Seen a Face." The novice musicians even tried their hand at songwriting and attempted, without much success, to put music to a few ballads Emmitt's father had written about outlaws. Hirshberg remembers another Emmitt-sung cover they regularly included in their set: "There was a Billy Joel song Drew used to sing, 'Travelin' Prayer.' We did not know enough at the time to despise it. The reason it attracted our attention is it had a banjo in it. It was a piece of shit song. I think even Billy Joel thinks it's a piece of shit song." It seems when the Emmitt–Hirshberg duo ended a few years later, so did Emmitt's version of this song, as there is no evidence of him ever playing the song with any of his other bands since, though one can always cross one's fingers and hope. Even at that young age, Hirshberg noticed Emmitt's superior talent was clearly advanced beyond kids his age. Hirshberg recalls how he was generous with his playing, doing exactly what was required in each song and allowing room for others to play.

As so often happens with childhood friends, Hirshberg and Emmitt grew apart due to the normal reasons one changes friends in high school; new acquaintances, girls, and distance. Hirshberg also thinks his lack of desire to practice was frustrating to Emmitt, who was striving for perfection. He remembers Emmitt calling him and asking why he did not come over to play music anymore. Hirshberg says, "I just danced around his question and said, 'It doesn't sound good anymore.' He said to me, 'Of course it doesn't sound good, you don't ever come by to practice.' I remember that phone conversation clearly and his exasperation with me."

Throughout his early teens, Emmitt played mostly guitar before getting into the banjo. In addition to his acoustic duo with Hirshberg, he played electric guitar in a series of garage bands throughout high school. The chance to play music live provided an outlet and escape for Emmitt, who admits in an understated manner, "High school was an interesting time for me." His parents were going through a divorce, which led Emmitt to move out of his parents' house and in with his older brother when he was seventeen. Before they stopped playing music together and grew apart, Hirshberg recalls bonding with Emmitt not only over music, but also over their difficult situations at home: "We both had these dysfunctional families and we felt connected because of that."

Emmitt attended Boulder High School for two years, during which time he often ditched school in his friend's van to go to the park to party and play music all day. His many absences from school led to him being expelled. Despite this major bump in the road, Emmitt's mother remained supportive of his music. He says, "She was amazing and saw the vision where I was headed [musically]. She said, 'Stay home and play guitar.'" Therefore, for his entire junior year of high school, Emmitt worked odd jobs, stayed home, and practiced. It was a time that allowed him to focus on his craft and begin to hone his own, personal style. For his senior year, he enrolled in a local, alternative high school called the September School. The independent school, with its small class sizes and focus on individual development, was perfect for Emmitt, who struggled in a traditional school setting. "It was awesome. I had a songwriting class. I had a class on field botany. I had a class on great American authors. I had algebra. I had these great teachers and I finally did well in school." One of his teachers was the school's principal, Joe Sundrum, who taught the songwriting class. Sundrum was a musician and played in a local band called the Chutney Brothers. He was also good friends with another local Boulder band, Navarro, which was one of Emmitt's favorite bands. Navarro found their greatest success in the seventies when they served as Carole King's backing band, touring regularly with her and playing on a pair of her albums. Sundrum invited Navarro's two primary songwriters, Mark Hallman (who also played with another longtime Colorado resident, Dan Fogelberg) and Robert McEntee, to come to school to help teach his songwriting class. "Those guys, especially Robert, had a lot of good things to say about songwriting that stuck with me," says Emmitt. "Then Navarro played a benefit at the school and I got to meet them and I thought they were rock stars. They were an amazing band. They were a great band. They were a huge influence on my music for sure." At the benefit, Emmitt also met Navarro's rhythm section, drummer Michael Wooten and bassist Rob Galloway. Over the ensuing years, the pair played with several local bands Emmitt often saw. Their strong playing resonated with Emmitt, as they later served as the rhythm section for Leftover Salmon during the band's earliest, formative years.

The positive and creative atmosphere of the September School had a dramatic effect on Emmitt, who had previously struggled in school. His interest piqued in academics for the first time, he buckled down and finished high school in 1978. After high school, he went onto pursue a music degree at the University of Colorado. However, the traditional school setting again did not mesh with Emmitt's independent, nonconformist, creative spirit, and he left after one semester. He worked a string of odd jobs, including a stint with the forest service, but nothing stuck until he began working as the groundskeeper at a local preschool. He gained more responsibility over the years and began working in the classroom. He found he really enjoyed working and helping kids and thought of becoming certified as a teacher and making a career of it. His career plan took another step forward when he picked up a woman who was hitchhiking. She worked at a local Montessori school and said there were job openings there. He applied and was hired as a teaching assistant. He found his struggles as a student made him able to relate easily with other like-minded students. He became the director of afternoon programs and taught music classes. It was a job that, in addition to the satisfaction of helping other students who were struggling as he once had, allowed him the freedom to work during the day and keep his nights free so he could still play music. He would work at the Montessori school through the 1980s, rising early to make it to school every day, while staying out late at night to play gigs with his bands.

Emmitt found the pull of bluegrass starting to become inescapable. Not only was it the music that spoke to him, but also the atmosphere surrounding it he found appealing. "I realized there was a whole culture attached to it. I loved the scene of people getting together around the campfire and playing. That's what got me."[3] Emmitt began to immerse himself in bluegrass. He was studying the genre's masters, explaining, "I got into the Stanley Brothers before I got into Bill Monroe, strangely enough. When I began going to the Rocky Mountain Bluegrass Festival I got exposed to a lot of bluegrass there. Bands like the Seldom Scene, who became a big influence, Don Reno, the Bluegrass Cardinals, some local bands like the Bluegrass Patriots, and Front Range. All kinds of really great traditional bands. I was also getting into Hot Rize, New Grass Revival, and David Grisman. Grisman's playing was a big influ-

ence on me." He was spending as much time picking and playing bluegrass and traditional music as possible. The rapid growth of his skills
exhibited his devotion to practicing and honing his craft. In his late
teens, he discovered the instrument he would redefine with his innovative style. His mom, who was extremely supportive of her son's musical
endeavors, bought him his first mandolin. With joy, he recalls, "She
bought me an $80 Kentucky Mandolin. She just felt I should have one,
which was a great idea." Emmitt was mostly familiar with the mandolin
through the occasional Led Zeppelin tune, such as "Going to California," or "The Battle of Evermore," on which Jimmy Page and John Paul
Jones play the instrument. With this unlikely starting point, Emmitt
began his exploration of the mandolin. In 2014 at the Telluride Bluegrass Festival, Emmitt, through an introduction from longtime friend
Sam Bush, met John Paul Jones and let the rock legend know of the
influence he had on the young, budding mandolin player. Emmitt says
the mandolin "really spoke to me, and I put the banjo down at that
point. I saw Hot Rize and they changed my whole view of what bluegrass could be." He saw them play at the Bandshell in Boulder a short
while later in 1980 and approached Tim O'Brien about taking lessons
from him. O'Brien was impressed with Emmitt's advanced skill, much
of which he first picked up from a Jesse McReynolds mandolin instruc-
tion book. Emmitt only took a handful of lessons from O'Brien, but the
two developed a bond lasting for forty years.

Emmitt's next musical partner, who became part of his first real
working band, came when a singer and her husband were looking for a
place to live and saw an ad Emmitt and his brother placed for a room
they were renting in the house they shared in the foothills outside of
Boulder. Emily Cantrell and her husband Mark moved into the Emmitt
brothers' house in early 1981. She and Emmitt clicked immediately.
Cantrell remembers how "Drew just whipped out his guitar and we
started playing and singing together. We just hit it off musically and I
thought, 'Wow, this guy has a great voice!' We both liked California
country rock songs like 'Desperado' by the Eagles, and 'Night Rider's
Lament' by Mike Burton. We also liked traditional and progressive
bluegrass—we listened to a lot of the Seldom Scene. And we had both
grown up in Tennessee." Despite the age difference between the two
(Emmitt was nineteen and Cantrell was twenty-six), she recalls their

musical connection as being special as they had "an even spirit between them."

Cantrell and Emmitt realized they were both natural harmony singers and their voices meshed perfectly. They were performing around Boulder at parties, restaurants, and bars. Playing as a duo throughout the fall of 1981 and into the summer of 1982, they secured regular gigs at Jose Muldoon's, a Mexican restaurant no longer existing, and a local bar, the Hungry Farmer. Their sets reflected the pair's shared interest in bluegrass, including old-timey traditional songs and covers of some of their bluegrass heroes like the Seldom Scene.

At one of Cantrell and Emmitt's regular lunchtime sets at the Hungry Farmer, a young local musician, Michael Slingsby, who was on his lunch break from his job as an architect, happened to catch their set. He noticed Emmitt was playing a Gibson Hummingbird, the same guitar he owned. When Emmitt and Cantrell took a set break, Slingsby approached Emmitt to talk about their guitars. The two quickly realized they were kindred spirits, and the seeds of a long friendship were sown. In this long-lasting friendship Leftover Salmon found one of their first and most loyal fans in Slingsby, who was present for many of the crucial events in the development of the band. Because of this and his willingness to help his friends in any way he could, he was often wrongly thought to be the band's manager, even though he has never filled any official role with the band. Many times over the earliest years, the band asked him to fill the manager role for their various projects and help with booking shows, but he says, "The truth is I was never suited for that type of thing. I am not a manager type guy." Still, at early Salmon shows, Slingsby usually could be found working the door, checking IDs, collecting the cover, or helping the band load and unload their gear. The band jokingly referred to him as Manager Mike from the stage, adding to the confusion. Slingsby says when people asked him if he was the manager, his response was always the same, "I managed to show up most of the time." Slingsby says on one occasion he was compensated for his services. After a late night of helping the band haul their gear in and out of the venue, Emmitt handed him a dollar and said, "There, now you are a paid professional."

Slingsby and his roommate, Glenn Keefe, who played bass and worked at the same firm as Slingsby, were hosting a party at their house in Left Hand Canyon in Jamestown, a small town a few miles north of

Boulder, the weekend after Slingsby and Emmitt first met. Slingsby invited Emmitt and Cantrell to attend. Like many of the parties in the area at the time hosted by musicians, most of the guests brought their instruments and the sweet sounds of bluegrass picking filled the evening. As they played late into the night, Emmitt and Cantrell connected with Keefe and banjo picker Nolan Farmer, who was Slingsby's brother-in-law at the time. Slingsby says he recognized that even though "Drew had only been playing the mandolin for a short time, he was already better than anybody you could find around. He was the kind of guy who could walk into a bluegrass picking circle and instantly raise the level of musicianship of everyone there." Emmitt, Cantrell, Keefe, and Farmer bonded as they played that night. Cantrell says they realized, "We sound like a bluegrass band, so perhaps we should form one." With Cantrell on guitar, Emmitt on mandolin, Keefe on bass, and Farmer on banjo, they christened themselves the Porphyry Mountain Band. The name came from a local mountain near Jamestown, where Keefe and Slingsby lived.

Shortly after forming, the Porphyry Mountain Band saw an ad looking for a bluegrass band to play for two weeks at the grand opening of a new May D&F Department Store in downtown Denver. "We applied and got the job. We meshed during those two weeks because we were performing several times a day, every day," says Cantrell. Upon returning from Denver, they added Emmitt's banjo teacher, Glen Henderson, to the band on fiddle, and hired Eric Holle on banjo to replace the departing Farmer. They began to play regular gigs at the bars around the local ski areas. Cantrell says they also played a lot of parties and weddings because Emmitt was "really well connected and had lots of friends."

The Porphyry Mountain Band's sets at the time pulled from some of Emmitt's favorite bands, including the Johnson Mountain Boys, an often-overlooked powerhouse from the bluegrass hotbed of Washington, DC. Emmitt says, "Not many people, even knowledgeable bluegrass fans, are familiar with the Johnson Mountain Boys, but they were a great, great, truly amazing band. Without them and what their music brought to me, I doubt I would have fallen in love with bluegrass." The Seldom Scene also heavily influenced Emmitt, and he included many of their songs in his sets. He was particularly enamored of the Seldom Scene's mandolinist, John Duffey. "Many people probably do not notice

An early publicity shot of the Porphyry Mountain Band on West Pearl Street in Boulder, Colorado, in 1982. From left, Glenn Keefe, Eric Holle, Emily Cantrell, Drew Emmitt, and Glen Henderson. Courtesy of Emily Cantrell.

his influence on my playing . . . At the time I listened to him intently and studied his tone. I liked his tone more than any other mandolinists."[4]

With Hot Rize leading the way, and young, up-and-coming bands such as the Reasonable Band, Gold Rush, and the Bluegrass Patriots making a big noise, and major bluegrass festivals in the region like the Telluride Bluegrass Festival and RockyGrass, bluegrass was experiencing a serious jolt of energy and enthusiasm in the Rocky Mountains in the eighties. Colorado's Front Range corridor was turning into a hotbed of acoustic music; there were regular jams, festivals, and picking parties. There was a growing, supportive network of venues like the Gold Hill Inn, the Stage Stop, and the Millsite Inn, which provided a welcoming environment for this type of music. "It was a great time to be playing bluegrass in Colorado," says Cantrell. "In the early eighties bluegrass was hitting a wave and becoming more popular, especially around Boulder."

The Porphyry Mountain Band would rename themselves the Tractors, due to their name often being mistaken for the Poor Free Mountain Band. Even with the name change, the band worked steadily in the area, taking part in the annual Telluride Bluegrass Festival band contest in 1984. "We didn't win," says Emmitt with a laugh, "that was the year every great Colorado bluegrass band entered. I think the Road Warriors won. The Bluegrass Patriots and Front Range were also there. It was like, 'Oh great we are up against all the best bands, really professional bands.' We did well, but we didn't win."

Shortly after the band contest, and despite the band starting to find greater success, Emmitt's time with the Tractors came to end. Cantrell, mostly by default due to her age, always served as the band's leader and primary singer, but Emmitt's undeniable drive, talent, high-energy performance style, and desire to take the band's sound into a more progressive realm, similar to what New Grass Revival was doing, hastened the end of his time with the band. Emmitt says, "Emily actually fired me because I was taking her spotlight. I had too much energy. She didn't like that, in her words, 'I was overshadowing her.'" Cantrell recalls the split came about mostly due to musical differences, as she "was called in a more traditional direction and Drew was moving in a more progressive direction." Cantrell continued with the Tractors for a short while longer without Emmitt before moving to Nashville, where she established herself as a solo artist. Cantrell and her husband would later appear as musicians in the classic Robert Redford movie *A River Runs Through It*. Despite the tensions often surrounding the end of bands, Cantrell looks back fondly on her time playing with Emmitt and recognizes, even at that young age, the unlimited potential he had.

> He was such a serious musician. Back then, we were having a great time, but were serious about the music. I had a lasting impression music was Drew's life. We kind of all knew we desired to be on bigger stages and to be professional musicians; it was not just a hobby for us. Drew has the X factor. You know you are hearing something special. I loved singing and playing with him. I always thought he would go far in the world of music. When we parted ways, he was experimenting with saxophone, as well as other instruments. I wouldn't have been surprised at any musical direction he took.

Emmitt says he was "really sad" following his dismissal from the Tractors and played in some local country bands to fill the time, which he called an interesting experience. He did not stay away from bluegrass long, though, as former bandmate Nolan Farmer, who left the Tractors before him, asked him if he wanted to sit in with the Left Hand String Band, a band Farmer and Keefe had recently joined. Local musician Keely Brunner formed the group in 1982, in the small town of Niwot, near Gold Hill, where Emmitt lived at the time. The band's name came from a left-handed Arapahoe Chief, Chief Niwot, who was called Chief Left Hand for short. Around Boulder there are many things named after Chief Left Hand, including Left Hand Canyon, Left Hand Brewing Company, and Left Hand Grange Hall, where Hot Rize played often in their early years.

Brunner was a longtime part of the local bluegrass and folk scene in Boulder since moving from Pennsylvania in the early seventies. He was a skilled guitarist with a sweet swinging voice, and played in several bands in the area, including Town and Country Review, which featured a young Tim O'Brien on fiddle. Town and Country Review was the first band O'Brien played with in Boulder after he moved from West Virginia in 1974. O'Brien met Brunner through the Folk Arts Music store (now called HB Woodsongs) which has long been at the center of the string band music scene in Boulder, serving as a hub for local musicians to connect through. He worked there with two of Brunner's Town and Country Review bandmates, Ritchie Mintz and Ned Alderman, who owned the store. O'Brien says, "Keely was a good friend. He was a lot of fun to play with. He was adventurous musically. He liked a little smoke and a little drink. He was a good guy, who was a great singer and a solid guitarist."

Brunner lived in Left Hand Canyon outside of Boulder and hosted regular picking parties centered around this growing group of bluegrass musicians in the area. These musicians were not playing for an audience at the time. They were simply playing for themselves at parties and having a good time while doing it. They were developing the skills that helped this talented collection of musicians, including Brunner, O'Brien, Dobro player Buck Buckner, fiddler Danny Elmore, and Dan Sadowski—better known as Pastor Mustard, the longtime MC of the Telluride Bluegrass Festival—to create a scene rooted in bluegrass but stretching into something different. Brunner was instrumental in helping to create and foster this scene. He would often record his friends performing impromptu shows in his living room, dubbing cassettes of these shows and passing them around. "He loved music and he loved singing and he loved picking," recalls O'Brien. "He was in the business of making that happen however he could."

Brunner's hosting of regular Sunday afternoon picking parties was a way he made music happen at the time. He was responsible for bringing people together and provided a supportive environment to the creative musical experimentation in the air. "People were taking chances within the music there because they felt comfortable to do and try different stuff," says Randy Kelley, another local musician who regularly attended those parties. "We had so much fun and there was this willingness to do goofy things. We could be playing a fairly traditional bluegrass tune and the banjo player could start going off in a different direction, and we would all follow him."[5] Much as with other cities or areas that became musical hubs defined by one particular musical style, Colorado became entrenched as the place to be for anyone who was inclined toward progressive bluegrass or string band music. The flood of transplants, in addition to the locals who were already playing this type of music, helped to foster a scene built around local gigs and parties that served as a breeding ground for a plethora of musicians looking to form bands.

Benny Galloway, a singer and guitarist, who would find fame as a songwriter and with his band the Wayward Sons, moved to the area in the late seventies and was part of this exciting time of exploding bluegrass music in Colorado. He experienced many of those parties in Left Hand Canyon:

> I was surrounded by so much music and so many fun-loving folks; I couldn't help but be entirely absorbed. What a scene. Everywhere we went, any day of the week, it was always about pickin' tunes. What a unique situation; there couldn't be a better place for a songwriter to practice his trade and perform new material. It was easy for the songs to take on a mind of their own. Drums, no drums, plugged in, not plugged in, the sky was the limit. I was convinced I not only found the Holy Grail of acoustic-style music, I had fallen right into it. I met people who would help shape the way I wrote, played, and performed. In turn, we became more than friends. We became family, a musical family.[6]

This bluegrass scene and musical family continued to develop over the years, furthering blossoming with the start of the Telluride Bluegrass Festival, RockyGrass Festival, Rocky Mountain Folk Festival, and many others, and was firmly established in the Boulder region by the time Farmer invited Emmitt to sit in with the Left Hand String Band in 1984. The gig was at a bar only a mile away from his house, so he agreed to come and sit in with the band. Emmitt's sit-in left such an impression on the band, when their mandolin player quit shortly after, they asked Emmitt if he would like to join full-time. He agreed and joined the group, which at the time included Farmer on banjo, Brunner on guitar, and Keefe on bass.

Brunner, who originally formed the band, was quite a few years older than Emmitt and initially served as the lead singer, as the band's sound was built around his folksier, more traditional bluegrass leanings. However, Emmitt, with his electrifying stage presence and strong songwriting, was soon fronting the band and, in his own words, "Kind of made it my own." Slingsby had been friends with Brunner for years and was familiar with his talents, but when it came to the Left Hand String Band, it was clear to him who powered the sound of the band: "I have always thought of Drew as the driving force in the Left Hand String Band."

In bassist Keefe, Emmitt found a willing conspirator in his desire to push the boundaries of traditional bluegrass music and to experiment with a more progressive style. Emmitt liked to play rock 'n' roll in a bluegrass style, and Keefe, who played a short-scale, solid-body electric bass, was perfectly suited for the task. Bluegrass legend O'Brien says the pair were "Two peas in a pod as adventurous, bluegrass jammers." Keefe was highly intelligent and had an intense love for music. He was a key element of the band as he helped book their gigs and served as the band's soundman during live performances, adjusting the sound from a personal monitor-board onstage. "Glenn and Drew and their good friendship at the time, they were the glue of the Left Hand String Band," Slingsby says. "It was Drew's band, but Glenn was instrumental. Glenn did all the booking, he did sound, and he played bass. The same was true of him in the early days of Leftover Salmon. I cannot emphasize that enough. None of it would have happened without him."

In addition to the evolution in sound and style, the band also saw its lineup change when banjo picker Farmer left shortly after Emmitt joined. The band replaced him with Gerald Bozarth from another local band, Gold Rush, who had found some success over the previous years.

The band's lineup further expanded again in 1986 when Bozarth invited his former Gold Rush bandmate, Dobro player Al Goll, to sit in at one of the band's regular Tuesday-night gigs at the Walrus Saloon. Much as with Emmitt a few years prior, the sit-in went well, and they extended an invitation to Goll to join the band full time. Goll, who had recently settled back in the area after a few years of living in Hawaii, was already a key cog of the bluegrass scene in the area. He was friendly with the guys in Hot Rize and often sat in with them at local shows.

Emmitt joined the band two years before Goll, and while Brunner was still in the band at the time Goll joined and doing a good portion of the singing, the band was now fully Emmitt's vision, and Goll noticed it immediately upon joining. "Everything was centered around Drew," he says. "We were doing a lot of his originals. He was a great writer back in the day and still is. It was more than just his talent as a singer and mandolin player. He had this aura about him. He was always positive, a smile on his face, very optimistic and just kind of drew you into his presence. People were drawn to him." As demonstrated over the years with Hirshberg, Cantrell, and anyone else who he played with, Emmitt's infectious energy pulled all those he encountered into his inspiring orbit and into whatever his latest musical adventure was at the time. This would continue, as his influence is clearly seen in the transformation of the sound of the Left Hand String Band. When he first joined, they adhered to a much more traditional sound, but Emmitt was beginning to get deeply into Sam Bush and New Grass Revival, and it was reflected in the evolution of the band's sound through Emmitt's developing, progressive songwriting.

Since their formation in 1971, New Grass Revival was at the forefront of the progressive revolution in bluegrass music. Even more so than Hot Rize, New Grass Revival was pushing forward the traditional sound of bluegrass music into uncharted realms. They incorporated lengthy jams into their songs, much the way psychedelic bands of the sixties did. They peppered their shows with covers far outside the normal bluegrass canon, including everything from Bob Marley to the Beatles to Townes Van Zandt to Jerry Lee Lewis. They also began spreading across the stage in the style of rock bands, with each member having their own microphone as opposed to jockeying for position around a single microphone. It was not only their music and how they played it setting them apart from other traditional bluegrass bands at the time, but also their style and dress. They ditched the usually conservative buttoned-up suit aesthetic for a more hippie, friendly look with their long hair, bushy beards, and scruffy jeans. With their nontraditional approach to the music and the way, they seemed to revel in bucking convention, "New Grass Revival was breaking ground by resynthesizing the folk and popular elements of bluegrass."[7] For Emmitt, who was equally inspired by both rock 'n' roll and bluegrass, the discovery of New Grass Revival marked a transformative moment for the young musician. He says, "Hot Rize was what gave me the inspiration to play bluegrass and mandolin. Tim O'Brien was my first big influence. When I discovered New Grass Revival it was even more up my alley. Once I saw Sam Bush play that was the vision. It was like playing rock 'n' roll with bluegrass instruments. Combining rock and bluegrass—because I was equal parts rock and bluegrass—became the vision. That vision became Leftover Salmon." Bush's singular style on the mandolin would have a huge influence on Emmitt, as his desire to combine bluegrass and rock was shaped by Bush's role as an originator of progressive bluegrass. Years later after their meeting, Bush, whom Emmitt calls, "His ultimate mandolin hero," would serve as a mentor and continue to inform his style. This change and style taking place was noticeable to O'Brien who, while not always around due to his hectic touring schedule with Hot Rize, still made time to see the Left Hand String Band and sit in with them when possible. He says, "Drew liked to play rock 'n' roll songs with a bluegrass style. He steered the band toward more what he plays now. He was changing the sound of the band. It was obvious he had a lot of energy."

Leftover Salmon was still a few years away, and the Left Hand String Band was missing two key players who would help to create and define Salmon's sound. Despite this, the Left Hand String Band's sound was progressive, and in a live setting, it was even a bit reckless. With this progressive approach to bluegrass music, they steadily built up a sizeable following. They played at the Rocky Mountain Bluegrass Festival (later called RockyGrass) eight times between 1983 and 1993. They also held several regular residences over the years, including a regular Tuesday-night gig at the Walrus Saloon in Boulder. In 1986, they picked up another regular residency at the Gold Hill Inn. The Gold Hill Inn was an old log house that was converted into a hotel and gourmet restaurant. It hosted live music for a short stretch in the seventies but had

The Left Hand String Band (from left): Keely Brunner, Gerald Bozarth, Drew Emmitt, Glenn Keefe, Al Goll. Courtesy of Emily Cantrell.

stopped until the Left Hand String Band paid the historic venue a visit. "We kind of re-started the music scene there," remembers Emmitt. "They weren't doing music there anymore. They did it years before and bands like the Dillards and the Ophelia Swing Band played there. We were going there, setting up and playing acoustic. That turned into them inviting us to play a regular gig and set up a P.A. That was our bread and butter. We played there once a month in the summertime and it was slammed. It was this huge party. We would put posters everywhere. We plastered the entire county with posters. It became kind of a big deal."

To capture the energy and excitement of their slammed shows at the Gold Hill Inn, the Left Hand String Band recorded a live album there in 1987. The resulting *Live at the Gold Hill Inn* was only released on cassette, and it is extremely hard to find copies of now, but it perfectly captured the youthful energy and excitement of a band on the verge of something big. The Left Hand String Band's regular gigs at the Gold Hill Inn also exposed them to an influential fan in Craig Ferguson. Ferguson was heavily involved in bluegrass in the area, including working with the Telluride Bluegrass Festival, becoming its director in 1989.

He was a fan of the Left Hand String Band and a regular at their shows at the Gold Hill Inn. Emmitt had been trying for years to get the band into the lineup for the Telluride Bluegrass Festival, which is one of the country's premier bluegrass festivals. At first, he tried talking to the festival's original promoter, Fred Shellman, but noticed, "He disappeared whenever I would go over to talk to him." When Ferguson took over as director, Emmitt knew he was a fan of the band and thought an easier path to be able to get the Left Hand String Band added to the lineup. Ferguson told Emmitt they should enter the annual band contest because he was sure they would win and gain a spot as part of the lineup the following year. Emmitt stood his ground, insisting that based on what they already accomplished they should be added to the lineup, not because of how they performed in some contest. Ferguson eventually relented, adding the band to the lineup in 1990. The Left Hand String Band would play the Telluride Bluegrass Festival every year after that, from 1990 to 1993.

Dobroist Goll was in the band as they were building up momentum and a fan base. He left right before they played Telluride for the first time, ending up as a highly in demand player in Nashville, but recalls the excitement surrounding the band before he left, not just from fans, but also from fellow musicians. "Tim O'Brien would sit in with us every Tuesday if he was in town. He sat in with us a lot. We did a big festival in Boulder, the Chaqua Park Festival in 1987, and he joined us for that as well. It was a lot of fun. It did not seem to be work at all. We made a little bit of money and had a big following. It was just great fun to be doing it. I loved it."

The Left Hand String Band's sound, while not as unhinged as Leftover Salmon is when they are at their live best, does exhibit the take-no-prisoners energy and gas pedal mashed to the floor speed that would become trademarks of Emmitt's playing. Their music was more akin to fellow bluegrass progressives John Hartford, David Grisman, the Dillards, Hot Rize, and New Grass Revival. These musicians were folk and rock influenced and were expanding the traditional bluegrass sound started by Bill Monroe into the stratosphere with their volume and style, as they incorporated influences far outside of the normal bluegrass world. This, despite the absence of drums, gave this progressive, bluegrass style a more rock 'n' roll flavor. It was a flavor the Left Hand String Band was deeply immersed in, with Emmitt remarking from stage during their appearance at the Strawberry Bluegrass Festival in 1991 the music of the Left Hand String Band was "rock 'n' roll blue-grass."[8] This rock 'n' roll bluegrass sound that morphed into Leftover Salmon found itself a better fit in the Boulder music scene beginning to sprout around bands including Big Head Todd & the Monsters, the Samples, and Acoustic Junction, who were finding willing, adventurous ears at the University of Colorado, which was located in Boulder. These other Boulder bands pulled from a diverse range of music influences and were following a DIY approach, defined by their widely differing musical styles, and united by their always-evolving go-for-broke live shows. They would later be lumped under the wide-ranging, loosely applied jamband label, which would also be applied to Leftover Salmon. They were bands, writer and jambands.com founder Dean Budnick explains, that "share a collective penchant for improvisation, a commitment to song craft and a propensity to cross genre boundaries, drawing from a range of traditions including blues, bluegrass, funk, jazz, rock, psychedelia and even techno."[9]

The Left Hand String Band, led by Emmitt's instantly recognizable songwriting, clearly shows the roots of what would become foundational building blocks of Leftover Salmon's music. During his time with the Left Hand String Band, Emmitt was a prolific songwriter, penning many tunes, including "Get Me Outta This City," "Just Before the Evening," "Valley of the Full Moon," "Gold Hill Line," and "Stop All Your Worrying," that would carry over to Salmon and become fan favorites and live standards of the band. They also began playing covers Emmitt continued to play throughout the rest of his career. Slingsby remembers how Emmitt played traditional bluegrass tunes but could find something completely new in them. He would take a simple tune like Jimmie Skinner's "Doin' My Time," and turn it into a musical exploration that leaves even the progressive New Grass Revival version of the song, which was Emmitt's inspiration for covering it, in the large improvisational wake he creates every time he performs it. Early live shows of the Left Hand String Band, while highlighting the strong and distinctive songwriting skills of Emmitt, also shone a light on the differences between them and Leftover Salmon. While Emmitt's original style clearly stands out and is reminiscent of Salmon's high-octane energy, the absence of future front man Vince Herman's frenetic, ringmaster stage presence and banjo picker Mark Vann's uniquely powerful playing clearly loom large.

The Left Hand String Band's sole studio album, 1991's *Get Me Outta This City*, which included Vann and bassist Keefe, is the direct predecessor of Leftover Salmon. The addition of Vann's visionary banjo picking brings in an element that clearly echoes what Salmon would become. Hot Rize's Charles Sawtelle produced the album and it is dominated by Emmitt's strong songwriting. The absence of Herman's influence looms large as the final missing piece of the Leftover Salmon puzzle. While the music on *Get Me Outta This City* comes across as progressive bluegrass, the relatively straightforward versions of "Get Me Outta This City," "Just Before the Evening," "Gold Hill Line," and "Stop All Your Worrying" are a reminder of the inspired directions Salmon would later take with the same music.

The first of the missing Leftover Salmon parts appeared in Emmitt's orbit in 1985 on a Tuesday evening when the Left Hand String Band was playing one of their regular gigs at the Walrus Saloon in Boulder. The sign out front advertising bluegrass music caught the eye of a bearded guitarist who had just driven across the country from West Virginia with his buddy, Lew Prichard, in a 1963 Volvo station wagon. The bearded guitarist says they got to Boulder and, "There was a sign in front of this bar that said, 'Bluegrass Music Tonight—Left Hand String Band,' so we hung out until the show happened."

The bearded guitarist, Vince Herman, had recently left West Virginia University six credits shy of graduation, and was heading west to spend a few weeks in Colorado. He was looking to experience a music scene more progressive than the one he was a part of in Morgantown, West Virginia, during his college years. His friend Prichard had been to Boulder and the Telluride Bluegrass Festival before, and his recommendation, along with Herman's discovery of Hot Rize, led to him settling on Colorado. "I moved from West Virginia to Colorado chasing the Hot Rize scene," says Herman. "Charles Sawtelle was an absolute guitar god for me, right up there with Clarence White and Tony Rice and all that on the guitar. Hot Rize was instrumental for me in coming to Colorado."[10] Prichard says, "We weren't sure what we what would find. Our plan was to go there and see what was going on. We planned to go there and do some busking. Just see what we could do for ourselves, to get some music going on." For Herman, he thought he might "move to Boulder for a couple of weeks and then go to Nicaragua. It was the time of the Iran Contra thing and I was going to go join the Sandinistas and learn Spanish and come back and go to graduate school."

Herman and Prichard found lodging for the night and hung around out front of the Walrus Saloon until the show started. There were maybe a hundred people at the show, and Herman remembers, "The Left Hand String Band was kicking ass." The pair waited around until after the show, introduced themselves to Emmitt, and talked some music. "It was just meant to be," recalls Emmitt, "He came to see us play and I was one of the first people he met in Boulder. The Left Hand String Band was the first band he saw in Boulder."

Herman was duly inspired by what he saw the Left Hand String Band doing that night. "I thought, 'Damn, it would be fucking awesome to be in a band making as much money at night as you do doing your job during the day. It would be fucking killer.'"

Chapter 2

VINCE HERMAN

Vince is a master. He is one of the most masterful front men I have ever been onstage with, and he is one of the only front men I have ever been onstage with where I felt like I didn't need to do anything.—*Reverend Jeff Mosier (Aquarium Rescue Unit, Blueground Undergrass)*

Sitting backstage at the Hot August Music Festival in Cockeysville, Maryland, in August 2016, Vince Herman is flipping through a stack of old pictures he brought along in a worn, leather satchel. A large industrial fan sits in the corner of the room and does its best to try to stifle the unrelenting heat and humidity blanketing the day. Every time the fan oscillates across the room, hands fly to the table to keep the numerous pictures spread across it from being blown around. Bandmates Andy Thorn and Alwyn Robinson flank Herman and marvel every time he pulls out another picture of a much more youthful version of himself from the stack of photos. Howls of disbelief erupt from Thorn and Robinson when a picture of a twenty-something Herman skiing through a pair of trees is revealed. "You skied?" asks Thorn with clear surprise. Herman just laughs and continues flipping through photos. Finally, Herman pauses as he comes across a picture of himself as a three-year-old in 1965. In the black-and-white photo, he is seated on a couch, a well-decorated Christmas tree in the background, a toy guitar in his hand, a sense of swagger in his step, and a sly smile on his face. Herman looks up from the picture with a laugh and a similarly sly smile on his face and declares, "Not much has changed for me since." Not a truer statement has ever been spoken. A few minutes after looking at that picture of himself as a child, Herman is onstage with Leftover Salmon, guitar in hand, huge smile on his face, ripping through yet another blistering set at a music festival, just as he has done since Leftover Salmon first formed in 1989. He bounces around the stage the whole show with a seemingly endless supply of energy to burn. He engages the audience and pulls them into his party, much the way he did as a child when he performed shows for his mother's card club, dancing and singing as he stood on the table. He is a true entertainer and has been his whole life. For Herman, performing live is just a continuation of a life surrounded and defined by music.

That life of music began in Carnegie, Pennsylvania, a small town located eight miles west of downtown Pittsburgh. It is best known as the home of Football Hall of Famer Mike Ditka and Baseball Hall of Famer Honus Wagner. Herman's family roots run deep in the area as they have lived in Carnegie for four generations. He was born May 28, 1962, into a strict Irish Catholic family as the youngest of seven children. His parents' strictness meant his brothers and sisters were not allowed to take part in the hippie movement swirling around them in the late sixties and had to hide some of their more out-there musical tastes. His siblings found a way to express their desire to experience the hippie movement by dressing their younger brother Vince up as one. They dressed him in a wig, boots, and gave him a plywood guitar with rubber-band strings. While in costume, he would dance and perform in the family's living room. Despite his parents' aversion to the hippie trends and music of the time, Herman's family was a musical one. His mother was always singing around the house and his dad sang in church. It was his grandfather, though, that Herman looked up to the most: "He would sing on holidays when he had a drink or two. He was the real musical inspiration when it came to entertaining."[1]

As the youngest of seven children, Herman says his parents "were a little slacker with me," but he still at times listened to smuggled cassettes provided by his older siblings. "My older brother was into Motown, so that was the first stuff in my ears. Then it was the British Invasion, the Rolling Stones, all those kinds of things. A little later, it was the Doors, Traffic, Cream, and David Peel & the Lower East Side," Herman says. "That was the tape [David Peel] hid in my brother's Chevy Nova under the seats so my parents wouldn't find it. As the

A three-year-old Vince Herman, Christmas 1965, proving not much has changed. Courtesy of Vince Herman.

youngest, I absorbed a lot of music." Herman soon wanted more than just pretending to play the guitar and asked his parents if he could start taking guitar lessons. They agreed and he began in the third grade. He took lessons from a local accordion player who was a member of a polka band. The accordion player was not much of a guitar player, and Herman says the only real lasting impact was to teach him how to read music. For a short time, Herman took piano lessons, but says it was mostly because he knew it would bug his sister. Ever impatient and active, Herman's guitar skills did not advance as fast as he wanted when he first took up the instrument. It was not until he got extremely sick and was laid up at home in bed for a couple of weeks he saw the progress he desired. His parents, looking to occupy him while he was home sick, bought him a guitar songbook. With nothing else to do but practice, his skills began to grow exponentially as he learned the different tunes from the songbook. While the practice and lessons from the book were beneficial, the always-energetic Herman soon grew bored with learning from a book. He was motivated to learn and play but was not interested in simply mimicking what he saw in the book. He wanted more. He wanted to create his own music. He wanted to learn to live and breathe the guitar. "I was like fuck that," he says. "I started teaching myself how to play these chords, melodies, and all that." As his skills grew, he developed the confidence to start his first garage band in middle school. When asked if he served as the front man for that group, Herman answers with his characteristic laugh, "Nah, we didn't quite make it that far."

Herman first discovered bluegrass music as middle schooler when a friend had him listen to a Doc Watson record after school one day. Soon after, he saw David Bromberg & His Big Band and "the hook was set."[2] For Herman, what he calls "the real pivotal point" of his musical evolution came when he attended the Smoky City Folk Festival at Schenley Park in downtown Pittsburgh in 1977. He saw a group of people "who as far as [he] could tell were strangers to each other playing these tunes together and having a blast with this common repertoire they all knew." That group of players included members of a local band, Devilish Mary, and throughout the jam session they played songs from the old-timey, bluegrass canon, which resonated with Herman. He had not brought his guitar along and instead stood there transfixed at the communal interplay between the musicians and thought to himself how he wanted to learn to do that. Just like his future bandmate, Drew Emmitt, who at the same time was discovering bluegrass across the country in Colorado, it was the social aspect of the music that resonated with Herman. The ability to have an experience shared through music was a life-changing moment for Herman. "That just blew my mind. I realized that's the kind of fun I want to have playing music. The texture and the tunes were great, but the thing that grasped me first was the social context of it." He began to seek out this new strain of old-timey music that was mostly unfamiliar to him up to that point in his life. As he began to gain confidence and develop as a musician, he started to attend and play at various acoustic open-mic nights around town featuring a similar style of music. Later in high school he would attend his first bluegrass festival, where he drank a little moonshine and watched Bill Monroe sing, "Walls of Time."

While in high school he began hanging around Jack Gabing, whose older brother Bob was a local musician. Bob's long-running band, the Blues Orphans, was well known for their eccentric style. Their blues-based sound blended rock, polka, punk, bluegrass, and just about everything else into an irresistible, tasty musical stew. The Blues Orphans' music is laced with the sharp humor of Gabing's lyrics, which often starts with a serious topic, but is told with a heavy dose of sarcasm and includes songs such as "Unplug That Telephone," "Gangsta Lovin'," "Tie Dye Redneck," and "Smart Phones, Dumb People." The band's lineup is in constant motion, growing and shrinking over the years; sometimes having horns, sometimes not, but at the center was always Bob and his enigmatic presence. Bob would start playing some weird lick or guitar riff, leaving the band unsure of what song he was going to begin, forcing them to hold on and to try to follow his lead. This unpredictability made Blues Orphans shows a swirl of excitement where the crowd might break into a giant samba line parading around the venue. Herman was greatly influenced by Bob's ability to be completely free and unrestrained onstage and the audience reaction he could instigate. In an interview with *American Songwriter* in 2012, Herman was asked about his favorite songwriters and he named the usual suspects: Jackson Browne, Todd Snider, and Woody Guthrie. Then he added, "But my real hero is Bob Gabing from my hometown of Carnegie, Pennsylvania. He writes hysterical anthems that have inspired me for years."[3] Bob's influence on Herman would come into focus over the years as Herman's growing stage presence and songwriting reflected those qualities he admired in Bob and the Blues Orphans.

In the eleventh grade, Herman joined a well-established local band, Eddie and the Night Riders, and played his first paying gig. After his discovery at the Smoky City Folk Festival, Herman was mostly focused on bluegrass and old-timey music, but Eddie and the Night Riders played outlaw-type country music; Waylon Jennings, Johnny Cash, Willie Nelson, and similar bands popular at the time. Despite the musical differences between what the Night Riders played and what was moving Herman musically at the time, the opportunity was too good to pass up. For the teenaged Herman, he was fine playing whatever, because

Eddie and the Night Riders played regular gigs at places like Archie's Gone Country on Route 51 in Pittsburgh, and he got a chance to experience life in a real band. He says, "I did all the important shit you were supposed to do. I used my mother's eyeliner to accentuate what little mustache I had. I used the bass player's ID so I could actually drink beer, and I got a blow job at set break."

Herman lasted a few months in the band, but "knew that as I got toward my senior year in high school I was actually going to have to go out and get a job if I didn't go to college. So, I decided to go to college." He enrolled at West Virginia University in Morgantown, West Virginia, in 1980. The acting department was having scholarship auditions, and Herman, who was named "Most Talented" in his senior class at Carlynton High School, decided to try out. He did not earn a scholarship, but

Vince Herman in his high school yearbook from his senior year, where he was named Most Talented. Courtesy of Vince Herman.

still decided to study acting his freshman year before changing his major to anthropology the following year. Herman's interest in anthropology was ignited when he "realized if I wanted to do theatre, I should know something about the world and I realized I was fucking clueless. So, I went in the direction of trying to figure what people are all about." To help expand his view of the world, Herman, who felt he had not experienced much since he was born sixty miles from where he ended up going to college and never ventured outside of the area, hitchhiked to Seattle at the end of his sophomore year in 1982. From there, he found his way to Juneau, Alaska, and obtained employment on a fishing boat where he worked for three months. That season turned out to be one of the lowest prices for fish in years, so he did not make much money while in Alaska. It did not deter him from looking back fondly at the trip, calling it, "the adventure of a lifetime."

While at West Virginia University, Herman says he gained his real education through the music he was experiencing at the time. He had seen the Grateful Dead a few times in high school, but began to connect with them during college, calling them, "a major influence on my music." Herman loved the unpredictability of Grateful Dead shows, how the band could so expertly seem to find the fine line between improvisation and rehearsed ability. At a show he attended with his college roommate with a head full of acid in May 1980 at the Hartford Civic Center in Connecticut, the Grateful Dead employed a crowd-pleasing participation trick that struck a chord with him. The last song of their set was the Buddy Holly classic, "Not Fade Away." As the band finished the song and left the stage, the crowd continued to chant, "No our love won't fade away," over and over until the band came back out. "I love that trick," says Herman, who pocketed the memory and started to incorporate similar ideas and what he learned from Gabing into his developing stagecraft. The show was also significant for a certain red-headed guitarist in attendance that night who was experiencing his first Dead show. Trey Anastasio, who would go on to form the seminal jamband Phish, was in high school nearby at the Taft School and went to the same show with friends. As with Herman, the evening resonated deeply with Anastasio. "It was like getting hit in the head with a baseball bat," he declares.[4]

In addition to the Grateful Dead, Herman began digging deeper into bluegrass and old-timey music while in college. He was part of a traveling labor history show where he had the opportunity to tour with some of his professors and perform music for different audiences around the region. Herman helped create a soundtrack for the show featuring music inspired by the old-timey sound. Despite the outward goofiness Herman often exudes, the labor history show represents who he really is: a deeply thoughtful musician who, like his folk music heroes, loves singing songs about the struggles of the workingman. While at West Virginia he also was experiencing old-timey music at its roots and learning from some of the genre's masters. He says, "I got absolutely absorbed in the old-time scene. I got to play with guys like Melvin Wine, Mose Coffman, J. P. Fraley and all these great characters that made West Virginia a paradise to me."[5] He was regularly attending a number of the folk, bluegrass, and old-timey festivals in the area. Herman's college friend Lew Prichard remembers how on their annual trips to the Galax Fiddler Convention, the roots of Herman's masterful front-man persona were starting to emerge: "He would just come up with these hilarious songs and go off. He was fun to be around and jam with. People would stop and crowd around him and listen."

At the West Virginia State Folk Festival in 1983, Herman had what he calls, "The most profound musical experience of my life." He was up all Saturday night at the festival picking guitar and partying with the hard-driving string band, the Bing Brothers. As morning started to rear its head, Herman found himself standing knee deep in a creek as the sun was starting to peek over the horizon, with a small group of his musical heroes singing gospel songs to welcome in the new day. He says there might have been one or two instruments, but it was mostly a cappella. "It was Hazel Dickens, Alice Gerrard, Michael Kline, the Bing Brothers, Lorraine Duisit from Trapezoid—who was a major, major influence—and Tina Liza Jones from Trapezoid. We were the last ones up. It was a powerful moment. Those singers in that group just meant the world to me." Playing with his idols reinforced the idea in Herman that there need be no wall between fan and band. Music is a communal experience and should be shared by everyone.

In was not only old-timey music Herman was discovering during his college years. He also began to get deeply into Cajun music and was fortunate enough to be able to learn from Dewey Balfa, a musician from Louisiana often referred to as the Bill Monroe of Cajun music because of the way he helped introduce the style to a larger audience.

Herman met Balfa at the Augusta Heritage Festival in Elkins, West Virginia, in 1982. "Dewey did more to expose Cajun music to the world than anyone," says Herman. "I learned you laugh and cry when that music gets in you deep. He was an amazing musician and a profoundly heartfelt guy. That's how the washboard got in my ear."[6] Cajun music began to exert a strong influence on Herman's diversified musical style.

Herman also met a local musician, Vince Farsetta, while in college who shared the same all-over-the-place musical tastes and who influenced Herman greatly. Farsetta was a New York native who hitchhiked to West Virginia in 1972. He fell in love with the state and the traditional, Appalachian-type music he discovered there and settled permanently in Morgantown. Farsetta played around Morgantown and the surrounding area with his band Small Axe. Herman was a big fan of Small Axe. Their high-energy live shows left a lasting impression on him. He says, "Vinnie Farsetta was a huge influence. He wrote great tunes. Small Axe was the shit. All the chicks were there. It was where I learned how to play rowdy music. Small Axe taught me how to get a crowd pumped up and sweat hard before they got out the door." Farsetta remembers Herman always seemed to be around at his shows and the two eventually connected and became friends. Herman's upbeat personality and eagerness to play music drew Farsetta to him. "He was the happiest guy around. He always wanted to play tunes. He was always ready to pick." Farsetta's singular songwriting style drew from a wide range of influences, including reggae, calypso, ska, and string band. All those disparate influences were laced with Farsetta's sharp sense of humor and tied up into one uncommonly original sound that had a long-lasting impact on the teenaged Herman. Many of the obscure covers he first learned from Farsetta, including "Zombie Jamboree," "BooBoo," and "Carnival Time," ended up in the Leftover Salmon catalog and became some of the band's most popular songs. Even some of Farsetta's original songs found their way into the Salmon canon, including "L.E. Minet," and "Jokester." All those songs were on an album Farsetta recorded in 1985 called *For the Times*. Farsetta passed on a tape of the album to Herman while he was still at West Virginia University, and it found a spot in constant rotation on his stereo. It would leave a lasting impression on Herman's musical development as the style and songs became ingrained in his musical DNA.

Herman was not just attending wild, energetic shows while in college, he was also creating them. He incorporated his vaudevillian and theatrical background into his developing stage persona and began to seek out people who were willing to join him onstage in nutty and crazy endeavors. He was clearly influenced by what he saw Farsetta doing with Small Axe and worked to find different and creative ways to involve the crowd while playing shows. He played in a variety of bands in college, though their shows were mostly limited to local house or fraternity parties. No matter where he played, he tried to make each show more than just a concert you came to and watched. Instead, he tried turning them into a big musical party where the crowd was as much a part of the show as the band. One of his bands in college was Captain Jelly & the 'Nuff, whose slogan was, "Because too much is just enough," and incorporated some of those crowd interaction tricks Herman picked up from Farsetta and the Grateful Dead. Throughout the show, Herman would lean into the microphone and ask the crowd, "Who is Captain Jelly?" The crowd would yell back with great enthusiasm, "I am Captain Jelly!" Despite this bit of inspired crowd interaction, Captain Jelly & the 'Nuff only played together for about six months. They never made it out of the fraternity party scene that made up the bulk of their shows during their all-too-short existence. Years later, Herman heard a poorly dubbed tape from one of Captain Jelly's few shows and called it frightening. For a short time, Herman was the front man of a band called Free Beer. Farsetta says, "He put the name, Free Beer, on posters around campus. It said Free Beer and wherever they were playing and people showed up thinking they are getting free beer only to find out it was the name of the band."

Most of Herman's experience playing live music in college was at parties around campus. "He had a crew of people around him who were just very eclectic, very wild," remembers Farsetta. "They put on ladies' dresses with their hairy chests sticking out and would play a party. It didn't matter to them. Those guys like to get naked and play. Shenanigans not many people do. They played with unbelievable energy." Among that eclectic crew was a pair of brothers, Fred Prichard and his younger brother Lew. According to Herman, Fred was a "seriously funny writer and all-around hysterian." Fred played with Herman in a variety of guises throughout college and would later leave his mark with Leftover Salmon, penning, "Rodeo Geek," for their first album, *Bridges to Bert*, and the live staple, "Cactus Flower," which appeared on 1995's *Ask the Fish*. His younger brother Lew first encountered Herman at a party in the spring of 1984 and the two soon were playing music regularly together. The pair did not have a name for their loosely assembled band, which usually was just Herman and Lew, but occasionally incorporated other musicians as well. Instead of arranging regular gigs, they developed a reputation for spontaneous, guerrilla-style shows that might erupt anywhere on campus or in downtown Morgantown. Often, they grabbed a pair of chairs and headed to the student union. "We would set them up next to each other and stand on them and start playing. Pretty soon there would be a crowd all around us," says Lew Prichard. "It was the same kind of stuff Vince was doing at Galax which drew crowds."

One of these spontaneous shows took place at a local restaurant, the Boston Beanery, in downtown Morgantown, and showcased Herman's growing mastery as a commanding presence in front of a crowd. Prichard, Herman, and few other musician friends barged into the restaurant with their instruments and began playing. Instantly they drew a crowd. The crowd gathered around, the musicians began to get rowdy, and the restaurant's manager intervened, telling Herman and his crew they had to leave. Never one to let a good party end, Herman led a stream of people out of the restaurant pied-piper style while continuing to sing and play. He led the now-mobile party to an empty spot behind the restaurant where he and the band kept the party going, drawing an even larger crowd that continued to get rowdier and rowdier. The cops were called and Prichard recalls, "They had a dog with them and it looked like it might become a dangerous situation." Herman sensed the tension building and looking for a way to defuse it, began singing a rousing version of "God Bless America." The gathered crowd joined in, inspiring the approaching police to stop and start singing as well. Herman, with his perfect reading of the crowd and the potentially tense situation, won over the police over with his patriotic gesture. After the crowd cheered the end of the song, the once fierce-looking cops, now with a laugh and a smile on their faces, simply asked the crowd and band to please leave and disperse. Herman's inspired response was just one in many growing examples of his developing skills as a front man.

By the fall of 1985, Herman was still six credits shy of graduating. He had more credits than required for graduation but had not passed his advanced Spanish class requirements he needed. He decided he needed a change of scenery and a life-altering experience before finishing his schooling. He was also living in the attic of a house with no heat and the impending winter cold was forcing him to reevaluate his living situation. "Morgantown was wearing kind of thin," he says, "and I wanted to go somewhere with a music scene that was more progressive." He was pretty politically charged at the time and inspired by the Iran-Contra affair and the United States involvement with the Contras, and wanted to head to the border of Nicaragua and El Salvador and serve as a Witness for Peace. The Witness for Peace activist organization opposed Ronald Reagan's support for the Nicaraguan Contras and sent U.S. citizens to Nicaragua to see the effects of the U.S. government's military policy firsthand. Herman wished to make a difference with the activist group and, as a bonus, master the Spanish language while there so he could come back and test out of the advanced Spanish class he was missing, enroll in graduate school, and pursue an advanced degree in anthropology.

To satisfy his desire to experience a more progressive bluegrass scene before heading to Nicaragua, Herman and Prichard thought they would take a road trip to Boulder, Colorado, and hang out there for a couple of weeks and soak up the area's music. Prichard had been out to the Telluride Bluegrass Festival the year before and spoke highly of the area. Herman was also greatly influenced by the bluegrass music emanating from Colorado at the time and says, "Tim O'Brien was my inspiration to move from West Virginia to Colorado. To see Hot Rize and be part of that bluegrass scene." In addition to playing a progressive bluegrass style, at the core of who Herman was at the time, Hot Rize also occasionally played sets as their alter-ego band, Red Knuckles and the Trailblazers. Red Knuckles played comedy-fueled sets in a Western Swing style that showed how humor could be incorporated into music and was a very appealing concept to Herman, though the connection between the two bands was initially lost on him. The first time he saw Red Knuckles and the Trailblazers play at Mountain Stage in Charleston, West Virginia, he had no idea it was Hot Rize in disguise, and the revelation they were the same band was mind-blowing and a great influence on his stagecraft. Hot Rize and Red Knuckles's freewheeling approach gave the crowd permission to have fun. Herman would also pocket this concept and start to use it whenever he had the chance to perform for a crowd.

Herman and Prichard left Morgantown for Boulder during the last week of October in 1985 in Prichard's 1963 white Volvo station wagon. The pair drove straight through, stopping only for food and gas. They took turns driving, one napping in the back while the other drove. When they reached the Colorado border they stopped off at a diner and fortified themselves with a big western breakfast to get them through the final few hours of their trip. They first stopped in Denver to see a friend of Prichard's, but both agreed it did not quite feel right there, and they continued on to Boulder. Upon arriving in Boulder, they found a place to stay for the night, then headed downtown looking for a place to grab a beer and a burger when they saw a sign out front of the Walrus Saloon advertising, "Bluegrass Music Tonight—Left Hand String Band." They parked Prichard's Volvo out front of the bar and waited around until the band came on.

The Walrus Saloon was a small bar on the corner of 11th and Walnut Street in downtown Boulder that hosted live music throughout the years and where the Left Hand String Band played a regular Tuesday-night gig for a couple of years. While Herman loved the old-timey music that was the dominant sound in West Virginia, he was ready for a change and to expand his musical horizons. His first night in Boulder at the Walrus did just that. "I walk in and they were playing progressive bluegrass, and I thought, 'Man this is exactly what we are after here,'" he recalls. "I thought these guys were really good and there must be a big scene in Boulder if this is what I can find on a Tuesday night." The evening struck a chord with Prichard as well: "I really liked Drew's singing that night. He had a way of playing the mandolin we later called the bumblebee lick because he played all these notes and it was so fun to hear. He would take off on a break or solo and just start playing all these rapid notes." Herman and Prichard stayed until the end of the show, when they introduced themselves to the band; it was just a casual introduction, in which they said hello and briefly talked about music. "It's kind of weird to get out of your car, walk into a place, and find someone you will play with for the next twenty-five years," says Herman.[7] Herman documented that first meeting with Emmitt in a small well-worn notebook that served as a journal for his trip out from West Virginia. In an entry happily declaring, "Boulder! Great town, Great

Luck," and listing such mundane daily events as eating and going to the post office it read, "The Walrus. The only place in town with a string band, and we find it on the day that, that band is playing!"

Following that show, Herman and Prichard began to settle into the area. They at first lived in a storage unit they rented for a month until they found permanent housing. Immediately they jumped into the local music scene, spending many a long afternoon busking on the Pearl Street Mall in downtown Boulder and playing at local parties as the Vince and Lew Show. They also continued to play spontaneous shows as they had done back in West Virginia. "We would bust into a fraternity party and start playing something like an acoustic version of a Talking Heads song and people would start cracking up," says Prichard. As they had back in college, they played each show with unpredictable zaniness. Emmitt remembers many parties around town when the pair played in nothing more than their underwear. Occasionally they added local fiddler Susan James to their sound whenever they were lucky enough to score a paying gig. Herman's plans to head to South America changed for good, "when I met this girl and before long we were having a baby." Within a few months, they were married. The relationship was doomed from the beginning as the liberal Herman says, "We were just from different worlds. Her father was an executive at Exxon. I remember going to dinner at their house and it was the first time I had seen a pepper grinder and I was sitting there shaking that thing and they were looking at me like, 'Where is this kid from?' It didn't work out too good, but we have a great son."

With the plan of heading to South America to join the Witnesses for Peace in Nicaragua no longer a real option, Herman began to permanently settle into Boulder and find his place in the local music scene. He got a job at a local seafood restaurant, which helped provide a small but steady income. His travel partner, Prichard, did not have as much luck finding steady employment and not gotten married in the short time he was in Boulder. After nine months, he left Herman in Boulder to head back home to West Virginia.

For Herman, his job at the seafood restaurant not only provided a paycheck, but also many a meal for him and his friends. Each night, he took home any food too old to serve and would throw it all together and cook a big meal with it. He would buy some beer, invite friends over, and play music all night, falling asleep for a few hours before waking up to be at the restaurant at 5:30 a.m. to start prepping for the day. Always the welcoming host, Herman invited every player he met in Boulder to attend his picking parties. To help compile the invite list, he used "Buck's List," which was named for local musician, Daniel "Buck" Buckner, who Herman called, "an inspiration to the whole Boulder scene." "Buck's List" had the names and phone numbers of all the players in the area. In those pre-internet days, this list was an invaluable tool for musicians in the Boulder area when trying to find musicians to fill out a band for an upcoming gig or simply gathering people to invite to your next party. Buckner died in 2003, but his list lives on as "Buck's Bluegrass Hotline" at local Boulder radio station KGNU as a calendar of all the bluegrass events in Colorado.

With the help of "Buck's List," Herman's parties become large, extremely popular affairs. You could expect to see everyone there from players just starting out, to well-established local stars like Emmitt and the Left Hand String Band, to national acts like Nick Forster of Hot Rize, who still lived in the area and was a regular attendee. It was at one of these parties in late fall of 1985, shortly after Herman settled in Boulder, that he and Emmitt first played together. After their initial meeting at the Walrus Saloon, Emmitt and Herman went their separate ways, but as Herman settled into Boulder permanently and his parties became popular events, they reconnected at one of them. Neither of them recalls anything particularly memorable or spectacular their first time playing together. It was like any other party at Herman's house. It was crowded, there was lots of beer and weed, it was a rowdy time, and the playing went on all night because there was no time for sleeping when everyone was feeling fine.

Emmitt and Herman's friendship deepened as they began seeing each other more and more at parties and various gigs around town. As hard as it is to imagine given Herman's penchant for playing loose with the rules and always looking for a good time, for a brief stretch he worked as the doorman and bouncer at the Walrus Saloon. He often worked on Tuesday nights when the Left Hand String Band played their regular residency. He and Emmitt got to know each other better through those long shared nights. Musically, Herman continued to play mostly at house parties, while Emmitt was still regularly gigging with the Left Hand String Band. In 1987, a few years after Herman arrived in Boulder, Keely Brunner, the original founder and guitarist of the

Left Hand String Band, had decided to leave the band. Emmitt began casting around town to find Brunner's replacement. He settled on two potential guitarists, Herman and his friend Steve Burnside.

Burnside and Herman each auditioned for the band and were both told they did not get the job. With a laugh Herman says, "I reacted kinder to the news than Steve, so they hired me. I don't know if that was the plan all along, Drew and I never talked about it later, but that's how I remember it. Steve and I are still good friends to this day." Even though they hired Herman, the Left Hand String Band would still sometimes use Burnside as a guitar sub whenever they needed help filling a show. Despite Herman's growing ability as a front man, he stepped back and served as the band's guitar player, only singing the occasional harmony. The band was fully Emmitt's vision at this point, as he was the front man and focal point onstage. Herman's skills were not going unnoticed, though. Emmitt recognized his rare talent and abilities and realized the Left Hand String Band might not be the best place for him to display what he could do. He says, "I liked his stage presence and showmanship. I thought his forte was to be the front man. He was kind of a nutcase entertainer and good guitar player. He has a style like no one else. He is not technically an amazing guitar player, but he is a powerful player that can get a crowd going, which works better in a situation like Leftover Salmon with drums and loud instruments, but maybe not so much in a bluegrass situation like the Left Hand String Band. I saw this and thought, 'This could be something cool.'" Herman was also sensing the possibilities of what might become from a combination of Emmitt's approach to bluegrass and his own musical influences. "They had an aggressive approach to bluegrass, sort of a New Grass Revival sound, which I liked," he explains. "I was into stuff like polka, Cajun, and jug band music, but we shared common ground. The old-time music was where my heart was and whatever kind of band I was going to get into had to be roots oriented."[8]

The Left Hand String Band's live set list at the time showed Emmitt's influence on the group's direction as it was chock-full of songs he had written. A handful of those songs, including "Gold Hill Line," "Get Me Outta This City," and "Just Before the Evening," would later resurface as a regular part of Leftover Salmon's set. The Left Hand String Band reflected Emmitt's desire to find ways to combine rock 'n' roll and bluegrass. While their sound still adhered to a progressive bluegrass

Left Hand String Band show August 8, 1987 (from left): Eric Holle, Drew Emmitt, a beardless Vince Herman, and Glenn Keefe. Courtesy of Vince Herman.

style like what New Grass Revival was doing, they also began incorporating rock covers by bands like the Allman Brothers Band and Little Feat into their sets. Emmitt noticed the positive reaction of the crowd when they played those covers. The audience stood and danced with uncontrollable excitement for the acoustic versions of the rock songs as well as the more aggressively played traditional tunes, which was in sharp contrast to the subdued way crowds usually watched bluegrass shows with seated pleasure. Emmitt began to realize the possibilities of removing bluegrass from its traditional bonds and playing it in a more liberating setting and style. During Herman's tenure with the Left Hand String Band, this vision was beginning to be explored. They played rock covers, started messing with the arrangement of many of the traditional tunes in their sets, and began to develop Emmitt's songs into live, musical beasts. Despite this exploration, the ability to truly play without rules and labels was not fully realized until the creation of Leftover Salmon. For all the boundaries the Left Hand String Band pushed and stretched, they never completely broke free to create something entirely new. They were still a straight-ahead bluegrass band that played with an intriguing progressive lean.

Herman played with the Left Hand String Band for about a year and a half, between 1987 and 1988. They eventually fired him because he says, "They found a better guitar player." Emmitt jokes another reason they had to replace Herman was because he was constantly breaking guitar strings and spending half the show on his knees trying to fix his guitar. The better guitar player they found to replace Herman was Rob Wheeler, the Assistant District Attorney for Clear Creek County, who Burnside says was, "A killer guitar player who easily outplayed anything Vince and I could contribute." Despite being fired, Herman looked back on his time with the Left Hand String Band fondly. "I loved it," he says. "I was just psyched to be out playing gigs." There were no hard feelings after the firing. Herman and Emmitt remained friends, hanging out socially and picking together whenever the opportunity arose.

Around the same time as being fired from the Left Hand String Band, Herman got divorced from his first wife. The dual shock of the impending unknown both musically and in his personal life led him to the decision he was going to commit to music full-time. While dealing with the stress of finding a new place to live and setting up visitation times with his young son, Herman decided now was the time to commit himself to music full-time. "I jumped off the cliff after and decided I was going to play music for a living no matter what from then on out." There was a little voice in the back of Herman's head saying you cannot play music for a living and urging him to find real work, but he now knew it was time to ignore that voice. He moved in with a friend who owned a landscaping business and who let Herman work with him occasionally. Knowing his rent was covered, Herman set out to start his own band and secure as many gigs as possible.

Herman started a new band, the Salmon Heads, which was built around Herman and fiddle player Hugh Robertson and born from their shared love of Cajun music. Robertson was a friend from West Virginia who also made the trek west to Colorado to experience the growing music scene there. Robertson was familiar with Herman's talent for party fun and had been urging him to start his own band. Since his earliest days in college, Herman was entranced with Cajun music and the party atmosphere its accordion-dominated sound created. The accordion was long a part of Herman's life, even before he discovered

Cajun music in college. Raised in western Pennsylvania, with its large population of eastern European immigrants, polka music and the accordion were omnipresent for Herman growing up. It seemed to him it was the norm to have a polka band at a wedding, and he grew up thinking you could not get married without one. Now with the chance to create a band in his own vision, he wanted to incorporate that accordion sound that was such a huge part of the fabric of who he was. The Cajun music he discovered in college and its heavy reliance on the accordion only validated Herman's musical roots and he now wanted the Cajun sound and the accordion to be at that center of the music his new band, the Salmon Heads, would create. In addition to this Cajun sound, he still wanted to be able to blend all the other music that moved him over the years, the ska and calypso he discovered through Vince Farsetta and Small Axe, the bluegrass and old-timey music from West Virginia, and the adventurous spirit of the Grateful Dead. Much like with Emmitt and his desire to create something more progressive with the Left Hand String Band, Herman's vision for the Salmon Heads was not fully formed until he combined forces with Emmitt.

The inspiration for the Salmon Heads' name came from a brief time when Emmitt and Herman were living together in Gold Hill in Emmitt's house. Herman had left the seafood restaurant he was working at and found a job selling seafood at the Table Mesa shopping center in Boulder. When possible, Herman brought home food from the market to feed his hungry housemates. Occasionally the only leftover items to bring home were the heads of the salmon that had been removed. The resourceful Herman would remove the meat remaining on the heads and use it to make a soup or some other type of meal. The fridge at Emmitt and Herman's house was usually full of leftover salmon heads, just waiting to be eaten. "One day, on a very fun mushroom-filled afternoon," recounts Burnside, "Vince and I decorated the outdoor picnic table at his house with place settings and all, donned our favorite thrift-store tweed coats and ball caps, and placed cigarettes in the mouths of the salmon heads we used to decorate the table." To remember this momentous creation, they took some pictures of the two of them seated at the table with the salmon heads. The picture shows a grinning Herman and Burnside, psychedelic smiles plastered on their faces, sitting down for a meal, surrounded by bottles of beer and fish parts, a salmon head smoking a cigarette affixed to Herman's ball cap. Later when he was trying to come up with a name for his new band, those pictures served as an inspiration for Herman, as he settled on the moniker the Salmon Heads.

Herman had begun hosting a pair of regular weekly jams: Tuesday nights at the Boulder Inn near the University of Colorado and Thursday nights at the outdoor shed at the house he and Emmitt shared. Both attracted large gatherings and, inspired by Herman's good-time leadership, often turned into raging, late-night affairs. As Herman and Robertson were beginning the group that would become the Salmon Heads, they looked to these jam sessions and the core group who shared in Herman's enthusiasm for creative insanity. From those jam sessions, they recruited John Stubbs on bass, Gerry Cavagnaro on accordion and harmonica, and Dave Dorian on washboard. Occasionally they added the percussive talents of Herman's old neighbor Linda Phillips on triangle and washboard to augment their sound. Stubbs would

On a very fun mushroom-filled afternoon, Vince Herman (left) and Steve Burnside (right), at the house in Gold Hill shared by Herman and Drew Emmitt, take the photograph that became the inspiration for the Salmon Heads name. Courtesy of Vince Herman.

be replaced on bass after the first couple of gigs by Burnside, who "Had a fretless bass and was eager to put it to use."

At their inaugural show on the Hill in Boulder, the Salmon Heads with their odd conglomeration of a lineup that included acoustic guitar, washboard, and accordion, were asked to not come back after the first set by the show's promoter, who told them, "What you do is not college music, please leave." Later that night, a brick was tossed through the window of the offending venue. Herman defiantly declares it was not he or anyone else in the band who did it, but word still got around it was. Whether they did it or not, it was believed they did, and people now wanted to come see this band so badass they threw a brick through the window of a venue that insulted them.

The Salmon Heads were the perfect distillation of who Herman was at the time. They were a Cajun jug band that incorporated a good dose of humor into both their songs and performance. "It was a lot of Jim Kweskin kind of stuff. Lots of stupid and funny jokes," says Herman. With this desire to infuse his new band with all the widely divergent styles moving him so, Herman looked to incorporate many of the odd songs he first learned from Farsetta into the band's setlist. "There were a bunch of songs I learned from Vinnie I did with the Salmon Heads that are still part of the Leftover Salmon repertoire," Herman says. "Like some of his cool calypso covers like 'BooBoo' and 'Zombie Jamboree.'" The band also included a bunch of David Bromberg material and tunes from the old-timey underground scene. They even included obscure covers of Pousette Dart's "Amnesia," and the Special's "A Message to You, Rudy." "The band was very high energy and we were all into costumes," states Burnside. "There was no way we were going to be as good or as tight as the Left Hand String Band, but we, probably rightly so, thought we had more personality, hilarity, and entertainment creativity. Mostly we were an electric jug band and followed Vince's lead. He was always improvising and knew the next tune that was going to be played before we even finished the one we were on. Everybody laughed at Vince's hilarious wordplay and incessant improvisational banter. I played the straight man to the star."

Herman's dedication to attempting to play music for a living no matter what obstacles were in his way was tested a few months after the Salmon Heads started. He was still working at the market selling seafood, and the Salmon Heads had a gig scheduled for an upcoming

The Salmon Heads in front of the Gold Hill Inn (from left): John Stubbs, Gerry Cavagnaro, Dave Dorian, Linda Phillips, Hugh Robertson, Vince Herman. Courtesy of Vince of Herman.

weekend. Herman asked his boss if he could have time off to play a gig. Instead of giving him the time off, Herman's boss gave him an ultimatum: "You are going to have to decide if you want to sell seafood or play music." Herman's response to his boss was immediate and to the point, "Well shit, thanks for putting it on the line like that. I'm out of here." His desire to make music for a living having been tested, Herman rightly felt proud about keeping his commitment to his dream, but knew he still had to pay the bills somehow. He helped with his friend's landscaping business when he could or would find whatever kind of odd job was available to help make ends meet. He says, "I did every kind of work imaginable, from working on fishing boats to construction. I tried the real jobs but they just weren't for me." This daily struggle when he wandered around the street, with no money, and nothing to eat—Herman says he lived close to poverty—only sharpened his dedication and resolve to make a career out of music. Still, he says, "It required a lot of faith."[9]

The Salmon Heads began to gain some attention for their high-energy shows, and while not an exact fit for the exploding bluegrass scene happening at the time in Colorado, they exhibited enough of an old-timey sensibility they were able to find an audience in the local bluegrass scene. They started getting gigs at some of the surrounding ski areas and in local bars and restaurants and soon landed a regular weekly gig at the legendary J.J. McCabes. McCabes was a local Boulder pub well known for hosting live music, including an early Phish show in 1990. Bassist Keith Moseley, who would go on to become one of the founding members of Colorado jamband The String Cheese Incident, moved to Boulder in January of 1989 and was just beginning to become entranced by the progressive bluegrass sound so pervasive in the area at the time. He caught quite a few of those early Salmon Heads shows at McCabes. "I just showed up looking for something to do one night," recalls Moseley of the first time he saw the Salmon Heads. "I may have heard the talk this was the new local band to check out. I remember Vince doing his thing and Gerry playing accordion with them. I was struck by this cool, Cajun, zydeco, dance thing I hadn't had any exposure to. I remember the good time, party, dance vibe they created and thinking, 'Wow, this sounds so new to me.' I wasn't tuned in to that kind of music. But right away I was captivated and wanted to know when they were playing again." Besides the unique style of music the Salmon Heads were making, the other draw for people was Herman, whose on-stage style of hysterics and zaniness was now fully on display and starting to attract an audience. Moseley was one of those fans who was struck by Herman's unparalleled antics at the very first Salmon Heads show he saw at McCabes, "I remember thinking, 'Who is that crazy front guy?' He was quite an entertainer even from early on. He was great at delivering a song and getting people up and excited."

The Telluride Bluegrass Festival in 1989 featured a lineup of bands and musicians who were broadening the bluegrass sound into a bold, modern direction, much the way the Left Hand String Band and the Salmon Heads were trying to evolve the sound they loved so much. These bands were stretching the bounds of the label, newgrass, that was being used to describe this forward-thinking sound. Included among these forward-thinking bands at Telluride in 1989 were Hot Rize, New Grass Revival, Jerry Douglas, Béla Fleck, Peter Rowan, David Grisman, Sam

Bush, and Alison Krauss. Noticeably absent from the lineup was the Left Hand String Band, who had built up a head of momentum over the previous few years. Despite a valiant effort from Emmitt, who spent much time over the previous years trying to convince festival director Craig Ferguson to add them, the band still was left out of the lineup. Ferguson, despite being a fan of the Left Hand String Band, instead suggested they enter the band contest. He felt they would easily win the band contest, which would guarantee them a spot on the following year's lineup. Emmitt did not want to enter the band contest. He felt they had more than paid their dues over the previous years, amassing a good-size following in the region, and that Ferguson should add them based on their merit to date, not on their performance in the band contest, which they viewed as another audition they had already passed. Ferguson, despite Emmitt's objections and arguments to convince him otherwise, did not add the Left Hand String Band to the 1989 lineup. Also absent from the lineup was Herman's Salmon Heads, though their absence was not as much of a surprise as the Left Hand String Band. The Salmon Heads were still in the earliest stages of band development and just starting to build their fan base. While they were gaining a lot of attention for Herman's outrageous stage antics and the masterful way he commanded an audience, they still had not assembled enough of a following to warrant their addition to the lineup.

Despite not playing the festival, members of both bands were still in attendance. Their appearance at the festival was not something new. They and their extended group of friends had regularly been traveling to Telluride to experience the festival every June for years and partaking in both the daily lineup of music as well as the campground jams taking place every night. These campground jams were just as important to some as the music played onstage during the day, and go on all night. Flyers were distributed when you entered the Town Park Campground—the main campground for the festival—warning if you stayed there you were not going to get any sleep due to the nonstop playing and partying taking place. Festival attendees would create elaborate setups and multilevel camps to enhance their ability to party after the sun went down. These camps reappeared each year in June for the festival and were known by nicknames such as Camp Tucson or Tarp-a-rama and were adorned with signs proclaiming, "If it ain't got strings we don't want to hear it," or "Tune it or Die!" As one could expect when

Emmitt and Herman were involved, their crew's camp, nicknamed Camp Howdy (a reference to a story Peter Rowan tells before his song "Free Mexican Air Force"), was a regular, buzzing hive of all-night picking, partying, and general mayhem throughout the festival. Each night after attending the festival their group would head back to camp, "light a big ole fire and start having a pick," raging all night until the early morning. That camaraderie and picking with friends was, for Emmitt, his chief reason for attending the festival each year. He says, "We came for the music and to see the festival, but our focus was to be in the campground and pick all night around a campfire with our friends."[10]

The music at the Telluride Bluegrass Festival did not end when the main stage closed each night. Besides the regular jams and picking circles taking place around the campground, the music moved into the bars littering downtown Telluride for intimate shows with the bands from the festival or smaller bands who were still trying to make their way into the festival's lineup. These smaller bands were groups like the Left Hand String Band and the Salmon Heads, who, as they had done for the past few years, booked shows at a couple of the local bars in Telluride, the Roma and Fly Me to the Moon. These late-night shows, while a great way to introduce themselves to a new, wider audience, did not in any way stop them from partying at Camp Howdy. The only difference being, on nights they had shows booked, the partying and merriment would not get started until three in the morning when they returned from the bars. "We would just come back later and do the same thing," remembers Michael Slingsby who was a regular part of Camp Howdy. "We would fire up and go to dawn."

Even though the Left Hand String Band was not part of the lineup and Emmitt had told festival promoter Ferguson that Left Hand String Band would not take part in the annual band contest, that did not mean that Emmitt was going to be completely absent from the festival's daily schedule. He thought the concept of the band contest was "ridiculous," and to show his contempt, he decided to put together a group to compete in the contest. To say Emmitt wanted to enter a group to compete is a complete injustice to the idea of competition. "We entered the band contest with the intention of losing it as kind of a joke," says Emmitt. "We wanted to have twenty people onstage, but we didn't have quite that many. I think we had thirteen." Emmitt rounded up many of his friends who were part of Camp Howdy to take part with him in the contest, as well as including some of the Salmon Heads. He would also find a banjo player sitting beneath a tree while he was walking the campgrounds whom he would ask to join him as part of the contest. That chance meeting with the banjo player would prove to be a life-altering encounter for both Emmitt and later Herman as they unknowingly found the final piece of the Leftover Salmon puzzle.

Chapter 3

MARK VANN

He opened a lot of doors for bluegrass banjo players the world over with his groundbreaking technique and the fearless energy and the presentation he laid on audiences. Totally pioneering stuff.—*Larry Keel*

"Down in front," yelled Mark Vann at the mountain partially blocking his view of the rising sun, his verbal explosion shattering the early morning silence. His three companions on this hike, his wife Jennifer, Drew Emmitt, and Vince Herman, burst out in laughter. Its joyous sound echoed off the surrounding mountains. "That is when we knew," says Herman, "this guy shouldn't be building decks in Virginia, he should be moving to Colorado to play music." The four decided to hike Bear Creek Falls, just outside of Telluride, to celebrate the newfound friendship of the three men. They had met earlier in the weekend in the campground at the 1989 Telluride Bluegrass Festival and spent the previous two days playing music at the festival, in the campgrounds, and around town. Emmitt, Herman, and Vann instantly recognized a shared prankster spirit and a humorous exuberance for life. The hike was the perfect capstone to their meeting. Despite the instantaneous musical connection the three experienced over the course of the festival, it would still be a few months before the three of them would finally take the stage together as Leftover Salmon, and even longer before Vann settled things in Virginia and moved to Colorado permanently, but the seeds of what were to come were first born that weekend in June at the

Telluride Bluegrass Festival and blossomed on that early morning hike to watch the sunrise.

Vann was born December 28, 1962, in Rockville, Maryland. Music was constant in the Vann household as the entire family played some sort of instrument. His father, Bryant, played guitar, his mother, Ricki, the upright bass and piano, and his brother, Mike, the mandolin. Vann remembers there were always other instruments lying around the house to play, including recorders, autoharps, and clarinets. Instead of watching television while growing up, Vann says the family played music for fun instead. His first instrument was a ukulele his grandmother gave him when he was eight. At age nine, he discovered the instrument that would go onto to define the rest of his musical life, or perhaps it is more accurate to say he discovered the instrument he would spend a lifetime redefining.

On July 4, 1972, Vann's family went to the Festival of American Folklife held on the National Mall in Washington, DC. The festival was filled with exhibits, dancers, and musicians. Among all of that, Vann saw iconic banjo picker Carl Pagter playing. His mother Ricki says, "He sat down on the grass under the elbow of this banjo player and didn't take his eyes off him for hours. His fingers never stopped moving as he watched." Transfixed by the playing of Pagter, Vann stayed at the stage all day, only occasionally moving so he could see Pagter's fingers from a different perspective, and thus try to discern how the sound so intoxicating to him was created. The next day, Vann approached his parents and announced, "I want to play banjo more than anything in the world, can I have one?" His parents noticed his rapt attention to Pagter's skillful playing the day before and how when he came home he tried to emulate that playing on his ukulele. They decided he was serious about learning to play and purchased him one.

Vann dove headfirst into the banjo. He obtained a copy of the definitive home lesson book, *Earl Scruggs and the 5-String Banjo*. Using that and records he slowed down on his turntable, he taught himself how to play. For Vann, he was all about the banjo and to him there was no greater master to learn from than the legendary Earl Scruggs. "For the longest time, Scruggs was all I listened to—just trying to dissect that and going through the book. I slowly branched out and started hearing other kinds of banjo players," says Vann. "I got into bluegrass because that was what the banjo was in. It wasn't that I heard bluegrass first and decided to be a banjo player."[1] Vann would lock himself away in his room and practice for up to eight hours every day. His parents noticed how fast his skills were developing. His mother wondered if he was naturally gifted like his grandmother, a musical prodigy who could play "the harp, piano, and anything else she touched." They signed him up for lessons, but quickly discovered he was already too advanced and gifted for restrictive, basic lessons and taking them only seemed to slow down his progress.

Bluegrass music began to take over the young Vann's life, and he was soon exploring a world beyond Scruggs. He was "eating up" all the banjo he could, both traditional and nontraditional. When he discovered innovative banjo legend Tony Trischka he "freaked out" over his one-of-a-kind playing.[2] Along with Trischka and Scruggs, Vann was getting heavily into other banjo icons like Eddie Adcock, Pete Wernick, J. D. Crowe, Ben Eldridge, and Alan Munde. Bluegrass music and the banjo had such a profound impact on Vann he reckons he did not listen to any music without a banjo in it until he turned eighteen. Even years after he joined Leftover Salmon, his lack of knowledge about classic rock 'n' roll was always a source of humor for the rest of the band. "He didn't know anything about rock," says Emmitt. "We would say something about the Beatles, Pink Floyd, Led Zeppelin, or some classic band, and he would be like, 'Who?' We had to educate him about that. He only liked two rock bands, Rush and AC/DC. He hardly knew anything about rock. Besides those two bands, he only listened to music with a banjo in it."

Despite his lack of knowledge and interest in rock music while in high school, Vann was developing a nontraditional approach to the banjo that would greatly help when he began playing with Salmon years later. Much of this approach was influenced by his discovery of innovative banjo-master Béla Fleck. In 1981, when he was eighteen, Vann went to the nearby Birchmere theater in Alexandria, Virginia, to see bluegrass stalwarts the Seldom Scene, who were amid a twenty-year, Thursday night, residency at the club. However, on this evening one of the members of the Seldom Scene was sick, so the Birchmere asked the band who played the night before to stay and play an extra night. It was a bit of luck for Vann as the band, Spectrum, at the time included the young, hotshot banjo sensation Fleck. With his innovative approach

Fleck was revolutionizing the way the banjo was being played. Shortly after Vann witnessed Fleck at the Birchmere, Fleck left Spectrum and joined another forward-thinking, bluegrass icon, Sam Bush, in a new version of New Grass Revival, and together the pair continued to revolutionize bluegrass music. Their time together had a huge impact on the development of Salmon. Vann marveled at Fleck's immense talents: "It was just incredible, hearing him do the single-string stuff so cleanly and fluidly. I started getting into playing scales and single-string and trying to play the banjo in different kinds of music."[3]

After high school graduation, Vann headed north to Philadelphia to attend academically prestigious Haverford College. Vann was highly intelligent and much like in high school he continued to earn good grades his freshman year, despite expressing little interest in academics. Music was his driving passion, and he continued to play nonstop. His first year at Haverford, he found few musically like-minded individuals, so he mostly practiced and played by himself. At the start of his sophomore year, his class adviser introduced Vann to an incoming freshman named Greg Spatz, who had similar musical tastes. The pair met Spatz's first day on campus as he was moving in. That first introduction left a deep impression on Spatz. "He was wearing shorts, flip-flops, and a tennis shirt with the collar up and he looked pretty fit," remembers Spatz. "I had the impression he might be some kind of jock. This definitely turned out to not be the case. He had this gap between his front teeth and a big nervous, guileless smile, hair kind of falling over his eyes, a bit of a southern accent, an infectious goofy laugh, and a habit of saying, 'No way, no way,' about any kind of coincidental connection of exciting information." The two quickly fell into conversation upon first meeting, and Spatz says he was fascinated by Vann's disarming humility. The pair found an instant connection through their shared love of bluegrass. "I'm sure he and I played together that day," says Spatz. "I remember hearing him play as my parents and I schlepped in boxes and unpacked—Mark probably helped us with that, but mostly he sat in the doorway playing banjo for us." As Spatz listened to Vann run through Flatt & Scruggs numbers as he unpacked his boxes he was struck by the precision, sweetness, and clarity Vann played with. It was a level of skill that belied the young banjo picker's age.

As the college year got underway, Spatz and Vann discovered a musical chemistry between them and began playing as an acoustic, instrumental duo named Biloxi that featured Spatz on fiddle and mandolin and Vann on banjo. After a freshman year spent mostly playing by himself in his dorm room, Vann was hungry for people to play with, and Spatz proved to be the perfect partner. Spatz says, "The interesting dynamic between the two of us was Mark was a much more traditional player than I was. He knew everything from the Scruggs songbook, but not a lot of contemporary bluegrass beyond the Seldom Scene. I knew practically nothing on the traditional side of things and was passionate about the whole Tony Rice/David Grisman newgrass sound." The pair got hired to play occasional dinner gigs at some of the local restaurants on the Main Line in Philadelphia that paid them a small fee and allowed them to eat and drink as much beer as they wanted.

Spatz and Vann soon found similar, like-minded musicians at Haverford in John Flower, John Doan, Jim Baldwin, and David Bachus and formed a band called Farmer's Trust. Farmer's Trust was a "party band with a lot of Grateful Dead influences," that played a fairly conventional style of bluegrass. Their repertoire included a lot of Flatt & Scruggs, Old & in the Way, Seldom Scene, and traditional tunes, but at the same time they were willing to travel down a more progressive path. Farmer's Trust guitarist Baldwin says, "We revered the masters, and broke them down note by note, but fused our sound with what we were hearing elsewhere, bits of jazz and blues, and old-timey honky-tonk we'd drawl and get some laughs with and some classic rock."

Farmer's Trust played mostly around campus, at rugby team parties, and occasionally at the local nightclubs. For Vann, who was a notorious prankster and practical joker, the good-time atmosphere surrounding Farmer's Trust suited him perfectly. "There was definitely a party culture around the Farmer's Trust," admits Spatz. "I guess you could say we were in the leading vanguard of musicians blending traditional acoustic music with a Grateful Dead vibe. Of course, we didn't know were in any kind of vanguard, didn't think of ourselves that way, and no one knew who we were. We just liked having a good time and experimenting with instruments that didn't need to be plugged in." This experimentation was right in line with where Vann was musically at the time. But upon arriving at Haverford he was "Really getting into David Grisman right about then. The *Quintet '80* album was fairly fresh and I was devouring that stuff, even though it didn't have a banjo on it." He was also taking music theory courses and starting to expand his musical tastes. He explains, "It was a whole new way of looking at the instrument. You must have a lot of knowledge to be able to work around jazz tunes—scales and arpeggios, and leading chords, and things like that. You need to know a lot of this stuff to play outside bluegrass. I was devouring anything about music at the time."[4]

Farmer's Trust's at times experimental sound was pushed forward by the interplay and differing personalities within the band. "The band was six guys," says Baldwin, "So there were a lot of ideas floated all the time. Songs would break down, change, and become other ones before we knew it. We would throw down 'I've Just Seen a Face' and other rock classics with a gutbucket bass, and then step into the Seldom Scene's 'Muddy Waters.'" Farmer's Trust's music was both respectful and irreverent at the same time. The core of the band's instrumental sound was built around Spatz and Vann. "Greg and Mark were particularly skilled listeners," says Baldwin, "and technically amazing at both rhythm and lead. Those guys studied their instruments, were in touch with tone as much as melody, and harmonized with each other like they were singing." The synergy between Spatz and Vann's disparate musical backgrounds was what drove Farmer's Trust. Vann, who Baldwin complimented by saying, "He could play the banjo like his hands were made of iron and leather," tended to keep the band centered in the more traditional bluegrass sound, while Spatz pushed the band toward weird experimentation, with intricate arrangements and extended soloing. On the few tapes that exist of Farmer's Trust from this time, this synergy is fully evident, as well as the seed of who Vann would become as a musician. The Country Gazette classic song, "Hot Burrito Breakdown," was a regular part of Farmer's Trust sets and later became a signature song for Vann's years with Salmon. On those old Farmer's Trust tapes, where crowd noise threatens to overwhelm, it is easy to recognize the power and originality that even at that young age Vann played with.

The true leader of the experimentation in Farmer's Trust, though, was bassist John Flower. Spatz says, "John was sort of the ringleader for Farmer's Trust and for the party culture surrounding it. He liked challenging the status quo and leading people into various forms of mischief, mostly benign, usually involving drugs and various kinds of truancy. He is easily one of the smartest and most articulate people I have ever met and one of the most passionate lovers of music. When he'd turn you onto something musical he loved, his passion was pretty irre-

Mark Vann plays at Villanova University for a nuclear disarmament show with Farmer's Trust in 1983. Courtesy of Jim Baldwin.

sistible and would make your hair stand on end." Flower was a few years older than the rest of Farmer's Trust. He had graduated the previous year, while the rest of the band was still in college. Following graduation, he struggled to find a job, and at the end of Vann's sophomore year he decided to move to Virginia with his girlfriend. The timing was perfect for Vann, who had had enough of college despite his strong academic showing. He joked while in college that he majored in confusion, as he was never able to settle on an actual major and saw no path forward because of that. He explains, "I went to college because it was what I was supposed to do, but I always had the banjo kind of pulling at me and it just kind of won out after about two years."[5] Vann's decision to leave Haverford was unsurprising to his good friend Spatz. "He was the kind of student who got A's in every class he took from math to history, which is saying a lot at a school like Haverford, but he had no academic passion. His passion was for music and the banjo."

Flower and his girlfriend planned to move to the woods of Virginia and were going to live a minimal lifestyle. This back-to-basics existence appealed to Vann, so he decided to make the move with them. They moved to the woods in northern Virginia near the small town of Warrenton in Fauquier County and lived in a three-walled log cabin that was open to the elements and had limited amenities—no running water, plumbing, or electricity. The trio's Spartan lifestyle was not as Spartan as it seemed, though. While they did live in a shack that barely contained the outside elements, the land they were squatting on was located on Flower's girlfriend's parents' extensive property and was a short walk from their house, where they occasionally headed for showers and to do laundry. Still, this forced seclusion with few outside influences was a positive time for Vann. He did the occasional side construction or carpentry job to make a few bucks, but his real focus during this time was on the banjo, which he practiced almost nonstop. He had no electricity, no telephone, no bills, only an old car to get around in and a deep devotion to his instrument and music. He later told Emmitt, "[I] didn't have a job. [My] job was playing the banjo for eight hours a day. [I] would just play rolls to a metronome for eight hours a day, take a lunch break and get back to it." Years later, Emmitt noticed Vann's deep commitment his craft, "All that practice showed. His rhythm and timing were amazing." For Vann, the move into the woods was a chance for him to vanish into a musical cocoon, from which he emerged a pro with fierce focus.

While he was living in the woods with Flower, Vann occasionally headed home to Maryland. During one of these visits he met a local Maryland musician, Ed Schaeffer, at a house jam. Schaeffer had a well-established local band, Rattlesnake Hill, which had been playing in the area since 1980. It had recently seen some turnover in its ranks, and Schaeffer was looking to fill out the lineup for an album he was preparing to work on when he first met Vann. Vann's already prodigious skills had grown exponentially since leaving Haverford and devoting himself full time to practice in the cabin in the woods. This growth was evident to Schaeffer: "He had a machine-like delivery. He had such good timing. He was great. As soon I heard him, I went and told him about the project." Despite the obvious age gap between Vann and the rest of his bandmates—Schaeffer was in his late thirties, and the rest of the band were all at least a few years older than the just-out-of-his-teens Vann—he agreed to join. The band at the time included Schaeffer on guitar, Mike Phipps on mandolin, Willie Oldes on bass, and future Seldom Scene Dobro player Fred Travers. Vann was happy to be part of a group again, and Schaeffer noticed how much effort he contributed to working out the musical arrangements for the upcoming album with the rest of the band. Rattlesnake Hill headed into Patuxent Music to record with future Washington, DC, legend Tom Mindte who was just beginning what would become a prolific career in bluegrass as a musician, producer, and label owner. The resulting album, *19th Century Man*, was released in 1984 and was Vann's first recorded appearance on an album. The album was a straightforward, traditional style of bluegrass featuring none of the weird experimentation Vann was toying with in Farmer's Trust. Still, Vann's contributions to the album readily shine through, as his machine-like delivery and tasteful solos resonate with pure, traditional power. Vann also appeared on the live album, *Rattlesnake Hill at the Old Mill*, that was recorded during his brief tenure with the band. The four-song, live EP is an all-too-brief glimpse into Vann's already well-advanced banjo skills. By the time the live album was released, Vann had left Maryland and decamped back to the woods of Virginia.

During his, almost three years of seclusion in the woods, Vann took a trip to upstate New York in the summer of 1985. While on the trip, he met Jennifer Loud. Loud was intrigued by this highly intelligent man with a witty sense of humor who seemed to often downplay his smarts around others and developed a strong crush on him. As the two got to know each other better they formed a deep connection, with Vann falling in love with the dynamic personality of Loud. "He was utterly, giddily happy in love with her," says Spatz, "and brought back to the kind of goofy openness I remember from our first meeting by being with her." Loud eventually moved to Virginia to be with him. She lured him out of the woods and into a house they bought together. When he and Loud started dating, Vann was still doing carpentry work. After realizing the small local company he worked for would not be able to afford to pay him what his in-demand skills were worth, he decided to strike out on his own and start his own business. Vann and Loud opened their own landscaping and carpentry business called Woodscapes, which they ran for many years while living in Virginia.

In addition to the landscaping business, Vann also gave the occasional banjo lesson on the side to make a couple of bucks and help make ends meet. At one of these lessons, his student brought along a guitar-playing friend. After the lesson Vann asked his student's friend if he wanted to stick around and pick some. The friend, Larry Keel, quickly realized he and Vann were "kindred spirits." The two men were both like-minded progressive bluegrass players who approached their instruments with a similar out-of-the-box alternative style. It was clear to Keel Vann was a special talent. He proclaimed, "He was the most unique banjo player I ever heard." Keel also noticed Vann's insatiable appetite for practicing. Vann carved a mock banjo out of a block of wood. The head was the same size as a normal banjo, but the neck was much shorter. It had strings on it placed exactly as they were on a real banjo. "It would ride in his lap and he wouldn't have to hold it with his left hand and he could still drive with one hand," remembers Keel. "He practiced rolls while he would drive back and forth to work. He said it was meditation to practice his rolls all the time. It's those things that made him a completely different style of player."[6] This single-minded dedication by Vann to his banjo saw him developing a truly awe-inspiring set of skills, transcending what was normally thought possible on the five-string. Keel shared this intense dedication to perfecting his instrument as well and their shared intensity allowed a deep bond to develop between the two. "We both had the discipline and the homework down pretty good and were both interested in exploring new and different territories with our respective instruments," says Keel.

"Among all the pickers I was hanging out with at the time, Mark was totally unique. He was this amazingly creative, gifted person, and definitely a pioneer of a whole new style on the banjo."[7] Keel and Vann developed a close friendship and started working together in the landscaping business Vann owned. Keel says, "We were doing landscaping work, building decks, retaining walls, and customizing stuff. We also played music together a whole bunch and met a bunch of friends playing bluegrass in the area. It seemed we were picking all the time and had a great friend, John Flower, with us."[8]

Since moving to Virginia, Flower and Vann continued to play occasionally as Farmer's Trust with either some combination of local players, or on special occasions when the original members of the band would reunite to play a gig. Keel immediately fit in to what Vann and Flower were creating. "We had a blast together, playing music together, going to jams and parties," says Keel. Vann's reputation as a practical joker was also evident to Keel: "He was sneaky and full of mischief. He was always trying to get one over on you. Flower was a favorite target of Mark's pranks." Despite Vann making Flower a target of regular practical jokes, the trio recognized they were beginning to create something musically significant. The chemistry between Flower and Vann was already developed and refined from their time playing in college together. The dynamic emerging between Vann's innovative banjo rolls and Keel's unparalleled flatpicking guitar style was especially compelling. It was clear Keel needed to be in Farmer's Trust with Vann and Flower. They made the band into a permanent trio with Flower on bass, Keel on guitar, and Vann on banjo. Keel says, "We played a lot of private parties in the area and all kinds of things. We were good at creating. We had a different sound. We weren't just bluegrass; we were creating our own kind of music at that point."[9] They began to play the festival circuit in Virginia, West Virginia, and North Carolina and started getting some serious attention. Unfortunately for this new version of Farmer's Trust, they never got a chance to live up to their full potential as Vann headed west for what would be a life-changing trip—to the Telluride Bluegrass Festival.

In early summer 1989, Vann and Jennifer loaded up their pickup truck and made the cross-country drive from Virginia to Colorado for the 16th Annual Telluride Bluegrass Festival held over the weekend of June 22–25. It was Vann's second to trip to the legendary bluegrass festival, as he had gone the previous summer. Vann's goal for the weekend was to soak up the music and to participate in the festival's annual banjo competition.

Vann arrived in Telluride, set up camp, and headed over to get registered for the banjo contest. He breezed through the preliminary rounds on Thursday, June 22, and qualified for the finals being held the following morning. After the preliminary rounds, Vann retreated to his camp to practice his banjo, as was still his norm. He found a nice spot under a tree, sat down, and started playing. At the same time, Emmitt was wandering the campground on a quest to find a few more players to help him fill out the lineup for a band he was going to enter in the contest the following day. He viewed the contest as a joke and wanted to enter a band to illustrate this point. Frustrated at not having the Left Hand String Band selected to be part of the lineup, Emmitt was going to show his displeasure by making a mockery of the band contest. He entered the band in the contest under the name the Left Hand Salmon Spankers, as the band was a combination of the Left Hand String Band, the Salmon Heads, and another band, the Chicken Spankers. Emmitt wanted to have twenty people onstage when they finally took the stage, but even with parts of three bands, he was still short of the desired number. He was roaming the campgrounds trying to find some other players he could recruit to come and play when something caught his attention. He says, "I heard this incredible banjo playing. It was dead on, and the rhythm was perfect. I stopped and there was a guy sitting under a tree playing banjo. I introduced myself and said, 'Why don't you come be in the band contest with us?'" The banjo player Emmitt was impressed with was Vann, who was always up for a good time and a bit of adventure. He agreed to join them. It was not only Vann's perfect playing that struck Emmitt, but also his appearance. "When I met him, he had super short hair and a John Deere cap," remembers Emmitt. "He looked just like a country bumpkin. Later he became this very hip dude with long hair." The two continued to chat, and Emmitt, who was thoroughly amazed by Vann's banjo picking, invited him to come play at the Roma that evening in downtown Telluride. The Salmon Heads had a show booked there, and they invited Emmitt to join them for the evening. Emmitt knew the Salmon Heads enjoyed a spot of adventure and would not mind having a special banjo talent like Vann join them at their show at the Roma.

The Roma is one of the oldest bars in Telluride, first opening in 1897, and had long been a live music venue staple before closing and reopening as a high-end Asian-fusion restaurant in 2006. The downstairs bar hosted many an up-and-coming band on their way through Colorado for the first time. It famously was the location of Phish's first ever show in Colorado on July 28, 1988. It also was also a popular venue for bands to play during the Telluride Bluegrass Festival as the Left Hand String Band had done before and the Salmon Heads would be doing this year. As was often the case at Left Hand String Band and Salmon Heads' shows, they recruited their good friend Michael Slingsby to work the door and collect the cover. On this evening, he was helped by Vann's wife, Jennifer, who came with him to the show. This was a Salmon Heads show and featured Herman on guitar, Dave Dorian on washboard, Hugh Robertson on fiddle, and Steve Burnside on bass, but Emmitt, Vann, and bassist Glenn Keefe sat in with them for most of the show. The evening was a high-energy affair, made even more special by the presence of Emmitt, Vann, and Keefe. Herman and Emmitt had already begun developing an intense musical partnership, first at informal house jams, then more formally in the Left Hand String Band, and later in the party-hearty campgrounds at Telluride. The addition of Vann's banjo only added to the fiery energy coming from the small stage. Slingsby remembers the crowd getting worked into a drunken frenzy and chatting, "Roma, Roma, Roma," throughout the night.

The seven musicians squeezed themselves onto the small stage that night finding what little room was available for them and their instruments. Herman, always the jester, held court center stage while wearing a bright yellow hat with lips and a large floppy tongue embroidered on it. He was flanked to his immediate right by Emmitt with his long hair peeking out from beneath a cowboy hat. To Herman's left was Vann, hunched over his banjo in deep concentration in a sleeveless T-shirt looking exactly like the country bumpkin Emmitt thought he was when he first encountered him. In hindsight, it seems so natural to see those three in those stage positions together as this is how they patrolled the stage as a band for the next decade, but this was the first time the three ever stood onstage together and they assumed what would become their natural stage positions.

The evening was also memorable as the addition of Emmitt's mandolin and Vann's banjo created an entirely new dynamic. Despite the unique instrumentation of the band, an acoustic guitar, banjo, mandolin, fiddle, washboard, upright bass, and electric bass that did not seem to have a musical home, the seven musicians found immeasurable beauty in this odd configuration. With everyone's shared interest in bluegrass, Emmitt's desire to play rock 'n' roll, and Herman's deep love for a Cajun sound, something special happened that night. They found an entirely new musical dimension on which to exist. Herman says the Salmon Heads were simply a Cajun jug band, but this evening with Emmitt and Vann joining something changed, and this simple jug band that normally played humorous songs and calypso sing-alongs was reborn as a live, raging monster. Emmitt and Vann traded licks and solos back and forth, while Herman pushed his theatrical front man antics even further to the edge. Herman's guitar work is rarely recognized, as it is often overshadowed by his larger-than-life personality onstage, but

The Salmon Heads, with Drew Emmitt, Glenn Keefe, and Mark Vann, play the Roma during the Telluride Bluegrass Festival June 1989 (from left): Dave Dorian (partially obscured), Hugh Robertson (fiddle), Steve Burnside (bass), Drew Emmitt (mandolin), Vince Herman (guitar), Glenn Keefe (bass), and Mark Vann (banjo). Courtesy of Vince of Herman.

on this evening even his playing seemed to be something special and found a new level. With the Cajun clack of Dorian's washboard, the double bass power of Keefe and Burnside, Robertson's bluegrass fiddle, Emmitt's hyperactive mandolin, and Vann's machine-like banjo rolls all supporting Herman's unhinged antics, the roots of Leftover Salmon were all clearly evident onstage at the Roma. The energy among Emmitt, Herman, and Vann was unmistakable to the hundred or so patrons lucky enough to witness the first time these three shared a stage together. "In my mind," declares Slingsby, "it was the birth of Leftover Salmon right there. It took a while for it to get going, but that to me is the start." Herman agrees, "It was a Salmon Heads gig with those guys sitting in, but you could say it was really the first Leftover Salmon gig." Emmitt confirms, "That's pretty much where it started."[10] The entire band was buzzing both musically and chemically from the night and, as was the norm, they headed back to Camp Howdy after the show to continue the party. Emmitt describes the humorous scene that ensued when the well-lubricated band got back to camp. "Vince had like a hundred people following him through the campground to all these different campfires. It was nutty. I'd never seen anything like it. That was kind of the inaugural night of Leftover Salmon."[11]

The day following the show at the Roma was the contest finals. The individual finals were first, and Vann, despite the late night, again wowed with his inspired originality and inventive style that placed him in a class by himself and he easily won the competition. He would enter and win the contest again in 1994. The positive experience Vann had with the contest provoked him to convince his good friend Keel to head west from Virginia and take part, which he would do, winning the guitar contest in 1993 and 1995. After the individual banjo contest, Vann joined the Left Handed Salmon Spankers for their part in the band contest. The Salmon Spankers was the second band he played with in the band contest, as another group asked him to join as well. A quick change of his outfit between sets allowed him to be properly disguised for his double appearance. The Salmon Spankers set list reflected the disdain Emmitt had for the contest, as they played two cowboy type songs and an early version of the future Leftover Salmon tune, "Rodeo Geek," that was written by Herman's college friend Fred Prichard. As Slingsby says, "They had no chance, but they had a lot of fun." They finished a notable six out of seven bands. For Emmitt and Herman, the contest was simply a fun excuse to get together and play music during the day and further cemented the pair's shared sense of outlandish humor. There was plenty of picking and partying happening the rest of the weekend, so the Left Hand Salmon Spankers all scattered throughout the festival grounds after the contest. Some stuck around the main stage to check out the music, while others headed back to camp to rest up for the long night ahead.

Emmitt wanted to continue to play with Vann. The pair found a spot in the middle of the campground, sat down on a couple of logs, and started to pick. The connection between the two was deep and instantly recognizable. Slingsby joined the two to listen and was the only other person around when they began to play. He was struck by the almost telepathic way Vann seemed to be responding to Emmitt. He says, "I remember distinctly sitting with Mark and Drew and listening to them. There were so many times I was in position to see things we took for granted, but I understand now, why those moments are so important. Drew was showing Mark some of his songs like, 'Gold Hill Line,' 'Get Me Outta This City,' and 'Just Before the Evening,' and the first time through Drew played better leads on all those songs, better than he had ever done before with any other banjo player. I was so struck by Mark's musicianship. The musical rapport between Mark and Drew that afternoon was amazing, and only continued to grow from there." As the afternoon wore on and despite the magical, musical connection Emmitt and Vann were discovering, the pair stopped playing and headed back to their respective camps to grab a bite to eat and get ready for the night of partying to come with the setting sun.

Camp Howdy, being a group that liked to stay up all night and party, developed a solution for how they dealt with their fellow campers who decided to turn in early for the night to sleep and forgo the night's festivities. A large contingent would surround the tent of the Camp Howdy regular who was sleeping. Armed with their instruments and fueled from a night of partying, the contingent would proceed to sing and play and generally make quite a racket outside of the tent until their friend woke up and rejoined the festivities. The tradition had its roots in a late night a few years prior at Telluride. Slingsby had been chatting up a lady friend all night. As the night began to end, he was "surprised and bummed out" when she left him "at the door of her tent." The forlorn Slingsby wandered back to Camp Howdy in a "weird mood." Herman, and a few other friends were still awake, but "for Camp Howdy this was pretty mellow." Herman, looking to cheer his friend up and perhaps maybe stir up a little late-night excitement, suggested they grab their guitars and go and wake a friend of theirs on the other side of the campground. The small group stumbled through the campground, dodging tent stakes and guidelines as they maneuvered in the dark. They arrived at their friend's tent and belted out a rambling, out-of-tune version of "The Christmas Song (Chestnuts Roasting on the Open Fire)," which mostly was Herman singing, while everyone else sort of hummed along and sang the few words they knew as they all pounded away on their guitars. The tent sprang to life and the zipper flew open. Two sleepy heads popped out to see what all the commotion was, and Slingsby realized, "It was not our friends. We had the wrong tent." The sleepy folks who were abruptly woken up in the middle of the night by an off-key, drunken rendition of the Christmas classic found the whole event amusing. For Herman, it seemed to be the natural progression from his earliest day performing impromptu sets in the student union on a chair with Lew Prichard, to barging in to restaurants in downtown Morgantown to provide a surprise concert to the unsuspecting guests, to now musically ambushing random tents in the campground in the dead of night. Herman, Slingsby, and their friends spent the rest of the night wandering through the campground, swarming around tents and proceeding to serenade the sleepy campers inside with drunken singing until they woke up. On that first night, Slingsby says they probably had a nine out of ten positive reaction, which emboldened them to continue doing this again each night.

At first, they would bring instruments with them when they went around tent marauding, but over time, the idea of lugging instruments around the dark campground, late at night, often in altered states of mind, became a bit of struggle. Eventually their tent ambushing morphed into being done mostly a capella. It furthered evolved when Camp Howdy regular Mike Cutler suggested they sing the Austin Lounge Lizards song, "Anahuac" from the band's debut album, *Creatures from the Black Saloon*, as they vocally raided tents. This was often whittled down to simply singing the chorus, "Anahuac, Anahuac, it used to be my home, but it's not anymore," and the tradition of "Anahuacing" was born. "We'd sneak up on a campfire where a bunch of people were picking, and we'd run up with all our instruments and play 'Anahuac' loudly and out of key before we'd turn and run away," says Emmitt.[12] Over the years, it moved from this large-scale operation often including instruments, in which everyone in the campgrounds was a potential "Anahuac" target, to a more streamlined approached, singing a capella and generally focusing their sights on the crew of Camp Howdy. "Mostly after the first year we didn't do it randomly. We started doing it against each other. It became very hard to get sleep in our camp," explains Slingsby. "Some people in our group even had little secondary tents somewhere in the campground where they could sneak off to and get some sleep. They made sure no one knew where their tents were. It became a competition of who could get it worse." After Telluride, the Anahuacing would go on in condos and hotel rooms for years, often starting with a late-night call from Herman exclaiming, "What are you doing? You should be here!" Slingsby says despite the late-night calls and the intrusion of a pack of drunken friends singing loudly and off-key, you could never be mad, "Because when you got Anahuached it was a sign of love." The inspired chaos of Anahuacing was key to the development of Leftover Salmon. "That whole experience of Anahuacing in Telluride was really how this band was born," says Emmitt. "That kind of energy. We're just going to have fun and do crazy things and take it to the streets."

The Telluride Bluegrass Festival also provided Leftover Salmon with another long-lasting tradition that could trace its roots to the festival campgrounds. This tradition was born from one of Emmitt's favorite television shows and would provide the band with a rally crying from stage that would continue to echo on for years after its initial birth. One morning as Emmitt and Slingsby were walking into the festival grounds, Emmitt began saying, "Red hour, are you of the body?" It took Slingsby a moment to realize what he was talking about it, but quickly realized he was quoting an old *Star Trek* episode called "Return of the Archons." Both Emmitt and Slingsby were huge Star Trek fans and often talked about their favorite episodes. The episode Emmitt was referencing was about a planet Captain Kirk and crew visited whose inhabitants were living in a nineteenth-century style, with little or no individual expression or creativity. A mysterious dictator named Landru rules the people. This apparently peaceful society becomes berserk twice a year starting at 6 p.m., a time they call the "Red Hour." They call this chaotic period, "Festival." This "Festival" period of violence, destruction, and sexual aggressiveness is apparently the only time Landru does not exercise control over the people. In the episode during the "Red Hour," people are seen running through the streets yelling and screaming, breaking windows, starting fires, and engaging in all sorts of violent acts. During this, a man runs into the street and screams, "Festival! Festival!" He then runs off. When Slingsby first met up with Emmitt that morning on the way into Telluride festival grounds, Emmitt was talking about Landru and the "Return of the Archons," when out of nowhere he yelled, "Festival," catching Slingsby by surprise, who immediately broke out into laughter. It became the theme of weekend for the two good friends, who spent the whole time yelling "Festival" and amusing themselves. As with many things in the Leftover Salmon universe, this simple yell was soon picked up by their friends and grew into something well beyond a friendly inside joke. "It turned into this deep big festival yell," says Slingsby. "It was just something we did in the campground and it was a joke between us. It was just a code among our campground group. From there, it just progressed. Eventually Vince took it and did it all around the country. In Telluride, it had a life of its own. As the years progressed, you could be in the campground and yell, 'Festival!' and someone in another camp would yell, 'Festival!' and it would go around the campground. When the band was onstage I would yell, 'Festival!' and they would yell it back at me. Drew started it all." "Festival" has come to mean so much more to the band than just a silly yell from stage. The communal idea and endless fun of festivals are encapsulated in the "Festival" yell. It has come to be a greeting, a state of mind, the place to be. It represents all the band was and still is.

After Emmitt and Vann's afternoon campground picking session, Vann had gone back to his tent to relax a bit. He headed out later to see who else he could find to play with. It was a colder evening than normal, and Vann remembers, "The picking hadn't been great that particular night. I was kind of bummed out. I went to bed early, around eleven."[13] Perhaps it was the cold forcing people into the tents and the warmth of their sleeping bags earlier than they normally might have, because Emmitt, Herman, and their friends were experiencing this same lack of enthusiasm to party. They rounded up a crew and started "Anahuacing" some of their friends, waking them up and getting them to join the party. Vann says, "I was woken up about an hour later and heard this picking about forty feet from my tent that was just awesome.

I threw my clothes on and ran out there. It was Vince and Drew and a bunch of others getting all wild and crazy."[14] Emmitt and Herman were leading a large crew of Camp Howdy regulars around the camp "Anahuacing" tent after and tent and creating a giant, roving, mobile party as they moved around the campground. Vann grabbed his banjo and immediately joined in, picking and playing with Emmitt and Herman. The roving party, as it often does when Herman and Emmitt were involved, lasted all night. The large party was thinned down as sleep, as it always does, won out, until it was just Emmitt, Herman, Vann, and Vann's wife, Jennifer, still standing.

Not wanting to see the party stop and wishing to find a way to perfectly cap the weekend they just experienced, it was decided an early morning hike up nearby Bear Creek Falls to watch the sunrise would be the ideal way to end the weekend. It may have also been a way to get away from any other potential campers who were not happy

"The inaugural night of Leftover Salmon." Drew Emmitt, Vince Herman, and Mark Vann jam in the campground at the 1989 Telluride Bluegrass Festival shortly after their first meeting. Courtesy of Vince Herman.

about being unexpectedly serenaded by a drunken version of "Anahuac" in the middle of the night. "We walked up there at sunrise after carousing and harassing everyone in the campground," admits Emmitt sheepishly.

The group made it to the top of the mountain just before the sun rose for the day. They settled in, waiting for the dawn's early light, when they realized a mountain that stood on the horizon between them and the rising sun was going to partly obscure their view. As the early morning silence filled the air, Vann yelled at the mountain offending his view, "Down in front!" His companions were taken by surprise and initially shocked as the dawn's waking quiet was broken by the outburst. That initial shock was quickly replaced with laughter, as Emmitt recognized a familiar mischievous spirit. "It was our first experience with Mark and his humor and his personality, which was very quirky and witty. I think that is when we realized he was going to fit in." Herman and Emmitt knew they had met a similar soul. It was not just the shared musical vision of what they could be that bonded the three. It was also the immediate personal connection they felt. It was clear whatever the future held for them musically they needed to face it together. Interestingly, while Herman felt right away Vann "shouldn't be building decks in Virginia anymore, he should be moving to Colorado," to play music, the idea of the three of them joining forces at that point was not discussed. The Left Hand String Band and the Salmon Heads were still two separate entities and despite the magic evident the night before at the Roma, the idea of combining the bands was not even a thought yet. The Left Hand String Band was by far the bigger of the two bands, and Emmitt asked Vann if he wanted to take over the banjo role. Vann agreed. He would head to Virginia, settle things at home, and then head back to Colorado. The addition of Vann solidified what the Left Hand String Band was doing with Emmitt, Keefe, and guitarist Rob Wheeler, and seemed to signify even brighter days ahead for the band. The day following their hike as Emmitt prepared to head home to Boulder and Vann back to Virginia, Herman and the Salmon Heads drove to Durango to play a show at Farquahrts.

The importance of not just the Telluride Bluegrass Festival, but music festivals in general, for the development of the music and personality of Emmitt, Herman, Vann, and Leftover Salmon cannot be overstated. Bluegrass festivals provided a chance for them to find their place musically and understand how to connect with fans. They spent many years as fans at these festivals themselves, watching their idols play onstage and seeing how they related with audiences and spending countless hours playing in campground jams and trying out some of those same ideas. These festivals provided some of the earliest collaborations between the Left Hand String Band and the Salmon Heads, marking the genesis of what was to come. The festival campgrounds also provided a fertile place for the audacious humor and antics of Emmitt, Herman, and Vann to evolve and flourish, becoming a natural part of who they were both off- and onstage. Herman says for him, festivals are an almost religious experience, a chance to get together with friends new and old and celebrate the importance of music for life. Festivals provide the opportunity to take a holiday from reality and gather with your tribe, turn it up, crank it out, and enjoy the community of it all. For Leftover Salmon, festivals became an essential part of their outlook on life. "Festivals are what we got now," declares Herman. "For some of our culture it is pro or college sports, for me it is all about the gathering at festivals. Festivals allow us to gather and celebrate the essence of what we all do and the joy of being alive."

After the Telluride Bluegrass Festival, Vann headed back to Virginia to get things in order with his business and abandon his normal life as he prepared to move to Colorado and join up with the Left Hand String Band. While he may have been in Virginia at the time, his heart was already in Colorado. In his handwritten personal calendars from the year it was almost as if he was trying to put Virginia behind him and get to Colorado as soon as he could, as all the pages from February to September 1990 are ripped out, with the first entry for September happily reading, "MOVE TO COLORADO!!!" His impending move brought an end to Farmer's Trust. Keel and Flower would continue forward, replacing Vann with Will Lee and adding Danny Knicely on mandolin. They called their new band Magraw Gap. Magraw Gap would find great success over the ensuing years, even winning the Telluride Bluegrass Festival band competition in 1996. Keel would leave Magraw Gap and begin a solo career that has seen him become one of the most revered flatpicking guitarists around. For Emmitt and Herman things went back to normal. They continued to play shows, hang out together at parties, and pick whenever possible. The Left Hand String Band were in a bit of a holding pattern as they waited for Vann to join them, so they only played the occasional show. Throughout the fall, the Salmon Heads continued to regularly gig in the surrounding area. Occasionally they would have their friends from the Left Hand String Band join them. "There were a few times we jammed together," recalls Emmitt of the transition period before Vann arrived in Colorado. "Glenn and I ended up joining up with the Salmon Heads and jamming. One time was in Fort Collins and another at the Millsite just north of Boulder." Those two shows, while featuring the earliest incarnation of Leftover Salmon, Herman, Emmitt, Keefe, Dorian, and accordionist Gerry Cavagnaro, are also drastically different, as Dorian only played washboard for the pair of shows and were not the true vision of rock 'n' roll bluegrass they would come to be. That vision finally took flight a few months later in December of 1989 over the course of a couple of shows, climaxing with a gig on New Year's Eve.

The Salmon Heads had lined up a couple of gigs in Telluride a few days before Christmas, and another one on New Year's Eve at the Eldo in Crested Butte. Both gigs were long drives from Boulder, as Telluride was six hours away and Crested Butte was four. "Some of the guys in the Salmon Heads didn't want to go that far for the gigs, and Vince was scrambling to put a lineup together," says Emmitt. "Glenn had the idea to put the two bands together and be more of a rock band. It was the first time those two bands had gotten together and played with a drummer. Before we just had Dave on washboard." These gigs were simply a fun excuse to get out and play with some good friends. The lineup for all the shows was the same as it was earlier in the fall: Emmitt, Herman, Keefe, Cavagnaro, and Dorian. The key difference being Dorian was now playing a full drum kit.

For the two Telluride shows, the band rented a condo they could stay in for the two-night run. As it was the first time they all played with a drummer they wanted to rehearse to figure things out. The rehearsal did not go so well because "within the first twenty minutes they were all blasted, and just started writing down names of songs they knew on a piece of paper." They ended up with a list of songs they all partially knew but did not know the beginnings or ends for them. So that night, they played one long medley for an hour and half. One song after another with no stopping, while Herman looked down at the piece of paper with all the songs they knew written on it, changing from one to the other on the fly. This nonstop musical party clearly left an impression on the gathered crowd, as the next night there was a line out the door to get in.

The following week, the same group gathered for the four-hour trip to Crested Butte to play the Eldo on New Year's Eve. "One of the clearest memories I have is driving to the gig with Drew and thinking, 'Man, this is cool,'" says Herman. "This is the start of something new." Emmitt and Herman, who were riding to the show together in Emmitt's truck, were discussing what to call this conglomeration of the Left Hand String Band and the Salmon Heads, when Herman in a moment of pure simplistic, inspiration blurted out, "Leftover Salmon." A solution so straightforward and simple it made perfect sense. Combine the names of the two bands and move on. Emmitt reflects on that burst of inspiration he has lived with ever since. "We laughed and said, 'Okay.' We didn't think it was going to turn into anything at that point. We thought we were just going to be together for that gig." [15] Herman agrees, "I really thought it'd only last one gig." [16] Despite this uncertainty of this new band's future for Herman, the drive to the show was filled with much optimism about the future for the two young musicians. Perhaps it was the impending New Year or the wide-open possibilities looming ahead for both. Herman states, "There was a definite sense of onward to the future going into that gig we both felt on the ride there."

With a handful of shows together over the past few months and the experience of playing together as a band the previous week, the newly christened group worked up many songs and had a large repertoire from which to pull, so figuring out what to play was not a problem. With the addition of drums, how they would present that material was an easy decision as well. "We just said, 'Let's take bluegrass, crank it up, add drums, and that will be Leftover Salmon," explains Emmitt. [17] Their set list for the Eldo show was more refined than it was the week before in Telluride, and pulled from both the Left Hand String Band's and the Salmon Heads' usual song catalog. "It was really natural to combine those two bands," says Herman.

While the exact set list for the night has been lost due to the ravages of time and fuzzy memories, Herman and Emmitt both recalled they played Emmitt's "Gold Hill Line." Herman is also sure they played a few other Emmitt-penned tunes: "I certainly knew them from my time with the Left Hand String Band, and Glenn was the bass player in that band. We would have taught Gerry the few tunes and he would have played harmonica on the tunes where the accordion didn't quite work." Among some of the other songs they are both certain were played were some of the tunes Herman first learned from Vince Farsetta back in West Virginia, like "Zombie Jamboree" and "BooBoo." They also played traditional bluegrass songs, including "Little Maggie," and a slew of covers, including "Gimme da Ting," by calypso legend Lord Kitchener, "Voodoo Queen Marie," by the Holy Modal Rounders, and "She Took Off My Romeos," by David Lindley. This eclectic mix of songs was a strong opening statement of who Leftover Salmon was to become.

It was not just the song selection that made the evening special, it was also the energy crackling in the air that could almost be tasted by the band. This crackling energy was sparking an intense reaction from the crowd. "The response at Crested Butte was off the hook," says Herman with a similar bolt of energy. "We found the older the song we played, the more old-time bluegrass it was, the rowdier the crowd got. The slam dancing taking place was just out of hand. People were just flailing across the room. We looked at each other onstage like, 'Whoa,' we could be on to something here." This response was not foreign to Emmitt. He had begun noticing the reaction at Left Hand String Band shows when they cranked up the tempo on some old traditional tune or when they threw an Allman Brothers Band or Little Feat song into their set and the usual sedated bluegrass crowd would come to life. He recognized a similar reaction at the Eldo, and his immediate feeling was like Herman's, "This could be very cool." As if the bluegrass gods knew what was happening at the Eldo, in Oakland, California, the same night, Salmon's musical forefathers, New Grass Revival, were playing their last show opening for the Grateful Dead. Unbeknownst to both audiences, the torch was passed.

Leftover Salmon's blistering show also tapped into the energy prevalent in the ski towns that dot the mountains of Colorado and found a willing audience for this new brand of high-energy bluegrass, which they soon christened slamgrass. "I guess the thing unique for a bluegrass band was to have drums and playing a kind of aggressive slam dancing, with kind of a punk edge," Herman says. "At the time in Crested Butte that struck a chord with the community, you know? The slam dancing thing just went off that first night. And all the energy was in there, in the ski community at the time, we just kind of harnessed it."[18] This new sound was something unheard before and a refreshing change from other rock bands who dominated the Colorado ski towns at the time. The ski community gave them an audience open to this new high-powered sound and a strong network of venues within these ski towns that supported live music. Those venues, in that pre-internet age, communicated with each other regularly about what bands were drawing crowds and what bands to book. When Leftover Salmon walked offstage after the first night, they were already an in-demand band. "The ski circuit as it was in 1990 was we played our first gig on New Year's Eve and the next day we had six other gigs," explains Herman. This immediate reaction was not lost on the band and the potential it seemed to hold for them. As they quickly began to gain popularity they found they had trouble describing this new, hybrid sound to bar owners and promoters who were looking to book them and promote their shows. "The guys at the doors at these ski towns didn't know what to say when people asked what kind of music we played," laughs Herman who recognized calling it electric bluegrass did not cut it. "So, we came up with the phrase, 'Polyethnic Cajun Slamgrass.' That enabled us to include all the musical directions in our heads. Growing up in the sixties and seventies we had so much in our heads—not just rock 'n' roll and bluegrass, but also cartoon music, jazz, show tunes and so on." [19]

Among the initial gigs Salmon got offered was a two-night run at the Zephyr in Salt Lake City, Utah, and the Mangy Moose in Jackson Hole, Wyoming, in February of 1990. Vann was not around for the December shows, but had come back to Colorado for a visit and was camping in Emmitt's yard around the time of the Zephyr and Mangy Moose shows. There was some discussion between Emmitt and Herman about whether Vann should join Leftover Salmon as well as the Left Hand String Band. "I had to convince Vince because he didn't think we needed a banjo player," recalls Emmitt. "I remember him asking me, 'Do we need a banjo player?' I said, 'Yeah, I think we do.' At that point, Vince wasn't all that into having a banjo player; he was leaning toward a more Cajuny-rock band sound and I was more into a bluegrass-type thing. I told Vince we should have him sit in and see how it works." The Vanns followed the band from Colorado to both shows.

He joined the band the first night in Jackson Hole at the Mangy Moose, marking the first time Emmitt, Herman, and Vann played as Leftover Salmon together. The following night, Vann again sat in with the band. The connection they experienced over the summer was still

Leftover Salmon plays their first show with Mark Vann at the Mangy Moose in Jackson Hole, Wyoming, February 1990 (from left): Vann, Glenn Keefe, Drew Emmitt. Courtesy of Vince Herman.

there. "He started playing with us and it sounded good and it made sense," says Emmitt. "After Mark sat in with us, Vince was sure." "It was a no brainer. He was so good," admits Herman with excitement. "I always like high-energy music, it makes people dance and get rowdy and the banjo always helps with that." With that Vann was now in both the Left Hand String Band and Leftover Salmon. He headed back to Virginia one last time and returned to Colorado in September of 1990 for good.

Upon Vann's return, the Left Hand String Band was by far the more established of the two bands and seemed destined for much bigger things. Herman says, "The plan was they were going to build the Left Hand String Band into a national touring act, but Leftover Salmon took that energy and ran with it." Emmitt, Vann, and Keefe split their time between both bands. The Left Hand String Band by far had the larger and more prestigious gigs, while Salmon was still playing small clubs. Emmitt says, "At that point Salmon was just this kind of party band. It

Leftover Salmon plays their first show with Mark Vann at the Mangy Moose in Jackson Hole, Wyoming, February 1990 (from left): Vince Herman, Dave Dorian, Gerry Cavagnaro. Courtesy of Vince Herman.

wasn't a serious thing yet." The Left Hand String Band was beginning to get some serious attention and was booked to play the main stage at the Telluride Bluegrass Festival in 1990. The festival program guide for the festival that year hailed their developing style of "traditional, progressive, and original bluegrass as the true Rocky Mountain style."[20] While the Left Hand String Band was playing the main stage at Telluride, Leftover Salmon was relegated to playing the bars in the evening after the festival ended for the day. The Left Hand String Band was clearly on the rise and posed for bigger days. Plans were made to enter the studio and record their first album with Hot Rize's Charles Sawtelle producing.

While Emmitt was splitting his time between the two bands, Herman's attention was now focused entirely on Leftover Salmon, as the Salmon Heads fizzled out as soon as Leftover Salmon started. Salmon Head bassist Steve Burnside says there was no end moment for the Salmon Heads. The remaining Salmon Heads were left in the dark about the future of the band and what their role might be going forward. Burnside was already growing ambivalent toward the Salmon Heads as he was finding new opportunities himself and was not too concerned with the future of the band. "I encouraged them to go on and form something new," he says. "I didn't think it was going to go anywhere, and I didn't hold it against them." The Salmon Heads' final show was December 10, 1989, a couple of weeks before the first Leftover Salmon shows. Despite Herman's clear affinity for the Salmon Heads, a band he created in his own vision, it was clear once Leftover Salmon started it marked the end of the Salmon Heads. "The Salmon Heads only played smaller gigs, local Chinese restaurants, and J.J. McCabes. We didn't really get out of town. We didn't play Denver. It was mostly a Boulder thing. After New Year's when Salmon started playing the ski areas and got all this work, the Salmon Heads just kind of folded," he says. After the Salmon Heads' demise, Burnside reflected on their legacy, "We had some good gigs and played around the Boulder area, on the mall, got in the local student newspaper, made T-shirts, and created an area-wide reputation that would lay the foundation for Leftover Salmon later."

In retrospect, it is often easy to lump the Left Hand String Band and Leftover Salmon together as if they were one band sharing two names. Yes, they shared members in Emmitt, Keefe, and Vann and musically covered some of the same landscape, but they worked as entirely different entities and were thought of as such by both bands. They shared some musical sensibilities and occasionally played the same Emmitt tune, but their approach and sound were altogether different. The Left Hand String Band, even with the addition of Vann's inventive banjo, were still at their best an intriguing progressive bluegrass band, akin to Hot Rize or Tony Rice, while Leftover Salmon was developing into something wholly original, something never heard before—a true bluegrass rock band. They were two separate bands and thought of as such. "With the drums and the more rock, bluegrassy thing, Leftover Salmon was a different sort of band then the Left Hand String Band," says Herman, "and they mostly played to different audiences." At an early Leftover Salmon show at the Fox Theatre on April 18, 1993, after ripping through a version of Emmitt's "Just Before the Evening," which was long a part of the Left Hand String Band's set, Herman clearly differentiated between the two bands. He remarked from stage, "That's

off the Left Hand String Band album, *Get Me Outta This City*. Catch
the Left Hand boys at the Telluride Bluegrass festival this summer."[21]

As the summer of 1990 approached, Vann was preparing to relocate
to Colorado, the Left Hand String Band was gearing up for their first
main stage appearance at the Telluride Bluegrass Festival, and Leftover
Salmon was steadily touring the ski towns of Colorado building an audience and a reputation as one of the hottest new bands in the state. The
possibilities seemed limitless, but change was just on the horizon for
both bands.

Chapter 4

MICHAEL WOOTEN

I was a big Michael Wooten fan. Wooten played with such a touch that he could drive a band, but still make it sound really musical. He was the engine. He had such a great touch on the drums. Always smiling. Super professional. He elevated the band to the next level.—*Keith Moseley (String Cheese Incident)*

Since New Year's Eve 1989 and the arrival of Mark Vann from Virginia to Colorado permanently that summer, both Leftover Salmon and the Left Hand String Band were regularly playing shows and the "level of both bands went up so high," says longtime band friend Michael Slingsby. As Drew Emmitt was involved in both, he decided to quit working at the Montessori school where he was teaching and devote his energy to music full-time. "Salmon was just starting and we were doing like weddings and parties. We did ski-town kind of gigs. It was a risky move to quit my job," he explains, "but I had a feeling somehow it was all going to work." He remembers walking out of school for the last time with all his instruments tucked underneath his arms, heading out the door and on his way to a gig. He never returned to working a regular day job every again, as music was his sole focus. Despite the uncertainty, it was a dream come true for Emmitt. He had struggled and worked for the previous decade to create a life in music, and now he had not one, but two bands that seemed capable of achieving the success he worked so hard to obtain. He knew all he had to do was reach just a little bit higher for it.

The arrival of Vann marked a new chapter in the long history of the Left Hand String Band. Emmitt and Glenn Keefe now had another member in the band who was not only as talented as they were, but as willing as they were to get adventurous with bluegrass. His arrival also changed the dynamics of the band. Emmitt and Keefe were long the dominant personalities in the Left Hand String Band, but Vann's immediate connection with Emmitt pushed Keefe aside a bit. While he was still responsible for most of the managing and booking duties, a power shift occurred and Emmitt and Vann were clearly the driving force of the band now.

Offers for better shows and festivals were beginning to roll in for the Left Hand String Band. They were invited to play a showcase at the International Bluegrass Music Association's annual convention in 1992, and it seemed big things were happening. They decided now was the time to make a studio album and capitalize on this wave of enthusiasm. Emmitt had a backlog of songs he had refined from years of playing them live and felt they would translate well in the studio with the right help. They enlisted longtime friend Charles Sawtelle to produce it and to help capture the energy the Left Hand String Band was known for. Sawtelle was a skilled producer and a great choice for the band. He was the guitarist and a founding member of Hot Rize, and extremely familiar with the progressive bluegrass sound Emmitt was going for. He had been friends with Emmitt for years, and because of this relationship and his talents, his selection as producer was an easy one. "It was always wonderful to work with Charles," says Emmitt. "He was such a wonderful human being and so incredibly knowledgeable in the studio."

The resulting album, *Get Me Outta This City*, released in 1991, was a perfect representation of the Left Hand String Band, capturing the band's signature progressive bluegrass style. The album featured eleven tracks, "Get Me Outta This City," "Back Door Romance," "Just Before the Evening," "Stop All Your Worrying," "Dreams," "Gypsy," "Time Stands Still," "Keep Your Mind Open and Your Mouth Shut," "Falling Rock," "Gold Hill Line," and "Homefires." Those tracks were well known to fans of the Left Hand String Band as they were all a regular part of their set. Almost all those songs have become familiar to a legion of Leftover Salmon fans, as most have found their place in the band's extensive catalog. With the presence of Vann and Keefe and the deluge of Emmitt's own written songs that found their way into the Salmon repertoire, *Get Me Outta This City* almost serves as the first Leftover Salmon album. For Slingsby, the album, and particularly the version of "Dreams," was a revelation of the special chemistry developing between Emmitt and Vann. "The banjo Mark did on 'Dreams' is among my favorite I ever heard him play. He was the first banjo player that could play it like that with Drew. He was just so pure. He was an incredible rock 'n' roll banjo player, the best on the planet. His lead on it just takes me back and absorbs me." Jambands.com said, "With the release of *Get Me Outta This City*, Emmitt and his cadre attempted to fill the void created by New Grass Revival's 1989 dissolution. The successful amalgamation of reggae and bluegrass on 'Just Before the Evening' and the David Grisman-inspired instrumental "Dreams" revealed a band with untrammeled potential."[1]

The album would resonate with future String Cheese Incident bassist Keith Moseley. Moseley moved to Boulder in 1989 and became enthralled by the Left Hand String Band. He was heavily influenced by them, saying, "They were accomplished pickers and some of my earliest introduction to bluegrass music." He owned a copy of *Get Me Outta This City* on cassette, and says, "I really liked the title track and 'Gold Hill Line.' It was especially interesting as it talked about the old railroad line which is now a popular hiking and mountain biking trail I used to ride a lot." While Moseley was a fan and inspired by the Left Hand String Band, he was even more excited by the possibilities presented by merging the band with the Salmon Heads, "I thought this is going to be powerful, that band is going to be awesome. The addition of Mark just made me think, 'Wow, what a strong lineup.'"

Even though the possibilities seemed limitless for the newly formed Leftover Salmon, they and the Left Hand String Band were still functioning as two separate bands and, while the Left Hand String Band was forging ahead, carving out their place in the bluegrass world, Leftover Salmon was beginning to make strides as well. The connections Salmon made with the various ski towns and the music circuit they supported were paying off with more and more shows and an audience that grew each time they came to town. Moseley moved from Boulder to the ski town of Crested Butte and was playing bluegrass guitar in the Whiskey Crate Warriors with Michael Kang and Paul Lee. Salmon's potential was clear to him. "Having seen both of the old bands, I was excited about Vince and Drew in the same band. They were both charismatic front men of their bands, so I was sure the new band was going to be a home run." Moseley reckons that over the first few years of Leftover Salmon he saw them around fifty times, often when they came through Crested Butte or one of the other ski towns in the region. "They would come through several times a winter, and it was always a big event," he explains. "It was like Salmon is coming to town, I can't work late Saturday night! They were a big deal for everyone in town. Everyone would be excited because Salmon was coming. We must get off work. We have to plan our party schedule. We had to make sure we were ready to go, because they would just light the place up." Moseley's future String Cheese Incident bandmate Michael Travis agreed, "I thought they were the best band I had ever seen. They were the soundtrack for my winters in Crested Butte."[2]

Those early, formative years of Leftover Salmon were a learning experience as they were just starting to figure out how to tour their brand of bluegrass music and take it to a wider audience. Former Salmon Head bassist Steve Burnside witnessed the evolution of the band from its earliest days and says, "They were pretty loose at first, but gradually upped their game with better players, better gigs, and some pretty funny shows with hilarious antics that the local scene of community clowns, hangers-on, and alt-bluegrass enthusiasts assisted with."

The ski towns Salmon played provided a ready-made crowd that was perfect for their party sound and unrestrained energy. Salmon took advantage of this willing audience. Often, they played a happy-hour set in some remote town like Steamboat Springs, then made the multiple-hour drive back to Boulder, where they would play another show later that night. Their schedule at the time was a dizzying array of nonstop trips, crisscrossing the state from show to show with multiple-night stands at the numerous venues in the ski towns, like the Inferno in Steamboat Springs, the Jackalope in Vail, Purgatory in Durango, and the Idle Spur in Crested Butte. Over the first couple years, the band played with a limitless amount of energy and an unmatched work ethic. Before the internet and YouTube, you had to be seen to be known and discovered. Salmon was making sure they were seen by everyone. In 1991, their first full year as a band with Vann, they were already playing more than 170 shows. This was in addition to the Left Hand String Band shows Emmitt, Keefe, and Vann were still playing. As well as the acoustic trio shows that Emmitt, Herman, and Vann occasionally played under the name Salmon Creek. Despite being born out of the bluegrass world and coming to exist in the jamband world, Salmon opened for a wide-range of stylistically different bands over their early years including No Doubt, Ziggy Marley, the Radiators, and the Cherry Poppin' Daddies.

The party environment of the ski towns proved to be the perfect location for Salmon to hone their sound and stagecraft. Herman's ability to drop humorous references about current events or to twist the lyrics of some well-known song, like the Rolling Stones' "Paint it Black," into a paean to pot-smoking, singing about "Big green sticky-buds," and the band's gung-ho attitude toward partying both off- and onstage, only served to endear them to the rowdy, ready-to-party-all-night ski bums. Emmitt's blistering mandolin and guitar work combined with the addition of drums was a key to their success in those rowdy bars where dancing and having a good time was the name of the game. "The band was right at home in the ski-town scene," remembers Moseley, who first met and connected with the band after one of their shows in Crested Butte. "I definitely remember meeting Vince and Drew at some after-party in Crested Butte and hanging out and having some drinks and smoking a joint. I was probably gushing a little too much about how great they were and how into the band I was. It seemed like a super natural fit for them to come play the ski circuit and mix it up with the fans after the shows. It seemed they were right at home there as some of those after parties went late and pretty long into the night and morning." Fans in the ski areas knew that when Leftover Salmon was in town their raucous live show would keep them out all weekend, howling at the moon, dancing to the rhythm of a Cajun tune, and hoping Monday did not come back too soon. To Herman, it was clear they were attracting a certain type of fan who fed off the band's infectious, never-ending party intensity. He points out, "As opposed to most traditional music audiences—sort of polite and laid back—our crowd is definitely scragglier, rowdier and probably a bit drunker. The audience tends to jump up and down a lot."[3]

The energy with which Leftover Salmon played onstage and partied off-stage meshed perfectly with the adrenaline-fueled attitude of those who moved to Colorado looking for an active lifestyle and the next good run. "Leftover Salmon reflects the attitude of Boulder," notes Hot Rize's Tim O'Brien. "It's sunshine, rock climbing, and skiing. Outdoorsy stuff, alternative lifestyle, hippified. There was a good bluegrass scene in Fort Collins, Boulder, and Denver. They kind of took that and ran with it." Before they were known for their notorious festival antics—all-night jams, guest-filled sets, and partying until dawn—Salmon was already doing that at every show they played, no matter how small the club. Much as they would later in their career, Salmon loved to tap into the sense of community so pervasive in the bluegrass world—holding house jams and campground picks and inviting friends and fellow musicians to join them onstage whenever possible. Bill Nershi, future singer and guitarist for The String Cheese Incident, was just a local ski bum at the time who often played at the bottom of the mountain as skiers waited for the ski lift. He met Salmon in the early years of the band because he says he never missed a show when they played in his area. He says despite being nothing more than a "local après ski guy," the band invited him to sit in whenever they were in town, and Herman would often "sing my name into all of the songs," throughout the night.[4]

As the Left Hand String Band continued to forge ahead, Emmitt was exploring a musical freedom with Leftover Salmon he had not experienced before, which allowed him to rediscover the music of his youth and get in touch with the guitar again. As he got deeper and deeper into bluegrass, Emmitt made the conscious choice to stop playing the electric guitar, which, looking back, he says was a "silly" decision. The more popular the Left Hand String Band got, the more Emmitt focused on the mandolin and acoustic instruments. By the time Salmon was beginning, he realized he had not played the electric guitar in years. He brought along his electric guitar and an electric mandolin a friend of his made for him to a few early Leftover Salmon gigs and realized, "One of the great things about Salmon is I can bluegrass and rock 'n' roll at the same time. Anymore that is not such a big deal because many people are doing it now, but at the time nobody else was doing it. It was a completely foreign concept to people." In addition to adding electric instruments to his arsenal, Emmitt was discovering new ways to use those weapons that helped define his singular style and Salmon's sound. He had been fooling around playing slide on his acoustic mandolin for a few years and was intrigued by the possibilities. The real eye-opening moment came when he "brought the electric mandolin to the band, hit the distortion pedal, started using the slide and a whole new sound was born." It was revelatory moment for Emmitt, who felt he struck musical gold with this simple, yet stunning sound. "It is not hard to do," says Emmitt with a sly laugh, "but no one else thought to do it." This style made an impact on those who looked up to Salmon. String Cheese Incident mandolinist Michael Kang was hugely influenced by what Emmitt did with the electric mandolin in a bluegrass setting and even had his mandolin built by the same maker who built Emmitt's, but he recognized the uniqueness of what Emmitt was doing with the slide and how distinct it was to Salmon's sound. He told Emmitt, "That slide mandolin thing is you, I am leaving that alone." Emmitt's screaming style of slide work is reminiscent of the late, great Allman Brothers guitarist Duane Allman's slide guitar. The uniqueness of playing slide on an electric mandolin allowed Emmitt to play with a bluegrass soul and a rock 'n' roll heart as he straddled the gap between the two diverse genres. In doing so, he built a bridge between bluegrass and rock 'n' roll and in the process helped Leftover Salmon create an unimaginable sound that was not entirely bluegrass, not entirely rock 'n' roll. This sound started to find a home among similar musically rebellious bands like Phish, Widespread Panic, Shockra, and the Aquarium Rescue Unit, who were fusing disparate musical genres into a mind-bending mix.

Emmitt was not the only one adjusting his arsenal of instruments as Leftover Salmon was beginning to hone their sound. While Emmitt was discovering new sounds to coax from his mandolin and rekindling his love for the electric guitar, Vann, whose background was almost exclusively in acoustic string music, was trying to figure out how to play an acoustic banjo at the volume necessary to not get lost in a band with drums and electric instruments. "There was a definite learning curve," says Herman about Vann's transition to amplified music. Vann experimented with a variety of techniques and ideas to help increase the volume and decrease the feedback of his acoustic banjo. "I tried several different pickups and bought an amplifier," he explained, "but I couldn't get the pickup loud enough without EQ-ing the heck out of it. I got a parametric equalizer, but I just couldn't get it but so loud before the feedback would be hellacious."[5] He hit upon the simple solution of stuffing towels or pillows inside the body of his banjo to help deaden it and to reduce the feedback. This was clearly only a temporary solution, and Vann continued to look for other alternatives. He played this way for the first year of the band until he noticed that Béla Fleck played a

Deering Crossfire electric banjo and could play as loud as an electric guitar without any feedback. Fleck was also able to use his banjo with electronic effects and pedals. He had all the convenience and abilities of an electric guitar, but with a banjo sound. Vann was sold on the potential of the Deering and quickly acquired one. Shortly after acquiring the Deering, he heard of another electric-style banjo made by Nechville. He tried one out and liked it so much he had a custom one made. The resulting banjo came to be known affectionately as the Stump because of its finish and hulking appearance. Vann once lovingly described it as "a hunk of wood with pickups."[6] It was a thing of rare beauty and in Vann's hands, it became something even more special. The Stump, along with the Deering Crossfire, rounded out Vann's musical arsenal and helped solve the problem of bringing an acoustic instrument into an electric setting, allowing him to get up to rock 'n' roll volume. They both gave him many options as to what kind of style he could play. "If I want to play bluegrass, I'll play the Deering," explained Vann. "If I want a long sustain sound, or a real, hard rock 'n' roll sound, I'll go for the Nechville."[7] In a band like Leftover Salmon, with their eclectic mix of styles, this ability to move in many directions was an absolute necessity. Vann approached the electric banjo as a completely different instrument than his acoustic one, just as the electric guitar is completely different from an acoustic one. "Rather than trying to just play banjo things on it," he says, "I've tried to find things that would bring out the uniqueness of the instrument. I've ended up doing a lot more single-string stuff and starting to cop some electric guitar techniques; whole-note bends and double string bends and playing two strings at once—I kind of do the single-string thing, but with two strings to get harmonies."[8]

With Vann's instrument difficulties worked out, Leftover Salmon's progressive sound begin to take shape. With his background in his college band, Farmer's Trust, who experimented with bluegrass and found new directions in which to take it, Vann was a willing conspirator when it came to messing with the DNA of the genre. "He was totally open to it," recalls Emmitt. "As traditional a player as he was, he was open-minded to being progressive. He very much became a rock player. I was playing electric guitar a lot and I think he was copying what I was doing and applying it to the banjo." For Vann, his willingness to experiment and break away from the traditional sound he was rooted in was not the problem. The problem was his limited vocabulary when it came to any kind of music outside of the bluegrass realm. Salmon, while rooted in bluegrass, Cajun, and old-timey music, was clearly beginning to find a more rock-oriented sound, incorporating rock 'n' roll covers and electric instruments into their musical stew. For Vann, many of the covers they played or musical references they used were outside of the bluegrass realm and foreign to him. The rest of the band took the time to enlarge his rock 'n' roll vocabulary, introducing him to the rock music they took for granted. As Vann was introduced to the world of rock 'n' roll, he began to adapt new ideas. "Playing the banjo in a rock 'n' roll band is a whole other thing. I tried to develop a few techniques, like strumming. You can't just play eighth notes all the time for a blues tune. I love playing rhythm, sometimes more than soloing," he says. "Actually, the hardest part about playing rock banjo and all these other kinds of music wasn't playing lead but finding ways to play rhythm. It wasn't a three-finger roll, because that just doesn't work on a lot of music."[9]

As Leftover Salmon began to create their own style and find a place existing between the bluegrass and rock worlds, they discovered other advantages to this odd combination of sound and worlds. At the time, in the late eighties and early nineties, few bluegrass bands could tour and play clubs across the country. It was just an accepted fact bluegrass was played in places where you sat down. Bluegrass bands did not play places where you could stand and rock. They were mostly confined to the bluegrass festival circuit that existed in the summer and the occasional gig at a theater or club over the winter. Salmon discovered their hybrid sound that was part rock, part bluegrass allowed them to do both. Emmitt says, "As a bluegrass band no one was able to tour. Hot Rize was the only bluegrass band that could play clubs and theaters. Nobody else had a clue how to tour as a bluegrass band. Nobody would hire bluegrass bands in clubs. It was revolutionary; we figured out how to tour as a bluegrass band and how to make it work. We showed a lot of bands how to do that. What we did was bring both worlds together where we could play festivals, bars, and theatres, and play the kind of music we wanted. It was like we had the vision and it all came together. Instead of being exclusive and playing one or the other we got to play both and that was an amazing thing." Herman agrees, "At the time four-piece bluegrass bands weren't playing in bars and doing the things Salmon could. At the time bluegrass was pretty much a festival gig or a wedding gig. Some bar gigs but not a whole lot. I think Salmon being more diverse and leaning toward more rock 'n' roll had a little more marketability."

Over time, they found a more-than-willing audience for this odd musical conglomeration among the same fans who were flocking to similar bands, including Phish, God Street Wine, Béla Fleck & the Flecktones, and moe., across the country. The addition of drums to the band's bluegrassy sound gave their music a broader appeal as it began to subtly creep into the land of rock 'n' roll. This made their music more accessible to people who initially might have been turned off by the thought of bluegrass music, but now found themselves grooving and slam-dancing to energetic versions of traditional bluegrass tunes like "Little Maggie," "Whiskey Before Breakfast," or "Rocky Road Blues." Vann says that the band's uncommon sound "happened accidentally and just kind of naturally. We never sat down and said, 'Well, bluegrass isn't making us enough money, let's go and make a rock 'n' roll band.'"[10]

As the band's sound and identity began to solidify, their lineup was starting to experience its first changes. Over the formative years of the band, there was a bit of ruthlessness as the core three of Emmitt, Herman, and Vann would continue to tinker with the lineup, always searching for the perfect combination. The first change came a few months after the band's initial gig when another local drummer, Josey Wales, replaced original drummer Dave Dorian. "Dave was primarily a washboard player and he went to a kit for Leftover Salmon," explains Herman. "He wasn't real practiced on the kit, so it was new for him. There were some definite rhythmic difficulties."

Accordionist Gerry Cavagnaro followed Dorian's departure shortly. Cavagnaro was a carpenter and busy with work. As the band's travel schedule increased, it was difficult for him to make gigs. His replacement was Boulder-based accordion and keyboard wizard, Joe Jogerst, who was invited to join the band by his friend, bassist Keefe. Jogerst's arrival in the band was a key moment in the evolution of Leftover Salmon, as in addition to playing accordion and continuing their Polyethnic, Cajun style, he also played keyboards and could fatten out the band's sound and bring a more rock flavor to what they did. Herman says his addition was "another step on the way to making the sound of the band bigger."

An early publicity shot of Leftover Salmon in 1991 (clockwise from top left): Vince Herman, Josey Wales, Glenn Keefe, Mark Vann, Drew Emmitt, and Gerry Cavagnaro. Courtesy of Vince of Herman.

As the lineup solidified with the addition of Jogerst, Salmon began to find great success in the emerging Boulder music scene. The area was ripe for live music. It had a large audience between the surrounding ski areas and the University of Colorado who were hungry for new exciting music. "The late eighties and early nineties the music scene was really exploding for bands like us," says Jeep MacNichol, who played drums for the Samples at the time and was one of Boulder's most popular bands during this explosion of live music. The area's venues that supported music like this, J.J. McCabes, Tulagi's, the Dark Horse, and the Walrus, were soon joined by the newly opened Fox Theatre and the refurbished Boulder Theater, helping to create a vibrant music scene in downtown Boulder. Acoustic Junction's Reed Foehl says, "It was The Samples, Big Head Todd & the Monsters, Leftover Salmon, and us. We were playing all the time in the area, honing our craft. We all went on to sign with major labels and garner national success. We put Boulder on the map as a place where kids looked for new music." In addition to those bands Foehl mentioned, there was a host of other Boulder-based bands who were making noise both locally and nationally, including Band Du Jour, Zuba, Water, The Winebottles, Doug & the Thugs, and Zestfinger. They found varying degrees of national success over the years and were all a key part of the hugely important Boulder scene of the nineties as many of their members, including Dave Watts, Bill McKay, Liza Oxnard, and Sherri Jackson, moved on to bigger projects.

It was not just the bands drawing attention to Boulder. The recently opened Fox and Boulder theaters saw their reputations grow exponentially as well, becoming a draw for national touring acts. The Fox, in particular, was receiving lots of attention culminating in 2013 when *Rolling Stone* magazine named it the fourth best music venue in the United States. Over the years, the Fox and Salmon developed a close relationship, as the band played at the venue countless times. Salmon played there so much it was often joked that because of all their sold-out shows, they kept the new theater open and able to stay in business during the venue's early years. It was not just the performance space for the Fox receiving national attention; it was becoming recognized among bands and music insiders for its immensely talented staff and crew. It was commonplace for national acts looking to fill out a spot on their road crew, or to find a lighting or sound person, or hire someone to take on a management role, to scoop up various staff members from the Fox because of how well versed they were in the business.

The Samples' MacNichol says the music was well received in Boulder because, "At that time, when Friday or any night came around for a Colorado University student the first thing they would do is look in the *Colorado Daily* or at one of the kiosks on The Hill or on Pearl Street to see who was playing. If nothing was going on there would be word of mouth about a party going on with a live band." This thriving scene convinced Boston drummer Dave Watts that Boulder might be the place to move to make a living in music. He says the first time his band, Shockra, was playing the Fox Theatre, "Leftover Salmon was sold out at the Boulder Theater and Band Du Jour was playing to a packed house at Tulagi's right next door. It was that night I realized Boulder had such a great scene and I could definitely make a living as a musician there." As the Boulder scene was teeming with so much talent, it was not uncommon to randomly come across a backyard party filled with some of the area's best musicians during a mind-blowing jam. "I remember stumbling into a backyard party with this band I had never seen playing before," recalls MacNichol. "It was one in the morning and there was a three-piece band. There was a strobe light in the grass shining on the band. The guitar player was dressed like Batman in a black cowboy hat and was just ripping Stevie Ray Vaughn–like solos. It was Big Head Todd, and that was one of their first shows in Boulder."

Much as Hot Rize and the Telluride Bluegrass Festival did for bluegrass in Colorado in the eighties—making it a desired destination for bands and fans alike—Leftover Salmon and their friends in the Samples, Acoustic Junction, and Big Head Todd did the same for Boulder in the nineties. A slew of younger, like-minded bands, including The String Cheese Incident, Yonder Mountain String Band, The Motet, Shanti Groove, and Rose Hill Drive, formed in the area over the years and followed the path they blazed. "We were all so ready to work and hit the road playing music," says Foehl. "It wasn't about hit singles. It was more about cultivating a grassroots fan base."

The development of the Boulder scene was a microcosm of the rest of the country. The similar scenes beginning to flourish in college towns and cities were supportive of live music and focused on a growing crop of new bands who were incorporating wide-ranging influences into their music. These band's primary focus was on their live show. Each night they played a different set list, jamming and improvising their songs into new directions, creating something new. This creation on-stage each night saw a growth of the taper community. The taper community was made up of music fans who recorded shows they went to and shared those tapes around through friends and other tapers. This allowed the music of these local and regional bands to spread around the country and develop fans in far-flung places they had yet to tour in. This community had its roots in the tapers at Grateful Dead shows. Due to the Grateful Dead's constantly changing their set lists and the improvisational jamming they engaged in each night, fans taped shows so they could relive those moments and share them with their friends who were unable to attend those shows. This new crop of bands was engaging in similar styles of improvisational jamming night to night and fans began taping shows so as not to miss any of it. From this developed a highly passionate fan base. The organic, fan-friendly following that sprouted was not unique to Boulder, but also flourishing across the country in similar cities like Athens, Charlottesville, New York City, and a slew of small college towns across the Northeast. MacNichol recognized the growing significance of this scene: "The music and going to see these bands live is about the only thing college kids did at the time. There were no distractions like YouTube, iPhones, and a million other options like there are today. Because of this, college kids got into their bands. Almost like sports fans. They followed them, talked about them, sent home cassettes to their friends in other states, bought their T-shirts, and shared their music when they went home on Christmas break. There was an intense passion from the fans for all those bands at that time." These cities and college towns found diverse bands like Widespread Panic, Phish, the Black Crowes, Ominous Seapods, All-Good, and Blues Traveler all beginning to find common ground among the fans and community they shared despite the differences they had stylistically and musically.

Much like the rest of the country, the scene in Boulder was built on bands who shared a common approach to making music, but who all came from different backgrounds. While musically diverse, these bands often played together, creating a unified feeling. Among the Boulder groups, the members of Leftover Salmon, despite their laid-back demeanor, were beginning to garner reputations as serious musicians. "The styles of the bands in Boulder at the time were somewhat varied with a mix rock, blues, folk, and reggae. And all incorporating extended jams," explains MacNichol. "What I think was unique about Leftover Salmon is they were the first band to play bluegrass. Really serious bluegrass. There were many bands with talented players, but the Salmon guys were the guys who really knew their shit. I remember watching one of their early shows with a buddy and commenting this is not a band you want to jump onstage and jam with unless you know your chops."

For the next couple of years, the lineup of Emmitt, Herman, Jogerst, Keefe, Vann, and Wales worked steadily, developing their original, adrenaline-fueled, slamgrass style into a must-see event drawing larger and larger crowds every time they visited the ski towns that made up the bulk of their shows. They played with a reckless abandon, having nothing to lose and everything to gain. Each night, their sets were filled with inside jokes only a select few got, but with every show that changed, as more and more got it. In 1990, Salmon settled into a regular residency at J.J. McCabes playing every other Tuesday. The supportive nature of the musicians in Boulder was on full display when Herman suggested to his friend Reed Foehl from Acoustic Junction they play the opposite Tuesday at the club. Foehl agreed and the two bands alternated weeks. Despite playing on opposite Tuesdays, there were many sit-ins and guest appearances with each other. Among all the Boulder bands, but especially between Salmon and Acoustic Junction, there was a real sense of camaraderie.

They also were playing regularly at the Stage Stop in Rollinsville, a small town just south of Nederland. The Stage Stop was an old barn built in 1868 that served many uses over its life before being converted into a bar hosting live music in 1972. It boasted the slogan, "The Stage Stop, serving hicks, hippies, and bikers since 1868." The Stage Stop is remembered by those who were lucky enough to catch Salmon there as having a floor that literally bounced a couple of inches up and down as the band blasted through their set. On one night after ripping through a particularly rowdy song that had the floor bouncing even more than normal, the owner approached the band and informed them they were not allowed to play that song anymore. The Stage Stop was convenient as it was walking distance from an old yellow cinder-block schoolhouse Herman called home at the time. The schoolhouse had four classrooms. Three of the rooms were being used as bedrooms for Herman and his two roommates, while the fourth was a grow room for their weed, which was remembered by all who sampled it as being "really, really good." The schoolhouse was home to some of the band's most legendary parties. Often these all-night parties followed a Leftover Salmon show at the Stage Stop, after which everyone stumbled over to the schoolhouse to continue the revelry, making a huge bonfire out of the old cabinets in the school and partying until dawn. The years at the schoolhouse were immortalized with a photo of fifty or so of the band's closest friends one morning after a long night of partying. The bleary-eyed crew assembled on the front steps of the school for their "class photo," under a handwritten banner proclaiming the "Class of '91."

During these years, Salmon also began hosting their own alternative to the Telluride Bluegrass Festival, the annual Telluwhat Festival. They organized a bunch of pickup bands with frustrated musicians who were not invited to play at Telluride and had music from noon to midnight. Everyone who showed up received a backstage pass. The grounds—

which was at first the backyard of a friend—were patrolled by staff with radios made from cereal boxes with foil antennas. Like Telluride, they held daily workshops, including such indispensable ones like how to open a beer with four common household items or how to tie a cherry stem with your tongue. As Telluwhat grew over the years, they realized they had to get permits for stages and bathrooms. They found a way around it when it was discovered you could get temporary permits for a wedding. "So, we married people," says Slingsby, "or more specifically Vince married people. We would find a couple ready to get married, have a ceremony, and that would satisfy the requirements."

Early shows were always an unpredictable blast of energy that could explode into any number of wild directions. At times, Herman would leap offstage to lead the crowd in a conga-line-style parade, often referred to as the Crested Butte Mambo, out of the venue and down the street. Sometimes these parades served a functional purpose, like when the band played past their curfew and needed to get everyone to leave the bar. Other times, when the mood would strike, the band would rile the crowd into a frenzy and lead them out of the venue and down the street to the other bars in town and bust up the sets of the other bands playing that night. They would then lead the crowd back to where they had begun and finish their own set. Over the years these parades could be known to erupt almost anywhere—in the campgrounds, in hotels after shows, or even on a random Tuesday in downtown Nederland. This air of unpredictability and the band's relentless pursuit of crazy created an unmistakable good-time party atmosphere that made the crowd part of the show. Salmon showed real care for their audience at each show, creating a shared sense of loyalty between band and fans. They did not just make art and hope people showed up, they reached out as entertainers and established a connection to the audience. Fans knew when Leftover Salmon was coming to town it would be a huge party. Every night, Salmon broke down the wall between performer and audience and made the conscious decision to let the audience not only be part of the creative moment, but also to at times literally *be* the creative moment. Unlike so many other bands, Salmon recognized it was the performer's responsibility to start the fun every night. They would take the stage in a swirl of frenzied energy, not waiting to see what kind of mood the audience might be in on that night. Salmon wanted to party. They wanted the crowd to be part of the party and they made sure that happened. Every night, Salmon took a mere musical performance and made it into a life event. They proved you must have a high level of talent to be able to seem that loose.

Leftover Salmon's growing reputation led to the opportunity to record their first album in 1992. They settled into rehearsals to get ready for the album, but before they entered the studio the band again was faced with turnover in their lineup. As he did with the Left Hand String Band, Keefe served as Salmon's primary manager since their inception, booking most of their shows. He also acted as the band's soundman, running sound from stage while they played. This gave him a fairly large say in band decisions. He was integral to the growth of the band through those formative years, but as the years went on the rest of the band felt his commitment to the continued growth of Salmon was not the same as theirs. This tension festered for a while. The breaking point came when Keefe missed a rehearsal for the preproduction of the upcoming album. The band had had enough and decided to let him go and find a new bass player. "Glenn didn't seem committed," says Emmitt. The band was also not happy with Wales. "We felt we needed a

Vince Herman (center in cape) leads the crowd in parade formation during a New Year's Eve show at the Fillmore in Denver, December 31, 1999. Courtesy of Vince of Herman.

better drummer, to be quite honest. Josey was fine, but we felt we needed something more in a drummer, so right before the record we made the conscious decision to get a different rhythm section for various reasons."

The decision to replace Wales was an easy one for the band. He was with the band for less than two years, and Emmitt says, "He did not have much input on things; he was just along for the ride." Keefe was a different situation altogether. He and Emmitt had been together since 1982. Over the years, they played together in the Porphyry Mountain Band, The Tractors, The Left Hand String Band, and now Leftover Salmon. Up to that point, no other musician had shared as much time onstage with Emmitt as Keefe. Keefe, unlike Wales, did have a quite a bit of input in band decisions. He was an original member who had played with Emmitt for almost a decade. To fire him from the band was difficult not only because of his longtime association with both bands, but also because of the deep personal relationships he had with everyone. For Jogerst, who was brought into Leftover Salmon by Keefe, it was a decision that nearly thirty years later, is still difficult to deal with. He says, "It is a very sensitive and personal subject which I don't like to discuss." For Slingsby, it was an even harder decision to deal with,

> Me being best friends with both it was so tough for me. The sole reason Glenn was kicked out of the band was musical. They wanted a better bass player. They did invite him to stay on as manager, but of course when you are a musician and used to being onstage, it hurts to say they want someone better. I can't overemphasize Glenn's part in building the band. He did all the legwork. He did all the booking. He did all the sound. Everything like that. I understand the decision on Drew's part. In terms of a causing a rift, it broke up Drew and Glenn's friendship. Glenn didn't go to Leftover Salmon shows anymore. I felt so much for Glenn, but intellectually I understood. I felt guilty going to shows after Glenn left, but I was able to maintain my friendship with both.

Keefe's exit from Leftover Salmon also hastened the end of the Left Hand String Band. They played a few final shows they already had on the books and made an appearance at the Telluride Bluegrass Festival the following year, but going forward Left Hand String Band was no more. The band's guitarist, Rob Wheeler, was a local district attorney and was finding it more and more difficult to make shows, so instead of trying to replace a bassist and a guitar player, Emmitt and Vann ended the Left Hand String Band and focused all of their energies on Leftover Salmon. Over the ensuing years, they would occasionally play shows billed as Left Hand String, but it was usually some acoustic variation of Leftover Salmon, often opening for themselves. It was many years before Emmitt and Keefe shared a stage again. In an interview with the local paper *The Daily Camera* following the dismissal of Keefe and Wales, Herman in his own way tried to explain their exit, saying, "They put a forkful of potato salad in their mouths and just disappeared."[11]

The loss of Keefe opened the door for Vann to become more involved on the business end of Leftover Salmon, something he had shown interest in previously. He had a brilliant personality and no problem expressing his often strong opinion on how things should be done. This combined with his natural intelligence made it easy for him to take over Keefe's role as manager. "Mark kind of fell into the role of running the band and being the business coordinator, manager, and booking agent," Emmitt says. "Booking tours, taking care of finances, writing checks, Mark became the guy that oversaw everything. He had the mind for it and Vince and I didn't want to do it. He came into a position of great power in the band." This position was not without some difficulties over the years. Despite making some extra money for the added responsibilities he took on, Vann often felt he was working harder than everyone else in the band. These feelings surfaced when the band was home from tour. While everyone else in the band could get away and enjoy their free time, Vann was often in his home office occupied with the business side of the band. Still, Emmitt thinks any issues caused by Vann's workload was something the band was always able to handle. "We were always good friends. We were all equal partners of the band. There was a bit of underlying tension, but we all had our roles," explains Emmitt. "Mark was kind of in charge and he liked it that way. I always felt my role was more as the songwriter because I was writing more songs than anyone else. Vince was fronting the band and being the entertainer. Mark's role was being the business manager." In the early days of the band, much of the day-to-day financial information was kept in Vann's handwritten daily calendar. Vann was meticulous in his role as business manager, documenting every expense the band accrued. In his handwritten calendars, there were entries for everything from $2.50 for batteries, to $6.25 for an oil filter, to $3.03 for envelopes and postage, to $50 for pot.

As Vann settled into his new role as manager, the band still had the issue of replacing their entire rhythm section. The sting of the firing of Keefe left Emmitt unhappy on a personal level, but the bottom line was the decision to replace him was the same as it was to replace original drummer Dave Dorian with Wales, and then to replace Wales. It was to bring up the level of the band's music. To make the band better. Which was always the goal for Emmitt and Salmon. The search for a new rhythm section focused on the vibrant music community that existed in the Boulder area at the time, and particularly, the rhythm section from legendary Boulder band Navarro.

Navarro had found great success in the seventies, and Emmitt declares they "were my favorite Boulder band." They were part of a scene in Boulder extremely vital throughout the seventies when many high-profile musicians lived in the area. They often came to work at Caribou Ranch studio. Caribou Ranch was built in 1972 in a converted barn on ranch property in the Rocky Mountains near Nederland, not far from Boulder. The studio would establish itself as one of the premier recording facilities over the next decade. Over the years, a procession of rock royalty recorded there, including Elton John, John Lennon, The Beach Boys, Chicago, and many, many more. Their presence helped raise the level of many of the bands in the area, as opportunities seemed more plentiful and perhaps a little closer than before. Emmitt was a teenager at the time and greatly influenced by the music swirling around. He says,

> The Boulder music scene has a really rich history. There were a lot of great bands that came through; the Nitty Gritty Dirt Band, Jerry Jeff Walker, Stephen Stills, Joe Walsh. A lot of guys lived around Boulder or up in Nederland or Gold Hill. There were also great local bands like Chris Daniels and the Kings. Lots of great guitar players in the area, like Tommy Bolin, who went to Boulder High. When I was a teenager all I wanted was to be part of the Boulder music scene. That was my biggest dream, which is funny now when I think of it. At the time, the Boulder music scene was so vital and amazing it was like if I could just be part of this scene it would be amazing.

Guitarist Bolin's first group was the bluesy-rock band Zephyr formed in Boulder in 1969. Bolin only stayed with the band for a few years before moving onto to play with the James Gang and later Deep Purple. Zephyr continued without Bolin, revamping their lineup and finding new, national success. One of the new additions to their lineup was drummer Michael Wooten, who joined in 1971. Wooten, who was born in 1947, moved to Colorado in 1967 after a stint in the Navy. He established himself as a well-regarded fixture of the Boulder music scene. He played with Zephyr for a couple years, appearing on their 1972 swansong album *Sunset Ride*, recorded with engineer Mal Addey of EMI and Beatles fame. Following the demise of Zephyr, Wooten joined up a with another Boulder-based band, Slumgullion, whom he played with from 1972 to 1973. He parlayed that opportunity into backing up country-rocker Chris Hillman for three years while also playing in an early version of Firefall, before hooking up with what would be his longest-running band of the decade, Navarro.

Navarro was built around songwriters Mark Hallman and Robert McEntee, powered by the dynamic rhythm section of Wooten and bassist Rob Galloway, and featured Richard Hard on flute and sax and Miguel Rivera on percussion. They toured nationally since their inception and gained a modest following, but by 1976, they felt they had run their course as they were not able to channel their cult following into something larger. They were burnt out from years of slogging it out on the road and were ready to call it quits and move onto other endeavors. "The band had been real popular around Boulder for years, but we'd taken it as far as it could go," declared Wooten in *Rolling Stone* magazine in 1977.[12] Navarro had a few final shows scheduled in their hometown and then were going their separate ways when they received an unexpected lifeline. Legendary singer-songwriter Carole King was recording at Caribou Ranch and in need of a band. On the advice of friend and Colorado resident Dan Fogelberg, she caught one of Navarro's last shows and was duly impressed. She was unaware the band was planning to disband and reached out to see if they might be interested in working with her. The band recognized that this opportunity was too good to pass up, decided not to break up, and instead went into the studio with King. Something clicked between King and Navarro and a musical partnership formed. She was drawn to the band and declared in her autobiography, *A Natural Woman: A Memoir*, "Their musicianship was inspired and full of energy."[13] With King's unmatched songwriting and Navarro's inspired energy, they recorded two albums together, 1977's *Simple Things* and 1978's *Welcome Home*. Drummer Wooten helped cowrite two tracks for *Welcome Home*. They recorded a third album with King in 1976, often referred to as the "Lost Album," that was never released due to a dispute with her record label. The band toured with King for the next few years before parting ways. The time with King rejuvenated Navarro. Building on the momentum they rediscovered playing with her, they released a pair of albums, 1977's *Listen* and 1978's *Straight from the Heart* on Capitol Records. Despite their time with King, and the connections and recognition that came with it, neither album took off the way they hoped and the band called it quits for good at the end of the seventies. Wooten stayed busy hooking up with R&B legend Bobby "Blue" Bland during the eighties and recording one album, 1985's *Members Only*, with him.

Emmitt would see Navarro live when he could and was lucky enough to meet the band's primary songwriters Hallman and McEntee while in high school when they taught a songwriting class at the September School, the alternative school he attended. He met the rest of the band, including the rhythm section of Wooten and Galloway, a short time later at a benefit Navarro played for the school. As Emmitt got older and established himself on the Boulder music scene, he came to not only admire the band's work but also came to know them as friends and musical peers, especially Galloway and Wooten. Even after Navarro ended, he still paid attention to what they did musically around town. "Over the years they were in several bands around Boulder I went to see, especially Michael," remembers Emmitt. He bonded with bassist Galloway, when they became roommates for a brief stretch. In addition to his time with Navarro, Galloway, like Wooten, had a long history in the Boulder music scene. Prior to his time in Navarro, Galloway played with seminal Boulder band Magic Music. Magic Music is often viewed as the forerunner to the jamband scene that flourished in the nineties in Boulder region. Magic Music was a collection of talented hippies who were always on the cusp of making it big, but a series of poor record deals and bad luck relegated them to the footnote of music history; a band who almost made it. But to a generation of musicians in Boulder, they were the epitome of what could be and an inspiration to many in the Front Range region.

As Leftover Salmon began looking for a new rhythm section, they heard Galloway and Wooten were both available and interested. "We knew we had to hop on that," says Herman. "We knew they played at a different level. They were legit players." With the addition of Galloway and Wooten, Salmon saw their rhythm section instantly become a strength of the band. This was crucial, as they were heading into the studio for the first time and Galloway and Wooten's years of experience proved invaluable. Emmitt recognized how important they were to the growth of Salmon: "They played together for years as a rhythm section so they were locked in. That sent us in a whole new direction having those guys." Jogerst agreed, calling them, "A very valuable addition."

Wooten was an immense addition to the band. Emmitt says, "He was a great drummer. He was a groove player. He was excellent at supporting the song and playing the music." It was not just musically, though, that Wooten had a positive influence on the band. "Michael not only expanded the sound of the band with his percussive drumming," explains Jogerst, "but he also took on the role of what I would best describe as a father figure, always caring for the well-being of all the band members." He was an easygoing guy, who was always pleasant to be around. When the band was cooped up on long bus rides, this was almost as important as the musical talent he brought to the group. "He was a really fun guy to hang out with," says Herman, "and he had a lot of insight and incredible history. It just felt we were lucky to land a guy like him. We always felt honored." Wooten, with his years in the music industry, also had a sense of how things should be handled properly. When things were not being done appropriately, he had no problem speaking his mind. Foehl was familiar with Wooten from his time on the Boulder scene, recognized the knowledge and experience he brought to Leftover Salmon, and calls him, "The wise old owl in the band." The String Cheese Incident's rhythm section of bassist Keith Moseley and drummer Michael Travis both witnessed firsthand Wooten's contributions to Leftover Salmon, as they saw many of those early shows with Wooten. Moseley remarks Wooten "elevated the band to the next level. He was more seasoned. He was the professional." While Travis says Wooten, "Was the cream of Salmon's sound. He was so in the pocket, such a smooth bluegrass pocket, and wonderful guy."[14] Quite simply the addition of Wooten's drumming was a quantum leap forward in the sound the band produced. His calm, nurturing personality and the wisdom he brought from years of experience in rock 'n' roll were also highly valued additions.

With the problem of the rhythm section settled, the new lineup prepared to head into the studio to work on their debut album. The band was firing on all cylinders and was especially feeling it after a run of shows they played at Farquahrts in Durango, Colorado. They had played at Farquahrts many times previously, but after their residency there in April 1992, Jogerst says, "The band clicked like never before." This residency also provided a name for the upcoming album and a mantra Salmon would repeat for years to come onstage. As was the norm at the time, they had a mailing list for people to sign up for near the stage during the run at Farquahrts. After one show, they were looking over the list and saw someone had written, "State Bridge is the Best." State Bridge being the name of another venue in the area. The handwriting was messy and they interpreted it as "State Bridges to Bert." Vann found it particularly amusing and kept saying repeatedly, "There is a bridge, there is Bert, it's a Bridge to Bert." "We were in a lively state," laughs Emmitt, "and we looked it at and went off on this tangent of there is the bridge, there is Bert. It is a bridge to Bert. It came to mean, you get on the bridge and it will take you somewhere, then there is Bert and that is the outcome or something good. Then it just became Bridges to Bert." Bridges to Bert became a mantra for the band and their growing fan base. It was a term that took on many meanings, but when used by fans helped to identify those who "got it." The band's fans latched onto the term, using it to describe a variety of things. Herman, during live shows, regularly incorporated it into the lyrics of songs and as a part of his often-hilarious stage banter. "It made a lot of sense to us," says Emmitt. "We thought we discovered the meaning of the universe."

With the feeling the band was starting to fire on all cylinders and the inspiration of the discovery of the Bridges to Bert and the many layers of meaning it held for the band, Salmon headed into the studio. They were going to finance the album themselves and through loans from their friends. Herman would later proudly declare, "We were able to pay all of our friends back pretty quickly. The album sold a lot more than we thought." They decided after their revelation at Farquahrts to name the album *Bridges to Bert*. With financing and the name of the album chosen, they got to work.

The band had already begun preproduction work when Galloway and Wooten joined them, so they only had one rehearsal with the pair to get them up to speed on the material they had chosen for the album. Much of the material was a steady part of their repertoire for some time. The Emmitt-penned "Just Before the Evening" was long a regular part of Left Hand String Band and Salmon shows and was thus extremely familiar to the everyone in the band. Some of the obscure covers Herman picked for the album, including "BooBoo," "Zombie Jamboree," and the Fred Prichard tune "Rodeo Geek," he had played since college with various bands including the Salmon Heads and were second nature to most in the band. For the newer, original songs the band was working on, Jogerst says, "The writing part came together spontaneously, as we were jamming at live shows." "Head Bag," a collaborative effort born from a zydeco progression Jogerst came up with on accordion, combined with a frenetic banjo line from Vann with words by Herman based on the 1992 Los Angeles riots, exemplified this spontaneity. This freewheeling writing style pulled from all corners of the musical spectrum and effortlessly incorporatingf references to a vast array of musical genres would come to be one of the band's defining personality traits. The goal with the one rehearsal left before entering the studio was to get the new rhythm section of Galloway and Wooten familiar with the songs. They provided the pair a rough demo of the tracks so they could prepare for the rehearsal at Emmitt's house. The band set up in the living room and went through the songs. Herman, with a noticeable sense of awe in his voice, remembers how Galloway and Wooten, who had never played any of the songs with the band before, "just nailed them the first time. They were pros. It was a whole different level of playing." This helped ease some of the pressure and nervousness that the band was experiencing prior to entering the studio.

They headed into Colorado Sound Studios in Denver in the last week of May 1992 to begin work. As with the Left Hand String Band's *Get Me Outta This City*, good friend Charles Sawtelle from Hot Rize was going to be the producer. Everyone in the band was a fan of Hot Rize and admired Sawtelle's work. The familiarity of being friends and, for Vann and Emmitt, having worked with him previously, made Sawtelle the ideal choice to be producer of the record. "Charles was the nicest person and took us under his wings," recalls Jogerst about the band's time in the studio. "Except for some remastering James Tuttle did toward the end of the project, most of what *Bridges to Bert* is came from Charles influence and producing skills."

With Sawtelle's steady hand and mentorship leading the way, Leftover Salmon began work at Colorado Sound, for what was a week and a half of recording time. For Herman, the presence of Sawtelle was reassuring. It was his first time in the studio, and he admits he was a bit "panicked." Some of Herman's uncertainty upon entering the studio was when he realized he was going to need to write words for the songs he had written. Up to that point, Herman who is an extremely instinctive performer, made up lyrics each night based on the audience or events surrounding the show. Other times he was just "speaking gibberish" when performing them. He knew now he was going to have to write actual words for his songs that would be immortalized forever on an album. It was not until just a few days before they were set to enter the studio he finally finished the words for all his songs. He also says he realized that, "Recording is like the Olympics for musicians. You must be at your best. You must be as precise as possible. It was my first time in the studio and it was a frightening thing. Thankfully, Charles was really good about reminding us to relax, telling us we were just there to play music."

On the first day in the studio, as the band was getting settled and starting to sort out their gear, Jogerst sat down at the grand piano and begin playing a brooding atmospheric piece with snippets that sounded as if they could have fit right at home in the soundtrack to the 1970s classic sci-fi thriller *Rollerball*. It caught the rest of the band's ear and they encouraged him to expand on those simple ideas. Jogerst refined it by adding a Hammond organ and synth to it. The liner notes for the album summed up the moment, "The first day in the studio was chaos—Joe wasn't—so he recorded this great opus to Bert. It bridges the tomorrow with the yesterday."[15] The two-minute instrumental born from that chaotic first day, named "Bridges of Time," helped set the table for the rest of time in the studio. On the album, "Bridges of Time" served as the introduction for "Nothing but Time," as Jogerst's cascading piano run dissolves into the gentle strum of an acoustic guitar. For a band whose roots and soul were in bluegrass music, "Bridges of Time" was a statement that from here on out, they would be so much more. Herman praised the instrumental piece and recognized its out-of-nowhere birth, calling it "unexpected." The *Stanford Daily* commented on this declaration of musical purpose in its review of the album. "On 'Bridges of Time' Leftover Salmon use the keyboard to follow the ancestral line of music. When the music switches from a random chord progression to a medieval fugue to a Renaissance sonata and then to a New Age piece, all taste of Leftover Salmon's prominent Cajun spice is left behind."[16] While "Bridges of Time" did introduce yet another musical dimension to the band's ever-widening arsenal, it was not true all taste of their Cajun spice was left behind. In fact, it was quite the opposite. The addition of Jogerst's accordion helped accentuate the Cajun sound Herman was so enamored by, most notably on the zydeco-inspired track, "Bosco Stumble." Jogerst also stood out on another instrumental track, the Russian folk tune "Dark Eyes," which helped prove the accordion was the "hip instrument for the '90s."[17]

The real stars of the album though, were Leftover Salmon's nontraditional, sideways approach to bluegrass music and the innovative avenues they were beginning to explore. Wooten's drumming was instrumental to this evolution. Ever the consummate professional, Wooten's decades of experience and refined style gave Salmon's music a solid base and beat over which to work. He played with a sly, subtle, laid-back touch, which propelled the band forward with a relaxed, grooving roll that had a pronounced swing to it. This gave it a danceable heartbeat and allowed the organic, rootsy soul of their music to shine through with sustained clarity.

Despite the relative lack of studio experience for the band, besides Galloway and Wooten, the sessions were, according to Jogerst, "Very relaxed, without pressure and a lot of fun. It always felt like a family, not just with the band, but also with everyone at Colorado Sound." Emmitt says the recording, "Flowed pretty well, because most of the songs we had been playing for some time." He said this was especially true of "BooBoo," "Zombie Jamboree," and "Just Before the Evening," which had smooth births as they were part of Emmitt and Herman's musical catalog the longest and the most familiar and comfortable for the band. "BooBoo" even features the rare appearance of Emmitt playing flute. Not everything on the album went as smoothly as those tracks. Emmitt cites "Bosco Stumble" and "Tu n'as pas Aller," as being particularly difficult. "They are the rougher tunes," he explains, "probably because I was playing fiddle. I was pretty new at the fiddle. I could do a much better job today." Even with some of his reservations about his fiddle playing, Emmitt admits, "I think a lot of the album is good considering." Vann especially shines on the reworking of the traditional fiddle tune "Over the Waterfall," which was becoming a showpiece for the band live when it was paired with fellow traditional tunes "Green Thing" and "Whiskey Before Breakfast." The collaborative "Head Bag" and Emmitt's "Just Before the Evening" also stand out as solid, well-crafted tracks on the album. "Just Before the Evening," with gorgeous backing vocals courtesy of Emmitt's wife Renee, was previously released on the Left Hand String Band's *Get Me Outta This City*. The song is a beautiful ode to the moment between day and night, that time when the worries of the day just fade away. It was written when Emmitt was living in Gold Hill and would hike up to an area called the Crow's Nest, which provided a 360-degree view of the surrounding region. He often headed there to watch the sunset, and wrote "Just Before the Evening" on one of those hikes.

Another standout track on the album was "Pasta on the Mountain," which from its first appearance onstage with the band became a live anthem of sorts for Leftover Salmon. The song evolved, as so many of their other songs have, onstage as Herman would make up words as the band jammed and vamped behind him. Starting with a silly rap about Kraft Macaroni and Cheese, it soon took on elements of the Grateful Dead's "Fire on the Mountain." From there, Emmitt says, "It became 'Pasta on the Mountain' and meant various things relating to marijuana. It became a kind of hippie anthem," and was extremely well received and loved by the band's ever-growing fan base. Despite its beloved status in the Salmon repertoire, its inclusion was met with some skepticism. Producer Sawtelle was unsure it should be part of the album. "He tried to talk us out of doing it," says Herman. "He said the rest of the record kind of fits together and then there is this song from out of nowhere. He just thought it lived in a different neighborhood. We held firm, and it certainly has become a live staple for us." The studio had a whole library of sound effects and the band dug deep into it as they finished the song. "We went crazy with the effects," Emmitt says with a laugh, "we added car crashes and breaking glass. It is an interesting version of 'Pasta' for sure."

Looking back, it is easy for a band to be overly critical of their early studio efforts. They, unlike fans, can see every flaw and bum note youth and inexperience brought to the album, whereas fans tend to focus on the positives. Emmitt is able to look back and put *Bridges to Bert* in proper perspective: "It was our first real studio effort, and we were all green at recording. I think we were proud of it at the time, but we felt it didn't quite capture what the band is live. It has some good moments considering we were pretty brand new at recording." Herman agrees, "It was a great experience, and I think the album has held up pretty well over the years."

With the clarity of hindsight, Emmitt recognizes some of the limitations they encountered in working, Sawtelle, who while extremely knowledgeable about how to record bluegrass, was not as comfortable recording a more rock 'n' roll sound. "Working with Charles was wonderful and we learned a lot working with him in the studio. At the same time, he really didn't know how to quite capture how hard edge we could be or how rocking we could be. I don't think the album has the rock or edgy sound it could have." Still, the choice of Sawtelle was the right one for the young band. The rocking, edgy sound Emmitt was hoping to create and combine with the band's bluegrass roots was present, perhaps not as pronounced as he hoped for, but it was still there on the album. It was a foreign-sounding concept in 1992 to add drums to bluegrass and pair it with calypso and zydeco. It was just not being done. By anyone. Therefore, to be able to find a producer who knew how to properly capture those sounds on an album was difficult. Bassist Galloway jokingly called this mix of sounds and styles, "Biodiversity."[18] Boulder's *Daily Camera* highlighted this diversity in their review, stating, *"Bridges to Bert* has enough polish for purists and enough zany energy for the crowds that pack Leftover Salmon nightclub shows. The album is a stew of musical styles buoyed by Galloway and Wooten's unflinching funky rhythm core."[19]

The description the band had begun using for their music and that adorns the cover of *Bridges to Bert* summed up perfectly this seemingly indescribable sound, Polyethnic Cajun slamgrass. At a show in Warrenton, Virginia, in 1996, Herman from stage explained what this description of their music meant to the band: "We call this style of music Polyethnic Cajun slamgrass and that means we can pretty much do whatever we want."[20] And that is just what they were doing, both on- and offstage, where they were developing well-deserved reputations as legendary partiers.

This musical mash-up of sounds became the central point in any review that followed *Bridges to Bert*'s release. These reviews often start by making some food-related joke or pun about the band's name, before referencing their bluegrass and string-band roots, then commenting on the band's wide-ranging influences. Today this incorporation of such wide-ranging, diverse styles is something done much more commonly, but at the time there were few bands this eclectic who were incorporating such obscure and nonmainstream styles such as bluegrass, zydeco, and calypso into rock music. The *Louisville Music News* seemed to perfectly understand what Salmon was going for, asserting in their review of *Bridges to Bert*:

> These boys have a great, anarchic sense of humor, but they never let it get in the way of the music. From traditional Irish and Yiddish tunes to their own originals, this sextet rivals NRBQ for eclectic taste and general fun-loving nature. If there is any downside to this record, it's the dizzying diversity. From zydeco to bluegrass to Southern rock to Cajun romp to a Grateful Dead/Steve Miller send up, you barely have time to catch your breath before the band clambers off in a completely new direction. Fortunately, the music itself is so well executed it seems worth hanging on through the whole white-knuckle twists and turns.[21]

Upon the album's release in the fall of 1992, that was celebrated with a release party at the Boulder Theater November 20, it began getting some airplay on the influential Boulder radio station KBCO. While KBCO played a few tracks from the album, it was an outtake from the sessions called "Alfalfa's," a funny, whimsical tune Herman wrote about working at a local health food store in the Boulder area, that received the most attention. "It got a ton of airplay," says Emmitt. "It was just this funny tune Vince wrote to the melody he got off a Mormon album called, *When I Grow Up I Want to Be a Mormon*. He turned it into when I grow up I want to work at Alfalfa's. It became this huge anthem in Boulder. It is what a lot of people knew us for and it wasn't anything what the band was like. It was a surprise for some people who came to hear that song because we would almost never play it live because it wasn't one of our better songs." The decision for KBCO to pick up and play "Alfalfa's" never sat well with Emmitt, who felt the radio station, which was hugely influential in the region and enjoyed good relation-

Leftover Salmon plays the Little Bear Saloon in Evergreen, Colorado, in November 1992, just prior to the release of *Bridges to Bert* (from left): Joe Jogerst, Drew Emmitt, Vince Herman, Rob Galloway, and Mark Vann. Courtesy of Vince Herman.

ships with all the local bands, never showed the amount of support he felt they should for Salmon. "It angers me because we got a little support from KBCO, but not much," says Emmitt. "They kind of picked Todd (Big Head Todd & the Monsters) as their darling, which is great and did really well for him, but if we had ever gotten any kind of radio play it would have made a huge, huge difference."

Following the release of *Bridges to Bert*, bassist Galloway decided to leave the band. He had a young family at home and had recently started a business specializing in constructing energy-efficient houses and buildings that was beginning to take off. He only played with the band for a about a year, but it was a crucial time as he replaced original bassist Keefe and helped them get through their first studio experience with his steady approach and years of experience. For Galloway's replacement, they looked to a bassist Wooten had recommended, Chris Engleman, who he had known since the seventies. They had never played in any bands together but jammed together plenty of times over the years and shared the occasional gig. Wooten invited Engleman to come jam with the band and see how it worked out. At the time Engleman was (and still is) the house bass player for the eTown Radio show band. The eTown Radio show is a nationally syndicated radio broadcast hosted by Hot Rize's Nick Forster and broadcast from downtown Boulder. Back then, the eTown Radio show had a season of tapings that ran from September through May with the summer off. After jamming with the band and finding a musical connection, Engleman thought, "It would be fun to give it a go with the boys, with the understanding by the end of the summer I would decide to stay with the band or go back to doing the eTown show, as well as doing my other freelance gigs I was doing." Engleman played his first shows with the band at the end of April 1993, before getting ready to hit the road with the band for the summer.

Before heading out for the summer, the band acquired an old yellow school bus from a wholesaler in Colorado Springs, which they planned to convert to a touring bus. It was a step up from their earlier touring vehicles, which at times included a 1978 Suburban the band packed to within an inch of its life with all their gear, a 1973 red cube van, and a big white box truck. The school bus came directly from a school system, so the band felt they were getting something mechanically sound as it had only four hundred miles on it when they purchased it. Its insides would be redone by Vann via his carpentry skills and would include bunks, but that first summer it was a bare setup. Nothing more than a couple of seats with all their gear stowed in the back. Engleman recalled the bus, later christened Bridget, "was pretty funky at the time, not fixed up much in any way." It had no amenities, like heat or AC. It had no radio. Shocks were almost nonexistent. And it struggled to get above 60 mph on the highway. Still the bus provided a freedom and space the band had not had before. Herman says, "We just fell in love with it. Just to have a space that was the band's space was a whole lot better than driving around in a Suburban with a PA in the back and all of us crammed in it." The band all took turns driving, but again the addition of Wooten would shine through as he soon took over most of the driving duties as he had driven large vehicles while in the Navy. "He was a pretty conscientious guy and sober," says Herman, "so that was a bonus."

Bridget the school bus was not the only addition to the band's traveling arsenal during this time. They also obtained a three-foot-tall head of the McDonald's character Mayor McCheese. The head was originally liberated from a Denver area McDonald's in the late eighties by a friend of the band. It ended up in Herman's possession when the friend was moving and going to get rid of the head. Herman instead took it and it found a place with Leftover Salmon on their bus, onstage, and in the campground. Wherever they were, it was, unless it was missing, which happened frequently. It became their Zen cohort. It meant everything and at the same time it meant nothing. "It's a burger," states Herman. "It's pretty fucking serious." It became one of their most prized possessions and would grace stickers, posters, artwork, and be viewed as a member of the band. It is central to Salmon lore and part of many pranks, kidnappings, and jokes over the years. It was used for gambling, with everyone throwing money in a pot and whoever could heave the head closest to the target winning the money. When the band was on tour in the South, it was tethered behind a boat and dragged around a lake as people attempted to ride the Mayor without falling off. It was ridden down ski slopes. It was suspended from the ceiling at New Year's Eve celebrations. It was passed around by the crowd during shows. It was involved in a low-speed drunken golf cart chase at High Sierra Music Festival when moe.'s Rob Derhak attempted to run off with it. It may have even helped a fan smuggle some pot across the border from Mexico. It was kidnapped by fans and fellow bands. One kidnapping led to a woman taking naked pictures of herself straddling the Mayor and sending them to the band. Thankfully she had the sense to cover her face as the band photocopied the picture and hung it around town with the caption, "Have you seen this cheeseburger?"

These kidnappings of the Mayor led to the tradition of it being returned in some grandiose style. Once a group of fans demanded five hundred pounds of feed corn in exchange for its return. Another time, it was taken hostage by the High Sierra Festival people and kept missing for quite some time. It was returned to the band when they were playing at the Great American Music Hall in San Francisco. While the band was onstage, a parade erupted in the crowd, being led by someone in a "crazy-psychedelic jacket with The Mayor on their head." The parade wound its way up on to stage. The head was removed to reveal Del McCoury Band fiddler Jason Carter, who proceeded to join the band for the rest of the set. It was later revealed the Mayor was held in Ronnie McCoury's garage during his long abduction. The Mayor has

Mark Vann (seated left in hat) and Vince Herman (seated right), along with Mayor McCheese (center), take the ferry to Nantucket for a pair of Leftover Salmon shows at the Muse in July 1995. Courtesy of Vince of Herman.

even helped bands come together. Dango Rose from Elephant Revival says he kidnapped the Mayor off the rooftop of Planetmind in Nederland. At the time, Rose was in a band called High on the Hog and they were playing at the Winfield Bluegrass Festival in Kansas shortly after. He took the Mayor with him to Kansas, where its appearance attracted Bonnie Paine over to see what it was all about. The chance meeting led to them starting Elephant Revival. Rose says, "One might say, Mayor McCheese helped bring us together."

Leftover Salmon thrived while Engleman was in the band, their live shows seeming to get better and better each night as the band worked out their stagecraft and benefited from the power and vast experience of Engleman and Wooten. Despite this, Engleman realized the life of a hard-touring musician was not for him. "I was the 'old' guy in the band—I was thirty-eight at the time—even though Michael Wooten was actually older than me. It is just Michael was a more youthful older guy than I," recounts Engleman. "I was not comfortable roughing it on these school bus tours. It was during that tour I decided I wanted to go back to doing my eTown gig starting in the fall. I had a lot of fun with

The Mayor enjoys some down time from the road and tries his hand at water-skiing. Courtesy of Johnny Pfarr.

Leftover Salmon, but I just needed to make a choice. I liked the house band eTown gig as I get to play with so many different people and I get to be home. I don't mind traveling, but that 'on the road' thing is wearying. And even just the two months or so, I could feel myself being more tired than usual." The band tried to make accommodations for him and make his time with them on the road a little easier. They let him fly out to their destinations instead of partaking in the long bus rides from Colorado. While the rest of the band slept on the bus, they got him a motel room. On the rare occasion when the band splurged on a motel room for the entire band, they always let Engleman have the bed, while everyone else slept on the floor, in the chairs, or even the bathtub.

Knowing Engleman was not long for the band, Salmon was always on the lookout for his potential replacement. On one of their first West Coast trips, they made a stop at the Oregon Country Fair in Veneta, Oregon, in July of 1993 and saw their bass-playing future in the guise of a "twenty-year old Jaco Pastorius freak."

Chapter 5

TYE NORTH

Tye was my little brother. He had a genuine desire to make the music as good as it could be. Positive and beautiful spirit. Dedicated, friendly and professional. He was twenty when they hired him. Sweet man he is. We got into some great grooves putting those guys up on a silver platter.—*Jeff Sipe (Aquarium Rescue Unit)*

"I did not even hear a note of Leftover Salmon until I met them at the Oregon Country Fair," says Tye North. It was July of 1993, and North was preparing to play his first show with Kpani Addy and Aba-Ni Aya, a West African highlife dance band from Ghana, at the fair. North was twenty years old and still living at home in Portland, Oregon, with his dad, Roger North, who played drums in the humor-driven folk band, the Holy Modal Rounders. Roger, a graduate of M.I.T., originally worked as a structural engineer before embarking on his music career. He first played with Quill, whose most high-profile gig was Woodstock in 1969. The band disbanded shortly after the legendary festival and Roger went to play with folk artist Odetta, before joining the Holy Modal Rounders. During his time with the Rounders, he combined his engineering skills with his music knowledge and developed the North Drums. North Drums used a unique horn shape designed to project the sound outward so the audience could hear the most direct qualities of the drum. Roger passed those same inventive and musical qualities down to his son.

Growing up, North was surrounding by music, as his dad was constantly playing and there were always other musicians around. This exposure piqued his interest. "I didn't go to music school and that sort of thing," he says. "I got into it because I liked the music. My dad didn't push it on me, so it made me curious."[1] Like his dad, North first played drums and percussion before switching to the guitar. He switched to the bass when he joined a band in high school who already had a guitarist, but no bassist. He had trouble finding quality instruments to use because he was left-handed. He looked to remedy this problem by learning to make his own quality guitars and basses. His interest in building instruments served two purposes. First, it gave him an intimate knowledge of how instruments were made and allowed him to produce quality gear that suited his needs perfectly. Second, it gave him something to fall back on if the playing side of music did not work out for him. For the young musician, though, he did not want to think about the second option. He knew what he wanted; he wanted to be a touring, professional musician: "I didn't want to have something to fall back on. I didn't want to have to fall back."[2]

North was deeply into jazz and greatly influenced by legendary bassist Jaco Pastorius and says, "Despite my background with the Holy Modal Rounders, and that kind of folk-Americana music, I didn't know about any of that stuff. I didn't know about bluegrass, I didn't know who Bill Monroe was. I was into jazz and a bunch of other stuff at that point." He had no connection to or familiarity with Leftover Salmon, until that July day at the Oregon Country Fair when the girlfriend of one of the members of Kpani Addy and Aba-Ni Aya suggested they go check them out. North says, "It was the first time I ever heard their name."

Leftover Salmon played their set at the Oregon Country Fair and then looked to find other musicians to jam and party with. The Oregon Country Fair is a very "out there" festival and lends itself to an extremely creative environment that finds all kinds of offstage jamming and insanity happening. It is "the best gathering of artists, vaudevillians, musicians, architects, fire jugglers, nudists, and dreamers assembled anywhere on the planet." In this creative environment, Salmon settled into an intense jam in the musicians' camping area. North was part of it and says, "Mark Vann was the first musician I met in the band. We were just jamming and I had never played with a banjo before and here I was with someone who is one of the best in the world. That was a crazy weekend for Leftover Salmon. What happens at Country Fair stays at

Country Fair. It was wild. It was mind opening." North made an impression on the band as well, who was on the lookout for Chris Engleman's replacement as they knew he was leaving at the end of the summer. "He was a young kid in a bandanna with very long hair and way into the Jaco Pastorius thing," says Emmitt of his first impression of North.

Salmon wanted to hear more of this young kid. They had a run of shows through Oregon the following week ending in North's hometown of Portland at the Belmont Inn. Plans were made for him to come to the show and play with the band as a live audition. After, they headed back to North's house to hang out and see how they all got along. They were impressed with his playing at the Belmont and, despite the large age difference between North and the rest of the band, they all clicked personally. "We thought he was cool and invited him to join," says Emmitt. Herman says they considered a few other bass players, including Chris Que from Hypnotic Clambake, but after meeting North realized he fit the bill perfectly and, even more importantly, "He was very enthusiastic and hungry. He was willing to drop everything, move to Colorado, and join the band. He had nothing entangling him. He was ready to jump on the bus and go." North readily agrees, "I got the gig because I was totally flexible to play and willing to travel."

North had a month of commitments with Kpani Addy and Aba-Ni Aya lined up, but he was so excited to get on the road with Salmon he only played one more gig with them before packing up and heading out to Colorado to join them. By August, a month after first meeting Leftover Salmon, North relocated to Colorado and moved into the ranch near Gold Hill most of the band called home at the time. Engleman enjoyed his time with the band but realized life on the road was not for him. Those early days touring were hard times for Salmon. They were away from their young families for long stretches and were making little money. They often lived off the money they made each night to get them to the next gig. When they finally returned home after weeks away, it was with very little to show for their hard work. "I had no negatives as to why I decided to leave the band, other than I was not great at keeping up the energy of touring in the school bus," Engleman says, "but that was my problem, not anyone else's."

To help prepare for his new role with Leftover Salmon, North gave himself a crash course in their music. He listened to *Bridges to Bert* and a live cassette of a show from the Fox Theatre. He admits the thirty or so tunes he learned from that brief introduction left him woefully unprepared for the band's expansive catalog that found them stopping on a dime and changing course midstream during live shows as they moved from song to song. North reckons over his first year in the band he learned another three hundred-plus songs. It was not just the number of songs he had to learn that created such a steep learning curve for him, but how to play the various styles and genres that made up the sound of Leftover Salmon. The rest of the band easily floated among these styles as it was the music at their core, but for North much of it was foreign to him at the time. While he had some exposure to this Americana sound through his dad and the Holy Modal Rounders, North devoted himself deeply to the sound of his idol, bass legend Jaco Pastorius, and thus narrowed his musical repertoire. "It was definitely a molding process to get him to be the bass player our band needed," Herman says. "Tye was really into Jaco and that is how he heard the bass and we had a different kind of thing going on. He had to adapt. Bands all have a different boogie woogie. You have to bring all of yourself to the table, but you also have to see how the rest of the band moves and works." Much of the musical tension came from the disparate backgrounds of their rhythm section, the straight classic rock 'n' roll of drummer Michael Wooten and bassist North's deep interest in jazz. North knew to fit in with Salmon, "I had to learn how to do what they did."

His first year in the band was a difficult time for the young bass player. North was struggling to learn the vast song catalog and diverse musical styles already second nature to the rest of the band. He recognized the steep learning curve ahead of him and knew to survive in Salmon he had to cram a lifetime of learning into a few short months. "There are plenty of musicians who don't know how to play all those different styles and only learn some of these styles, which are all very different," says North. "Leftover Salmon did all of that stuff and mashed it into one kind of thing. I had to learn all of it."

North was also struggling with the large age gap between him and the rest of the band. He was only twenty, while the rest of the band was in their thirties, and in the case of Wooten in his forties. In addition, as he was not even twenty-one yet, North says unless the band was playing a show, he was not able to get into some of the venues where they played. To the rest of the band, he was still the young kid they plucked out of some Afro-rock band in Portland. They spent much time during the first year giving disapproving looks, reminding him not to overplay, just be the bass player and to not do all the other fancy stuff he often wandered into; to instead just lay in the pocket and support the music. North says he was feeling pressure from the rest of the band and knew they were actively talking with other bass players to replace him. "It was painfully stressful. Tears every night," he recalls. "It was like Miles Davis being in Charlie Parker's band. Every night I wanted to quit, but I didn't want to quit. Every night I was in fear of losing my gig and having to pack up my bags and go home. That would have been awful."

North forged ahead and continued to grind away at each show that first year and saw small improvement each night. He adopted a work-manlike approach, practicing constantly to find the place where his style became one with the band. Like his idol Pastorius, North refused to back down from a challenge. It was a slow, painful process but one starting to pay dividends as the good nights began to outweigh the bad. The idea of having to pack his bags seemed to get further and further away with each show. His confidence took a bit of a hit at an early show when the band's bus left without him, the rest of the band thinking he was sleeping in his bunk. It took two hours for anyone to realize North was not on the bus. Crisis was averted when a couple of friendly hippies could drive a seething North to the next show. For someone who struggled with feeling accepted in the band early on, this was not what his already shaky confidence needed. "Tye was the young kid and the band liked to pick on him," remembers Acoustic Junction's Reed Foehl, who saw many of North's early shows in their hometown of Boulder. "They rode him tough, but he always came through and he settled in nicely. He was so nice and eager to learn."

During this formative time with Leftover Salmon, North befriended another local bass player who was learning the bass and experiencing his own struggles. Following the path Leftover Salmon blazed where they combined bluegrass and rock was another Colorado band, The String Cheese Incident. When String Cheese first started in 1993, bass player Keith Moseley made the switch from guitar to bass and experienced many of the same struggles North did. The pair talked frequently and helped each other through some rough times musically. "As I was coming up and learning to play bass he was a big influence for me and a good friend," says Moseley. "He was a mentor even though he was younger. He was a much more accomplished player."

"It was about a year into it, that it took me to make it solid. When things started to gel we began to tear things up," proclaims North. After months and months of intense work, one day, it just all seemed to click. North remembers the moment when he knew he finally won the band's confidence. "One day at a gig Mark turned around and said, 'You are doing it!' Sometimes learning is incremental, it is not always clear how much you are improving. Then someone says something you know. It might have only been 10 percent different from the night before, but that is when I got the nod. I heard them saying, 'He got it. He can do it.' At that point, I earned my gig." Herman recognizes how difficult a time it was for North as the rest of the band might have contributed to those rough times: "Tye was so young when we added him and we probably beat him up a bit as the little brother." With North's musical difficulties figured out, Salmon got an offer to join a like-minded, similarly adventurous band, the Aquarium Rescue Unit, for their spring 1994 tour. This would be Salmon's first time touring on the East Coast and a chance for them to take their slamgrass style to an audience outside of Colorado and the surrounding region.

The Aquarium Rescue Unit formed in Atlanta, Georgia, in the late eighties. The band was born out of weekly jam sessions hosted by the enigmatic Bruce Hampton, who was often referred to simply as the Colonel. Out of these sessions, a collection of uber-talented musicians emerged and formed the Aquarium Rescue Unit, a genre-busting and era-defining band whose long-lasting influence can still be seen today in such groups as Leftover Salmon, the Tedeschi Trucks Band, Phish, Dave Matthews Band, Widespread Panic, and countless others. The band was led by the otherworldly personality of Hampton, who dropped knowledge and long-lasting life lessons on all those who he met just as easily as he bestowed nicknames on all those who circled in his orbit or accurately guessed one's birthday upon first meeting. The Aquarium Rescue Unit's lineup was an all-star roster of talent featuring Oteil Burbridge on bass, Jimmy Herring on guitar, Jeff "Apt. Q-258" Sipe on drums, Matt Mundy on mandolin, and Harold L. Jones, better known as Count M'Butu, on percussion. The band for a short while also featured Charlie Williams on guitar and "The Reverend" Jeff Mosier on banjo. The Aquarium Rescue Unit's music was a car crash, but because of their immense talents instead sounded like an outer-space symphony that made a glorious, inspirational racket. As their stature grew, the Aquarium Rescue Unit became spiritual leaders of a burgeoning group of bands who at first had no unifying name, but later were grouped under the broad umbrella of the label "jamband." For the bands starting to gather under this jamband label, Hampton proved to be the perfect mentor and spiritual leader. He believed music should be reflective of your life; that you should play with no ego, finding a place where you can get out of the way and let the music come through you and go where it needs to go. For these jambands who were incorporating elements of improvisation and creating something new each night onstage, Hampton's lessons were the perfect guide.

At the time in the late eighties and early nineties, before the jamband label was being used, there was no defining name for this loose collection of bands. They all shared many of the same characteristics in their approach to making music. *Rolling Stone* magazine in a feature profile on the Spin Doctors noted the similar characteristics. "The bands have a handful of things in common, including the fact none of them were born to be styled. The groups all thrive on live music. They all tour until they drop and then tour some more. But they all sound entirely different and make different use of the improvisation tradition handed down by the Allman Brothers and the Grateful Dead. Blues Traveler, for instance, offers brute force, where the Spin Doctors offer agility."[3] Unlike other musical movements or scenes that usually developed around a singular style or sound, or in one city or location, this developing jamband scene was not united by one such common sound, style, or place. These bands found their musical differences served to unite them. "This was a breeding ground for diversity, creativity, and a family of musicians who had great affections for a wide range of styles, especially older styles the radio and TV had forgotten about," says guitarist James "Fuzz" Sangiovanni from Deep Banana Blackout, which was one of these early jambands. "I saw variations of classic funk, soul, R&B, and blues—like we were doing—and sixties/seventies psychedelic rock, prog rock, jazz, folk, bluegrass, and so on." These bands shared a DIY attitude and improvisational approach to their live shows, which more so than crafting studio albums became their primary focus. Salmon was getting swept up as part of this scene as they shared some of the same traits with these bands they viewed as peers.

This scene had its roots in the always evolving live shows of bands such as the Grateful Dead, the Allman Brothers Band, Santana, Cream, and Little Feat. These jambands often incorporated similar elements of improvisation during their live shows. This idea of improvisation took on many different meanings. From night to night, the arrangement, structure, and sonic nature of their songs were experimented with, creating unscripted and unplanned moments of musical spontaneity and creation during each show. Varying and changing their set lists each night also allowed bands to create a unique experience at every show.

Within this growing scene were bands that touched all corners of the musical realm. There was the southern-rock boogie of Widespread Panic and the Black Crowes, the blues swagger of Blues Traveler, the spacey banjo-jazz of Béla Fleck & the Flecktones, the free-flowing exploration of Phish, the reggae-infused sounds of the Samples, the jangly-psychedelic groove of the Spin Doctors, the prog-rock of moe, and the bluegrass-based soul of Leftover Salmon. Hampton proved to be the perfect mentor for these bands. "When we started playing with Bruce all these preconceptions of music genres went away," explains guitarist Jimmy Herring, who played with Hampton in Aquarium Rescue Unit and would go on to become one of the preeminent guitarists of the jam scene, playing with everyone from the Allman Brothers Band, to Phil Lesh, to Widespread Panic. "Music just became music. There were no lines between genres. There is no difference between jazz and blues, it is the same thing, it is just music. You began to view music that way after playing with him. Everything was open to him. It was just such a beautiful time." Hampton was a force of nature both on and offstage, inspiring not only with his larger-than-life personality, but also with the way he approached every show he played. Herring continues, "Bruce wasn't an instrumentalist. He didn't even view himself as a musician. He viewed himself a vocal expressionist. The one thing he was in touch with, that few people who you meet are, was he could be himself. He could play himself. He didn't always sound the same. How he was feeling inside, you could hear it in how he played. If he was having a great day you could hear him play a certain way. If he was happy or if he was tired or if something bad happened you could hear it too. That is what music is supposed to be, it is supposed to be a reflection of life." Through this belief and ability to channel his daily life into his music, Hampton moved mountains onstage every night. He believed in being "out" when playing music, to have no ego, and to not let oneself get in the way of the music; to be totally free. Hampton was the fulcrum between bullshit and the mysterious. Hampton called this philosophy he created and espoused, and that Salmon followed, Zambi. It is a style and an idea that much like Hampton is almost impossible to describe with mere words. It is an idea that one who knows will recognize when they see it. Or not. On a drive near his Oregon home Herman explains Zambi. "You see that crosswalk," he says. "You see the traffic light? That traffic light is Zambi." If you think about it long enough you get it. Or you don't. That is Zambi.

For Salmon and these other burgeoning jambands, this idea resonated deeply with them and they all began to follow this same template and the lessons Hampton shared with them. These lessons had an especially profound impact on Salmon as they were tugging at the preconceived notions of musical genres with the way they toyed with the DNA of bluegrass and rock. Hampton proved to be a huge influence on many in this growing scene musically, philosophically, and as a friend and father figure. Meeting someone like Hampton and the cadre of musi-

The "twenty-year-old Jaco Pastorius freak," Tye North, and the "Father of the jamband scene," Col. Bruce Hampton jam onstage during the H.O.R.D.E. tour, August 5, 1997. Courtesy of Vince Herman.

cians who shared these ideals helped validate what Salmon was doing and the music they were creating. "The quote unquote jamband scene wasn't called anything at that point," says Emmitt. "We weren't called that then but looking back I am thankful to be part of the jamband scene."

All the diverse bands of this scene slowly developed into a multi-genre, many-fingered, American music animal even bluegrass and Left-over Salmon found a home in. "We definitely felt a lot of kinship with all those bands" explains Emmitt, "because we were getting out there and testing the waters and playing the same venues. We got to see [Widespread] Panic here [Crested Butte, Colorado] at the Eldo with two hundred people and we met them that night. I remember touring around Colorado and Phish was playing some of the venues like the Boulder Theater or the Inferno in Steamboat. We were all the same level at that point. Phish was starting to get bigger, they were already bigger on the East Coast, big, but not huge. Panic was bigger in the South. The next thing you knew those bands took off and blew up. It was interesting to watch the whole thing happen."

Over those formative years of this new scene, Salmon did more than almost any band west of the Mississippi to help usher in the modern jamband movement. Through those early years, they toured with many of those first jambands, including Blues Traveler, Widespread Panic, From Good Homes, Max Creek, Schleigho, Moon Boot Lover, Agents of Good Roots, Béla Fleck & the Flecktones, and Aquarium Rescue Unit. Among those countless shows were many a shared stage. There was an all-night rager in 1995 in Albany, New York, at an under-at-tended show at Valentines with moe. The exact details of the evening have been lost due to time, cloudy memories, and the extra effort both bands put into having a good time that night. But everyone is sure there was a heavy rainstorm the night of the show and the roof of the venue began leaking, causing parts of the ceiling to peel off during the show. "It was a rowdy mess," says moe. bassist Rob Derhak. "We had some sort of dance competition. Drew took a piece of the ceiling and some-how I was awarded that piece of ceiling as a prize." There was a surprise sit-in from Trey Anastasio from Phish at the Rialto Theater in Tucson, Arizona, in 1999, at which Anastasio tried to lead the crowd through his band's trademark meatstick dance. During the show, Herman an-nounced that after the show they would all reconvene in the streets in parade formation to continue the party. The evening ended with Salmon and Anastasio continuing the good times at a local house party in town. There were countless all-night jams and never-ending parties over the years awash with music, booze, and drugs. The partying reputation of the band grew to be "epic." Salmon may have been bluegrass onstage, but they were definitely rock 'n' roll off it. Despite the party atmosphere that the band encouraged, they had an unmatched work ethic and a real commitment to their craft that allowed them to distance themselves from their peers.

It is unclear who first coined the term "jamband" for this scene, though it is generally considered to have been popularized by writer Dean Budnick with the release of his book, *Jam Bands: North America's Hottest Live Groups* and the start of his long-running website, jambands.com. Budnick would also come to popularize the one-word use of it, explaining, "I think it carries more grace than jam band. I like the fact that it is a neologism. We're not just trying to say, 'Hey, look at these bands, they jam, they are jam bands.' There's more to it and I feel that jambands suggests a flow, a fluidity that marks the music it tries to encapsulate."[4] The term was an easy way to categorize the bands existing loosely on the same musical dimension. It is a description that can be polarizing among both bands and fans. For some, they want to avoid the negative connotation applied to the label, that these bands are simply stoned Grateful Dead wannabes, noodling away on lengthy self-indulgent jams that serve no other purpose to but to help facilitate someone's psychedelic adventure that evening. At the same time, it is a convenient way to identify these bands. Maybe they all do not jam in the sense of true free-form improvisation like the Grateful Dead or Miles Davis did each night onstage, but they all take chances every night during their shows. For Herman, it was something simpler, "To me the jamband word just meant there would be people with long hair at the show. It was a code for hippie music. Blues or funk or improv or bluegrass, all those things were acceptable to the ears of the long haired." This music was most definitely associated with what Herman called "the long-haired" and had a hippie aesthetic to it, both in attitudes and style. When Salmon fell in with the emerging jamband scene, they found a home that not only liked what they did but also encouraged it.

Chris Castino, guitarist and singer for the Big Wu, a band who emerged in the wake of those first jambands, was in college at the time and active in this developing community. He recognized the influence the earlier hippie generation was having on this new scene. He explains, "Thirty years after the 'The Summer of Love,' hippies still functioned as the 'turner-ons' of a sort of a genre that still clung to the sixties in many ways. If the seventies were excess, the eighties were electronic, and the early nineties were angst-filled, the sixties were seemingly a golden age of musical synthesis. There were jazz concerts on college campuses, a revival of folk and bluegrass music, and renewed appreciation for the old bluesman; add in the drugs—psychedelic or otherwise—and it became the primordial soup from which would emerge the jambands of our time."

These jambands are often negatively thought to simply play long songs that go on and on, but that is a lazy description and one that does not speak to the true nature of what these bands accomplished each night. Many bands play lengthy songs, but for jambands it is not simply the length that defines them. The last track on Hüsker Dü's classic album *Zen Arcade*, "Reoccurring Dreams," is fourteen minutes long and no one ever confuses them with a jamband. No, the defining factor for these bands is not long songs that get lost in the haze of some overexuberant guitarist wailing away in a long meandering solo that never seems to get anywhere. It is their willingness to take chances live. If those chances materialized as a twenty-minute drum solo, a lengthy full-band improvisation, a vocal jam, or a three-minute burst of slam-grass energy, it was the experimentation and openness to try anything onstage that tied these bands together under the jamband label. It is true many of these bands played lengthy versions of their songs, but as Emmitt dryly notes, "We weren't playing songs for a half hour. We will stretch out sometimes, but it wasn't our focus." Salmon noticed a difference in their audience, as their shows, while still musically audacious, often required more attention to the songs and what they were trying to say within them each night. It is often easier to lose oneself in an altered state of mind to a spacey, twenty-five-minute jam as opposed to shorter songs where one is focusing on the interplay and listening to what each instrument is saying. While the band were fans of a little psychedelic adventuring themselves, this was not always reflected in their music, which stayed grounded to the earth with a rootsy flavor and eschewed trippy, free-form exploration. "We were able to build our own fan base of people who thought like we did," says Emmitt, "that liked songs and were more into it for the music instead of the fancy light show and being out of their minds on hallucinogenic drugs, which is great. We have some of our music that definitely caters to that as well, but that wasn't our focus."

The other distinction between Salmon and their jamband peers was their choice of material from which they pulled cover songs. While all the bands spoke the same musical language, and shared many of the same influences, Salmon was by far the most bluegrass influenced. As the band was jamming more in their shows, they again found it was the traditional tunes that stirred up the crowd the most. "We might play a twenty-minute song onstage," says North, "but that song was 'Doin' My Time' by Bill Monroe. That was the tune we started getting freaky with the most with some weird riffs I had come up with. There was some weird instrumentation and we would just take it into the sky."

This reliance on less rock-inspired covers also served to further distinguish Salmon. Despite this unique, often unfamiliar sound, Salmon found a way to make it work in a way that made sense to ears accustomed to a more rock 'n' roll sound. "Drew, Vince, and I all come from bluegrass," says Vann. "That's how we learned to play—years of picking bluegrass and nothing else. The next thing you know we are all electric, but we still dig playing bluegrass tunes, but we also play in clubs expecting to hear rock or something they can relate to. So, we'll do what they can relate to, then we'll do what we like, and then we'll do all this other stuff. And for some reason it works. We could never have planned it that way. We do work hard and think about what's happening to us and how to manage it, but we never sat down and said, 'Hey, we'll take the market by storm by making a Polyethnic Cajun bluegrass band.'"[5]

Among the bands in the jam scene, Salmon was the most original sounding as they were coming from a bluegrass background and had fewer sonic similarities to the Grateful Dead, who many bands in the scene were clearly emulating. "We love the Grateful Dead," says Emmitt, "but we weren't coming from a place of being a Grateful Dead cover band, which is pretty much how a lot of other jambands started. Panic played a bunch of Grateful Dead covers. Phish was kind of following that paradigm. We weren't following them. We love the Grateful Dead, but we didn't play any Dead covers then. Our covers were bluegrass, zydeco, and Cajun. It was a completely different way of going about it." For Salmon, they were not worried about fitting into some well-defined musical box. They were only interested in learning, creating, having a good time, and reaching as many people as they could, which they did through nonstop touring.

The live development of some of the tunes in Salmon's catalog, especially the Vann-penned, "Funky Mountain Fogdown," showed the influence of the jam scene they were ensconced in. The length and depth of improvisation within "Funky Mountain Fogdown," while never to be confused with one of Phish's mind-bending jams, showcased how Salmon could stretch and improvise like their peers. This improvising often included wacky antics from Herman that finds him leading the band through various teases and snippets of other songs he weaves in and out of. Emmitt, with his imposing arsenal of mandolin, guitar, and fiddle, steadies the band on this uncertain musical journey. This sense of improvisation found its way into other songs in their catalog. Just witness any live version of "Whispering Waters," "Ask the Fish," or "Pasta on the Mountain," that could stretch almost to a breaking point, for proof. While Leftover Salmon have their moments of inspired jams, they usually packed their sets with twenty-five to thirty songs hovering around the five-minute mark. Emmitt says, "We were more about playing songs than jamming for an hour." This was unlike many of their peers at the time who might play fifteen songs a night, all over ten minutes in length. Does this discount Salmon as a jamband? Hardly. They took mighty chances onstage each night. Their chances did not always manifest themselves in the form of otherworldly improvisation. More often, it was the way Salmon played outside of accepted musical norms, bluegrass songs with drums, rock songs with a Cajun feel, full-blown accordion solos existing next to ripping banjo runs, or an old-time traditional tune played at breakneck speed. It was the way they effortlessly mashed it all together in their energetic live show, segueing between songs as Herman composed new lyrics on the fly, ditching planned set lists, and seeing where their muse and the crowd would take them.

For Leftover Salmon and other similar bands, not being shackled to a desire or need to be radio friendly and having to appeal to the lowest common denominator allowed them the freedom to experiment nightly with something entirely new. They lived outside the mainstream. They were not measured by album sales or chart positions. They were instead measured each night by their highly invested fans who followed the bands from town to town treating each show as wholly new experience. "I can't imagine playing the same thing, the same way two hundred shows a year," says Vann. "That would drive me crazy. It drives me crazy to do it twice sometimes. I think of playing music as more of a conversation than a recital. If I asked you to repeat something you just said, chances are you wouldn't say it in exactly the same words. You would paraphrase it. And if I asked you to repeat it a third time, you would do it again, probably not the same. To me, that is how music is. You have to make a point musically, and maybe you have the same basic idea you're working around every time you solo, but there's so many ways to say the same thing that I can't imagine wanting to say it the same way every time."[6]

Using the model of the Grateful Dead as their template, jambands built an audience through touring and ever-evolving live shows. They were not reliant on one hit to break them. They were using live shows as their preferred medium to reach fans. It changed the way they presented themselves to the listener. Instead of prescribing what they felt the crowd should hear by focusing on studio albums, they focused on live shows, which allowed them to play off the crowd, crafting something new each night. This allowed fans to develop a deep personal connection with the band from the live experiences they shared each night and gave fans a reason to attend multiple shows in a row since each night was something new. A community between both bands and fans began to develop, uniting bands scattered across the country.

Jambands built their fans one show at a time, winning new converts every night they played. Unlike in the past, when bands relied on a major-label contract and a hit album to provide financial support and to help them build a fan base, they now found through this developing community and nonstop touring they could circumvent the usual label influences and create their own rabid fan bases. This in turn allowed bands, despite never having major-label or mainstream attention, to earn a decent living through playing music, which is the obvious, desired goal of any band. The trade-off was that these bands had to tour constantly, as they did not generate the same income from album and merchandise sales. For bands in their party-hearty twenties, they did not think twice about this. They packed the van (or school bus) with the band, their gear, and the crew and hit the road for weeks or months at a time, traveling from coast to coast playing shows seemingly every night. The number of shows these bands played a year was staggering. Between 1990 and 1994, Phish averaged 124 shows a year, while Widespread Panic averaged a whopping 153, with a high of 175 in 1990. Salmon was just getting started in 1990, but they were true road warriors and were playing upward of 170 shows shortly after starting. They kept this relentless pace up for the remainder of the nineties, hovering around the 200-show mark for many years. Many of these bands thrived doing this. Though years later, the hard living from constantly being on the road and party after party would catch up with them, as many struggled with family issues and addictions. For many, what were once vices, now became habits. For some in the Salmon family, this became true.

The growing tape-trading community of live shows helped jambands to grow as well. For fans of this loose collection of bands, new music spread among them like a virus. When trading tapes, they tacked on a few filler songs of a different band to help introduce the recipient of the tape to new music. At this time, tape trading was also evolving from cassette tapes to rewritable CDs, which were proving to be a more efficient medium to share music. Even more importantly, jambands started relying on the nascent internet at the time. The internet provided a crucial role in the development and promotion as fans and bands alike could connect on early chat rooms and listservs, where they could discuss last night's set list or make plans for get-togethers at future shows. "We were in a world where we subconsciously were operating a Grateful Dead template with taper-friendly shows and dancers," says Jeff Mosier, who was a part of this growing scene first as member of Aquarium Rescue Unit and later with his own band Blueground Undergrass. "There was not even the word jamband when we started. As the internet grew, this scene got bigger and bigger and grew into what it is today."

This framework allowed fans to form a community around a band, while also allowing bands to be able to establish audiences in far-flung places they had never visited before. Like the ski-town circuit Salmon tapped into at their outset, this network, which included many college towns, did much the same. It provided a ready-built audience who communicated and spread music with their friends at other colleges, creating a ready-made touring network. These fans also often provided cheap lodging and maybe a meal. In turn, a close personal relationship developed between bands and their fans. This bonded them in a way that was unique compared to other music scenes. Deep Banana Blackout's Fuzz witnessed this community firsthand: "I realized quickly the jam scene was a welcoming, open-minded, music loving, fun-loving community, and bands who were outside the mainstream, like us, could find an enthusiastic audience and a home." As jambands traveled around the country, many of their shows took place on campuses or in fraternity houses. Soon, these shows moved into a new crop of jamband-friendly venues including the Wetlands in New York City, the 8x10 Club in Baltimore, the Bayou in Washington, DC, the Fox Theatre in Atlanta, the Warfield and Fillmore in San Francisco, Trax in Charlottesville, and the Fox Theatre in Boulder who supported and encouraged this music. These venues were supportive of the scene and culture springing up around the bands. They allowed concerts to be taped, were tolerant of shows longer than the norm, and often looked the other way at the indulgence of a joint or two by the crowd.

These bands also inadvertently benefited from the passing of Jerry Garcia in 1995, which ended the thirty-year run of the Grateful Dead. His death also ended the gigantic network of fans that followed the band from city to city, with their mobile marketplace—affectionately referred to as Shakedown Street, after the Grateful Dead song—a bustling, functioning community and marketplace. With the demise of the Grateful Dead, many of those fans looked to find new bands and communities who shared the ideals they lived on Dead tour and found them among many of the new jambands who looked to the Grateful Dead for inspiration. Journalist and Grateful Dead historian Blair Jackson examined this post-Garcia migration of fans in his book, *Garcia: An American Life*:

> Where did the tour heads go? By the time Garcia died, some were already following the popular band Phish, a tremendously skilled, vibrant, fun-loving, and eclectic quartet with a penchant for jamming, big grooves, and playing long sets of highly improvisational music. Phish is more like the Grateful Dead in approach than sound, and though there was an overlap of fans for years, Phish has always attracted its own, mainly younger, crowd of non-Deadheads, too. A similarly obsessive subculture has grown around Phish, too, with ta-

pers and statisticians and merchants and hard-cores who hit entire tours. Other commercially popular bands that attracted followings of young Deadheads in the mid-nineties were the Dave Matthews Band and Blues Traveler. The next tier of less mainstream groups admired by many Deadheads for their jamming prowess included Rusted Root, moe., Widespread Panic, God Street Wine, String Cheese Incident, Zero, Max Creek, Leftover Salmon, and Medeski, Martin, & Wood. None of these bands sound like each other; mostly they share a sense of adventure and musical daring that is attractive to Deadheads.[7]

Part of Salmon's appeal to many Deadheads had to do with the highly inventive, improvisational style of banjo picker Vann. His style resonated with them because they were so tuned to Garcia's style of playing. Vann and Garcia approached playing live in a similar way with how they both built phrases and improvised passages. The similarities might have stemmed from Garcia's early interest in playing the banjo and how diligently he pursued it before focusing on the electric guitar. Salmon also proved to be a good fit for many Deadheads looking for a new musical home due to the way they combined so many styles of American music together creating a timeless sound, much as the Grateful Dead had done before them. Chad Staehly, who plays keys in Hard Working Americans and Great American Taxi, and who discovered Salmon following the passing of Garcia, says, "They were danceable and most of the lyrics were in the folk tradition we loved about the Grateful Dead."

Leftover Salmon's East Coast tour with Aquarium Rescue Unit in the spring of 1994 was the first time they would get to experience many of these jam-friendly venues and see this growing scene and community outside of Boulder. The tour also highlighted another characteristic of these jambands, Col. Bruce Hampton. Herman with a laugh and his tongue firmly planted in cheek, declares, "I think the common, unifying factor among these bands is the accepting of Bruce Hampton as our lord and savior. I think Bruce is the wheel that everything revolves around." Hampton's roots stretch back to the sixties when he made guest appearances on two Frank Zappa albums, 1967's *We're Only in It for The Money*, and 1968's *Lumpy Gravy*, to opening for the Grateful Dead in 1970, to when good friend Duane Allman helped Hampton secure a major-label record deal for the Hampton Grease Band. Hampton is the legitimate bridge between those bands who were the god-fathers of the scene, the Grateful Dead and the Allman Brothers Band, and the first crop of bands part of the jamband movement. Hampton's influence and guidance is revered and cherished by all in the scene. Bands felt they arrived when they finally got the nod of approval from Hampton. String Cheese Incident bassist Keith Moseley recalls a show early in the band's career when they were playing with Hampton. During String Cheese's set, Hampton sat in a chair on the side of the stage checking them out. As they finished and were walking off, Moseley says, "I remember Bruce telling us, 'I think you boys are going to do all right with this.' I thought, 'Awesome,' Col. Bruce thinks we are going to do good. He is giving us his blessing and approval, we are onto something here. He was such a strange and inspiring musical cat, and we were so tuned into what he was doing, that to get his blessing meant a lot." Guitarist Derek Trucks, who first played with Hampton as a twelve-year-old guitar prodigy, bluntly states, "He is the father of the jamband scene."[8]

The tour with Aquarium Rescue Unit (ARU) was an eye-opening moment for Leftover Salmon. Besides being their first East Coast tour, the chance to play with the mind-blowing talent of ARU was like witnessing a religious sermon every night. "Each night we played our set and got a good response," says Herman, "and then those guys came out and we just sat there with our jaws on the floor going, 'Oh shit. If this is what bands sound like outside of Colorado we are screwed.' Jimmy Herring, Oteil Burbridge, and Jeff Sipe, that was frightening. That was a major trip for us there." Herman's sense of awe was shared by his tour mates in ARU who were just as impressed with Salmon's sound as they were with ARU's. "It was just amazing to hear a rock group driven by a banjo. I was shocked," gushed Hampton. "They were just great cats. They were innovative. They were loose and would take chances. I couldn't believe they were playing bluegrass changes over rock music. A banjo-driven rock band? They were the first one I had ever heard. They also had an organ in the group, which was just crazy. Acoustic guitar, mandolin, banjo, bass, and organ, it just didn't make sense. I had never heard an organ, banjo band. It doesn't work, but it worked for them." Bassist Burbridge even went so far as to question why Salmon was opening for ARU, and not the other way around. The two bands found they were musical soul mates, sharing the same intrepid spirit and playful nature. "I was blown away by them," says ARU guitarist Herring. "The minute we heard them and played together we were instant friends. All the guys in the band are top-notch musicians and they had this awesome way of electrifying bluegrass. We would watch their set every night and be like, 'These guys are cooking!' They would sit in with us. We would sit in with them. It was such a beautiful period of time where music was the universal language and got us all together."

The two bands found an intimate, easygoing chemistry. This led to onstage interactions between the two bands almost every night. ARU drummer Sipe says, "They were as zany as ARU in their own ways. It was a good double bill. They would sit in with us often, always bringing a surprise." Often those sit-ins involved Emmitt, who ended up joining ARU almost every night onstage as their mandolin player, Matt Mundy, left the band the prior year due to his aversion to playing an electric instrument and not been replaced yet. For Emmitt, he was slack-jawed every night he took the stage with them, proclaiming, "Standing next to Jimmy and Oteil onstage is like being next to Zeus when he is throwing thunderbolts." Emmitt also made a mighty impression on ARU as his talents as a multi-instrument threat were becoming well recognized within the jamband scene. Sipe says they considered asking him to join as Mundy's replacement, but realized it was not fair to ask Emmitt to leave what he was creating with Salmon. "We couldn't ask him to quit what he built, and decided he was better off not joining." Despite not joining ARU, just having the interest and utmost respect from a band like ARU was a major boost. North says, "His confidence shot through the roof, knowing a band like that wanted him."

The tour was also extremely beneficial for North and his development as he could spend quality time with ARU's otherworldly bassist, Burbridge. North absorbed as much as he could from the extraordinarily talented bassist. "That tour was a big part of my growth," says North. "Getting to see Oteil thirty times. To hang out and play with him. It was a huge amount of training."

Following their two-week run with ARU, things started taking off for Salmon. They saw their touring schedule greatly increase as they were introduced to a whole new audience who were clamoring for Salmon's return visit. Ever the eager road warriors, Salmon were more than happy to oblige: they immediately followed up their March visit to the East Coast with another trip in May. Starting in Columbia, Missouri, with a show at the Blue Note, they began traveling north for shows in Chicago, Iowa City, multiple nights in Wisconsin and Michigan, before starting to snake east with shows in Ithaca, Burlington, and Worcester. They then headed south, stopping in Knoxville and Winston-Salem before winding up in Atlanta. Their tour found them with few off nights as they played twelve shows in eighteen days and was a grind, as the band was traveling and sleeping in Bridget, the converted school bus they had purchased the previous summer. Springtime on the East Coast, especially as they began to travel down South, can be hot, humid, sticky, and quite uncomfortable when traveling in a school bus with no air-conditioning. Still, the band was thrilled to be touring and willing to take their slamgrass anywhere people were willing to listen. "We had a limitless amount of drive," declares North. For Salmon, it was an exciting time. They were rolling down the road in their mobile party pad, Bridget, stopping almost every night to play a show and winning over new fans. After the show, they piled back into Bridget, drunk and dirty, where they partied as they rolled on through the night and headed further on down the road. To limit the amount of stops they made, they often stood on the steps by the front of the bus, opened the door and urinated as they continued truckin' on down the road. To keep from stopping, they also employed what they called the "dead man switch," where the replacement driver changed places with the driver by sliding into the seat at the same time the driver stood up, passing off the controls as they barreled down the highway. "They were going to do it no matter what," says Hampton. "They were working so hard it was just unbelievable. They never slept. They would tour ferociously. It seemed they would do eight, nine gigs a week. You would see them and know they hadn't slept in four days."

Not everyone was enjoying themselves though. The expanded touring schedule was hardest on keyboardist Joe Jogerst, who seemed to lose the enthusiasm he experienced early on with the band. He says, "The first two to three years, when we toured Colorado, it felt like a family and I have very fond memories. Unfortunately, this changed when we started touring nationally." The end for him came at a stop at the Chameleon Club in Atlanta in March of 1994 when he finally had enough and decided to the leave the tour and the band. He explains, "The conflict between the band's intensive touring schedule and my family life became too great." While the band may have sensed some of

Jogerst's unhappiness on the road, as there was some building tension, his abrupt decision to leave the band hours before a show with his gear already set up on stage caught them all off-guard. "No one really wanted that to happen," says North. His decision to leave forced the band to a crossroad. "I don't think we knew how we could go on without keys and accordion, because accordion was such a big part of our sound at first," admits Emmitt.

Salmon decided to push on as a five-piece with Emmitt, Herman, Vann, North, and Wooten. While the band still maintained their blue-grass-based sound and continued to incorporate many styles into their repertoire, Jogerst's leaving pushed the band toward a more rock-oriented sound as they played as a stripped-down five-piece without the familiar accordion sound they had used for so long. The band found this new configuration suited them and they liked what it allowed them to do musically. North says the band was, "killing it" following Jogerst's departure. Instead of the musical uncertainty they thought would come with the departure of Jogerst, they instead found a new comfort and excitement in their live shows that was easily recognized by their audience at the time.

Still they were playing each night to mixed numbers. Some nights shows were packed, other nights sparsely attended. No matter, they played each night as if they were the biggest band in the world. This helped them book bigger and better shows, and they were offered a headlining spot at the most revered of venues for jambands, the Wetlands in New York City, October 1, 1994, with moe. opening for them. Emmitt recalls the insanity of navigating Bridget into Manhattan during rush hour, and the even greater surprise when the line to get into the show was wrapped around the block. This caught the band off-guard, as they were still relatively unknown at the time in the Northeast. They later found out the crowd size was aided by a strong rumor circulating that it was a secret Phish show. There might have initially been some disappointment in the crowd when Phish did not take the stage, but Salmon did not let the opportunity pass by and threw an all-night party into the wee hours of the morning. Herman was in rare form and weaved snippets and teases of other songs as well as countless references to smoking illegal substances into their twenty-nine-song show, which connected with the Wetlands crowd.

The band wanted to capture this newfound energy they were discovering each night and made plans to record a live album, *Ask the Fish*, at one of their favorite venues, the Fox Theatre in their hometown of Boulder, over Halloween weekend 1994. As if recording their first live album was not difficult enough, the band was going to be celebrating Halloween and playing in full costume. "It was a little challenging," says Emmitt. "I was in a full wizard costume with these giant sleeves and a hat. It was a little hard to maneuver." Despite the difficulties playing in costume, the band enjoyed the pageantry and humor of it and it became a tradition for the band to dress up in outlandish costumes throughout the years.

At the time of recording *Ask the Fish*, the band was amid an extremely creative period and the song selection for the album reflects that, as even though the album came just a year after *Bridges to Bert*, it was chock-full of newly written songs and included brand-new arrangements of a fistful of old-timey tunes the band reinvented in their own vision. Emmitt's two brand new tracks "Lonesome Road" and "Bend in the River" show a considerable growth and maturity in his development as a songwriter. "Lonesome Road" was a contemplative look at life that had a timeless feel and would establish itself as a standout track on the album and a crowd favorite for years to come. His other contribution, "Bend in the River," was a full declaration of love Emmitt had written for his wife, Renee, about their recent wedding. Its lyrics were an accurate description of the couple's nuptials. Its joyous, upbeat lyrics and melody would become a classic for the band and one of their most popular songs.

Herman, while never the prolific songwriter Emmitt was, still contributed the new original "Stay Away Monday," which was fast becoming a fan favorite with its lyrics about partying all weekend that resonated with the band's fan base. Herman was also a serious musicologist and always discovering new music to include as part of the band's repertoire. He was completely open to wherever and from whomever he might find new music. This could include obscure covers, old traditional songs, or discovering some new unknown songwriter who moved his soul. Acoustic Junction's Reed Foehl, witnessed this ability to find new music firsthand when they were both young, struggling bands in Boulder. "I think he is one the of best all-time song collectors. He is always pulling songs out of the air, always including guests as part of the show.

Just a selfless musician." On *Ask the Fish* Herman included two songs by songwriters from his personal orbit whom he first met in college. One was a twenty-two-second blast of energy, "Cactus Flower," written by his former bandmate from college Fred Prichard, who also contributed "Rodeo Geek" to *Bridges to Bert*. The other inclusion was from longtime friend Vince Farsetta. Farsetta had a great impact on Herman's development as a musician. The Farsetta-penned tune "Jokester" Herman had chosen to include on the live album had become one of their most popular live songs, but unbeknownst to Herman at the time had a personal connection to him, as it was a song Farsetta composed about him. "I wrote that song about Vince," says Farsetta with a subtle chuckle, "but he didn't know that when he recorded it. It was about him. He is the Jokester. Carefree and happy, always having fun. Listen to the lyrics, 'Runnin' wild, you goin' all the time/ Always laughin' and actin' in mime/ No time for whinin' when you are feelin' fine/ Always dancin' and talkin' in rhymes.' It's just the way he is. It blows my mind."

Herman had also written words for a handful of traditional songs that the band reworked to fit their live shows. One of those songs, "Ask the Fish," was born from a recent party the band held and would provide the album with its name. At the party, Vann came across a copper can opener in the shape of a fish. Much like when the band first discovered the bridges to Bert, Vann was in a lively state of mind after having a few cocktails. He proceeded to walk up to everyone at the party with the fish can opener and ask, "Would you like to ask the fish? You would like to ask the fish." It became yet another long-running inside joke for the band as they used a picture of the can opener as the cover of the album and early copies of the album included a plastic replica of it. When the band was messing around with the arrangement to an old-timey tune called "Old Cluck Hen," Herman made up lyrics about environmental concerns and incorporated the "Ask the Fish" line. The song, "Ask the Fish," became a live beast which the band uses as a launching pad for many sonic adventures onstage. Over the years, the song was accentuated with everything from squeaking rubber fish bath-toys, the celestial sounds of the waterphone (a water-filled metallic instrument Vann resonated with a fiddle bow), to North singing bass notes in the monastic tradition, to a variety of otherworld effects courtesy of Emmitt and his mandolin and electric guitar. "Ask the Fish" is something new every show as Herman improvises lyrics referencing popular culture, other songs, the geographical location of that show, the venue, the nearest rivers, and the vibe of the crowd. Some of the same phrases pop up every time, but lots of new territory is explored in the song every show. Herman spouts some new improvisational poetry, making up verses and modifying old nursery rhymes to suit the purposes of the fish. Often his new lyrical material for "Ask the Fish," which could cover everything from local issues to environmental concerns, came from time spent before the show when Herman wandered around the local area to find out what was going on and what was on people's minds. "We would hear Vince rattle off news articles about stuff he had read," North says. "He was consuming a lot of the local culture when we toured. He would walk around college campuses and pick up on local stuff and what was happening with local politicians and that shit would come out at the gig. Vince would go off and all that stuff would come spilling out. His memory and ability to retain all and have it come out in lyrics that night is why he is so brilliant." Herman is influenced by the moment every time he takes the stage. An article he reads earlier in the day becomes new lyrics later that night, a casual conversation over a joint with a friend becomes a change to the set list, a look at old pictures backstage may become the reason he tells the story of how he and Emmitt first met.

The finished live album perfectly captured who Salmon was in concert at the time. For many, it is still their peak live recording as they were starting to flex their improvisational muscles. The *Atlanta Journal* declared, "The Boulder, Colorado, quintet is swimming upstream in the music business—blending Americana styles with jam-oriented live shows that appeal to fans of like-minded artists such as Phish and Widespread Panic. Their newest live album, *Ask the Fish*, is a testament to Leftover Salmon's stage antics, foot-stompin', long-winded spontaneity. Guitars, bass, and drums mingle with a washboard, waterphone, fiddle, and electric banjo in a cacophonous uproar of original and rearranged traditional bluegrass."[9]

Salmon was riding a wave of momentum and touring at a torrid pace. Every night was a shocking burst of energy and creativity. They were part of a collection of like-minded bands such as Phish, God Street Wine, Aquarium Rescue Unit, and Widespread Panic, who were pioneering this new jam scene. It was truly a magical time. Despite playing mostly in rock clubs and finding a new audience whose experience and exposure to bluegrass was often limited to what they heard Salmon play, they did not forget their roots. In 1995, they were invited to play at two of the biggest bluegrass festivals in the country. First, over the weekend of April 28–30, they made their debut at one of the preeminent bluegrass festivals in the country when they played MerleFest in Boonsboro, North Carolina. Vann says the band had some apprehension about playing such a prestigious bluegrass festival in front of a crowd who preferred a more traditional sound, which was miles away from what Salmon was doing. "You know, we had drums," says Vann, "we were plugged in, and we didn't know how they were going to react. I'd been at festivals where the audience all got up and left when they saw an electric bass. I remembered how people booed the Osborne Brothers when they first came onstage with an electric bass."[10] Salmon did not have to worry. With their Polyethnic Cajun slamgrass style on full display, they made an immediate impact on the more traditional leaning bluegrass crowd. "They were unknown but they got into MerleFest that year," remembers Hot Rize's Tim O'Brien. "They made a big impression. They played all over the place that weekend. They sold something like 1,500 CDs over the weekend, something unheard of, some crazy number for the weekend. It made everyone else stand up and listen. They had a big party Sunday night when they found out how much they sold. It was like, 'Wow, this is working for us.'" O'Brien also recognized the impact Salmon had on the crowd as he noticed an entirely new audience who followed Salmon from the jam scene into the bluegrass world. "It was the young kids. This is when you started seeing kids with dreadlocks play hacky sack at the big events. It was a new move. It was a new feature in the audience." Salmon's impact led to them being invited back to play the festival the following year, which was memorable as it led to an introduction to one of the band's biggest musical heroes.

Sam Bush from New Grass Revival had long been a huge influence on Emmitt's mandolin playing and musical choices. That following year in 1996, at MerleFest, Emmitt, along with a host of other mandolin pickers including Bush, Chris Thile, Jimmy Gaudreau, and Shawn Lane, were part of a workshop called Mando Mania, where the panel of mandolin masters would demonstrate various techniques and styles for the audience. During the workshop, Emmitt was asked to demonstrate what slamgrass was. Emmitt says, "I played a Monroe-ish mandolin straight bluegrass thing, then I went into the intro to 'Reuben's Train,'

Leftover Salmon plays the Hill Side Stage during their first appearance at Merle-Fest in April 1995 (from left): Drew Emmitt, Michael Wooten, Vince Herman, Tye North, and Mark Vann. Courtesy of Vince of Herman.

which is breakneck, crazy stuff. It got everyone's attention. Sam looked over at me like 'Whoa, who are you?'" Later that day, Salmon was hanging out on Bridget, which was parked among all the fancy, high-end tour buses, when they saw Bush walk by. "He was walking the other way and he turns and gets a funny look on his face and grabs his chin in thought," says Emmitt. "Then he started walking straight to the school bus. He gets on, whips out a bowl and says, 'I assume it is all right to light this up here.' We ended up telling stories and picking tunes and having a great time." That night, they connected again at a party held by a mutual friend of theirs, and a deep friendship was born. Emmitt says, "We found we have all these things in common. He was into rock 'n' roll and electric guitar and so was I. We were similar people. It was just a great experience. From then on, whenever we saw Sam we get him onstage with us. He has played on several of our records. He has played on my solo records. There have just so many great experiences with him." Bush agrees with Emmitt's feelings, simply stating, "Drew is my mandolin brother. I can't tell you how much I love him." Over the course of MerleFest, Bush found a kindred musical spirit in Salmon, who while sprung from a bluegrass world, came to exist in a newgrass landscape home to Bush. He recognized a similar energy to his own in Salmon. Their willingness to load up an old school bus and drive anywhere reminded him of his early days with New Grass Revival when they toured in an old converted bread truck. "I liked the excitement, energy, and drive they had. They came from a world where they were studying bluegrass. I have always said if you want to be successful in a newgrass style you must know bluegrass and be aware of how those instruments work together. They were doing it in a way that differentiated them from other bands in that style. I realized after the first time I sat in with them my right hand couldn't move fast enough to keep up with them. I had to switch to fiddle. I could keep up with them on the fiddle."

The other festival in the summer of 1995 that cemented their bluegrass roots was the Telluride Bluegrass Festival in June in their home state of Colorado. It was an extra special moment as they had spent so much time as young struggling musicians there watching their idols and picking all night in the campgrounds. Emmitt's Left Hand String Band had played the festival for the previous four years, but this was the first time Leftover Salmon graced the stage at the legendary festival. It was a full-circle moment for the band who saw its roots sprout six years prior at the campgrounds at Telluride and in the bars around town. It marked the start of a run, with Salmon playing the Telluride Bluegrass Festival sixteen times over the next twenty-two years.

Following their appearance at MerleFest and Telluride in 1995, Salmon was becoming a major draw on the road and at festivals across the country. Festival promoters knew they were getting so much more when they booked Salmon. Whereas most bands play their set and move on, Salmon was just getting started when they finished their set. They could be counted on to commandeer a golf cart and storm through the campgrounds whipping the crowd into a frenzy as they led all-night jam sessions that snaked through the campgrounds. The idea of the late-night tent set at festivals was practically created in response to Salmon's antics. This attention they were receiving was despite the lack of a promotional push or retailing expertise from a major label. They were also getting little support from radio stations across the country. Influential rock station KROQ in Los Angeles even dissed them, saying, "They stink as badly as their name."[11] In spite of this lack of support, Salmon were selling out shows at some of the premier venues across the country. In that pre-digital age, they had amassed a mailing list of more than 13,000 names all compiled from a clipboard left at their merchandise table during shows. The band was ranked in the top fifty nationally for average box office gross per city. Box office gross is one of those fancy business terms that basically means lots of people were willing to fork over money to see them. This was accomplished without the help of a major label. They were doing all of it by themselves in an old yellow school bus they drove to every corner of the country. This made those major labels start paying attention. The thought of having the support and distribution of a major was appealing. Since their earliest days, they had been hustling hard to sell CDs and merchandise at every show. They often frequented local record and music stores while on the road to see if they might take a few on consignment. The band welcomed the idea of having a real support structure.

Some of their peers, including Phish, Widespread Panic, Blues Traveler, Big Head Todd & the Monsters, and Dave Matthews had already made the move to major labels and it was clear Leftover Salmon was soon to follow. "We were being courted by several major record labels," recounts Emmitt. "It was insane. We were the hot item. It was before a lot of the other jambands like The String Cheese Incident, moe., and Strangefolk, started to hit. At that time, we were the heart of the feeding frenzy. We were the new thing." They were being courted by Atlantic, Sony, Capricorn, Hollywood Records, and Island. Salmon had long valued their independence and self-managed since the beginning, but with this increasing interest, they recognized the need for a manager who could help navigate the tricky waters of dealing with a major label. They were working with booking agent Armand Sadlier, who previously worked with Phish, Widespread Panic, Aquarium Rescue Unit, and the Samples, and was the go-to booking agent for jambands on the rise. He helped break those bands into bigger markets, but Salmon felt they were starting to hit some walls they could not get over and thought a move to a bigger booking agency could help overcome them. They did not have to look far. In their home state of Colorado was Chuck Morris, a longtime promoter, manager, and pillar of the music scene who had been working in the music industry since dropping out of a PhD program at the University of Colorado in the early seventies to manage a local club in Boulder. He established himself as a force in the music industry, managing everyone from the Nitty Gritty Dirt Band and Lyle Lovett, to Leo Kottke and Big Head Todd &

the Monsters. Morris would go on to collaborate with legendary Bill Graham in a management company that evolved into industry powerhouse Live Nation.

Salmon first met Morris when they played some shows he promoted. When they realized they needed bigger management, Morris seemed the ideal choice as they needed a powerful voice in dealing with the onslaught of major labels who were courting them. "Those labels don't want to work with you unless you have management," Herman says. "It is the way of letting them know you are going to be easy to work with. Most of the communication goes through the management not the artist. Chuck was definitely one of those gatekeeper types of guys."

With Morris onboard as their new manager, Salmon was hit with the full-court press of love from all the labels who desired their services. The labels flew them around the country, where they stayed in only the best hotels and ate the best food. "They all did pretty much the same thing. Put us up in fancy hotels and take us out for sushi," laughs Emmitt. "It kind of became a joke. We'll sign with whoever has the best sushi dinner." Hollywood Records, which was owned by Disney, brought them out to Disney World in California. Legendary manager Phil Walden from Capricorn, who managed such luminaries as Otis Redding, Al Green, Sam & Dave, and the Allman Brothers Band, flew out to a festival the band was playing and hung out on Bridget, wooing them. Atlantic Records flew the band to New York City. While there they also met with the president of Atlantic-Nashville, who told the band, "Give me one song and I will make you big in the country world too." It was a proposal the band found intriguing. While in New York, Atlantic also allowed the band to take whatever albums they wanted from the label's extensive discography. The jazz-loving North unsurprisingly took the John Coltrane collection, while Vann, who was still just discovering the rock music his bandmates had grown up with, snagged the Led Zeppelin box set. They later took the band out to dinner. While at dinner the band noticed an RV parked in front of the restaurant. "It was the guys from Hollywood Records," remembers Herman. "They just sat there waving at us all through dinner. Letting us know they were our guys." In the end, it came down to a slugging match between Atlantic and Hollywood, with the band choosing Hollywood. There was much excitement among the band about signing with Atlantic and being on the same roster as mega bands like Led Zeppelin and Yes, but there was some fear because Atlantic was so big they would not get the attention they needed. Hollywood, meanwhile, seemed to offer nothing but attention. The president of Hollywood Records was a bluegrass fan and they thought the personal connection would be helpful to the band. "They seemed to have a lot of resources and they did not have a lot of bands at the time as they were mostly into doing the Disney soundtracks," says Emmitt. "We felt we would get more attention." Hollywood also agreed to rerelease their first two albums, *Bridges to Bert* and *Ask the Fish*. "We got a lot more money to make records with," says Vann. "They also increased our visibility; our records were available in all the stores. They gave us a lot of freedom too. A lot of the nightmare stories you hear about the record labels coming in and wanting you to change everything wasn't true at all with those guys."

Upon signing, the band immediately headed into the studio to begin work on their first album for Hollywood. Hollywood hired producer Justin Niebank to helm it. Niebank was already a well-established engineer, having worked on albums by Neil Diamond, Billy Joel, John Mellencamp, Phish, and Hank Williams. Recently he had started producing more and worked with bands, Blues Traveler and Allgood, who were coming from a similar background as Salmon, and Hollywood felt he was the perfect person to handle the band's wide-ranging sound. The band headed into Kerr-Macy Studios in Denver with Niebank at the end of 1996 to start working on the new album. They completed the album at the home studio of Niebank in Nashville a few weeks later. Having Niebank on board was not only valued because of the experience he brought to the album, but also because Emmitt says having an outside voice involved is always good for the tensions that can arise within the band during the stressful work of recording.

The band was constantly writing and working up new songs during this time and had a backlog of new tunes ready to use for the album. This allowed them to get right into the studio as they did not have to write anything new before starting. They were simply choosing from their vast catalog. "We sort of looked to see what parts of our repertoire were and were not represented on an album," says Herman. "We cover such a wide base of stuff. We wanted it to be representative of our live show."[12]

The album continued to showcase the strong songwriting of Emmitt, as he penned five of the album's eventual eleven tracks. The other six

Vince Herman (standing left) and Drew Emmitt (seated) along with Justin Niebank (center) and Sam Bush (right) in Niebank's home studio during the recording of the *Euphoria* album. Courtesy of Vince Herman.

tracks consisted of the Vann instrumental "Funky Mountain Fogdown"; a cover of the Holy Modal Rounders "Euphoria," which would provide the album with its name; a Louvin Brothers cover, "Cash on the Barrelhead"; a traditional tune, "Ain't Gonna Work"; and two songs written by Herman's old buddy from Morgantown, Vince Farsetta, "Better," and "Mama Boulet." Herman says, "There was a pile of Vinny tunes we loved to play and they always got a real warm reception live when we played them. They were becoming signature songs and it seemed important to put them on the record." For Farsetta, who at the time had relocated to Nashville, where he was playing with the Flying Flamingos, the band surprised him with their decision to record his songs. Herman called him up one day and told him the good news. The band invited him to come to the session to watch them record. "It was a big honor to have them record those songs," says Farsetta. "They just tear it up. They are just perfect songs for them." Farsetta got an additional surprise a few months later while home making dinner one night. He had the television on in the background and was listening to *Entertainment Tonight*, when he heard "Better," come on. They were doing a piece on legendary ski and snowboarding filmmaker Warren Miller and his latest movie, *Snowriders 2*, which, unbeknownst to Farsetta, included Salmon's version of "Better." "There was my song on TV. I was so honored," says Farsetta. The movie would include three tracks from *Euphoria*, using "Highway Song," and "Euphoria," as well.

In addition to looking to friend Farsetta for material for the album, Salmon recruited some of their other friends to play on it as well. They brought in Sally Van Meter to add lap steel to "Muddy Water Home." Sam Bush added fiddle to "Highway Song," and "Funky Mountain Fogdown." The final guest on the album was British rock keyboardist Pete Sears. Since his earliest days in England, Sears has played with everyone from Rod Stewart to Jefferson Starship to Hot Tuna to countless others. Sears and Salmon first met at a party at legendary music promoter Bill Graham's house in Mill Valley, California. Salmon was hired to play at the party and Sears was immediately captivated by "their nontraditional approach to playing bluegrass."[13] Salmon and Sears developed a close musical connection after that initial meeting at Graham's house. Sears would occasionally sit in with the band as they had no keyboard player at the time. The occasional sit-in become more and more regular, and Sears would head out on the road with Salmon for a handful of tours over the years. There was even some talk of him joining the band full time, but Sears's always-busy schedule kept that from happening. Still, when they wanted a keyboard player for *Euphoria*, it was obvious who they would call. Sears lent his considerable talents to "River's Rising."

Looking back at the album twenty years on, Emmitt has conflicted feelings about the finished album. "I think there is some great stuff on there. Justin Niebank was an excellent producer. He was very good, but I feel like the album may be a little overproduced and didn't get a chance to breathe as much as it should. It didn't have as much of the natural sound that the band had at the time." Emmitt's reservations mostly were with some of the editing imposed by the label. He felt they edited the length of some of the tunes, but nothing was gained from the cuts. He was annoyed an entire section of "River's Rising" was removed. "It was supposed to have a fast part, a stop, and then have another fast part," explains Emmitt. In concert, the song used this drastic tempo change to devastating effect as it was becoming one of their most powerful songs live. With its swirling energy that would build to a crescendo not once, but twice, it was a surefire showstopper and always brought the crowd to the edge of euphoria. Emmitt had looked forward to crafting the same energy for the song in the studio and admits to being less than thrilled with the edited studio version. He was also disappointed when thirty seconds were edited off "Highway Song." He felt the edit was unnecessary, calling it "ridiculous," adding, "it did not make any difference into how much it got played on the radio." Emmitt, with the voice of the perfectionist that he is, tries to put the album in its proper personal perspective. "I don't want to say it's a disappointment, because I think it has some great stuff on there and it has some great-sounding stuff. Sometimes I will hear a cut from it and think that sounds good. There are some great moments, but I just felt it was too careful. I don't think it ever accomplished what they were trying to create for us and mold us into. There are probably some different opinions of it in the band. I feel I kind of got railroaded into it, because everyone felt it would get us more radio play. When you hear how it was recorded you can totally hear where the edits are. It is good and tight and concise, but I felt it was just too sterile." These conflicting feelings were being shared by many of Salmon's jamband peers who were struggling to find a way to harness the unpredictable energy they played with onstage each night and reproduce it in the studio. This was often made more difficult by the labels these bands were on, who were still existing in a well-defined, sterile approach to making albums and what they felt was acceptable for radio play.

Despite some of Emmitt's reservations about the finished album, Herman says the band "was generally psyched. It was our major-label debut and we thought we finally had some resources behind it." The album did see increased visibility beyond any of their previous releases due to Hollywood, as the label was able to get the album stocked in stores across the country and had a larger publicity reach than the bare-bones operation Salmon had functioned with for so long. Though, the band found out shortly Hollywood had no immediate plans to release a single from it or promote the album to radio. Still, following its release in March of 1997, *Euphoria* began to receive positive attention and reviews. *The Commercial Appeal* from Memphis, Tennessee, called the album, "Their best record to date."[14] It even began climbing up *Billboard*'s Heatseeker charts for new and emerging artists. A couple of tracks from the album, including "River's Rising," begin to find airplay on college radio and some of the better independent stations across the country. The lack of promotional support from Hollywood irked Emmitt, who felt the label insisted on the edits in the final mix of the album to groom it for a more radio-friendly release and then did not bother to push the album to radio. He says, "I felt like we were being pushed into a sound that wasn't exactly where our band was at the time. It was too careful. If we had gotten some radio support it would have made a huge difference in our careers."

Shortly after the release of *Euphoria*, drummer Wooten announced to the band he was leaving. "He was older than us," says Herman, "and we were driving in a school bus with no air-conditioning through Arizona in 110-degree weather. It was wearing on him more than us youngsters and I think that was the motivation. We were touring constantly and not in a very luxurious manner. For a guy who toured with Carole King and done the tops of the music world, I am sure it was hard to justify touring that way." Wooten agreed to stick with the band for a couple for months until they could find his replacement.

Chapter 6

JEFF SIPE

I used to watch him from the side of the stage when Aquarium Rescue Unit played with The Samples on H.O.R.D.E. tour. All the musicians from all the bands used to admire the musicianship of that whole band. Jeff was this mild-mannered, humble dude who basically schooled all of us. I had him write out a Latin groove he was messing around with in sound check one day, and he was more than happy to share his knowledge and show the specifics of the chop. At that time, many people referred to him as Jeff "Fives" Sipe, because a lot of his fills were combinations of fives. Solid drummer and person for sure!—*Jeep MacNichol (The Samples)*

"**W**e got here by floating down the river today," announced Vince Herman from the stage of the River Ranch Lodge in Tahoe, California, on July 9, 1997. "We are pretty charged up."[1] Leftover Salmon then unleashed a fiery version of "Ain't Gonna Work," which was perfect for a Wednesday afternoon. The show was noteworthy as it was the first with new drummer Jeff Sipe. Sipe was brought into the band to replace Michael Wooten, who had grown tired of the grind of hard touring. Salmon considered a few other drummers from their hometown of Boulder to help lower touring costs, but the Atlanta-based Sipe's talent was just too much to ignore. Salmon and Sipe had been friends since first meeting when they toured together in 1994 on Salmon's first East Coast tour with Aquarium Rescue Unit. Sipe's first show with the band came just three days after Wooten played his final show at the High Sierra Music Festival on July 6. In typical Salmon fashion, the band welcomed Sipe into the fold in a highly unusual manner. "I expected at least a full rehearsal or two before my first gig," recalls the drummer, "but no, instead we had rafts and boats floating down the stream as Drew played mandolin for me. These guys are fun-loving people, not at all formal. We ended the float at the stage where we set up and played." While they partied as they floated lazily downstream, Salmon taught their new drummer the songs he needed to know for their set later. On the afternoon float, Sipe got a grand introduction into the loose world of Salmon. To teach a new bandmate an entire set while partying as you floated down the river would have been an almost impossible task for any other drummer, but Sipe is a truly special talent who by the time he joined Salmon had established himself as one of the leading improvisational drummers of the jam scene.

Sipe was born in 1959 in Berlin, Germany, where his father—who worked as a makeup and disguise artist for the CIA—was stationed. He moved constantly as a child, as his father's unique job took him around the world, often to various exotic locales, even living for a time in Thailand and Vietnam. He was fascinated with music as child. In a sign of the things to come, it was often the obscure and weird that drew his attention, including a fascination with the bell ringing he heard in Buddhist temples. He learned to play the drums in the sixth grade while his father was stationed in Frankfurt, Germany. He moved back to the states for high school, living in Fairfax, Virginia. After graduating from Chantilly High in 1977, he moved to Boston to attend the Berklee School of Music, where he played with his fellow classmates Branford Marsalis, Bill Frisell, Mike Stern, Kevin Eubanks, and Steve Vai. Sipe and Vai even had a short-lived band together called Winter.

Following his time at Berklee, Sipe moved to Atlanta in 1983 and began teaching at the Atlanta Institute for Music. Shortly after arriving in Atlanta, Sipe met a collection of other like-minded musicians. Among them were a pair of brothers, Kofi and Oteil Burbridge, who played keys and bass respectively, and a pair of guitarists, Jimmy Herring and Charlie Williams. They played around Atlanta in various informal settings until they fell under the tutelage of Col. Bruce Hampton. Hampton was a charismatic, inspiring figure and soon formed a band with his new young friends. They played under a variety of names, usually including Arkansas followed by some weird title; the Travelers, Tourists, Florists, or State Birds. They increased the weirdness level when they added banjo picker Jeff Mosier into the fold. Mosier had no previous experience playing anything resembling rock music. He was a folk and bluegrass picker. One night while attending a David Olney show in Atlanta, Mosier was out front of the club during set break and heard a sound coming from the club next door. "It was just the oddest thing," remembers Mosier. "It sounded like a guy playing mandolin over a bad church PA, and there is an out-of-tune band playing with the guy. I thought maybe there are two bands. I asked someone, 'What is this?' He said that is Col. Bruce Hampton and the Arkansas Florists. I walk in and there is this guy playing the electric mandolin with his eyes closed and there was a weird group of musicians with him. One looked like a politician. There was a black guy with no shirt on. A guy sitting crossed legged on a table playing a whole bunch of keys attached with a fishing line. I was horrified."[2] Mosier got over his initial reaction when he realized they were playing a bluegrass tune he was familiar with by Dave Evans. He met Hampton and the band that evening and not long after joined the group.

This odd collection of musicians morphed into the Aquarium Rescue Unit, an eclectic band who were part of the vanguard of the emerging jam scene. Mosier would eventually leave and be replaced by mandolin virtuoso Matt Mundy. During this time, Sipe picked up his famous nickname, Apt. Q-258, from Hampton, who often christened those in his band with odd nicknames he felt truly showed their personality. Sipe's name came from a radio show Hampton often listened to hosted by evangelist Prophet Omega. Omega's shows were popular among touring musicians for their unintentional humor and weird sense of rhythm with which he spoke. His show was broadcast from Apartment Q-258 at 488 Lenmont, which he announced throughout his shows. Over the years, Hampton bestowed the shorter version of the address, Apt. Q-258, on Sipe, for a reason Sipe, with a laugh, says makes no sense, but in the world of Hampton was perfectly clear.

ARU was at the forefront of the new jamband scene, and Hampton was viewed as a spiritual leader. ARU never gained the popularity of many of the bands they influenced. They began to lose steam and fizzle out in 1994 when Hampton retired from the band. Following Hampton's departure, the rest of the band continued to tour for a few years, but they all began to get involved in other projects. The timing was advantageous for Sipe, as Wooten began to tire of the grind of the road

and Salmon was on the lookout for his replacement. While they auditioned a few other drummers, "We wanted Jeff," says Emmitt. "He was
our focus." Sipe was viewed as a superstar player with the ability to
elevate everyone around him. He often was the most talented musician
onstage but could play in such a way he would make everyone feel good
about where they were musically and because of that was able to raise
the level of an entire band. Salmon and Sipe had already bonded from
their tour together a few years prior and recognized the chemistry they
shared. For Sipe, who was enthusiastic to play with a band he shared a
musical curiosity with, it was also something much simpler. "For me it
was a chance to be employed full time with good friends and provide
for my wife and our soon to be new family."

With Sipe on board, the band began to find a completely new improvisational level during their live shows. He says, "I introduced different rhythms and dynamics to the group. It was always an experiment.
To me the banjo was the ride cymbal, the mandolin was the high hat
and snare drum. The bass was the bass drum. So, without being redun-
dant, I wanted to both back up what they had going on already and
invite new musical directions." Herman recognized the impact of the
inventive drummer, "Sipe was such a good player we were able to step
it up to a whole other level." Emmitt agrees, "He had a lot of drive and
a lot of chops. He brought a lot of excitement. It definitely pumped
things up a few notches." Despite Sipe's seemingly limitless talent,
there were still a few struggles when he first started playing with the
band. With ARU and his other side projects, he used much more intricate rhythm patterns, but with Salmon, they needed him to do something entirely different. Sipe had to strip down his thought process on
drumming when he joined. "I always took two-beat to be simple. I
never thought about it, never practiced it. Wow, I got a lesson when I
tried to play some bluegrass with them. It is one of the hardest things to
pull off and it seems so simple. It was a big challenge for me."[3]

For North, the addition of Sipe was a welcome change, as he and
Wooten struggled both musically and personally at times to find common ground and connect due to the wide age gap between them and
their diverse musical backgrounds. He says, "I feel Michael and I were
always fighting each other musically, but maybe that is what made it
sound so good. We have talked about it since then, and it's like, 'Wow, I
love you man.' We fought each other tooth and nail and did not have

any vocabulary that matched, because he came from this interesting songwriting, rock 'n' roll background. We didn't see eye to eye on anything, but we played two hundred gigs a year and did all this high-speed maneuvering onstage. We look back now and laugh, but it was stressful. There was lots of musical tension." Sipe recognized the work Wooten and North had done as rhythm section over the years and how Wooten's patience and steady playing made his own transition into the band much simpler. He also recognized how Wooten pioneered the difficult, two-beat style needed to play with Salmon, and with expert ease made it look so simple. He says, "Michael Wooten paved the way for me."[4] North says when Sipe joined, "The e-brake was off. We could just go. It was cool." This connection showed. Banjo master Danny Barnes and his band the Bad Livers did a monthlong run of shows with Salmon in 1999 and was amazed by Sipe and North's musical interplay onstage: "You couldn't touch those two guys for a rhythm section. As a music fan, even if their music was not your cup of tea in terms of song presentation and so forth, you could not deny those two were a force of nature. They could play as one person. You don't see that much in the jamband world, that level of musicality and improvisation. Often, bands will play to the audience and not to the muse or the music or to God or whatever you call that. What was John Coltrane playing to? He wasn't playing to make the crowd dance, he had a higher calling. That's the way I felt about Tye and Jeff, they were on another level." String Cheese Incident bassist Keith Moseley had been seeing Salmon for years also noticed this powerful chemistry. "We did a lot of touring together during the Jeff and Tye years. All the rhythm sections they went through had their good things, but Tye and Jeff were my favorite time. They were incredible, top-flight players. They could do things no other rhythm section I knew of could do. They could play the Latin beats and the funk and the zydeco with such authority and authenticity. It was an education to watch."

Salmon was building a head of momentum following the release of their first major-label album, *Euphoria*. "Big things were happening. We were selling out everywhere. We were the buzz band before some other bands came along and blew a little bit of that away from us," says Emmitt. Having the backing of a major label owned by Disney was advantageous for the band as they saw a big jump in record promotion and publicity, which began to expand their audience. *Dupree's Di-*

amond News, a magazine focused mostly on the improvisational and jamband scenes, clearly took notice of this momentum Salmon was building and the role Sipe's addition played in it. In their fall/winter issue of 1997, they declared, "Leftover Salmon is to Cajun/calypso/ bluegrass music what the Grateful Dead were to rock. This white-hot quintet stretches the envelope of the multiple musical genres they cover way open with long jams, high tempo, stick-in-yer-head melodies, and sweet bluegrass singing. They are certainly one of the hottest bands touring today. The recent addition of master groove rock drummer Jeff 'Apt. Q-258' Sipe will surely inspire this group to even higher heights."[5]

Following Sipe's first show at River Ranch, the band had an extensive list of tour dates lined up for the remainder of the summer and into the fall. The River Ranch show would serve as Sipe's sole warm-up before heading out on the road with Salmon. Sipe, ever the consummate professional, never missed a beat. Among the dates lined up was a high-profile spot on the upcoming H.O.R.D.E. Festival tour, which was slated to start two days after the River Ranch show.

The H.O.R.D.E. Festival or Horizon of Rock Developing Everywhere was started in 1992 by Blues Traveler, the Spin Doctors, Widespread Panic, Phish, and Aquarium Rescue Unit. The five bands were all part of the emerging jamband scene. They became friendly over the years when they crossed paths on the road, often opening for each other in different areas where one had a stronger following. They all desired to find a way to play in the larger outdoor amphitheaters over the summer months as opposed to the same clubs they played in relentlessly throughout the winter. They realized the simple economics of playing in a larger venue meant larger paychecks. The problem was none of the bands at that time quite had the influence or audience to make it worthwhile to arrange a full summer tour of those amphitheaters. One day John Popper asked Col. Bruce Hampton, "How would you have handled this in the old days?" Hampton told him they used to tour with five or six bands on the bill, with each band only playing thirty or forty minutes. This simple solution made them realize if they joined forces their combined power might be enough to make it financially feasible. After many informal discussions about the potential of the five bands touring together, they all sent representatives to a meeting at legendary rock promoter Bill Graham's office in New York City. Present at the meeting was all of Blues Traveler and Phish, Widespread Panic's John

Bell, the Spin Doctors' Eric Scheckman, and Hampton from Aquarium Rescue Unit. No managers or agents were allowed into the meeting, though they all nervously waited outside Graham's office. The musicians decided to organize a mobile festival throughout the summer where they would all get equal billing, the same amount of time on-stage, and equal pay. The musicians sealed the deal by shaking hands after ceremoniously dipping them in a jar of Vaseline Phish's Mike Gordon brought. However, a day later, after the managers got involved, this plan would change slightly. Bands would still all play the same seventy-five-minute set, but now be paid based on their draw in each market.

With the economics worked out, they began to develop a plan and schedule tour dates. "The idea was to find groups with strong fan bases regionally in different parts of the country," explains the Spin Doctors' drummer Aaron Comess, "and do a short tour with different groups going on at different times depending on what part of the country we were in." This approach underlines an overlooked aspect of the early jamband and H.O.R.D.E. scene, that they were a unified collection of bands, when in reality the bands were all part of a few regional scenes who shared similar characteristics. Again, Comess explains, "Every one of the bands were unique in their own way. That was what great about it. Although we shared similarities, our music was quite different from each other's. There was no competition at all, just a great vibe and lots of inspired music all around." These regional scenes and bands were scattered across the country. Blues Traveler, Spin Doctors, and God Street Wine from New York City. Aquarium Rescue Unit, Widespread Panic, and Allgood from Athens and Atlanta. moe., Ominous Seapods, Hypnotic Clambake, Deep Banana Blackout, and Strangefolk from the New England area. ekoostik hookah from the Midwest. Dave Matthews Band and Agents of Good Roots from Virginia. And Big Head Todd, the Samples, Leftover Salmon, and Acoustic Junction from Boulder. None of the Boulder bands were part of the initial year of H.O.R.D.E. but would be part of the second migration the following year. Samples drummer Jeep MacNichol, who played on the second year, recognized that despite the geographical differences among bands, "Those places had similar scenes to Boulder at that time and they generated huge local fan bases to take off from."

The first year, while not a financial success, hit a chord with a growing fan base and emboldened the festival to return for another go-round
the following summer. Three bands returned for the second year, Blues
Traveler, Widespread Panic, and Aquarium Rescue Unit, while two
Boulder bands, Big Head Todd & The Monsters and the Samples, were
added to the lineup. Over the ensuing years, Blues Traveler became the
de facto headliner for most years as the festival was John Popper's
project from the start. The lineup continued to pull mostly from the
jamband world, adding the Allman Brothers Band, Dave Matthews
Band, the Black Crowes, and Rusted Root over the years, but also
began to include bands who were not part of the scene that birthed
many of the original bands that filled the early lineups. Over the years,
it added such diverse acts as Lenny Kravitz, Beck, 311, G. Love &
Special Sauce, Primus, Natalie Merchant, Sheryl Crow, and Ziggy Marley among others. At a time when grunge was at its peak and Perry
Farrell's Lollapalooza was viewed as the gold standard of what a touring
festival could be, H.O.R.D.E., with its egalitarian approach, was finding
its place on the busy summer concert schedule. "The H.O.R.D.E. tour
was   kind   of   the   grassroots,   jammy   stepsister   of   Lollapalooza in every way," says MacNichol. "It was noncommercial, home
grown, underground and fan supported. Some bands were on big labels
and some not, but the success of the H.O.R.D.E. really had nothing to
do with the mainstream record label promotion like Lollapalooza. Lollapalooza was the streamlined tour bus with microwaves and TVs.
H.O.R.D.E. tour was more like the seventies Volkswagen bus with
stickers and a toaster oven."

Leftover Salmon made their first appearance on the festival in 1996,
playing ten shows on a run from Alabama to California. The following
year they again were added to the lineup and were one of the only
bands to play every date on the tour. The 1997 H.O.R.D.E. tour was a
coming-out party for the band. They were starting to get some attention
for *Euphoria* and they were hitting their stride with Sipe, who was
settling into his role. For many, the five-piece lineup of Emmitt, Herman, Vann, North, and Sipe was the most powerful incarnation of the
band. Chris Castino, guitarist and singer of the Big Wu, clearly noticed
this the first time he encountered Leftover Salmon on H.O.R.D.E. tour
in 1997, on which the Big Wu played three shows after winning a local
battle of the bands. Recalls Castino:

I was immediately impressed to see Jeff Sipe warming up—as he always does—on a full kit set up behind the main stage. All his limbs bounced like a marionette puppet. I thought, "Leftover Salmon is already better than I thought they would be and I haven't even heard them play." Where Vince and the band started to diverge was when they played tunes from the new album *Euphoria*. Whereas *Ask the Fish* felt liked it picked up where New Grass Revival left off, *Euphoria* felt like music to shake your ass to. It was fun and it was the perfect fit for a festival. In fact, this record defined festival rock. It was just what the doctor ordered when the mushrooms kicked in and you needed something upbeat to carry you through. It was raucous and often fast but it never forgot the three-part harmonies that defined bluegrass and the other accoutrements of Cajun, fiddle, and even rock music.

For Salmon, their life on H.O.R.D.E. tour was a dream come true. "It was epic," says Sipe. "Amazing vibe, with many great on-the-rise bands. It felt like the seventies, like original music was the focus and the main spirit for a lot of people. More of a tribe than a horde." The 1997 H.O.R.D.E. lineup featured an assorted roster of musicians including

Drummer, Jeff "Apt. Q-258" Sipe, who helped inspire the band to new heights, plays with Vince Herman on the 1997 H.O.R.D.E. tour. Courtesy of Vince Herman.

Neil Young, Beck, Ben Folds Five, Primus, Toad the Wet Sprocket, Ween, Soul Coughing, Mighty Mighty Bosstones, and Medeski, Martin, & Wood, among others. Each day, the band would arrive at the venue as blues legend Taj Mahal, who was also on the tour, was heading out to the local butcher shop to bring back all kinds of meat that he would grill and barbecue all day. "That was the focal point," says Herman, "going to hang with Taj. That barbecue all day long. It forged a lot of relationships." The band's set were usually later in the day on the second stage and thirty to forty minutes long. Occasionally they played on the main stage, but either way it left a lot of time for the band to hang out, watch other acts, and jam backstage with the other musicians. Col. Bruce would lead a group jam on the second stage at some point during the day, which most of Salmon would take part in. "Man, it was an amazing time for the band," recalls Herman. "It was a group of folks we still view as our contemporaries and musical buddies. To be with the guys from Panic, Neil Young, Morphine, and Col. Bruce. It made for some great camaraderie. It definitely taught us a lot about what the scene is all about." While most of the bands were outside of the public eye and the mainstream, they all found a home on the H.O.R.D.E. tour as it broke down music business barriers and created a musical revolution Leftover Salmon was at the forefront of. H.O.R.D.E. tour was Salmon's first big exposure to the rock world and playing in larger outdoor amphitheaters. They discovered many new bands on H.O.R.D.E. tour, especially Herman, who got deeply into the odd-rock stylings of Morphine and the all-female trio Cake Like.

One day on tour Vann invited Col. Bruce Hampton to come hang with him at their bus after both Salmon and ARU finished their sets. The two first met on Salmon's East Coast tour in 1994. Vann thought it was simply a chance to spend some time with a man who everyone on tour looked to for guidance and inspiration. It instead provided Vann with a weirdly profound moment, the likes of which seem to constantly swirl around Hampton. The pair was chatting when Hampton casually asked Vann where he was from and about his family. "He told me he had grown up in Atlanta," recounts Hampton. "I asked where and he gave me the address of my grandmother's house. It turns out we are like first cousins. I knew his father, but never met his mother. I told him about everyone who lived in the neighborhood and he just about fainted. I found out his father was my aunt's brother. Just crazy. We just sat there for twenty minutes and couldn't talk."

Emmitt also had a profound moment on tour, though it was musical and not as weirdly personal as Vann's. Throughout the first month of the tour, the band began hanging out with rock legend Neil Young. Young often opened the day playing an unannounced half-hour set on the side-stage as fans started to enter the venue. Most times only twenty or thirty people would be present for those sets. After, he would usually stick around and check out the bands that came on next. Emmitt remembers Young watching Salmon's set almost every day from the side of the stage in a "ball cap, jean jacket, and sunglasses." Young later, in an interview with Los Angeles radio station KROQ, gushed about his two new favorite bands he discovered on the tour: Primus and Leftover Salmon. Toward the end of the tour at a stop in Holmdel, New Jersey, on August 19, Herman visited Young's bus earlier in the day and invited him to join the band onstage. Young, as always, was elusive, telling Herman, "Don't get too excited. I don't want the guys to expect me to come and then I don't show up." During their set, Salmon was in the middle of a serious jam with Hampton as they worked through his signature tune, "Yield Not to Temptation." Herman says, "I was playing a solo and the crowd went nuts and I am thinking I must be killing it. I look over my shoulder and there was Neil right there ready to play some harp." Hampton also saw Young out of the corner of his eye standing there admiring what they were doing onstage. "I remember the look on his face was like, 'Damn, these guys are pretty good.'" Emmitt noticed the reaction of the crowd as well and turned to his right to have Young standing right next to him "like six inches from my face." He motioned Young onstage, who immediately joined on harmonica. After they finished "Yield Not to Temptation," Young stuck around for another song. Salmon launched into the Emmitt-penned, "Muddy Water Home," off their latest album *Euphoria*. "Vince was telling him the words and he was singing harmony with me," recalls Emmitt. "It was an amazing experience. After the tune, he was walking off the stage and he grabbed me by the shoulder and said, 'Thank you.' He came back out onstage, grabbed me in a big bear hug, and whispered in my ear, 'Thank you so much.' Then he walked off. It was quite an amazing experience. It was one of the highlights of my musical career."

Young was not the only one taking notice of what Salmon was doing. Throughout the tour, they seemed to garner more and more attention with each stop with their high-octane set that had only gotten more intense with the addition of Sipe. *Guitar World*, in their August 1997 issue, wrote, "Leftover Salmon is a shredder . . . with a schizophrenic knack for sounding like a different band every night of the week."[6] *Dupree's Diamond News*, who covered the H.O.R.D.E. tour extensively, also recognized what was happening every day during Salmon's set:

> Appearing for the entire tour were Leftover Salmon, with their pulse-elevating, spaz-grass. These guys often seemed a little on the schizoid side, moving from mellow Cajun swing to rollicking and unstoppable, atomic mountain-top wailing. In their allotted twenty-five minutes, the unreal mandolin strumming and yodeling of Drew Emmitt and the maddeningly precise electric banjo from Mark Vann appeared to lift the stage from the ground and send it spinning off into the atmosphere. Added to that was the intensity of a rightly placed new drummer, Apt. Q-258 (formerly of Hellborg, Lane, and Sipe; and Aquarium Rescue Unit), and you were left with a lot more than just stale fish.[7]

The *Fort-Worth Star Telegram* declared this about Salmon's appearance on H.O.R.D.E.:

> Late in the day at last summer's H.O.R.D.E. show in Ennis, you had three choices: A) listen to John Popper's endless make-the-dogs-howl harmonica solos as Blues Traveler closed the show, B) go home, or C) walk over to the second stage and catch a really good set by Leftover Salmon.
>
> The vast majority of the 20,000 or so there chose A or B, but C was the best option. Hailing from Boulder, Colorado, Leftover Salmon is one-part bluegrass, one-part Cajun/zydeco, one-part rock band—or, as they put it, "Polyethnic Cajun slamgrass," a palette wide enough to accommodate covers of Bill Monroe and Led Zeppelin and for the band to play both Laguna Seca Daze (where the Grateful Dead always stopped for at least one show per year) and the Telluride Bluegrass Festival.[8]

Following the H.O.R.D.E. tour, the band did not slow down, instead carrying the momentum into a full slate of shows in the fall. During this

The "e-brake was off." Leftover Salmon plays during the H.O.R.D.E. tour August 5, 1997. Courtesy of Vince Herman.

time, their longtime tour manager decided to leave the band to pursue other endeavors. For a band like Salmon who spent so much time on the road, having the right tour manager was essential. They needed someone who could manage a group of outsized personalities who all operated on different timetables and had different interests while on the road; in other words, they needed someone with the unique ability of being able to herd cats. Also, as they saw their touring scheduling continue to get larger and the venues they played bigger, they needed someone with a solid background and good experience in the industry. Two names emerged. One was Brian Harkin, who was working as the assistant tour manager for the Black Crowes, who was the first choice of manager Chuck Morris. The other one was Johnny Pfarr, a friend from Boulder who worked at the Fox Theatre and as the road manager for Acoustic Junction. Even though Morris was pushing for the bigger experience of Harkin, the band felt more comfortable with Pfarr. "I think they went with me because of the personal connection," says Pfarr. "Their well-known music and festival spirit, including their late-night antics, was something I very much wanted to be part of, and I thought I'd be the right guy to carry on that tradition." Pfarr's hiring also stayed true to the band's "family" values. More so than other bands, Salmon has maintained a close-knit family atmosphere that extends to their crew, and even includes ex–band members. Thirty years on, it is not uncommon to find the band, their crew, and countless friends hanging out backstage before shows in a loose, relaxed environment that is markedly different than the backstage of many other bands. Like all families, Salmon has their differences and disagreements, but it is far more common to find them spending time together both on tour and off then to find them arguing. For Pfarr, this was exactly what he was looking for. "I don't think I could work for a band with all that kind of other stuff going on. I wanted to be part of something that was more than just a well-pieced-together group where everyone was a hired gun," says Pfarr. With a laugh, he continues, "Those bands don't have much to say for themselves besides maybe a million dollars and a platinum record." Pfarr's hiring helped the band return to this all-encompassing environment. Some felt this feeling was missing with some of their previous managers who often excluded many of the band's longtime friends and fans from the backstage area in favor of their own friends or hangers-on. The hiring of Pfarr returned to the idea that friends were family.

Pfarr's first show with the band was June 16, 1998, at Red Rocks Amphitheatre in Morrison, Colorado, as part of the Telluride on the Rocks event featuring Béla Fleck & the Flecktones, David Grisman, Sam Bush, Tim O'Brien, and Mary Chapin Carpenter. As he walked them onstage, Pfarr thought to himself, "What a venue, what a band, what a high. I knew pretty immediately this was my family." Over the years, Pfarr's role evolved well beyond that of simply being their road manager. He became a highly valued and trusted member of their family and heavily involved in the business side of the band. Pfarr worked closely on the business side with Vann, who continued to run the business operations of the band throughout the years. The two would become very close. Pfarr says, "He was my best friend and business partner."

Also part of the crew at the time was Jeffree Lerner, who worked as the band's monitor engineer and stage tech. Lerner was also a drummer and percussionist, and the band often invited him onstage to sit in and lend his talents to their live shows. Lerner played close attention to Sipe, soaking up all he could from the drum master, saying, "Jeff Sipe was a huge influence and elder and pushed me to do what I am doing."[9]

Salmon's roots sound was not the music at Lerner's core, though, and he would leave his role with the band to join jamtronica act Sound Tribe Sector 9 as their percussionist in 1999.

In a further sign of change and bigger things to come, the band decided it was time to retire Bridget and upgrade their touring bus situation. Even though it was the right decision, letting go of Bridget was hard for the band. The old converted school bus had been with the band since 1993 and became part of their identity, serving so admirably as both a rolling hotel and mobile party pad. They took great pride in pulling up to the venue and parking it next to the big-time, full-fledged touring buses. While the bus had limitations—it was not properly geared to run on the highway (the band fried three transmissions over the years), it had no air-conditioning, and it had trouble getting over 60 mph, it was always full of music, laughs, parties, pot smoke, and for years was home. Keyboardist Peter Sears, who toured with the band briefly in the nineties, jokingly says, "It was sort of like traveling in a big yellow joint."[10] Bridget had been through rough times, like when they nearly froze to death while sleeping in it in the dead of winter in Vermont when the ice built up so thick on the windows in its unheated interior it had to be scraped off with a screwdriver. "We were coming into the coldest part of the country at the coldest time of the year," says Emmitt, "and I remember thinking this is insane. No one should be doing this. And no one was doing it. We paid some serious dues." But Bridget had seen even more great times, like when Emmitt, who was at the wheel, decided to surprise his sleeping bandmates after a show in Florida by continuing to drive south so they could awake to a sunrise in the Florida Keys that would take their breath away. For a while, they even towed a big plastic fish behind the bus to help raise awareness of environmental concerns of rivers and streams. To replace Bridget, the band purchased a real tour bus that came to be known as Barth, after the company that produced it. While Barth offered more conveniences than Bridget, it was in Bridget that Salmon established their identity. It ferried them around the country during their formative years when they were playing around two hundred shows a year. For three years, they spent over half the year on Bridget traveling around the country. "We went everywhere on that school bus," says Emmitt. "Every corner of the country. The strategy was to get out there and pound it. Go till you drop."

During this time Salmon also prepared to release their second live album. Seeking to further highlight the deep connection they shared with their fans, the band set out to compile an album that would allow the fans to have some input on the final track listing. Instead of recording every night and sifting through to find the best cuts, or as they done for *Ask the Fish* picking one show and going for it live that night, the band wanted to take advantage of the taper scene that had been supportive of the band and helped spread their music. Salmon petitioned their fans and tapers in their newsletter, on their website, and in local newspapers, to send in their favorite shows. The band assembled an album culled exclusively from those tapes. The resulting album, called *Taper's Reel* (also referred to as the *Ask the Tapers* album), featured twelve tracks recorded between 1991 and early 1998, and including a powerful version of Jim Messina's "Whispering Waters" that was becoming a live highlight for the band over the past year. They had tried to record a studio version for *Euphoria*, but were not quite able to capture the energy of the live version and ended up cutting it from the album. *Taper's Reel* captured the excitement of Salmon's live show, but there was some concern in the band over the quality of the recordings they used. As the release date for the album neared, concern over the quality began to grow. With a decision on what to do about the impending album still unresolved, review copies were sent out to various publications resulting in a lengthy review of the album in *Relix* magazine in June of 1998. With concern mounting over the quality of the album, Herman says as the release date neared, "the ball was dropped," and the album was never officially released.

Despite the positive attention Salmon was receiving for *Euphoria* and selling some hundred thousand copies relatively quickly, Hollywood Records was pouring more of its resources behind label mates Fastball and their hit song "The Way," and not providing as much attention to Salmon. While frustrating, Herman can understand Hollywood's approach: "Fastball was more mainstream music. We have always been into this folky-roots thing, which isn't always as marketable as compared to more mainstream rock 'n' roll. The roots thing has a bit of a stigma when it comes to the radio. Until AAA radio and Americana that stuff was an outlier." Despite this, the band continued to tour relentlessly. While their label was not fully recognizing the impact they were having, the band could see it each night with sold-out show after sold-out show. For those who saw Leftover Salmon during this time, they were lucky enough to witness a band harnessing the full intensity of their live powers. Every night was a psychedelic outburst of slam-grass energy and swirling mullets. Salmon was arguably one of the most exciting live shows at the time and a truly monstrous force onstage. Still, even with sold out shows every night, the band was not in denial of why some of their H.O.R.D.E. and jamband peers seemed to be making the move and to play to larger and larger crowds. With clarity often lost when trying to self-analyze, Emmitt accurately explains, "We were coming from a bluegrass tradition, more bluegrass than rock. Sometimes I think maybe because we didn't go quite in the rock direction we didn't get huge. We just kind of followed our own path for better or worse."

Despite Hollywood's growing lack of interest, the band and manager Chuck Morris had already conceived an ambitious follow up to *Euphoria*. Morris was the manager of the country-rock group Nitty Gritty Dirt Band when they released their groundbreaking album, *Will the Circle Be Unbroken*, in 1972. At that time, the Nitty Gritty Dirt Band were in a similar space to Salmon. They were a bunch of long-haired hippies living in the mountains of Colorado who loved old-timey, traditional music and were looking for a grand statement from their next album. *Will the Circle Be Unbroken* tied together two generations of musicians over thirty-eight tracks that found the younger rock-influenced Nitty Gritty Dirt Band playing with a host of country and bluegrass music legends, including Roy Acuff, Doc Watson, Earl Scruggs, Merle Travis, Vassar Clements, Jimmy Martin, and Maybelle Carter. The album introduced an entire generation of fans under the age of thirty to not only much of the music on the album, but many of the guests as well. Even though other bands, such as the Flying Burrito Brothers, the Byrds, and Poco, toyed with the country-rock formula, what they did leaned more to the rock than the country and old-time. *Will the Circle Be Unbroken* truly found the crossroads where those two musical identities intersected. The Nitty Gritty Dirt Band fully gave themselves over to the album, allowing each song and every guest to fully shine. The album catapulted them from simply being a novelty band to crossover stars who were nominated for multiple Grammy Awards, headlined the Ozark Music Festival to a crowd of over 350,000 and even shared the stage with Aerosmith. Morris envisioned a similar path forward from Leftover Salmon with a like-minded guest-laden album. He wanted to update the country and hippie combo and establish Leftover Salmon as more than just some hippie band with an odd name who played bluegrass with drums. He wanted to prove they could cross over to a much larger fan base. Morris wanted to introduce Salmon to a wider cross-section of fans by having them play with a host of legendary musicians who would resonate on an international level. "Chuck thought the album would give us an air of legitimacy in the music world outside the jam and H.O.R.D.E. scene," says Herman.

Morris and the band believed the ambitious idea they had for the album could be the crossover and breakthrough Hollywood wanted for the band. They knew they needed all the label's considerable financial backing to be able to pull it off. They wanted to get Randy Scruggs to produce it in Nashville and bring in a roster of guest musicians who ranged from A-list legends to like-minded peers. Hollywood was skeptical of the idea because of the potential cost to get all of the guests and because Herman says, "I don't think they knew what to do with *Euphoria*, the first record we gave them. It was maybe a bit too diverse to call it one kind of music." Morris used his vast influence to convince Hollywood to fully back the project. Emmitt recognized the importance of having Morris as their point man on the project: "That would have been a very expensive record to make with all the special guests and paying Randy to produce it. To Chuck's credit, he was able to make it happen."

With Hollywood on board, the band came up with a wish list of musicians who they wanted for the album. They looked to the original *Circle* album for inspiration. "I listened to the first *Circle* album a lot when it came out," says Herman. "Growing up in Pittsburgh, I assumed that a major role of music was to bring different generations together. That's the way it was with the polka bands there, but it sure wasn't that way with the rock bands I knew. One thing I like about the *Circle* album was the way it brought together musicians of different ages and different backgrounds."[11] With the idea of bringing generations together, they first looked to their friends and peers who they came to know over the years and reached out to Béla Fleck, Jerry Douglas, Sam Bush, John Popper, John Bell, Todd Mohr from Big Head Todd, and Taj Mahal. They then set their sights higher and looked to use their ace in the hole, producer Randy Scruggs. Scruggs previously worked with Waylon Jennings and was able to enlist the country great into the project. Scruggs was also able to recruit his father, banjo legend Earl Scruggs, which was a dream come true for Vann. Through Randy, they were trying to get Johnny Cash on board but were unable to make it work. They also brought in Lucinda Williams and in a sign of the circle being unbroken, Jeff Hanna from the Nitty Gritty Dirt Band made an appearance. The final list of musicians who appear on the album also included Sally Van Meter, Jeff Coffin, Reese Wynans, Jo-El Sonnier, and Del and Ronnie McCoury. "We felt like kids in a candy store being able to get all of our favorite bluegrass and rock musicians to play on this record," says Emmitt. The common factor among all the guests was they all had forged long careers coloring outside of the accepted lines. They were all outlaws, trailblazers, and revolutionaries. Leftover Salmon felt right at home.

The album would also prove Salmon's love for the communal aspect of music festivals as truly part of their identity and a defining trait of who they are. Salmon loves the camaraderie and bonding among fans and fellow musicians at festivals and wanted to incorporate that shared sense of community on *The Nashville Sessions*. Herman explains part of the idea behind the record was born out of those sit-ins that happen so often at festivals, "We get to say, 'Hey Sam or whoever, come on up for this one.' So, it's kind of like a festival on the record."[12]

In February of 1999, they entered Randy Scruggs's studio in Nashville to begin work. Like the Nitty Gritty Dirt Band had done nearly thirty years prior, Leftover Salmon was a newgrass-inspired band coming down from the Colorado mountains and visiting Nashville to make a record with musicians of all ages and all walks of life. The first order of business was figuring out what songs each guest would play. Whereas the original *Circle* album relied on an arsenal of traditional songs, Salmon was looking to use more of their own songs. Still, the same spirit was present. Emmitt says they were writing steadily and had songs that just lent themselves to the different artists. "I was lucky because I had about five songs I hadn't recorded yet that were perfect for the record." As they began to work out what songs they would record with which guests, the band also remained open to working with whatever songs their guests might pull out in the studio. "Sometimes, it was just us waiting to see what would come up," says Herman.[13] Out of the thirteen eventual tracks on the album, six were written by Emmitt, one by Herman and Vann, one by Vann, there was one traditional cover, and one each from Mahal, Jennings, Williams, and John Hartford.

Some of the original songs they used were written specifically with certain guests in mind. Emmitt says, "'Midnight Blues' I wrote thinking about the McCourys. I was thinking they should record it. I had even given it to Ronnie on cassette at one point." Vann had written "Five Alive" with the express idea of having Earl Scruggs play on it. While some of the other new songs just seemed appropriate for particular guests. "'On the Other Side,' was perfect for John Popper's harmonica," says Emmitt. "'Breakin' Thru' just lent itself to Jerry Douglas. I wrote a song with Randy Scruggs, 'It's Your World,' that was great for John Cowan's vocal and Big Head Todd's guitar. Vince had written 'Dance on Your Head,' which was perfect for Béla Fleck." Either way, the inclusion of such talented guests made each song a chance to simply put on a seat belt, hold on tight, and take off on a musical journey.

Reading Herman's handwritten notes from the sessions that were scrawled on scraps of paper he found lying around in the studio, the excitement for the sessions leaps off the page as he declares the band has "settled in for the musical adventure of our lives!" In his notes, he documents how smooth the process was for the band, explaining after the band loaded in, it jumped right into the first track, "On the Other Side," around 4 p.m. "Just before we start the first take," writes Herman, "Randy sticks his head in the door and says, 'Have fun.' And so, it will be. Two hours later we have the basic elements of the song down and are grinning ear to ear with how smoothly things work here in Scruggsville." Following "On the Other Side," the band began working on "Dance on Your Head." With North on an upright acoustic bass, the song starts going into new places they never visited before. Herman writes, "Drew gets some guitar raunch going and it's like water-skiing in a gravel parking lot, but funner." He adds that by 9 p.m., they have two tracks pretty much done and "we are so pumped even Mayor McCheese is grinning."

Over the course of the past two years, they had played well over three hundred shows, so they were already intimately familiar and dialed in with each of the songs they were going to record for the album, except for a few of the covers—Mahal's "Lovin' in My Baby's Eyes," Jennings "Are You Sure Hank Done It That Way?" and Williams's "Lines Around Your Eyes." This allowed the band to focus on the inclusion of the guest and to hone and perfect each song's structure for the album. Producer Scruggs proved invaluable. "He helped immensely by suggesting arrangement ideas and playing guitar," says Sipe. "He let us do our thing for the most part. We talked about approach to arrangement, solos, and whether to record to a metronome or click track, which I preferred. Some songs were not able to be performed to a click and they moved around a bit. It was tough to control the tempos because the core group was very organic in their approach to music in general. They moved like a school of fish."

The band decided to record each song individually, so the recording process took longer than normal as they did not lay down all the drum parts first and overdub everything later. Drummer Sipe liked this approach as he felt that, "The vibe on the album is more honest as a result." This decision to record each song individually also allowed the band the bonus luxury of getting to work extensively on each track with all the guests. In some cases, it was simply an excuse to spend quality time with good friends and make some great music. In the case of Mahal, Jennings, and Earl Scruggs, it was a chance to spend time with some of the band's musical idols. Hanging, playing, and partying with those idols was a unique opportunity that would provide a lifetime of memories. "It was a dream project for us. We were pinching ourselves every day," says Herman, who admits the band had to hold back on some of its usual jamming. "We just focused on the songs. We kept an ear for what was appropriate on the tunes and tried to make it sound good and clean. We didn't jump up and down for the recording. It's just such a treat to be playing with these folks that we just did it with a whole lot of respect in our head."[14]

Much like the Nitty Gritty Dirt Band was during the making of *Will the Circle Be Unbroken*, Salmon was completely open and willing to allow all the guests to be themselves and shine. They rightly realized, just as with *Will the Circle Be Unbroken*, the strength and power of the album would come from how Salmon integrated their varied roster of guests into the mix. Sipe remembers the band convincing Béla Fleck to just be himself and do what he would normally do. "He is a genius and he had so many great ideas that he kept apologizing and saying, 'Sorry, I am not trying to take over.' We were all ears. What a mind he has for organization and complementary parts. So logical and brilliant. Not to mention his virtuosity." Those traits and ideas shone on Fleck's two contributions to the album, "Dance on Your Head," and a cover of the John Hartford classic, "Up on the Hill Where We Do the Boogie," where Fleck's bouncy, inventive banjo line perfectly intertwines with Vann's banjo, giving the song a taste of the absurd, which for a Hartford song was perfect. Producer Scruggs also provide a special connection to the song as he had played on the original version on Hartford's *Aereo-Plain* album.

Jennings lived up to his oversized reputation and pulled up to the studio in a red and black Cadillac with a license plate reading, "Waylon." He strolled out of the Cadillac wearing a big black cowboy hat, red-tinted sunglasses, and jacket with embroidered roses on it. As he approached the band's bus parked out front of the studio, the first thing he asked was, "Got any beers on that bus?" Salmon had never played with Jennings, but knew they wanted to record his "Are You Sure Hank Done It This Way?" as an ode to doing things differently in Nashville. "That was something we were trying hard for," Herman says. "He heard some tapes and he liked what we were doing and that it was kind of a rock 'n' roll/country kind of thing. It fit him because he became a country star and was kind of pigeonholed in that category even though it was kind of far from where he stands musically."[15] The band had no idea for the arrangement of the song when they entered the studio, instead letting the moment take charge. For the vocals Herman and Jennings sang live together and Emmitt recalls it being an almost surreal moment to see his longtime bandmate singing with the legendary Jennings. As the band worked through his classic tune, Jennings, despite his larger-than-life, gregarious personality that often intimidated those who did not know him, made everyone feel at ease by telling them wild stories about he and Willie Nelson partying together in the seventies and of David Allen Coe blowing up a ticket booth at a festival that refused to pay him. Jennings would get the band to relax by jokingly telling them they were playing too fast. "He was such a classic character," says Herman with clear awe and respect. "Such dignity. Such an air about him, but at the same time he didn't give a shit. He was amazing. Made it really comfortable. I was excited to get to sing with him. He felt like a real comrade, even though he was this legendary cat." The finished track accentuated by Emmitt's fiddle and guitar was not the same old tune Jennings originally sung in 1975. It also answered the question—"Where do we take it from here?"—that Jennings posed in the song's lyrics as the new version featured a soaring duet with the grizzled, road-weary voice of Jennings and the expressive Herman updating the classic to reflect Salmon's own penchant for blazing their own path in the face of conventional musical norms.

The recording sessions provided Vann a chance to play with his all-time idol, banjo legend Earl Scruggs, father of album producer Randy. When Vann first discovered the banjo, he devoured the instructional book Earl had written. Vann says the chance to play with Earl "was a highlight for me."[16] Scruggs played a tape of what the band was working on for his dad, who liked what Salmon was doing and expressed interest in being on the record. While Earl had first gotten his start with Bill Monroe in the 1940s in the version of the Bluegrass Boys credited with refining and popularizing what came to be recognized as the traditional bluegrass sound, he also had a taste for the progressive, much like what Salmon tapped into. In the seventies, along with his sons Randy, Gary, and Steve, Vassar Clements, and longtime bandmate Josh Graves, he formed the Earl Scruggs Revue. The band had drums and toed the line between bluegrass and rock, helping create some of the template for what bands like Hot Rize, New Grass Revival, and later Salmon would follow. Earl also served as a link to the original *Circle* album as he played on both it and the 1989 sequel, *Will the Circle Be Unbroken: Volume Two*. For Vann, who first learned to play from the *Earl Scruggs Songbook*, it was a magical moment as he was now writing songs for the legend he had studied and looked up to for so long. Vann wrote a couple of tunes with Earl in mind, finally settling on an instrumental track named "Five Alive." "I wrote it with his style in mind," says Vann, "I was trying to channel him a little bit. I don't know how close I came, but I tried to write my version of something Earl might have written."[17] Scruggs passed a tape of the song to his dad, who impressed Vann with how prepared he was for the session when he entered the studio. "I didn't have to show him tab or anything," Vann says, "He showed up and was all over it."[18] Despite his quiet, reserved demeanor, the bluegrass icon long defied expectations with his revolutionary playing that inspired a generation of banjo pickers. The finished track chugged along with the soul of a traditional bluegrass song that sounded as if it had come straight from the front porch, then stopped off to say hi to friends in Colorado for a little high-country love. For Vann, the time in the studio with his musical idol was a bucket-list-type moment. After finishing the track, Vann walked out of the studio proclaiming, "Can you fucking believe it? I have been trying to play like Earl Scruggs since I was nine, and now here he is playing my song."

Whereas Jennings and Earl were a case of the band having a clear idea of what they wanted to perform when the guest arrived in the studio, Mahal was just the opposite, as Salmon, who bonded with the blues legend while on H.O.R.D.E. tour together, decided to just wait and see what happened when they all got into the studio together. "We had four or five Taj tunes we brushed up on," Herman says, "but we let him decide when he got there. We had no plan. We went in and Taj said he always wanted to do 'Lovin' in My Baby's Eyes,' with a more acoustic feel, so that is what we went after." As great as recording with Mahal was, the time spent with him hanging after they finished recording was just as exciting for the band. Mahal ended up staying most of the night jamming and talking about music on the bus. He wowed the band as he would easily glide from a traditional African-sounding piece to a "greasy, crooked, Delta blues thing," and back again. All the while he was explaining the traditions and nuances of all the different styles and how they intersected and intertwined with each other. For Herman, who is a serious music buff and always looking to learn a new song or style, it was a memorable experience. "He just blew my mind as a musicologist."

The only person they were not able to share the studio with was Lucinda Williams. She was one of the last guests brought into the project, and her schedule did not allow for her to spend time in Nashville with the band. Herman was enamored of her singing and excited to be able to bring her into the project. She sent the band a tape with a couple of her songs to choose from. "Doing her song 'Lines Around Your Eyes,' just seemed to fit," says Herman. The band recorded the track with help from accordionist Jo-El Sonnier, whose Cajuny flavor gave life and emotion to Williams's heartfelt lyrics. The band's take on her song was a timeless lament of love and a troubled relationship. The addition of Sonnier's accordion gave the song a desperate cry which was a perfect fit for the hurt in Williams's voice.

The album closed with a spooky take on the traditional gospel/blues tune, "Nobody's Fault but Mine" featuring Widespread Panic's John Bell on vocal and guitar. The band gathered in the studio late at night to start work on the track. They sat in the darkened recording room in a large circle to work on the arrangement of the song. A couple bottles of whiskey were passed around as they worked to help set the proper mood. As they rehearsed, the recording engineer placed a microphone in the center of the circle to capture the work in progress. As they got good and drunk and felt they had the arrangement down, they played the tune twice through. They retreated to the control room to listen to the playback and prepare for the final take. As they listened to the playback, it became clear they already had the final take. The rough take of their intimate, whiskey-fueled dirge, colored by Bell's gravelly, soulful timbre that chugged along with a languished, late-night pace was the perfect take. The simplicity and mood of the moment was captured with all its debauched flaws and was the perfect way to close the album. "All of life should be that uncomplicated," says Bell, recalling the blurry memories from the alcohol-fueled, hazy night. "I was truly honored to be included. I think there was beer involved and Col. Bruce Hampton was my chaperone."[19]

In addition to serving as Bell's chaperone, Hampton had also come into the studio to record with Salmon. In the typical Hampton way, he cranked up the weirdness level. He recorded one song called, "Six is Now Thirteen," that was Hampton ranting in the out-there way only he can, as he pontificated about salt and pepper allergies, mayonnaise, olives, and any other obscure thought trapped inside the weird world of his mind. The band played a strange, off-kilter mix behind his rant. Fleck and saxophonist Jeff Coffin joined in, providing their own peculiar additions to the musical cacophony. "It was really, really strange," recalls Emmitt. "Stranger than even a lot of our friends could deal with, so we ended up not putting it on there."[20] The song resurfaced in 2014 when it was included on a special vinyl edition rerelease of *The Nashville Sessions*. The liner notes for the vinyl edition included the disclaimer, "'Six is Now Thirteen,' is a view inside the universe of Bruce Hampton's mind. We were very frightened by this track fifteen years ago, so frightened we didn't include it on the CD. However, like a fine wine, it has aged well and is now suitable for consumption."[21]

All told, the band spent six weeks in Nashville, with about three weeks spent on the actual recording process. They hung with friends, saw lots of live music, and even had a huge dinner at Del McCoury's house with his family one Sunday afternoon. Even more importantly, they crafted an album that was a true work of art and represented the band's ambitious vision. Emmitt states, "As far as a piece of work that is the one I am most proud of." It was a glorious time for the band that they all look back on fondly. "I love this album. I have such a grateful and thankful feeling when I think about my friends and this recording session. I'm ready for a follow-up," says Sipe. It was a special moment for the band, something they had dreamed about since they first picked together in the campgrounds of Telluride. In his handwritten notes from the sessions, Herman declared, "We cannot believe this is really happening. It's beginning to sink in that today and tomorrow are the days we'll remember all of our lives."

The good times of the sessions and the time spent in Nashville was tempered by a dose of reality shortly after the band returned home to Colorado. During their time in the studio, they noticed Vann was struggling physically. While recording with Earl Scruggs, he was sweating profusely. At first everyone thought it just might be him being nervous around the banjo legend, but Sipe says, "He came out of the recording

Leftover Salmon with some of the guests that appeared on the Nashville Sessions in front of the legendary Ryman Theatre in Nashville (from left): (Back row) Reese Wynans, Jeff Coffin, Del McCoury, Ronnie McCoury, Drew Emmitt. (Middle Row) John Cowan, Mark Vann, Jo-El Sonnier, Randy Scruggs, Earl Scruggs, Tye North. (Front row) Vince Herman and Jeff Sipe. Courtesy of Vince Herman.

booth eyes wide and sweating and telling us he felt really weird." The band was worried what it might be, but Vann dismissed it until a few weeks later when he was back home in Colorado. He and his wife went to see David Grisman at the Fox Theatre the first weekend of March. During the show, his arm went numb. Again, he wanted to dismiss it, but when feeling did not return by the next day he finally went to the hospital to have it checked out. It was discovered he had a heart arrhythmia and his heart rate was fibrillating, speeding up and down drastically. He had a pacemaker put in immediately to help control this irregular heartbeat. During his recovery, Vann missed a monthlong run of shows in the South. To fill his spot, the band enlisted Billy Constable to fill Vann's banjo role. Herman would make mention of Vann's absence from stage at a show March 31, 1999, at the Elizabeth Reed Music Hall in Macon, Georgia, saying, "Mark is at home resting up. He has some health things to figure out, but he has it figured out and he will be back on our next tour."[22] After he recovered, Vann rejoined the band and they dove right back into their nonstop touring ways as they waited for the release of the new album in the fall.

The release of *The Nashville Sessions* in September 1999 gave Salmon a new air of legitimacy. It was hailed as the band's best album and received widespread acclaim. The *Rocky Mountain News* called it "an impressive leap forward."[23] Florida's *The Ledger* proclaimed, "This album is a classic."[24] *The Music Box* declared in a lengthy review, "*The Nashville Sessions* is Leftover Salmon's crowning achievement to date and for a disc so bloated with guest musicians the group manages to turn the affair into a stunning and seamless masterpiece."[25] Jambase.com labeled it, "A professional piece of art."[26] *Relix* magazine hailed the album and Salmon's growing stature: "Leftover Salmon has been regarded as one of the premier jambands of the nineties, but its roots have been inextricably embedded in bluegrass and country. *The Nashville Sessions* is one joyous album. The band crosses its Rocky Mountain wail with some pure Nashville country and bluegrass and the result is its best album to date."[27]

The album, as the band hoped it would, introduced a new generation of fans to their musical roots. Adam Greuel, from jamgrass band Horseshoes & Hand Grenades, was just a teenager when *The Nashville Sessions* was released, and acknowledges, "That album changed my life. Looking at the liner notes served as a newgrass encyclopedia that led me to chase down all those players' projects and to start researching them and finding all the stuff they did. In no small way Leftover Salmon was responsible for a newgrass and musical curiosity that lives strong in me today."

The Nashville Sessions was the perfect way to celebrate ten years as a band. The album showed a huge growth and maturity in the group's songwriting and playing. While they still enjoyed playing shows that were packed with jokes and gags that kept an audience entertained and coming back night after night, they recognized gags are part of a live show where you can "see people jumping around and can get swept up into that," but on an album, jokes can wear thin after repeated listening. Instead, on *The Nashville Sessions*, they focused on the presentation of each song and crafted a statement that was the perfect capstone to their first ten years as a band. Writer Geoffrey Himes noted this growth in a feature he wrote for the *Washington Post*, "Instead of ranging all over the stylistic map, *The Nashville Sessions* is unified by its emphasis on country and bluegrass flavors. And instead of sprawling at great length, the songs concentrate their improvisation into shorter, more focused arrangements."[28] *The Nashville Sessions* perfectly encapsulated who Leftover Salmon were and where they were going. It was a mature statement from a band not always known for mature statements. With the way they effortlessly brought a cornucopia of styles into their always welcoming musical tent, *The Nashville Sessions* was truly a grand celebration of American music and a defining moment for the band. One of the tracks from the album, "Breakin' Thru," has over the years evolved into the closest thing the band has to an anthem. It is a triumphant ode to perseverance and finally making it. It thoroughly summed up where Salmon was after the release of *The Nashville Sessions* as all of their dreams finally seemed to be coming true.

Chapter 7

GREG GARRISON

There are not many bass players out there that can lay down smooth jazz lines, the funkiest of funk, the bluegrass 1 and 5, and have a love and appreciation of the Grateful Dead. Greg is all that and more. I absolutely love his playing. Not only is he someone you can rely on musically, he's a great human being and a good friend I am happy to know.—*Adam Aijala (Yonder Mountain String Band)*

"We made this great record and we knew it was a great record. We knew we had made something amazing," says Drew Emmitt, "but it never got the attention it deserved. That was kind of sad. We felt if this doesn't get us to the next level, I don't know what will, because this is so great." Emmitt's frustration was stemming from what he viewed as a lack of support from their label, Hollywood Records, for their latest album, *The Nashville Sessions*. The album was steadily climbing up Billboard's Heatseekers charts and garnering critical acclaim across the country. Meanwhile their label seemed indifferent, providing what Emmitt felt was minimal support for an album he saw as a milestone as it bridged the gap between countless genres with its inclusion of an all-star roster of guests.

Much as with *Euphoria*, Salmon felt Hollywood Records did not provide the promotional support needed to help push their album. Some of the disconnect with Hollywood came from a massive turnover of personnel at the label that involved many of the people Salmon had developed a relationship with. With that connection gone, Salmon felt those who replaced them never figured out how to best promote the band. They still saw a great increase in publicity, marketing, and distribution over what they could do on their own and thus saw an increased visibility, but it seemed Hollywood did not put forth the effort needed to push the album to greater heights. Perhaps it was the age-old worry and stereotype of bluegrass music and the way people seemed to have negative preconceived notions about it. This idea was blown apart the year following the release of *The Nashville Sessions* with the release of the *O Brother, Where Art Thou?* soundtrack. The soundtrack used mostly modern recordings of traditional bluegrass, country, gospel, and folk music appropriate to the Great Depression time and Deep South setting of the film. It is not a stretch to say much like the *Will the Circle Be Unbroken, O Brother, Where Art Thou?* served as an introduction to bluegrass and old-timey music for a generation of new listeners. The soundtrack, which featured a roster of legendary musicians including Ralph Stanley, John Hartford, Norman Blake, and Emmylou Harris, became a bestseller, with sales of over seven million copies in the United States. It won multiple Grammy Awards in 2002, including Album of the Year. It singlehandedly proved there was a market for and interest in this style of music. Perhaps if *The Nashville Sessions* was released after it, Hollywood's attention and willingness to promote it would have been greater.

"After that record that was it with Hollywood," says Emmitt about the end of their relationship with the record label. "I am thankful Chuck Morris was able to get them to do another record with us. It served its purpose. That is when the record company came into play and did something good for us. Even though they could have done a lot more with that record. Still, we got to make a dream record." Salmon felt they benefited from the move to a major label and the exposure it provided, but at the end of the day they were an extremely independent band who long forged their own path and were always their own best advocates when it came to converting new fans. "We had run our course with them," reflects Herman. "We thought this was our chance to have a breakout thing that would set us on a newer path above and beyond our wildest dreams. It didn't quite work out like that. There was generally a feeling of let's get back out on the road touring and doing what we do best."

The band's break with Hollywood was also softened by a change they sensed was sweeping through the music industry with a move away

from major labels. "Major labels were losing their relevance and importance," says Emmitt, "and people were starting their own record labels,
which is what we have done since." Much of this change was due to the
rise of the internet and the control over all aspects of their career it gave
a band. It allowed bands to have a more immediate link to their fans.
They could now market themselves directly and get their music into
more hands via online sources and direct downloads. Herman remembers being perplexed at a meeting with Hollywood with all the various
department heads in which he noticed they did not seem to be recognizing this change happening. He says he asked them, "What's your
digital approach going to be? Are you moving into digital distribution?"
Their only response was they were getting rid of their warehouses for
shipping and fulfilling orders for CDs. Herman was underwhelmed by
their response. "They really didn't have any idea what the future was
going to hold. They seemed they had kind of thrown their hands up in
the air about how they were going to distribute and listen to music. That
kind of surprised me. We were sitting there with the heads of Disney's
record label and they didn't have a clue what their digital approach was
going to be. It was surprising. I figured they were just holding their
cards close to their chest. I thought they had to have a plan. They are
Disney. But you know things kind of evolved haphazardly and they did
not seem to have clue what was going to happen next."

Despite Hollywood's lack of attention and the end of their relationship with the label, Salmon was finding the style they had created and
refined over the past decade was starting to see many new, younger
bands follow in their always fun footsteps. The worry Hollywood might
have about bluegrass not being palatable to the masses was proving to
be wrong as there was a passionate growing interest in the jamband
scene about it. Bluegrass and roots music long had a home in the jam
scene as many of the bands infused their sound with strains of the old,
much as the Grateful Dead had done when they remade many traditional songs into their own image and introduced a plethora of traditional musicians and songs to a new crop of fans. Many of those fans
might have not been intimately familiar with a bluegrass and old-timey
sound but were eased into it by bands such as Salmon, Hypnotic Clambake, Blueground Undergrass, and Béla Fleck & the Flecktones. They
were discovering what it was about this traditional style of music that
was so appealing. These bands helped introduce a new generation of

fans to the possibilities of bluegrass music, proving it was much more than simple mountain music. They showed how it was a complex, thoughtful music that touched your soul.

While Salmon was by far the most versed in a bluegrass background and used it as a major component of their sound, as it was at the core of who they were as a band, other groups in the jam scene were also digging deep into the traditional well. Jam titans Phish were discovering this sound and beginning to incorporate it into their shows. This interest in bluegrass was sparked while they were on tour with Aquarium Rescue Unit in 1992. Phish guitarist Trey Anastasio says Matt Mundy of ARU passed on a copy of bluegrass legend Del McCoury's 1992 album, *Blue Side of Town*, to Phish. Anastasio says he and the rest of Phish listened to the album "fifty million times," in their van while on tour helping to set the bluegrass bug in the band.[1] To further expand their bluegrass vocabulary, the band invited banjo picker Jeff Mosier, of ARU, to join them on the road during their fall 1994 tour to teach them bluegrass. Mosier first met Phish when they played in Athens, Georgia, on the same evening ARU had a show in the area. After their set, ARU went down the street to see this other band they had heard so much about. Mosier recalls walking into the venue and seeing a weird group of guys onstage jumping up and down on trampolines. The weird guys were Phish and the two bands became instant friends that night. Shortly after meeting, Phish asked ARU to come north and tour with them in June 1990. A few years later, Phish asked Mosier to come on tour with them to help them develop their bluegrass skills. He joined the band from November 16 to 20, 1994. Over the weeklong run, Mosier would sit in with the band every night during an acoustic portion of the show, lending his banjo skills to a variety of traditional tunes. During the tour, he also taught them several traditional songs, including, "I'm Blue, I'm Lonesome," and "Long Journey Home," as well as helping to refine some of the bluegrass songs they had begun to incorporate into their sets. Mosier taught the band to play a variety of acoustic instruments that had a long-lasting impact on the sound of the band, especially over the following years as they began to add acoustic moments to their shows. The albums *Billy Breathes* and *Farmhouse* over the subsequent years carried the acoustic idea with them as they both incorporated elements of what they learned from Mosier. *Billy Breathes* features bassist Mike Gordon playing banjo, a skill he became more comfortable with after learning from Mosier.

As the jamband scene continued to evolve throughout the nineties, smaller, more distinct subgenres began to emerge. They all carried those same similar characteristics that first powered the jam scene: relentless touring, encouraging fans to freely trade tapes of live shows, the desire to investigate a combination of musical styles that seemed misplaced anywhere else, and nightly live improvisation onstage. Over the years, these bands began to fuse a wide range of styles onto the original jamband template. Leftover Salmon with their unique bluegrass-inspired blend were at the forefront of a new style that developed out of this and came to be known as jamgrass. Over time, as the sound evolved it would often be described with a simpler, wide-ranging, all-encompassing moniker becoming popular—Americana. The term "Americana" was first used in the mid-eighties and described bands incorporating elements of acoustic American-roots music styles, including country, folk, and bluegrass. This created a distinctive roots-oriented sound that exists in a world apart from the pure forms of the genres upon which it may draw. While acoustic instruments are often present and vital, Americana also often uses a full electric band. The style had its roots in sixties bands like the Flying Burrito Brothers, Poco, New Riders of the Purple Sage, and later work from the Byrds.

Despite its natural, straitlaced, buttoned-up, traditional tendencies, there has always been a rebellious, progressive side to bluegrass. This progressive side was built upon by bands who used bluegrass instrumentation and performance style as a foundation for what they did, but who did not adhere to a traditional bluegrass style. They applied this bluegrass methodology to their musical repertoire, which often drew heavily from contemporary rock music. This allowed these progressive bands to sound both youthful and traditional. This was like the approach Salmon took with their music when they first began. In the seventies, this progressive sound took form in the likes of John Hartford, The Dillards, New Grass Revival, David Bromberg, and David Grisman—all of whom Salmon looked to for inspiration and reveled in tweaking the accepted norms of the genre and giving a big middle finger to the status quo as they blurred the lines between bluegrass and rock. This blurring of lines was to the consternation of many in the old traditional guard. This consternation is ironic because while some of the old guard or more traditional fans try to ignore these more progressive bands—even going so far as to boo them at festivals if they dare bring an electric instrument onstage—this is a shame because those progressive musicians, who sometimes exist on the periphery of the genre, often introduce more new fans to bluegrass than many of the more traditional acts. For some traditionalists, it might be easy to dismiss Emmitt and Herman as bluegrass interlopers. Emmitt does so many things that go against the accepted norms of bluegrass music. He plays plugged in, uses a slide, and incorporates a wide range of pedals. But the reverence and respect for the tradition and history of the music that came before him is always at the forefront of what he does and the skill and intent with which he plays can wow even the most hardened bluegrass traditionalist. Herman, like Emmitt, is reverential of the traditions of the music. He is a true musicologist, always learning new tunes and digging deeper into the traditional sound that moved him so much when he first became immersed in it while in college in West Virginia. You would be hard pressed to find someone in a picking circle who knows more songs than Herman.

Those bands existing on the periphery of the genre clearly resonated with a young Emmitt, Herman, and Vann as they began to forge their musical path forward. When they started Leftover Salmon, they found it seemed natural to tweak the accepted norms and play with the DNA of bluegrass. They took what those progressive bands started and pushed it even further out. Like the bands they looked up to, who blurred the lines and reached across genres to introduce new fans to bluegrass, Salmon realized with their bluegrass-rock hybrid they were doing the same. "I just hope the band can turn people on to bluegrass," says Vann. "I am lucky to have a platform here for doing that. To be able to play bluegrass and banjo in front of a lot of people who never in their wildest dreams think about going to see a bluegrass band or banjo band. I think you've just got to quit whining about people's perception of the banjo and start showing them that it's different than what they think. You can't convince them. You got to show them. That's what I hope we're doing."[2] Salmon would change the rules in how you could present bluegrass music and, in the process, throw many of the stuffy, traditional confines of the genre out the window.

For Salmon, it was a natural evolution. As much as they loved bluegrass, they also loved rock, Cajun, and any number of oddly placed musical styles. They were not married to any one style. They loved it all and tried to play it all. David Bromberg is a clear predecessor, with his bluegrass-rooted sound and open willingness to incorporate elements from jazz, folk, blues, country, and rock into his music. John Hartford is also an important touchstone for the band, not only because of the inclusion of many of his songs in their sets (including "Up on the Hill Where We Do the Boogie," which is not only part of *The Nashville Sessions*, but also one of their most played songs live ever), but also for their seamless inclusion of humor into what they do. His quirky lyrics and anything-goes approach are clear inspirations.

In this scene, Salmon found a whole new generation of fans who were not raised on bluegrass and traditional music, but were ready and willing to dive headfirst into it. For many of these fans, their first exposure to bluegrass may have been through Jerry Garcia and his seventies bluegrass supergroup, Old & In the Way. Kagey Parrish of folk duo the Honey Dewdrops was one of those fans. He says, "Finding out about the various offshoots the Grateful Dead did—jug bands and bluegrass bands, Jerry Garcia's work with David Grisman—and branching out from there to Bill Monroe and older stuff from him. We had an interest in the Grateful Dead and realized they had an interest in doing more than just electric stuff. Thank God for them!"[3] Bluegrass bands and musicians tied to Garcia saw a change in their audiences over the years as more and more Deadheads began to flock to bluegrass shows after being exposed to it through Garcia's many offshoot bands and bluegrass friends. Hot Rize's Tim O'Brien recalls this change, "If you played a gig with Peter Rowan or David Grisman or Vassar Clements you could expect to see some of the Dead's audience. They would come see me play with Peter Rowan and would tape the show and start spreading it around. Pretty soon there would be other kids coming to tape your show and they started coming even if someone like Peter Rowan wasn't there. It kind of spread after that. It brought bluegrass into the jamming Deadhead community and it provided a place for someone like Leftover Salmon to flourish."

For many of these new converts to bluegrass, Leftover Salmon was exactly what they wanted their bluegrass to be—loud, raucous, delivered with drums and a taste of the old-timey, all played with a wink and a nod. Emmitt says, "We came from the bluegrass tradition, we weren't just a bunch of rock guys playing bluegrass. We played blue-

Leftover Salmon's progressive take on bluegrass continues to flourish as Mark Vann (right) and longtime friend Larry Keel (left), along with bassist Tye North play at the Ritz Theater in Raleigh, North Carolina 10/23/99. Courtesy of Johnny Pfarr.

grass and rock. We felt we were carrying on the tradition, but maybe bastardizing it some." This bastardizing of the original bluegrass sound, while offensive to some of the more hardline traditionalists who enjoy their bluegrass unplugged and polite, kept more in line with the original spirit of Bill Monroe when he first created the sound now recognized as bluegrass. Monroe mixed the fiddle sound he first heard from his Uncle Pendleton Vandiver with the country, gospel, and blues he was familiar with and ratcheted it up to a breakneck speed with his distinctive trademark mandolin to create what famed folklorist and musicologist Alan Lomax called "folk music with overdrive," in a 1959 article for *Esquire* magazine.[4] Leftover Salmon took Monroe's original approach even further, and, much like he did, added their own personal spin to it with drums and electric instruments. Drummer Jeff Sipe, who witnessed the band's birth from afar while still with Aquarium Rescue Unit, called their sound, "Very daring for the times."

Leftover Salmon began to incorporate more and more of the improvisational elements prevalent in the jam scene into their progressive bluegrass sound and an entirely new style began to emerge. This new style mixed the best elements of the music at the core of Salmon, the straight traditional bluegrass sound of Monroe, the irreverent humor and progressive sound of Hartford and New Grass Revival, and the loose inventive approach of their jamband peers. Salmon discovered their own musical landscape to inhabit. They had bonafide bluegrass roots born from years of campfire picks at Telluride but could also tap into an entire new generation of fans who only had a vague notion of traditional bluegrass through their inclusion of a rock-based sound.

Despite the lack of mainstream support, this new sound was finding a willing army of fans and a new crop of bands who were inspired by Salmon's fearless approach to music and beginning to emulate the bluegrassy, jammy style they pioneered. Keller Williams was introduced to this style at the Telluride Bluegrass Festival in 1995 when he first encountered Leftover Salmon on a cold and rainy afternoon as he shivered away in a borrowed hoodie. "It was a mixture of insanely fast bluegrass," recalls Williams, "combined with the speed and unbridled energy that was unmistakably pure, authentic, and immediately welcoming as it was accompanied by voices in harmony that came from crazy men onstage with mullets." No one combined the old-timey with the new quite like Salmon, and the sound they made was utterly infectious and inspiring. "One of the most popular types of bands on the jam scene is the bluegrass jamband. There are hundreds of them out there and some have risen to the top of the scene. There is no doubt Leftover Salmon paved the way for these acts. They all in one way or another owe their popularity to the inroads Salmon made on the scene," explains Dave Katz of ekoostik hookah, who witnessed Salmon's influence firsthand as they were both key cogs of the early jam scene and shared many a show and late night together over the years.

Yonder Mountain String Band's Ben Kaufmann says, "I boil it down to I saw Leftover Salmon open for Col. Bruce, and as a result I decided to drop out of school, move across the country, and try and put a band together." It was March of 1994 and Salmon was on their first East Coast tour opening for Aquarium Rescue Unit. At the time, Kaufmann was a nineteen-year-old film student at New York University who was into Phish and had recently discovered the Aquarium Rescue Unit through some live tapes he acquired. ARU was going to be playing at the famed Wetlands Preserve in New York City and a friend of Kaufmann's suggested they go. He also suggested they get there early to check out the opening band from Colorado which he had heard was pretty good. Kaufmann says, "The next thing I know Salmon comes out onstage and starts to play and my whole world altered. I had never heard them before. I never heard music like that before. I had become minimally aware of bluegrass—I sort of knew Béla Fleck & the Flecktones—but I had never seen anything like Leftover Salmon. They came out and it was 1,000 miles per hour right from the get-go. I remembered not being able to talk. I had no interest in interacting with my friends I was so absorbed in what was going on." Following their set, Kaufmann headed straight for the old VW bus that served as the merch table at the Wetlands and purchased *Bridges to Bert*. He says he had a moment of clarity in his life. "I didn't want to be in film school anymore. I didn't want to be in New York City. What I wanted to do was find out who this band Leftover Salmon was, where do they come from, and where do you have to live to make music with this energy and drive, and what I internally felt as a freedom. I began what would have been a many months process of investigating them."

Kaufmann's investigation resulted in him making the decision to move to Boulder, Colorado, and enroll in the University of Colorado so he could be near where this music that moved him so much was being made. Over the next few years, he immersed himself in the local scene and along with another young musician, Jeff Austin, was asked to join the Zukes of Zydeco, Steve Burnside's latest band. Burnside was a longtime friend of Herman and was an original member of the Salmon Heads. Through Burnside, Kaufmann would get to meet Herman and Salmon. During this time, Austin and another musician friend, Dave Johnston, worked at a restaurant called the Verve, which held open picking nights. Herman was a regular at these. Johnston recalls first meeting Herman at the Verve. "We hung out and had some beers, and thought, 'Holy cow this guy is a legend.' We were nervous, but it was a great time. Over the next couple of months, we developed a better relationship with the guys. Drew was still living in the Front Range and we would go see him there. One night we went to Vince's house for dinner and Mark brought an ostrich egg. It was bizarre and fun all wrapped into one." These new friendships would pay huge dividends, as

Kaufmann, Austin, and Johnston, along with guitarist Adam Aijala, would form Yonder Mountain String Band, a progressive bluegrass band who followed the example of Leftover Salmon and found they were able to exist both in the bluegrass and more rock-oriented jam-band world. Kaufmann says he has thought about that first night he saw Leftover Salmon and wondered, "what if?" What if he decided to grab a beer and miss the opener? What if he saw a friend at the bar and hung there until Col. Bruce came on? "If not for them, I couldn't even guess where I would be or what I would be doing," he says. "It would have altered the whole trajectory of my life."

Yonder Mountain mandolinist Austin, like other young musicians in the area at the time, looked to Herman as a mentor and someone who had traveled the road they were starting on and could provide insight-ful, sage advice. "Vince called one day and said come to my house," says Austin. "I came over and we sat in his kitchen and he said write all this down. He told me who to call, whose house to crash at, and how to get a foothold in every town we would tour through." Herman would take it on himself to recommend Yonder to promoters and festivals across the country, helping the young band establish a following in far-flung places they had yet to play and get booked into festivals where they were still an unknown act. "The first time we played High Sierra Music Festival in 1999 was because I stood in Vince's kitchen while he called Roy Carter (High Sierra co-founder) and then handed the phone to me," recalls Austin. "Yonder drove up there and played for free. Twice. We played the Berkshire Mountain Festival for free twice. We drove across the country four times for free, but it turned into an audience." Salmon often had Yonder open for them in the early days of the band. At a two-night run in Park City, Utah, at Harry O's September 29 and 30, 1999, Aijala says he got some sage advice from Emmitt he still relies on. "I was smoking a joint with Mark and Drew, and Drew said to me, 'It's all about the little things. Like when you get to a hotel and you can check in early, or a good meal on the road, or having clean clothes.' To this day whenever I am on the road and doing laundry I always think how it's the little things that get you through." Kaufmann agrees, and says Salmon's impact on the creation of Yonder was much more than just friendly advice about, "What the fuck to do, where do we go, how do we do it, and who do we need to know." He says,

I can say quite confidently that without Leftover Salmon there would be no Yonder Mountain String Band for a number of reasons. One, I wouldn't have moved to Colorado. Two, these guys were playing their music for years establishing Colorado and the Front Range as this epicenter for this experimental, kind of bluegrass, but kind of other things, rootsy whatever it is they do, Polyethnic Cajun slamgrass. They set it up. When we arrived on the scene it was like shooting fish in the barrel. It was almost cheating. You still had to pay your dues and log your miles and survive Wyoming in the winter, but the real leg-work had already been done. We show up and there are already people who were turned on and interested in what we were offering.

Yonder was not the only band looking to Salmon for inspiration and advice and traveling the path they paved. Another bluegrass-based band with drums was formed in Crested Butte in 1993 by a group of local ski bums. The band The String Cheese Incident was born from the same mold as Salmon. The String Cheese Incident bass player Keith Moseley was a big fan and asserts they were "A big influence" on the development of String Cheese, perhaps "the biggest influence in my eyes. By the time we started I had seen Leftover Salmon twenty, thirty, forty, maybe fifty times among all the various Boulder shows and the ski towns. They were my favorite band at the time. In a lot of ways, they were to me, what the Grateful Dead was to a lot of other people. They were kind of the breakout band for me in the terms of the music really speaking to me and going out and seeing them in multiple locations all over the state. Leftover Salmon was it for me."

Much like with Yonder Mountain String Band, Salmon served as mentors to String Cheese. Both bands incorporated many songs they first heard or learned from Salmon into their early shows. The String Cheese Incident recognized the importance of getting to share the stage with Salmon. The ability to play for Salmon's audience's ready and willing ears was an opportunity not to miss and they would let nothing get in the way when given that chance. Over Thanksgiving weekend 1994, String Cheese was invited to open for Salmon at Rafters in Crested Butte. String Cheese left Boulder for the long drive to Crested Butte. The roads were in awful shape due to the weather. Cars were spun out on either side of the road along the way, but nothing was going to stop String Cheese from getting to their gig. Moseley and guitarist

Bill Nershi were traveling together in Moseley's 1985 Toyota pickup truck with all their gear packed tight in the camper shell. The rest of the band was following a few minutes behind in another truck. On highway 50, right before Gunnison, Moseley and Nershi hit a patch of black ice. They skidded off the road and flipped the truck. Despite landing upside down, the pair was unharmed as their seatbelts held them in place. Their gear, which was tightly packed in the back, barely shifted. The two scrambled out of the car and waited for the rest of the band. They loaded all the gear into the other car and still made it in time to open the show. "There was no way we were going to miss that," says Moseley. "Opening for Salmon, nothing was going to stop us. Not even rolling the truck. We got there. We played our set. I remember thinking, the car accident is behind us. Now I am going to get my party on to Leftover Salmon. I don't have anything to do but get my buzz on and dance and that is what I am going do. We will deal with it all later. And that's what we did, we dealt with the truck the next day."

Salmon opened the eyes of many to what bluegrass could be and over the years there were many bands in the region who followed their lead, including Yonder Mountain String Band, String Cheese Incident, Shanti Groove, Elephant Revival, Head for the Hills, Floodplain Gang, and Runaway Truck Ramp. Bluegrass legend Sam Bush states, "One of the reasons Colorado youngsters love that fast bluegrass is because they heard Salmon doing it first." Salmon began humbly and created a model for the next generation of bands to follow. "When we started in the early nineties we were touring in an old school bus and had no idea what the hell we were doing and just made it happen," says Emmitt. "I think other bands were able to see that and think, 'Oh, well, maybe we don't need a record label. Maybe we could just get out on the road and start playing. When we started there wasn't another bluegrass-oriented band doing that. It was difficult. At that time, it was hard to convince people electric bluegrass was going to work."[5]

At that time, most of Salmon lived in Boulder and the surrounding area, including the mountain town of Nederland. Nederland's musical past stretches back to the days of Caribou Ranch and the long line of legendary musicians who passed through the studio's doors recording some of the seminal albums of the seventies and eighties there. The studio gave both national and local musicians a focal point around which to revolve. It was only a matter of time before the studio led to the creation of bands who fed off the energy emanating from there. Dango Rose from Elephant Revival recognizes this energy today in Leftover Salmon. "They are the most pure and authentic representation of that transfer of energy from the rock 'n' roll being produced at Caribou into the new style of bluegrass, jam-infused music being curated in the hills."

Many of the bands that sprouted in Salmon's wake did so around this area. The Samples' Jeep MacNichol noticed Salmon's growing importance for music in the region and how they were responsible for what was happening in "Nederland and for every bluegrass or bluegrass influenced band that has exponentially exploded since then." Nederland became a hot spot for this new jamgrass sound. Herman lived in the town and was often viewed as the unofficial mayor for the way he seemed to know everyone and serve as the focal point for music and fun taking place in town. He often could be found dressed as the King of Bacon or in some other ridiculous outfit leading a raucous parade full of costumed friends, freaks, and musicians decked out in capes, masks, and beads, who were playing everything from kazoos to guitars to French horns to washboards through the streets of town to help raise awareness of some cause, fund-raise for the community, or just for a good time. With Herman's presence in Nederland, young bands looked to him for guidance and help in establishing careers. This jamgrass sound began to migrate away from its home in the mountains and with the help of Salmon find converts across the country. Keller Williams became part of this community when he first met Boulder band String Cheese Incident and began to collaborate with them. "It always felt Boulder and Nederland had a tight community of proud pickers who would preach the positive praises of the Colorado high country," he says. "Leftover Salmon were always good to make sure the crowd knew where this music came from. I feel it's safe to say Leftover Salmon had a direct impact on bands like String Cheese, Yonder Mountain, Greensky Bluegrass, and Railroad Earth."

It was not an accident this style Salmon created and was inspiring so many young musicians took root in their home state of Colorado. Williams says, "Colorado seems to be a magnet for open-minded young people who love to dance to live music." In the nineties, there was an influx of forward-thinking people who were looking for a certain kind of lifestyle in moving to the state. There were many reasons Colorado was

A house-party jam at Vince Herman's house in Eldora, Colorado, in the late nineties with Vince Farsetta (with banjo), Mark Vann (obscured by Farsetta), Jeff Austin (center, with mandolin), filmmaker Eric Abramson (seated behind Austin), and Michael Slingsby (in hat, far right). Courtesy of Vince Herman.

becoming a sought-after destination. "I attribute a lot of it to the cannabis scene developing there," says Chad Staehly, who plays keys with Great American Taxi and Hard Working Americans, served as Leftover Salmon's archivist for a decade, and had moved to the region in the nineties to attend Colorado State and discovered all the area had to offer. "Outside of northern California, Colorado's [marijuana] growing scene was unrivaled and people were catching on. I think the craft beer movement was also a big part of it too. Couple that with the skiing, hiking, rafting, and the other outdoor activities and you have the ingredients for an adventurous lifestyle that appealed to many people. The alchemy in the nineties in Colorado was right for a band like Salmon to flourish." Salmon perfectly represented everything going on in Colorado at the time with their music and fans flocked to their good-time party shows. Drummer Dave Watts from the Motet was part of this rapidly growing scene since the early nineties when he moved to the area to pursue his music career and recognized those same traits that made Colorado such a prosperous musical scene. He says, "The Colorado scene has always been great because of the amount of support the fans give to local music. It seems healthy, happy people in a good economy consistently come out and enjoy live music."

Colorado was also welcoming of a more progressive bluegrass ideal. The Telluride Bluegrass Festival started in 1974 and was the precursor to the coming progressive bluegrass scene in Colorado. Tim O'Brien says the festival was begun by "some hippies from the mountains of Colorado who had gone to a traditional bluegrass festival and were inspired to start their own." The festival hired bands like New Grass Revival and John Hartford and people realized how much they loved that type of music and how rare they got to see it in the West. "It was a spontaneous combustion," says O'Brien, "a reaction. Someone has the smarts to start this festival in a beautiful place we all want to go and they put on all these musicians we want to see. It grew quickly. The audience was ready for New Grass Revival, they were ready for Strength in Numbers. It was modern, adventurous, but it had an acoustic down-home flair to it. All those conditions set up Leftover Salmon to come in and take the prize." The Telluride Bluegrass Festival was instrumental in the development of Salmon and their sound. "We formed as a band in the campground at Telluride," says Emmitt. "That's where we used to go watch all these bands that influenced us. It's a big family reunion every year. It's just an amazing time. Now we get to play with all these people we grew up kind of hero-worshipping; it's a really great thing."[6] Telluride was not the only festival in Colorado that was key to the growth of progressive bluegrass in the area. The RockyGrass Festival, held in Lyons, Colorado, also established itself as major bluegrass festival in the region. Much like with Telluride, the members of Salmon had been frequenting and playing at RockyGrass for years.

In addition to the festivals supportive of a progressive sound, the mountain and college towns that dotted the region were full of open-minded, ready-to-party music fans and ski bums, and provided countless places to play without having to travel far. Leftover Salmon tapped into the ski-town circuit at the start of their career to great success. "Colorado is a real rich, kind of fertile ground for music," explains Emmitt. "There are a lot of great places to play. There's the mountain towns, there's Boulder, there's Denver, there's Fort Collins. It's a great place to come and start a band without having to tour. People are very receptive, because they are ready to party and have a good time."[7] Salmon found their ability to tour as a rock band, despite being bluegrass-inspired, was a trait at the time unique to them. "As a bluegrass band, no one could tour," says Emmitt. "Hot Rize was really the only bluegrass band that could actually play clubs and theatres. Nobody else had a clue how to tour as a bluegrass band. Nobody hired bluegrass bands in a club. So it was revolutionary that we figured out how to tour as a bluegrass band and how to make it work. We showed a lot of bands how to do that."

As this jamgrass sound evolved and began to spread beyond Colorado's borders and infect other areas with its high-energy, good-time vibe, Salmon's peers in the jamband world were noticing the impact they were having. "Colorado has this jamband, bluegrass scene and Salmon were the beginning of that," says Rob Derhak, bassist for moe. "They were the first ones to do that. Their legacy is they started that. They put bluegrass in the jamband scene." Samples drummer MacNichol agrees with Derhak's assessment, "If Salmon hadn't started it and brought the bluegrass vibe into the public eye and maybe even into the mainstream some, I'm not sure any of the newer bands would be doing what they are doing to the level they do it."

The Reverend Jeff Mosier, banjo picker with the Aquarium Rescue Unit, formed his own band, Bluegrass Underground, after leaving ARU, inspired by the template Salmon had forged. "They were really huge influences for me on to how to run a band and what the hell is this music we are playing," says Mosier. "We were experimenting with a genre of music from the South and trying to force it into a Grateful Dead–affected hole. We all knew it existed because we had Peter Rowan, Old & In the Way, Hot Rize, and all these people who tried it." Leftover Salmon would take this progressive jam-infused take on traditional bluegrass even further than some of their newgrass predecessors could have imagined. Mosier referred to this sound as sonic bluegrass, explaining that, "We aren't afraid of volume, we don't use it at rock levels, but we do use it as part of what we do." He recognized Salmon's importance to the birth of this sound: "Leftover Salmon is the flagship for sonic bluegrass and remains so all these years later."

Sam Bush laughs when asked if Salmon is following in his footsteps and what he helped create with New Grass Revival or if they are the creators of something new. "It's all that. They follow in the New Grass Revival tradition, but they are also the elder statesman of the young slamgrass, jamgrass bands. Salmon started slamgrass. Railroad Earth, Infamous Stringdusters, Yonder Mountain String Band, Greensky Bluegrass, String Cheese Incident, and so many others all come across as influenced by Salmon." Quite simply, says Yonder bassist Kaufmann, "Salmon built the stage we all perform on." Kaufmann's bandmate, guitarist Aijala, agrees, "They set a path that gave us the balls to be able to even say we are going to play this kind of music and we are going to be playing in bars so we better plug in and be loud. They were the ones that made us go, yeah we can do this."

Another Colorado musician, Anders Beck, who would go on to find fame with Greensky Bluegrass, was living in Durango and working at a local music store in the late nineties and just beginning to try and find his own musical path when he first encountered Salmon. Much like the world-altering experience Kaufmann had when he first encountered Salmon at the Wetlands a few years prior, Beck would have a truly revelatory moment that helped shape his musical path the first time he saw the band live. He had been listening to "Salmon, Yonder, and a little Cheese," but was doing more of the traditional sound then. A friend had taken him to see Salmon at the Rico Theatre in 1999, a show at which Herman led the band and entire crowd out of the venue in a conga line to continue partying in the streets, before marching everyone back in. "I didn't know who any of them were then," says Beck, "it was a bunch of mullet weirdos onstage. It was like a group of Muppets. I thought these guys are crazy and they proceeded to burn the place down. I remember my exact thought was, 'You can do this with blue-grass instruments?' It absolutely changed my life because it was so fun and lawless, yet they were still playing bluegrass tunes, but they were playing them for ten minutes and getting weird as hell and I loved it. It changed my entire outlook on what could be done with this bluegrass thing I was getting into." Much as Kaufmann and a slew of other young, impressionable musicians had learned from Salmon on their initial dis-covery of the band, the key to their success and what they imparted to everyone who has ever seen one of their shows is music first and fore-most must be fun and fearless. "They taught multiple generations to not only be completely fearless, but to also be comfortable in the weirdness and the truth that is your own skin," says Austin. Salmon showed by doing all that, you can create a vibe that allows you to do whatever you want to do with music. There do not have to be any rules. You can throw a party and play great music. You can play a show with acoustic instruments where people will leave with their heads blown off. You can play a beautiful, touching song, and follow it up with the most ridiculous, silly song. You can pick a quiet tune and then rock the fuck out. "Salmon taught us it's OK to do all of that," says Beck, "It's not weird, it's music, it's fun and I have taken that to heart."

As Salmon found themselves at the forefront of a new style and in the position where they were being looked up to and emulated, they again were about to experience turnover in their ranks. After years of relentless touring, which saw the band playing upward of 175 shows every year since 1995, their rhythm section was beginning to become burnt out, and because of a myriad of things, both decided to leave. North says, "It had come to a point where we might have made some decisions I didn't agree with as far as where we were going. It was uncharted territory for everybody. Nobody knew exactly what we were doing with the record company stuff. There was more money involved. We [Sipe and North] were getting sick of the road." He had also gotten married in 1999, and being away from home was taking a toll as well. Sipe was also unhappy with being away from his wife and young family, and he and North decided to leave at the same time. North makes clear their decision to leave had nothing to do with a change in their relationship with the rest of the band. When asked if there was any personal tension, North says, "There was some, but it was brotherly love. Any bunch of guys stuck in a metal hot dog going down the road with each other for years and years on end are going to have some tension and stuff. It wasn't like, 'Fuck you I am out of here.' It was more, 'I can't do this for this reason and this reason. I am sorry.'" Sipe concurs, "It was a sad, but necessary move. I'm eternally grateful for their help though. They supported my family through the birth of my daughter." Even though there were no lasting hard feelings surrounding North and Sipe's departure, there was some surprise from the rest of the band about the timing of their decision. Despite the lack of support for *The Nashville Sessions* from their label, the band was riding a wave of popularity as they were being looked to as leaders of a new music style and were selling out shows at a rapid clip across the country. "We were what the buzz was all about for sure," says Emmitt, "It was an exciting time, and when Tye and Jeff decided to leave, it was difficult, because things were hopping and it was like, 'You want to leave now?'" It was decided the pair's final shows would be at the band's upcoming Planet Salmon Festival over the weekend of September 9–10, 2000.

Salmon had been through the uncertainty of lineup changes before, and while it was always difficult to deal with, tour manager Johnny Pfarr says the band took a positive approach. "Every lineup change adds another dimension than before, all bringing more diversity than before, none that trumped another, but ultimately we felt the current path was always the best." With this approach and once the initial shock of their rhythm departing set in, they started to think about potential replacements. For a drummer, they thought about Jose Martinez, to whom Sipe had introduced them the previous year at the High Sierra Festival. Salmon was playing a late-night show at the festival and mid-set, Martinez hopped on Sipe's drums. "He didn't miss a beat," recalls Emmitt. "When I finally saw him back there, I thought, 'Wow, he sounds pretty good.' It's worked out well ever since."[8] Originally from Venezuela, Martinez came from a jazz background and loved classic rock 'n' roll. Much like Sipe, it was an interesting background for a drummer who was about to play in a roots-based, bluegrass band. His rock 'n' roll and jazz background allowed him to play fast two-beat and hold it down for the rest of the band. Emmitt appreciated Martinez's skill set and how he propelled the band. "He was very loud. He just laid into it. He drove the band in a powerful way. He was very consistent. He had an extensive toolbox of drum chops and was definitely a formidable player." Martinez's easygoing demeanor was a valuable addition to the band's roster of strong personalities. Pfarr says, "Jose was a great addition. He was young, had a great heart and was easy to get along with."

While the band found the perfect replacement drummer, they had no idea what they would do for a bassist to replace North. They were actively auditioning players, but just could not seem to find the right guy until a CD came across their path from a bassist in another Colorado band, the Motet, a jazzy, Afro-funk band miles away from what Salmon was doing. Emmitt says they kept coming back to that CD. The CD was from a gig called the Hip-Bop Workshop and featured keyboardist Erik Deutsch, String Cheese Incident mandolinist Michael Kang, guitarist Ross Martin, drummer Dave Watts, and bassist Greg Garrison. Garrison was a jazz bassist who was working on his master's degree at the University of Northern Colorado, playing with the Motet, and doing the occasional wedding gig as a freelancer, when he heard about the Salmon opening. "Dave Watts (drummer and bandleader of The Motet) actually filled me in Tye was leaving and gave me his number," remembers Garrison. "I called him up to find out about the gig. He and I had both played with a lot of the same folks in the Boulder/ Lyons/Nederland scene and he heard good things about my playing, so he recommended me to the band when he found out I was interested." Garrison's diverse musical background, combined with a recommendation from his childhood friend, Jeff Austin from Yonder Mountain String Band, ensured he got the spot.

Garrison was born near Minneapolis–St. Paul, Minnesota, in 1974. A few years later, his family moved to Arlington Heights in the suburbs of Chicago. He says he did all the normal things kids do growing up in the suburbs, but he "always loved music and listening to records as a kid." The first stuff he listened to were the records he pilfered from his parents' collection, including albums from Jim Croce, Supertramp, the Beatles, James Taylor, and Michael Jackson's *Thriller*. He expanded his collection when he got a paper route in the sixth grade. "I would take the money I earned and sneak to the record store to buy Led Zeppelin cassettes before going home to give my money to Mom." Garrison was not just into listening to music but playing it as well. He started piano lessons when he was eight, switched to cello for a year, before switching to upright bass in the fifth grade. He got his first electric bass the following year. Garrison says he was first inspired to check out the bass by an older friend who played in a local heavy metal band in their neighborhood. He joined his first band in high school, an eighties hair-metal cover band named Teazin'. "And yes, that's a Z and an apostrophe in there," clarifies Garrison. In perhaps some foreshadowing of what would come for him in Salmon, who often sported otherworldly mullets, Garrison admits during his time with Teazin', he had "a good mullet." The rest of the band was unimpressed with his follicle accessories and asked him to get hair extensions. "Seriously," says Garrison, before adding, "but I never did." His tastes moved away from traditional rock and metal and were replaced by an intense interest in jazz. He began to study with two influential bass teachers in the Chicago area, Rob Amster and Nick Schneider, who gave him a foundation in music he still relies on to this day. Amster inspired him to "start listening to the right cats, Paul Chambers, Ray Brown, Ron Carter, John Patitucci, and to dig into the music theory associated with jazz and the bass." While Schneider "Kicked [his] ass and made [him] dig into [his] Simandl method book," which set him up for success by giving him a real substantial foundation by learning, "intonation, time, tone. To play with the bow. To listen to Ray Brown. To practice scales and arpeggios." These lessons combined to give Garrison a skill set that would serve him in no matter what kind of musical environment he played. Garrison's lifelong path in music was being set. In high school, he embraced the improvisational spirit that defines his playing, declaring in his high school yearbook, "I like the freedom of music; I can do what I want within a framework."[9]

In junior high, Garrison met fellow student Jeff Austin in English class. They would both end up going to the same high school, Rolling Meadows. The pair hung out a few times and traded some comics, but Garrison, who was a standout soccer player and award-winning musician and Austin who was an All-State performer in theatre and choir, only crossed paths occasionally while in high school. Garrison admits, "We were in different worlds. I was into sports, jazz band, and trying to get into trouble, while he was a theater guy. We honestly didn't connect until after high school was over." That connection took place at the University of Illinois where they both enrolled in fall of 1992. While at the University of Illinois, Garrison says, "We used to play a little together, which mostly consisted of us getting really baked on weed he'd bring back from Dead or Garcia Band tour. It was mostly just us sitting around with acoustic guitars, starting with Dead tunes and going from there. We'd play to entertain our friends primarily, but never did any gigging." During one of the many nights the two sat around and jammed, Austin says, "We were playing music, laughing our asses off, making up songs, and I started scatting and stuff. Greg told me, 'Don't ever stop doing that, do that all time, just make shit up, it is so fun, it is so cool.' Who knew it would become a cornerstone of my entire career." Garrison also met another musician, Dave Johnston, his freshman year at a party in the dorms where they lived. The two remained casual acquaintances until their junior year when they lived around the corner from each other and Johnston says they discovered a shared "enthusiasm for improvisational music like the Grateful Dead, the Allman Brothers, and Phish." Johnston had been getting deeply into the banjo, which he discovered his freshman year. The two could often be found playing in the front yard of Garrison's house with Johnston on banjo and Garrison on guitar. Eventually Johnston met Garrison's friend Austin at a party they all attended. Soon Johnston and Austin were playing to-

Greg Garrison in his senior year of high school. Courtesy of Greg Garrison.

gether in a band called the Bluegrassholes, whose slogan was, "We're a drinking band, with a bluegrass problem." Though Garrison never joined the band, he did play with them a couple of times when they needed a bass player.

Garrison found success his freshman year musically, he made the University of Illinois big band that was mostly comprised of grad students and was regularly picked up to play jazz gigs with some of the older, more experienced musicians. Despite the success he was finding musically, he says he "was a terrible student." He wound up transferring to Millikin University, where he "got his shit together." He returned to the University of Illinois the following year, where he became an honors student, which paved the way for his eventual master's and doctorate degrees. His second time around he also began to play with a few other bands, including the Rain Merchants, the Mighty Pranksters, and Organic Advisor, who Garrison notes had "a pretty good name for a jam-band, even by today's standards." While in college Garrison encountered Salmon's music for the first time. A friend of his had a live tape and wanted him to check out a version of "Pasta on the Mountain." Garrison had been going to Phish, God Street Wine, and Grateful Dead shows during college and was familiar with the jam scene. He was also already exposed to bluegrass which he had gotten into heavily, but he admits of his first exposure to Salmon, "I thought it was fun music, but it wasn't as jazzy or experimental as the Dead or Phish, and I feel bad saying this, it didn't really stand out to me." His opinion changed when he saw them live and realized "they were a hell of a live band."

Following graduation in 1997, Garrison relocated to Colorado to attend the University of Northern Colorado and begin work on his master's degree in bass performance, which he finished in 1999. While in grad school, he played with the Nederland Acid-Jazz scene at the regular Monday night sets where they ripped through jazz standards. These Monday night sets were hosted by legendary Nederland resident, "Michigan" Mike Torpie. Torpie was instrumental in fostering the area's music scene. He began throwing backyard parties in the mid-nineties that evolved into the annual NedFest. NedFest developed from a simple backyard party into a regular summer festival staple and has featured the likes of Keller Williams, Steve Kimock, Merl Saunders, Bill Kreutzmann, David Grisman, Particle, Dr. John, Sam Bush, Ricky Skaggs, the Duo, ALO, the Slip, Rob Wasserman, Stanley Jordan, Melvin Seals & JGB, Victor Wooten, and New Monsoon over the years. In addition to the Nederland Acid-Jazz scene, Garrison also reconnected with Austin and Johnston, who had both moved to Colorado. They all joined a local bluegrass band called Fireweed with guitarist Patrick Latella. Fireweed played in the local area, including a high-profile gig at the grand opening of the new Whole Foods in Boulder. Garrison did not stick with Fireweed long, and was replaced by bassist Ben Kaufmann when he left. Fireweed ended a short time later as Austin, Johnston, and Kaufmann left to start Yonder Mountain String Band along with guitarist Adam Aijala. One of Fireweed's last shows at the Fox Theatre in Boulder, opening for Runaway Truck Ramp, marked the first appearance of Yonder Mountain String Band as Aijala replaced Latella onstage midway through the show and they finished the set as Yonder.

Garrison also met drummer Dave Watts at the time after being introduced by guitarist Ross Martin. The two played together on a Tony Furtado gig in Boulder soon after first meeting. Garrison says he remembers, "Really digging [Watts'] playing as he reminded me of Ed Blackwell." Shortly after, Watts asked Garrison to join him for a short Colorado mountain tour with a band that later evolved into the Motet. "I think Eric Thorin had done the first one on bass, but couldn't do the second one," Garrison says. "The band was me, Dave, Ross Martin on guitar, Bill Kopper on guitar, and Scott Messersmith on percussion. Very different from the current Motet for sure." For Watts, Garrison's steady disposition, combined with his rock-solid playing, was vital to those early days of the Motet. "Greg has always been a very even keeled and focused personality, both on- and offstage," says Watts. "He's got a great sense of humor, which along with his easygoing attitude was helpful in those days of hectic touring and questionable gigs." Garrison played with this early version of the Motet for two years until Watts mentioned that North was leaving Salmon. Intrigued by the possibility of joining a band with a much larger national presence who toured regularly, Garrison reached out to North, whom he knew through the Acid-Jazz scene in Nederland. North recommended him to the rest of the band. At the same time Herman reached out to Austin looking for suggestions for new bass players. Austin knew Garrison was interested in Salmon. He provided a glowing recommendation of his longtime friend, telling Herman, "He is one of the best musicians I know and a good guy to hang with. I couldn't vouch for this guy more. I would give him a kidney. I would do whatever he needs." Austin's recommendation helped convince Salmon Garrison might be the guy they were looking for. Garrison connected with the band by phone via an assist from Austin, who put them in touch. Herman invited Garrison out to his place in Nederland for a picking session with him and Sipe. Garrison also visited Vann at his home to hang with him a bit. He convinced the band he might be the right choice, and they decided to fly him out to a show at the Barrelhouse Brewing Company in Cincinnati on August 14, 2000, for a live audition. Garrison wanted to make sure he was prepared and set out on an intensive crash course of the band's music. He went out and bought every one of the band's albums and began learning every song on them. He also connected with the local network of tapers and got himself a bunch of live shows. He says, "I made a huge list and made myself work on it for a couple of hours every night until I had the 1999–2000 Salmon repertoire under my fingers. As a bass player, you've got to know the songs."

Much as with Sipe's first show a few years prior in which the band taught him songs as they floated downstream in rafts, Garrison's live audition was similarly loose. He made his debut midway through the first set at the Barrelhouse on "Muddy Water Home" and played for the rest of the first set. Garrison says, "My audition literally consisted of Tye giving me his in-ear rig and a quick 'good luck.' No rehearsal, no nothing. Just 'Do you know this tune? That one too? Right on, let's play!' I still remember being nervous, which was making me push the time a bit, and Sipe giving me a smile and a 'lay back, my man' kind of look, which totally set me at ease." The band immediately recognized the work Garrison put into his preparation for the audition. "He knew things inside and out," says Emmitt, "We noticed how studious he was. He came prepared, he already knew a lot of our material." Emmitt feels that much as with Sipe and Martinez, Garrison's extensive background in jazz and playing with many bands helped him quickly assimilate into the band. "Coming out of playing with the Motet was a great place to start from coming into Salmon, because they play all kinds of stuff," says Emmitt. Even the bluegrass heavyweights, who Salmon looked to for guidance and admired so much, took notice of Garrison's limitless talent and chameleon-like ability to fit comfortably into any musical scenario into which he might be thrown into during Salmon's ever-evolving live show. Hot Rize's Tim O'Brien calls him, "A high-class, accomplished bassist," while bluegrass legend Sam Bush says, "He is obviously very educated. Anything you want to throw at him he can do."

Salmon had found their new rhythm section in bassist Garrison and drummer Martinez and while they were not officially part of the band yet, they invited both to come to their Planet Salmon Festival, which was North and Sipe's last shows, to sit in with them throughout the weekend. The festival featured music from some of the band's best musical friends over two days, including John Bell, John Cowan, Col. Bruce Hampton, Yonder Mountain String Band, John Brown's Body, Acoustic Syndicate, Derek Trucks Band, Maceo Parker, Rebirth Brass Band, Runaway Truck Ramp, Pete Wernick, and Jim Page. The weekend was a typical wild event. There was lots of partying, mischief, and music being made throughout the weekend. John Cowan says, "I remember it well. The last time I ingested any psychedelic properties—that I can remember—was probably 1985. I remember thinking, 'A lot of people are tripping out here. That's cool!' It was the first time I met John Bell and probably the first time I met Jeff Austin. It was kind of like Mayor McCheese meets Dr. John meets Kurt Vonnegut, and they go over to James Thurber's for cocktails."[10] For Widespread Panic's Bell he recalls a parade that snaked through the campground where he was, "Riding through the audience in a wagon wearing some freaky, wizard costume. I think we were throwing trinkets out to the people Mardi Gras style. Mostly, I was trying to keep from falling off that wagon."[11] For drummer Sipe, the weekend was a rollercoaster of emotions. For all the joy and excitement that came with every Salmon show, he knew his time with the band was coming to an end and says, "The music was exciting and as adventurous as it always was, but even more so because of the overwhelming feeling of my departure from the group as a full-time member. The familiarity with the songs and each other was completely comfortable, but the uncertainty of the future was hanging over me. It was bittersweet to be with the group because I knew I had to move on to build my family and my personal growth. Salmon couldn't offer full, equal membership even after nearly four years with them so I had no choice other than to look for opportunities to provide for my family. That said, I'm eternally grateful for all they did for me."

Following the Planet Salmon Festival, the band set out on a brief tour through the South opening for Robert Earl Keen with New Grass Revival's John Cowan on bass and Martinez on drums, while Garrison took care of previous commitments before joining the band. On the brief tour, the band was in the odd position of opening and playing with a lineup they knew was only temporary, so they decided to have a little fun and do something different. They moved away from much of their normal catalog and played a lot of old traditional bluegrass songs and New Grass Revival tunes, allowing Cowan to sing. They also played acoustic much of the time. It was a nice, low-stress break for Salmon as they prepared to hit the road full bore when Garrison joined. He played his first show November 10, 2000, at the Sangamon Auditorium in Springfield, Illinois, on a bill with Little Feat.

For a band who had seen so much turnover, the addition of Garrison proved to have a strong stabilizing effect both musically and personally. He is the epitome of what a bass player should be; steady, reliable, and rock solid. His steady personality both off and onstage was a welcome, calming influence for a band so often swirling in chaos. "To this day if Greg misses a change it is like, 'Oh my God!'" Emmitt declares. "It is shocking if he ever misses a note. He is meticulous and very well versed on the bass. He is not a fancy player, but is very solid, very musical. He always plays the right notes and always supports the song the way it needs to be supported. He is intuitive, especially when there is a jam going on. His ear is amazing. It is better when you play bluegrass to not be flashy and to just hold down the groove and play the right notes, and that is what he does." Garrison says his natural inclination to be the "mostly sober guy" in the room also was beneficial, "that, 'you were really holding things together tonight,' kind of thing." Bluegrass legend Bush has benefited from this inclination, saying with a laugh, "Greg has driven me home when I might have imbibed too much." The bassist says by the time he joined the band he had quit smoking pot, explaining that, "it never really agreed with me," but had no trouble being around the rest of the band, who were often indulging in some "Pasta on the Mountain." "I was a stoner in college," he says, "and I was totally down with the lifestyle and loose attitude surrounding the music. So, the 'party band' vibe didn't faze me at all."

Shortly after the addition of Garrison and Martinez, the band further augmented their lineup when they added keyboardist Bill McKay.

McKay had played with several bands including Band Du Jour, Beauso-
leil, and the Derek Trucks Band over the previous decade, and was well
known to Salmon from his years in the close-knit Boulder scene. It had
been years since they played with keys and there was some hesitation
on moving away from the five-piece lineup that was serving them so
well. Vann and tour manager Pfarr both spearheaded the idea as they
felt the band needed more firepower. Emmitt says he "personally was
not convinced we needed a keyboard player because I liked the five-
piece. I think Vince was of the same mindset." In the end, the strong
will of Vann won out and the band agreed to add keys. Pfarr suggested
McKay, with whom he was friendly from the area and felt would be a
great fit. When McKay joined, the rest of the band came around, as
they saw what he brought to the mix. "Once we started playing with Bill
it was great. We really enjoyed it. It was a nice addition," says Emmitt.
Still, there were some struggles for the band adjusting to McKay in the
lineup. They had long only had two lead singers, Herman and Emmitt,
who they had to consider when crafting each night's setlists, but the
addition of McKay meant there was another songwriter and singer
whose contributions had to be factored into the mix every night.

The addition of Garrison, Martinez, and McKay created a "new guy
faction" on the bus and helped ease their transition into Salmon. Martinez and Garrison clicked personally as both were serious jazz heads and
enjoyed freaking out the rest of the band on the bus by playing "some
late period Coltrane or Ornette Coleman or whatever." It took a while
for everyone to mesh onstage, and especially for Martinez and Garrison
to lock into a consistent pocket, but Garrison says, "The older cats were
patient with us and our growing pains. Some nights were pretty rough
for all involved for sure." The addition of the three musicians also saw
the band move slightly away from their bluegrass roots and become
more of a rock band who played with a roots background. "I think for a
while we became more of blues-rock band, which was fine," says Emmitt, who attributes much of the change to the addition of McKay. "He
definitely changed the flavor of the band for a while. He could play
bluegrass and many other styles but being more of Hammond player it
made for a heavier rock sound, which was great, but some of our fans
felt it wasn't really what the band was about."

As the band was changing their lineup, they sensed a change in
management was needed as well. They had slowly begun taking back

more control of their operations, as it just felt right when they had more control. They wanted a more hands-on experience from their management. Their current manager, Chuck Morris, had done great things for the band. He guided them with an expert touch as they negotiated the treacherous waters of their first major-label studio album. Even more importantly, he was the driving force in helping get their signature album, *The Nashville Sessions*, made; using his connections and influence to allow the band to recruit a roster of A-list musicians to make their dream reality. But it became clear Morris's attention was often being devoted to other projects. "Chuck was phenomenal with what he did in the music industry," says Pfarr, "but we might have just been a small blip on his radar." With that in mind, Salmon set out to find a new manager.

Chapter 8

JOHN JOY

John Joy is super. He is one of the greats. There is no nicer human being than him. He is an amazing guy.—*Col. Bruce Hampton*

In 2015, Leftover Salmon played the historic Stanley Hotel in Estes, Colorado, for the first time. The hotel was the inspiration for the Stephen King novel *The Shining*, and had served as the location for the film version starring Jack Nicholson and directed by Stanley Kubrick. Since 2015, the band has held an annual three-day event at the Stanley every March. The intimate nature of the event, which finds the band's most ardent followers descending on the hotel for a weekend extravaganza featuring multiple shows from the band, has been described as a gift from the band to fans.

Leftover Salmon manager John Joy originally had the idea the band should play their annual Halloween show at the famed location. His idea was to use the setup and location of the hotel along with the spooky imagery of the movie to create a one-of-kind Halloween event. It was one of many inspired ideas he has had for the band since he was first hired. "He is always thinking ahead," says Col. Bruce Hampton. "Salmon is lucky to have him, and he is lucky to be working for them. It is great chemistry. I could not do what he does. He is always on the case. Always thinking. Always brilliant." When Joy was hired in 2001, the Stanley was one of the first ideas he pitched to them. It was exactly ideas like this why Salmon hired him to replace Chuck Morris. Upon joining, Joy booked them to play the Stanley for the first time Halloween of 2001. But life, as it so often does, had other plans and the band would have to wait nearly fifteen years to be able to take the stage at the Stanley Hotel.

Joy first crossed paths with Salmon as a twenty-year-old ski bum in 1990 at the Jackalope in Vail, Colorado, after moving from his hometown of West Hartford, Connecticut, earlier that year. He made the move after one semester in college when he realized, "I was wasting my parents' money, because I didn't know what I wanted to do yet." He had some friends who moved to Colorado and in the fall of 1990, he joined them. "I wanted to be a ski bum," says Joy, "and I had this underlying plan to discover more about the Grateful Dead." Like so many other ski bums in Colorado, Joy first saw Salmon at a small ski-town bar, when the band was in its infancy. He was not yet twenty-one at that first show, so he had to sneak in. "A lot of my friends were very in tune with the band and friends with them," says Joy, "partying with them and hanging at the after parties. I was always a fan first and have remained a fan first. Trying to find my way backstage and hang out with the band was never a priority." Over the subsequent years, Joy says his goal was simply to afford his ski pass in the winter and get tickets for Grateful Dead tour. To help support himself, Joy did what many Dead-heads did he started a part-time business selling quesadillas in the parking lot on Dead tour. His part-time business provided enough money for his rent, his ski pass, and tickets for tour.

Following the passing of Jerry Garcia and the end of the Grateful Dead, Joy started to get involved in the business end of music. He and a friend promoted several music events around Colorado. During this time, he made his first trip to Jazz Fest in New Orleans. He says, "I discovered the most amazing city in the United States and some of the most unique places in the world. I fell into these small clubs that would go all night. I was at this club, the Maple Leaf, and the Rebirth Brass Band was playing. People were all decked out in costumes Mardi Gras style. The sun is coming in the window and the place is packed with people getting down to raw brass music. It was like a rave. A light bulb went off." Joy noticed there was a resurgence in this funk sound, but many of these bands were not really playing outside of New Orleans. The day after the Rebirth Brass Band show he started "banging on doors," until he connected with the Rebirth Brass Band. He would bring them and another New Orleans band, the Soul Rebels, to Colorado for a short tour he booked in the winter of 1998. He continued to book more and more shows for Rebirth around the country and eventually they hired him as their manager and booking agent. "That is how I got into the business," says Joy. He was working primarily as a booking agent but wanted to get more management. "The thing I learned over the years is the difference between a manager and an agent is you have creative control as a manager. That is what I thrived on, the creativity and the outside-the-box thinking."

Joy was introduced to Leftover Salmon in spring of 2000 through his roommate at the time, Scotty Stoughton, who booked some of the clubs in Vail and was a good friend of the band. Occasionally Stoughton would sit in with the band in a unique hybrid they called Rap Grass. "Scotty introduced me to the guys," says Joy. "I knew the band was having some issues and they weren't sold on their booking agent at the time. I wanted to get into management, but booking is what I built my business on. I told Scotty to put my name in the mix. I was trying to tap into them anyway I could." Tour manager Johnny Pfarr heard of Joy's interest and the two met up at Jazz Fest in New Orleans to chat about the spot. They hit it off when they realized they were from the same hometown but went to different schools. Over the next couple of months, Joy connected with the band at a few shows and festivals to see how they all got along. Pfarr, who was instrumental in helping hire Joy, says, "After seeing John as an individual and how much of a go-getter he was, it was clear he was the right guy to help us with the needs everyone in the band was speaking of." A few weeks later, "while back East visiting my folks, I got a call from Johnny," says Joy. "He called to say Vince fired Chuck [Morris] this morning and we want to bring you on for a trial as manager and see how it works. I was floored. I was barely making ends meet and they were going to give me a shot to be manager of the band. I'll admit I was green, but I knew I had the dedication and motivation to do it." When he was hired, Joy was more of a booking agent, and initially expressed his interest in the position, but he impressed the band so much they decided to bring him on as their manager. Since being hired Joy has validated Salmon's initial feeling that, despite his inexperience, he was the right man for the job. With the hiring of Joy, Salmon has enjoyed a special relationship with someone, to whom Herman says, "There is no doubting his commitment to the band and our personal lives. That is a rare and valuable thing to have in the music industry. It is a real blessing to have John Joy. There is no question about that."

After being hired, Joy agreed to work for free for six months to prove himself, though during that period the band tossed him some cash to show their appreciation for what he was doing. His first week on the job, Joy was sitting in his office when Herman, Pfarr, and Vann came storming into to talk some business. It was a shared office space and when the three of them busted in, they were oblivious to the rest of the office and "busted out a big bowl of weed." "It was a big comedy show," says Joy. "I thought, 'What am I getting myself into. Is this a test? Am I supposed to join them?' I am not the biggest pot smoker, but I always figured if you can't beat them join them."

Since starting in July, Joy had been busy and the band had scattered their different ways as they did when they came off tour. Plans were made for him to join the band at Salmon Fest at Rancho del Rio in Bond, Colorado, over the weekend of August 11–12, 2001, and it was going to be Joy's first chance to really interact with everyone in the band. The weekend got off to a weird start when a lighting truss col-

"No nicer human being." Manager John Joy works the phone in his office in early 2002. Courtesy of John Joy.

lapsed on the side stage and just missed slicing a B3 Hammond Organ in half, but after taking care of that situation things seemed to get back to normal with bands playing and people partying.

The weekend was a typical wild Salmon affair. Corn had become the unofficial theme of the festival. There was corn on the stage, around the grounds, in the dressing rooms, and there was a huge corn parade down the river with people on floats tossing corn to each and throwing it at the people on the shore as they floated by. Salmon's good friends from Fort Collins, who were known as Fort Support, even showed up in a pickup truck with the entire bed filled with corn. For Pfarr, despite the carefree hilarity of the weekend, most of his time was spent dealing with local law enforcement who were on site. There was a rave-style festival held at the same location a few weeks prior where someone died and there were a number of arrests. Pfarr says, "The law was definitely making sure things did not get out of hand." During the raft corn parade, Pfarr was standing on shore chatting with one of the police officers in charge, explaining how this was not the type of crowd to get out of hand. "Well, at least that's what I told him," says Pfarr. As they were talking, the parade floated by with Herman leading a contingent of naked hippies and people dressed in costume screaming, "Corn!" Parade participants were still launching corn at the shore and ten or fifteen corncobs flew toward Pfarr and the officer, landing at their feet with a thump. "I thought to myself this is not going to be good," says Pfarr, "then I busted out laughing, shrugged my shoulders, looked at the cop and said, 'Did I mention we like throwing parades?'" The officer gave a slight chuckle of amusement. Pfarr sensed a bit of an opening and invited him to join in the nighttime parade later. The cop returned and donned a costume but did not take part in the parade. Pfarr noticed as the night wore on, "He seemed to dig the music a lot." The next day when talking with his friends in Fort Support, Pfarr discovered one of the officers had eaten a piece of ganja-buttered corn. "I can't say for sure," laughs Pfarr, "but I believe it was my officer friend who became quite friendly as the night went on, who was dressed in costume and rocking out to Salmon who ate the ganja-corn. Needless to say, we had no issues with the police department the entire weekend."

It was not all laughs throughout the weekend though. Midway through Salmon's first set of the weekend, as they were ripping through "River's Rising," Vann left the stage saying he did not feel well. The

Vince Herman dancing with fans at the High Sierra Music Festival in 2001. A
common scene at any Leftover Salmon festival apperance. Courtesy of Johnny
Pfarr.

band chalked it up to exhaustion. They had a long cross-country trip
that day from Massachusetts, where they had played two shows at the
Berkshire Music Festival the day before. During the late show at Berkshire, Vann complained of not feeling well and left the stage partway
through their set. He was replaced by Yonder Mountain String Band's
Dave Johnston, who played the remainder of the set in Vann's place.
"Salmon came to me and said, 'We need you to fill in for Mark. He is
not feeling well and it would be really important to us," says Johnston.
"I told them, 'I am definitely not as good as Mark. I will just hang on
and do my best.'" When Vann complained of not feeling well, they did
not give it too much thought. The all-night partying that always accompanied a festival—and Vann was known to enjoy the late-night parties—
followed by the long trip back to Colorado could make even those with
the toughest constitutions get tired from time to time. Johnston says,

"There was nothing about what the guys said that made me feel it was some crazy thing. Mark did not feel well and he had to get out of there."

The second day at Salmon Fest, Vann said he was still not feeling 100 percent and thought about not playing. The band in their usual fun way came up with a humorous solution. Vann was hooked up so he could play remotely from offstage and sit down during the show. In his place, the band placed a large comfy chair in Vann's usual spot onstage. During the show, they brought up several longtime fans to "sit-in." They would take their place in the comfy chair and "sit-in" with the band, but not have an instrument to play. Meanwhile Vann was offstage and played the entire show. With the blindness of youth, Vann and the band did not think much about him not feeling well over the past few days. He had a pacemaker. He liked to stay up all night and push it to the extreme. It could have been any number of things. Vann's outsized personality made it easy to overlook potential problems. "Mark was just a fun guy to be around who had an amazing penchant for adventure in life," says Hard Working Americans' Chad Staehly. "We called him 'King of the late night.' He didn't believe in sleeping much."

Looking back, Joy says, "That was the first sign of Mark not feeling well. No one knew what to do. Did he need a medication adjustment? Is it a problem with the pacemaker?" Whatever it was, the band had a light touring schedule for the rest of August, which allowed a few weeks for everyone to rest and recover. During the down time, Joy had Herman, Pfarr, and Vann over to his house for a barbecue and to talk business about the upcoming tour. They hung for a bit, but again Vann was not feeling well and left early to go home. "No one thought anything of it," says Joy, "but it was still like he hasn't been feeling well for a couple of weeks now, what is going on?" With the nagging concern for Vann's health in the back of their minds, Salmon prepared for their upcoming fall tour due to begin September 12, 2001, in Houston, Texas.

The band set out from Colorado September 10 on their bus, Barth. Drummer Jose Martinez and keyboardist Bill McKay, who lived in Seattle and Atlanta, respectively, were due to fly out the following day and meet up with the band in Houston for the start of the tour. Following Vann's health misstep and a transition period as Joy settled in as their manager, everyone was looking forward to getting back out on the road and doing what they did best, playing live. "I was ready to get this machine rolling," says Joy. The fall tour would be the first he had a hand in scheduling since taking over as manager and he was looking forward to joining the band on the road later in the tour.

"I wake up to my clock radio on 9/11," says Joy, "the morning after those guys had taken off to the news of everything happening. My alarm went off after both towers had been struck, but I was awake to see them drop. It was insane. Suddenly this is what's going on. Things started getting canceled." As all of America watched the unfolding terror events in New York City and Washington, DC, Joy and the rest of the band, like the rest of the country, were in complete shock with no idea what tomorrow would bring. For the band, things were made even more difficult as they were in a bus away from their families in the middle of nowhere on their way to play shows they did not even know would take place anymore. Even if these shows did happen, they would be short a drummer and keyboardist as all the airports were closed and those two had not left to fly out yet. The show in Houston on September 12 was quickly canceled, but it was decided the band would play in Dallas on September 13. While it would be months before things across the country would even slightly resemble normal, Salmon knew they could at least provide a couple of hours, relief from the overwhelming coverage and news consuming everyone following the tragedy of 9/11. The band's show September 13 was minus Martinez and McKay, as they were both still on Greyhound buses rolling toward Texas. McKay arrived the following day for the band's show in Austin, while Martinez did not meet up with the band until September 17 in Tulsa, Oklahoma. For the shows in Austin and Lubbock, the band called on local drummer Pat Mastelotto, best known for his work with King Crimson and eighties rockers Mr. Mister, to fill in. For their show on the 13th in Dallas, the band returned to their roots and played a stripped-down show, heavy on bluegrass and reminiscent of what the Left Hand String Band had done a decade prior. The band opened the show with a somber Herman announcing to the crowd, "We are all in shock and we are going to do what we all got to do, which is to keep on keepin' on and playing music and making more love." The band started the night with the Bill Monroe classic "Blue Night," with the appropriate line "I can't keep from crying." The evening closed with a plea for unity and peace as the band led the crowd in a sing-along version of Bob Marley's "One Love."[1]

The full band was looking forward to reuniting and finding some sense of normalcy on tour after the country's world had been turned upside following 9/11, but that was not to be as again the band would deal with tragedy. One of Herman's brothers died, and he left the road to travel home to Pittsburgh to attend the funeral. Herman would miss two shows, September 17 in Tulsa and September 19 on Nashville. In Nashville, Salmon reached out to some of their friends in the area to help fill in for Herman. Sam Bush and John Cowan were available and sat in for much of the night. These marked the only two shows Herman ever missed with Salmon.

For new manager Joy, it was the most hectic, unsettling start to a tour. He was still working with a few other bands at the time, including the Rebirth Brass Band, and during everything going on with Salmon he was scheduled to fly to San Francisco for a Rebirth show at the Great American Music Hall September 21 and 22. He was going to meet up with Salmon the following week to spend some time on the road with the band. Further complicating things was how difficult it was to get in touch with the band at the time. This was 2001 and it was still a world where everyone was not yet carrying a cell phone. Salmon had two cell phones for the entire band on the bus with them, one for tour manager Pfarr and the other for the band to share. Joy says the band phone was mostly to keep the guys from getting lost after shows. He says, "Vince would go into the campground or wherever after a show to play some music and Johnny Pfarr would tell him what time the bus was leaving in the morning and then duct tape the phone to him."

The world-changing events of 9/11 and Herman's unexpected family tragedy made for one of the most difficult starts to a tour, but after Herman returned, the band seemed to get back into the groove and things seemed to return to normal again. "They are rolling down the road and everyone is in good spirits," says Joy. "It was a big relief after everything that just happened. We are back on track. It was the most derailed start of a tour, but finally for the first time it felt all the wheels were on the track." With a newfound sense of relief and optimism, Joy headed to San Francisco for his weekend with Rebirth Brass Band. That optimism was shattered a few days later when Joy received a phone call from Herman's then wife, Kimba, while in San Francisco. Joy had only met Kimba briefly and was surprised to hear from her. "She calls and almost breaks down on the phone," he says. "She tells me

Mark is sick. He just went to his mom's house. They took him to the hospital and they are sending him home from the tour. They think it was melanoma. This was the first time I heard the word. I didn't even know what it was then."

While on tour Vann had been experiencing dizzy spells, this and, combined with his pacemaker and the health issues he experienced the previous month when he was forced offstage, finally made it clear to his mom he needed to seek medical help. "Mark's mom was a nurse and had a maternal instinct he needed to get checked out," says Pfarr. Vann played with the band at Suwannee Music Park in Live Oak, Florida, before heading home to Colorado to get further tests. Herman says it was clear that something was wrong as he "just didn't have the energy to do it anymore." Instead of meeting up with the band on the road, Joy flew to Colorado to be with Vann. After several tests, Vann was diagnosed with stage 4 melanoma, a quick-striking, deadly form of skin cancer. Herman says the diagnosis "really got us by surprise." Vann immediately began to undergo aggressive chemotherapy. The intensive treatments drained his energy and made it clear he was not going to be returning to the road anytime soon. For close friend Pfarr, he says the news of the diagnosis and Vann's absence from the road "struck our hearts with a heavy dagger." Joy marvels at how long Vann pushed on before finally going to the hospital: "He was on a roller coaster of energy. Looking back, he was such a tough guy to be able to soldier and carry on. He didn't worry too much about it. He just kept pushing forward."

While Vann was back home in Colorado, Salmon was still on the road and had to figure out how to continue without their banjo player. They had a few days between their show at the Suwannee Music Park and their next one at the House of Blues in Buena Vista, Florida. Jeff Mosier's band Blueground Undergrass was already scheduled to open for Salmon the following two shows. During their off day, they reached out to Mosier to see if he was willing to stick around after Blueground Undergrass left the tour to fill in for Vann. He agreed and proved to be the perfect choice to help the band get through those first dates without Vann. "We were obviously devastated and those shows were going to be hard to play," says Herman. "Jeff seemed to have the sensitivity for that kind of thing. He was an aware kind of guy." Mosier played the remaining week of dates with the band during what would prove to be an emotionally draining time as the band tried to go out each night and put on a good face for the audience and be the fun-loving Salmon they always were, while on the inside being torn apart. Emmitt says, "Walking onstage that first time without Mark was one of the toughest things I've ever done in my life."[2]

Meanwhile Vann was going through treatment and fighting for his life. "It was pretty shocking," says Garrison, "to see someone who seemed so strong just physically fall apart in such a short time frame." For new manager Joy, his job changed instantly with Vann's diagnosis. "I knew my role had to shift from being a manager to being a friend." Since starting to work for the band, Joy most frequently dealt with Vann and Pfarr on all band business. Since its earliest days, Vann was involved as the band's business manager and over the years, even as they changed managers and hired the big name of Chuck Morris to run things, Vann had always been very involved on the business end. When he was diagnosed and began going through treatments, there was a huge shift on all fronts, music, business and social, due to the absence of Vann and his dominant personality.

Despite the emotional stress everyone was under, the band knew they had to continue to get out on the road and play. Their livelihoods and financial well-being depended on it. "We all knew we needed to keep on working, since nobody was really prepared, financially or mentally, to stop abruptly," says Garrison. They had no choice but to soldier on without their brother, knowing the desperate state he was in. Joy realized the differing nature of his job now, "After Mark got sick, I thought, 'How can I try and throw these crazy ideas out there when right now everyone just needs to survive?' I need to stay the course with whatever is going to bring the money in. Plus, the person who I brainstormed all these ideas with was no longer there to help."

Following the week-long run of shows with Mosier, the band had a month off the road. Whereas usually it was a time to relax away from the grind of the road, now Salmon's time was filled with worry about their comrade and preparation for an uncertain fall tour that was due to kick off on Halloween. "One of the first creative, out-of-the-box ideas I had when I first started was to do the show at the Stanley Hotel for Halloween," says Joy. "I had it reserved for Halloween proper that year and we were fired up about it. Then Mark gets diagnosed. Our conversations changed. How do I pick up the phone and talk about the future now with him?" Plans for the Halloween show at the Stanley Hotel were aborted. Joy says given the uncertainty around the band it was tough to commit to such a potentially costly endeavor and he was "afraid to roll the dice on something like that." Instead the band arranged a tour through the Southwest. They would play Halloween in Tucson, Arizona, and follow that with a couple of dates in California before heading home. With Vann still sidelined, Salmon recruited Tony Furtado to fill his banjo role.

The band felt helpless in their ability to help Vann as he battled cancer. They made the decision to organize four benefit shows billed as "Salmon and Friends," to raise money to help Vann and allow the band to spend more time at home as he went through treatment. Herman says, "The best thing we could do while Mark was sick was get a mess of people together to pick and throw some energy toward him." Pfarr and Joy started making calls to see what "mess of people" they could get to come play. Paul Barrere and Bill Payne from Little Feat became the first two to come aboard for the shows, as they were moved by the severity of Vann's diagnosis. With them on board, things snowballed and they were soon joined by an army of musical guests including Sam Bush, Béla Fleck, Peter Rowan, Sally Van Meter, John Cowan, Tony Furtado, Pete Wernick, Bill Payne, Paul Barrere, Todd Mohr, Michael Travis, and Bill Nershi, who all came to Vann's aid the best way they knew how, by playing music and bringing people together in a joyous celebration. Joy was amazed out the outpouring of support they received for the shows, "Every name in the bluegrass world, old and young, came out to support us. Even musicians and friends from outside that world."

Every night the shows were recorded and the tapes sent to Vann, who was finishing up his chemotherapy. They included messages from the crowd to Vann, like on the second night at the Boulder Theater which began with the crowd yelling, "Hey Mark, fuck that fucking cancer!"[3] Each night people could pay $10 to get their heads shaved in support or drop a couple of bucks in buckets placed around the venue. These shows culminated with a sold-out night at Denver's Fillmore Auditorium. Sam Bush, who was part of the shows, had fought through two bouts of cancer, and was personally familiar with the taxing and draining process involved with treatment. While in Denver for the Fillmore show he stopped by the hospital to say hi to Vann. Vann's frail appearance made him fully aware of "the gravity of the situation." He says, "As a cancer survivor, I always want to try to see my brothers going through it." That night at the Fillmore Pfarr says he remembers counting at one point twenty-one different musicians onstage. Pfarr told Vann to stay by the phone during the show. Pfarr called and held up the phone as all the musicians and the crowd of 4,000 screamed, "We love you, Mark," in unison. The outpouring of love and support for his close friend overwhelmed Pfarr. "The chills I got," he says, "I don't know how to describe it. It went so deep into my body. It was incredible."

At the same time as the benefit shows in Colorado, Phish's Mike Gordon helped organize another benefit, "Jammin' for Salmon: A Celebration of Life and Music," at B. B. King's in New York City with a roster of the band's East Coast friends including God Street Wine's Lo Faber, DJ Logic, John Medeski, Scott Murawski, and members of the Ominous Seapods and Deep Banana Blackout. The presence of so many of Salmon's cohorts from the early jamband scene reinforced the sense of shared community so prevalent among jambands and fans. "This type of community spirit is what brought me into the music world from the beginning," explained DJ Logic in an interview with *Billboard*. "It's all about sharing music and communicating with other musicians and fans. I don't even know Mark that well personally, but in light of all that's happened since September 11th, I think it's important to help out in the world anyway I can. He's a great player and I know he would do the same for me. The night was great, his spirit was with us, and I do think we all helped him just by being there and thinking of him, sending him positive vibes."[4]

Salmon followed up the fall benefit shows with a New Year's Eve blowout at the Paramount Theatre in Denver. On a night packed with guests and friends, Herman declared from stage, "We got the most special guest we could have. Mark Vann, the banjo man!"[5] Vann joined the band for a pair of songs to close out the first set, "Troubled Times," and "Better," which summed up the emotional state of the band, but optimistically pointed to a brighter tomorrow. While it was an emotional boost to the band to have Vann back onstage with them and to have his one-of-kind banjo picking reinvigorate their music, it was clear Vann was not going to be returning to the band. "Mark came to the show very sick," says Pfarr. "He was barely hanging on. He was very frail." Vann reemerged one more time toward the end of the show for "Whispering

Waters," a glorious, "Ask the Fish," which served to remind everyone of the genius of Vann's playing, before finishing things off with an encore of "Euphoria." Those final three songs of the night were the last three he ever played with Leftover Salmon.

The upcoming tour following their New Year's Eve run, was a monthlong trek up the West Coast followed by a quick jaunt east and back home to Colorado for a handful of shows in the mountains. Vann's condition and appearance at New Year's Eve made it clear he would not be heading back out on the road with the band for their winter tour, and again they reached out to Mosier to serve as a replacement for the upcoming tour. This was the first extended run the band had done since Vann had left the road, as the previous fall was mostly comprised of shorter runs of shows and one-off dates. The addition of Mosier's healing energy was invaluable to both the band and fans alike. "The Reverend Mosier was really the perfect person to go out with us as the first banjo player," says Emmitt. "He is a witty, funny, energetic person, and very spiritual and it made sense to have someone who was called Reverend be with us at that point. He made us laugh at a time when it was hard to find laughter anywhere."[6] The insightful Mosier fully recognized the role he needed to play on the tour, "My job became to make them laugh and get them through the shows. The crowd knew me well enough to know I wasn't going to be Mark Vann, so karmically I was perfect for that first tour. My job was to help them get through that time."

During the tour, Vann's condition deteriorated even further. "Mark's spirits started to get the best of him," says Pfarr. "I flew home off the road to walk around the hospital with him and just be by his side with him and Jennifer." Soon after, the cancer was found to have spread to Vann's brain. He decided he could not fight anymore. Everyone knew it would not be long now. Garrison says, "At first we were truly hopeful the chemo was going to work and Mark would be out with us again. But spiritually once we all knew he wasn't going to make it, things kind of fell apart."

As his condition worsened, Vann had been reluctant to have visitors as he did not want them to see him in his weakened condition. Pfarr convinced him to throw a party at his house. "Thirty to forty of Mark's closest friends spent the night with Mark celebrating his life," says Pfarr. Absent from the party was Emmitt, whose chance meeting with

Vann twelve years prior was the catalyst for everything that happened since. It was an emotionally draining time for all, and Joy says he thinks the gathering to say goodbye to Vann was, "More than Drew could face."

At Vann's everyone partied as hard as they could party into the wee hours of the morning. They spent the night laughing, picking, and feeling fine. It was a fitting farewell for Vann, who loved late-night parties. Even after getting his pacemaker installed, he still partied hard, much to the surprise of those around him. Even more fitting was for Vann to get everyone together. Since Salmon's inception, he had worked tirelessly for everyone in the band. "Mark was taking care of people until the end," says Herman. "He was beat, he was exhausted, but just knew we needed to have one more hang." Even right up until the end, Vann was involved in the business of Salmon and helping make decisions. As the night worked its way into the early morning, those still standing moved into Vann's office and were flipping through old photos when they came across one of a good friend of the band running across the tops of a row of port-a-potties. Vann looked up and declared that needed to be the cover for the upcoming live album they were in the process of mixing. The album, named *Live*, was released the following month and dedicated to Vann.

His weakened condition limited Vann's ability to play music throughout the evening, but Herman says, "That was a pretty special night," as Vann was up for telling stories. The evening was filled with lots of laughing, lots of living, and most importantly lots of love. "There were no remember this, or any goodbyes," says Pfarr. "It was all just smiles and hugs from some of the wonderful people who Mark had touched." Herman appreciated the special attention Vann paid throughout the evening to Herman's young son, Silas, who was seven at the time. This gesture was profoundly important to Herman, who says Vann, "Really passed along some energy to Silas that night."

A few days following the party, on Monday, March 4, 2004, Vann passed away. To help everyone cope with the shock of losing their brother, the band did what they do best and got together to play music, party, hang out, and remember Vann. A gathering at the Stage Stop in Rollinsville, where the band played so many of their early shows, was hastily arranged. The band invited all their close friends and family and had a "hell of a night." "It was a grand celebration of his life," says Joy. A few days later, a private, intimate memorial service was held at Vann's house on the horse farm he and his wife owned. As everyone gathered out back by a grove of trees that was Vann's favorite spot, to spread his ashes and say goodbye, a few of the horses on the farm came galloping over to where they stood. As if they could sense the sadness in the air and wanted to pay their respects, they lowered their heads and slowly walked toward the gathered group. "They came over to where we were and started kicking in the dirt as we were saying goodbye," says Joy. "It was a mystical moment."

Vann's loss was debilitating to everyone, and no one knew what direction the band was going to head. His passing reverberated in not only the surrounding Colorado music community, but well beyond the Rocky Mountains. "When those guys lost Mark," says Jeff Austin, "our whole community got fucked up by it. When he was sick and then gone, it threw the whole axis off. That was it. They were our heroes. They were our John Hartford. It was tough seeing how hard it was on those guys." The impact of Vann's passing still reverberates to this day. His one-time bandmate Larry Keel says, "I carry Mark with me in every note I play. So, there's a continued influence from his playing right there. He opened a lot of doors for bluegrass banjo players the world over with his groundbreaking technique and the fearless energy and presentation he and Leftover Salmon laid on audiences. Totally pioneering stuff." Acoustic Junction's Reed Foehl says, "He died much too young. He is a huge part of Salmon's legacy. We all miss him."

It was clear to all the impact his loss had on the band both personally and musically. Sam Bush says, "I really loved Mark a lot, and he obviously, of course, was a driving force in that band. Basically, I felt Mark brought the work ethic to the band. He was a true professional." His talent and his role in helping create Salmon's unique sound were well recognized, but the band was not just missing that as they tried to move forward. They were missing the balancing force to Emmitt and Herman. The third leg of the band's tripod. "Mark was such a great banjo player," says Hot Rize's Tim O'Brien. "He was also a great foil to Vince and Drew. He could keep up with them and challenge them every night to greater and greater heights and that is what has made Leftover Salmon so great."

Musically Vann's legacy was secure. In the pantheon of modern progressive bluegrass banjo pickers there is Béla Fleck, Tony Trischka,

"No one has ever done what Mark did with the banjo and no one has since." Mark Vann—December 28, 1962–March 4, 2002. Courtesy of Vince Herman.

and Mark Vann. "No one played like him. That's for sure," says Herman. Hard Working Americans' keyboardist Staehly, who had grown close to Vann when he worked as the band's archivist, says, "No one has ever done what Mark did with the banjo and no one has since. The different sounds and approaches he took with the instrument were unparalleled. It would take multiple lifetimes for most to get close to where Mark was with the instrument and how far he expanded it. It's absolutely mind-blowing what he accomplished in his short life." Legendary folk singer Jim Page had first met Vann when he and Salmon were part of a late-night jam at the High Sierra Music Festival in the mid-nineties and recognized Vann's extraordinary abilities. "Losing Mark was very sad. He was a very serious musician. I remember seeing him practice every day with his metronome. His sense of melody and adventure was so beautiful. He could deconstruct himself onstage in hilarious ways. He had all these weird effects on there. Wah-wah pedals on the banjo, stuff I had never seen before." Yonder Mountain String Band bassist Ben Kaufmann simply states, "He was a master. A magnificent musician."

Vann's influence has continued to resonate with all the musicians he met and mentored over the years. Mosier received invaluable help from Vann, who he says showed him how to rock on the banjo. "He told me, 'Mosier you got to do this and get that pedal straightened up and get some strings.' He turned me into a rocker." Mosier even admits that he now plays a solid-body Crossfire electric banjo because that is what Vann played. "He mentored me along on how to get up in the mix so that I would be a part of the band, not just some simple banjo plucking away in the background. I just loved him." Upon Vann's passing, String Cheese Incident bassist Keith Moseley recalled a picking session he had with Emmitt, Herman, and Vann early in his career. He had just bought his first upright bass and was learning to play it and says, "I was picking with the guys and thinking I can do this on my electric, but I can barely do this on the upright and here I am with Mark, Drew, and Vince. Mark was very encouraging, telling me, 'You got this. Stick with it, you are great.' I thought to myself, Mark Vann says I got this so I must be on my way. He was such an accomplished player. To get that vote of confidence from him early on meant the world to me."

As word of Vann's passing spread, friends and fellow musicians from across the musical spectrum all tried to come to grips with the loss of someone who lived a life full of energy, of enthusiasm for everything, who was always the life and heart of the party and the last one to go to bed. Some comforted themselves in the time they had with him and the music he made. Some were left to wonder could have been. "Mark was

the first guy I met in Salmon and while we had a lot of personal differences there was this deep love where we were inching toward each
other with our influences," says Tye North. "We will never know if we
would have been able to do anything with that."

For Greg Spatz, Vann's bandmate in his college band Farmer's
Trust, he comforted himself with having been able to reconnect with
his old friend. Since their time together at Haverford College, Spatz
and Vann, as so often happens over the years, lost touch and had not
seen each other for nearly ten years. In 2000, Salmon was going to be
playing at the Sandpoint Music Festival in Idaho. The festival was less
than an hour from where Spatz lived, and he drove out hoping to catch
up with Vann. The two former bandmates reconnected and rekindled
their musical conversation begun nearly twenty years prior in a dorm
room at Haverford. Salmon's set was delayed because of a thunder-
storm so the pair sat backstage talking and picking like they were eight-
een-year-olds again. "We were playing through all our old favorite stuff
and some new stuff, talking and taking up the musical dialogue pretty
much exactly where we had left it off," remembers Spatz. "It's kind of
astonishing how those strong musical connections last, it's like they are
in your DNA." Spatz would sit in with Salmon on fiddle for their second
set, allowing he and Vann to share the stage one last time. That day, the
two played like they were onstage at their old stomping grounds of
Brownies 23 East on the Main Line just up the street from Haverford.
Spatz says, "Though I had absolutely no idea I'd never see Mark again
after that day. I must say it is as fine a way to remember him as any I
can imagine, to be looking down stage left and seeing him there with
that big grin on his face and banjo down low where he liked it. Trading
solos back and forth with him. As far as I'm concerned, that's where
he'll always be. How I'll always think of him. I can't say either how
grateful I am to have that last day catching up with him, or how incredibly unfair it seems to never be able to do it again."

The month after Vann's passing the band released *Live* (pronounced
liv). It was a live album recorded the previous year at Salmon Fest in
Lesterville, Missouri. Emmitt says, "It's not the best live record we
could have made in my opinion. It's just like a snapshot of where we
were at that time. A lot of the tunes could have been better, but the
thing about it is Mark is on it and it's the last album with Mark and that
is definitely the significance of that record. It is a tribute album to him

in that regard."[7] Garrison agrees with Emmitt. "I think it's pretty uneven musically, but we needed to get something out that represented what Mark was doing in his last chapter with the band." The album included an inscription that summed up Vann's life, "Live Loud, Live Rowdy, Stay Up Late, Make Friends, Make Peace, Make Music."[8] Herman says, "One of the great comforts in trying to make sense of Mark's loss is he really lived big. He made a lot of friends, made a lot of music, and lived life to the fullest. He is a great example of how to live and the record is named that for him."

For Herman and Emmitt, they had to face the constant reminder of Vann's loss every night when they took the stage and glanced to their left where he stood for so long and as they listened for the familiar sound of his banjo each night, only to be left hopelessly wishing it would appear. Emmitt says, "It was difficult, very emotional. I've never not wanted to walk onstage before, but there were certainly some nights where I just didn't feel I could do it. It took every ounce of my energy to walk up onstage and pick up an instrument."[9] Each night was made more difficult by the upbeat nature of Salmon's music and the party atmosphere that surrounded their shows. "It was definitely kind of like putting on a mask to go out there," says Herman, "which didn't work out too well. I cried my share of tears the first couple of months playing without him. It was difficult. It was tough spiritually to get out there and play this music that has a real feel-good kind of vibe and have this sort of subtext of loss and tragedy floating around. It's definitely hard to surmount that hill there."[10]

The loss of Vann was also crucial to the business end of Salmon. Since Glenn Keefe left the band over a decade before, Vann had been heavily involved in the management of the band. Through all the various manager changes over the years, the one constant was Vann. He was instrumental in running the day-to-day business of the band. "Mark was a strong person and was the guiding force behind Leftover Salmon," says Garrison. "He ran the business, helped route the tours, made lots of the decisions, and was a huge musical force in the band. We all lost our direction when we lost Mark. Going back on the road after he died was necessary because we have to make a living, but it was really hard."[11] It was especially difficult for Emmitt and Herman, who since their earliest days were accustomed to the steady presence of Vann making decisions. Now the two men were left to adjust to a new challenging reality. Tour manager Pfarr had worked closely with Vann on the business of the band since first being hired and says, "The loss of Mark was difficult for me personally, because he and I basically talked eight times a day when they were off the road. He was the business manager and I was the tour manager and we were constantly talking about scheduling, what the band was going to do, money, budgets, and payroll. So, when he died it was a complete void for me. Not only did I lose my best friend, I lost my business partner and I felt a very, big, heavy weight on my shoulders to continue forward." Garrison helped Pfarr through the difficult times following Vann's death. Pfarr says, "When Greg joined the family, aside from his amazing musical contributions and sold rhythm, he was an awesome addition to me personally. Not just as a friend, but he was a business-minded musician like Mark. After Mark's passing left me emotionally empty. Greg's friendship, devotion to the music and our daily discussions about the business kept my spirit alive through a definitely difficult time for me."

After Vann's death, the band began to give serious consideration about a full-time replacement. Despite the success of the tour with Mosier and the chemistry they felt with him and the crackling energy and upbeat positivity he brought to the band, everyone knew he was only a temporary replacement for Vann. "I am a singer/songwriter who plays banjo as opposed to a banjo hotshot, which is really what they needed," says Mosier. "I never thought I would be in that band. When I went out with them my energy filled Mark's energy, but my banjo playing didn't fill the role they would need in the studio and going on to the next project. I wasn't expecting, and I don't think they ever intended, for me to be in the band. I never thought it was an audition or anything." Over the next few months, they continued to use a rotating cast of banjo players with Matt Flinner, Scott Vestal, and Tony Furtado, as they tried to figure out how to fill the hole left by Vann. It was an incredibly difficult time for everyone. Much like in the fall, they need to continue to tour to make money. While touring did allow them some escape from the emotional pain of losing Vann, each night onstage was a sad reminder of that loss. Emmitt says, "When Mark passed and we decided not to stop, but to go out with different banjo players, it was about the hardest time in this band ever. Trying to play without Mark and do what we do without having his role filled was so tough." This struggle was evident to all who saw the band at the time. Sam Bush says,

"For the first year when I would see them there was a hole. A sadness. They missed him. I missed him. We all missed Mark. We missed him and Jennifer being there. I felt there was a hole in the whole thing because he was such a huge force. It must have been incredibly painful for Drew and Vince, but they kept rocking."

Salmon knew they had to continue until they figured out where they wanted to be. "We knew we needed to keep working, at least for a while," says Garrison. "We had to give people time to transition to something else if they wanted to do that, we had to keep making money for Mark's wife, had to keep making payroll and quite honestly we felt Mark wanted the band to continue without him." It had been Vann's wish the band would continue without him, so they decided to do just that, but knew they needed to find a permanent replacement for Vann.

The "Big Three," Drew Emmitt, Vince Herman, and Mark Vann, doing what they did best in 1995. Courtesy of Vince Herman.

A few short days after his passing, the band got back on the road. At those first shows, friends of the band rented a limo to pick them up from the airport and drive them to the venue. For a band that has always had a family feel and an almost nonexistent line between band and fan, it was a chance for the fans to give back to the band and let them know there were good friends around, love abounding, and music to be played. Their friends let them know there was going to be a better day as they started the next chapter of Salmon without Vann.

Salmon had been treading water since Vann was first diagnosed, using a rotating cast of friends to take his place onstage. "We were just booking and performing and nothing was slowing down," says Joy. "Financially we had to keep going. Everyone depended on it for their livelihood. A replacement wasn't talked about. There were never any auditions or anything like that, we just filled the shoes so we could keep the train on the tracks. There was always a thought of what are we going to do, but nothing was discussed." At first, there was no pressure to decide on a permanent replacement as there was always a hope and belief Vann would beat this thing and return to the band and they would proceed forward. That unfortunately was no longer the case. They knew if they were to truly honor Vann's wish to continue they could no longer rely on friends and temporary replacements to fill the immense hole Vann left. They knew they had to find a way to turn the darkness into light.

"The transition was strange," explains Garrison. "Having different banjo players was a good diversion, but it never settled in musically doing things that way. Plus, for a while we were expecting to have Mark back. It's crazy to think it all went down in about six months—from diagnosis in September to his passing in March." Salmon knew they had to find a permanent solution. The question became, who?

Chapter 9

NOAM PIKELNY

It didn't take us long to realize this guy is a special talent on the banjo. What his career has become is fantastic. I think of him like Earl Scruggs. Scruggs refined this three-fingered style that was already there. He made it hyper refined and tight. Same with Noam. There are all these idiomatic ways to play the banjo; single string, melodic style, Scruggs style. Noam has figured out and brought to the next level the way to mix those styles and created this whole set of groundbreaking rules for how to incorporate those styles and make them connect.—*Dave Johnston (Yonder Mountain String Band)*

"**T**he thing about coming to this town," announced Vince Herman from the stage at the Canopy Club March 26, 2001, "is there are pickers all over this place. This guy here is a wild-ass banjo player. Tonight, we are going to have two banjos at once. Don't try this at home." Leftover Salmon then brought out a skinny, twenty-one-year-old student from nearby University of Illinois to play "Shenandoah Valley Breakdown" with them. The twenty-one-year-old student was Noam Pikelny, and he and Salmon had first met earlier in the day when he banged on the door of their bus, Barth, before the show. The band was relaxing after their soundcheck when Pikelny showed up. It was an unseasonably cold day—an all-time low of 12 degrees was reached—so the band invited him on the bus to chat a bit. Pikelny stopped by on the recommendation of some friends, Dan Broder and Ethan James, whom he and bassist Greg Garrison shared in common. Garrison had known Broder and James from his time at the University of Illinois when the two played with Jeff Austin and Dave Johnston in their college band the Bluegrassholes. When Austin and Johnston left for Colorado, the Bluegrassholes ended. Shortly after, Pikelny started at the University of Illinois. He met Broder and James, and the three were soon playing music together. "I entered school as a computer-engineering student," says Pikelny, "but quickly switched to the music theory department because I was having to do way too much homework and it was really getting in the way of playing music with some newfound friends."[1] This led to the formation of Waffle Hoss, a bluegrass-inspired band featuring Pikelny on banjo, Broder on guitar, Brad Decker on bass, and Pikelny's brother Motti on mandolin. Waffle Hoss combined the old-timey bluegrass Pikelny discovered when he first picked up the banjo as a nine-year-old, with the more progressive, jazz-inspired sounds of Béla Fleck that had become such a key part of his development as a musician. Pikelny's development as a musician continued through high school when he began taking lessons from Greg Cahill, a local banjo player who played in Special Consensus, one of the premier bluegrass bands in the Midwest.

Through Broder and James, Pikelny was introduced to Austin and Johnston when they came through Champaign a few years after leaving school with their new group, Yonder Mountain String Band, in October of 1999, to play at a small local club, Mike & Molly's. It was the first time Pikelny ever witnessed a band with bluegrass instrumentation playing in a rock style and having the crowd respond in kind. Seeing the energetic, rowdy dancing at Yonder's show began to tear down the notions of different styles of music for Pikelny, who realized music does not have to fit neatly into a well-defined box. He says. "It was an epiphany to me to see people responding as if they were at a rock concert, while the instrumentation was that of a bluegrass band. So, all of that started the ball rolling as far as me drifting back to the banjo and seeing playing music professionally as a possible route to take."[2]

Broder and James suggested Pikelny stop by and say hello to their old friend Garrison and the rest of Salmon when they came to Urbana, near the University of Illinois, on a cold March day. Pikelny had his banjo with him and within a few minutes he and Vann were picking away on some old bluegrass standards. Tour manager Johnny Pfarr says Pikelny "was very young, but an awesomely energetic individual who came highly praised among the inner bluegrass crowd." Things clicked so well between Vann and Pikelny as they jammed on the bus, they invited the young picker to join them for their show that night. It was one of the first opportunities for Pikelny to sit in with a national touring act and the excitement for him was visible onstage. Pikelny played Vann's second banjo, sharing leads and having a good time. "We really hit it off," says Pikelny, "and I think those guys put that in the back of their mind."[3]

At the time Salmon met Pikelny, the band was cruising. Their new additions of Garrison, drummer Jose Martinez, and keyboardist Bill McKay were finding their roles in the band. They were still riding a wave of enthusiasm begun with the release of *The Nashville Sessions*. The band had no reason to look beyond the next show, party, or festival. That is what managers were for. They just focused on the now. All that changed a few months later when Vann was diagnosed with cancer in September 2001 and succumbed to the ravages of the disease a few short months later. Salmon soldiered on with temporary replacements but knew that was not the solution. The band grew tired of trying to figure out what tunes they and the revolving replacement players had in common every time they hit the stage with someone new. They knew it was no way for the band to continue. For a six-month stretch following Vann's death, the band mostly relied on Matt Flinner to fill the banjo role. But Flinner, with his more traditional leanings and desire to focus on his mandolin work, was clearly not going to be the permanent solution. Herman says it was fun for a while as all the different players brought something new to the band, "But you get a little weary trying to remember what it is you know with whoever it is sitting in."[4] Since Vann's diagnosis, Salmon had used Jeff Mosier, Tony Furtado, Scott Vestal, and Flinner to fill Vann's immense role. Garrison says, "Each banjo player brought something different to the band. Mosier brought levity, humor, and wisdom. Furtado brought musicality, laid back friendship, and a Colorado connection. Vestal brought incredible chops and drive. And Flinner brought a combination of all these aspects." They were all extremely talented players and brought their own uniqueness to the band, but the constant change and uncertainty from night to night grew tiresome.

As it became clear they needed a full-time replacement, they began to weigh their options. All the players they used were extremely talented and more than capable of playing with Salmon, but they all had other bands and could not provide the commitment Salmon needed to fulfill their hectic touring schedule. Garrison says as they thought of potential replacements, they recalled the time Pikelny spent picking with Vann, "He obviously made an impression, and he was one of the first guys we thought about." The Yonder Mountain String Band guys had also been lobbying for Salmon to consider their young friend Pikelny as a potential full-time replacement. Yonder had come to know the talented picker through Broder and James when they and Pikelny had come to Colorado for Yonder's New Year's Eve shows the previous year. Pikelny impressed Johnston, who knew Salmon was looking for a permanent replacement. Johnston says, "I remember distinctly talking to Vince at his house and telling him there is this kid Noam Pikelny, you need to check him out."

A week before Pikelny was due to start classes the fall of his senior year in August 2002, Salmon called and asked if he wanted to come play some shows with them. "After two shows they offered me the spot," says Pikelny. "They asked if I wanted to stay on board and join the band. At that point, I was going back to school in a week to finish this music theory degree. My goal was to play music, find a group of guys to join up with and play the banjo for them. And here was this ridiculous opportunity to go on the road with this incredibly established band with one of the most loyal fans bases in existence and I couldn't resist."[5] The offer to join Salmon was a bittersweet one for Pikelny, who recognized the unfortunate circumstances that led to it. He says, "If history could've been rewritten where I did not get that gig, I would have wished it so because Mark Vann was a really great musician and a great human being."[6] Still, Pikelny knew it was a chance he could not pass up. He went back to campus, canceled all his classes, filled out all the paperwork to go on academic leave, and subleased his apartment. Within six weeks, he was living in a basement loft in Colorado in Johnston and Adam Aijala's house, where Aijala says, "We would hear him practicing in the basement all the time." For Pikelny, the move from college student to touring musician "happened very quickly."[7]

The decision to hire Pikelny in the end was an easy one. He was a supremely talented, ambitious musician, who, much like when Tye North joined a decade prior, was ready and eager to hit the road. "He was just a kid going to school and playing the banjo at the time," remembers Emmitt. "He came and sat with us on our bus, and he and Mark played together and we thought this guy is pretty good." Vann was impressed with him when they first met. When it came time to find a replacement, they remembered how Vann raved about him after picking together on Barth that cold day in Champaign. Pfarr says, "It certainly felt right once we made the commitment to him."

Yonder guitarist Aijala thought Pikelny was perfect for the job, "Mark was one of kind like Noam is. In my opinion, Mark's specialty was with the electric banjo and all the single-string stuff he could pull off. Noam is obviously an amazing single-string player. He can do anything. He has a bit of a different style than Mark, but both are super talented. I thought he was a super addition." Pikelny thinks Salmon recognized this similarity between his and Vann's playing. "I thought I was well suited for the job because Mark's playing on his electric banjo, was really influenced by Telecaster playing—the soul chicken-pickin' style of electric country guitar which was also one of my real loves. I was a huge fan of Albert Lee, Richard Flack, James Burton, and Brent Mason—those guys have played a bunch of Telecasters. I feel when I was first started playing Telecaster—and then came back to playing banjo—it really informed my style. That was something Mark and I had in common. I think maybe that's one of the reasons why those guys were drawn to me; the songs on the electric banjo, where it wasn't just plugged-in bluegrass banjo on overdrive."[8]

The band also liked Pikelny's fearless approach to music. He was unafraid to take chances, and with Salmon that was a necessity. "He's got a real distinct voice, and he takes it out there," says Herman. "He's not worried about stepping out on a limb and being able to find his way back."[9] To help Pikelny with his transition into the band, Salmon archivist, Chad Staehly, compiled a collection of CDs with various versions of songs so he could get a full sense of what Vann's role musically was with the band. Staehly did the same for Garrison, Martinez, and McKay when they first joined the band as well. Staehly says, "I remember Noam sending me an email a couple of weeks later and he was just blown away by Mark's playing, like jaw on the floor blown away. He thought Mark was light-years ahead of most and couldn't believe some of the things Mark did in the context of the banjo."

The addition of Pikelny helped revive some of the drive and excitement Salmon lost when Vann died. In an interview at the time, Garrison said Pikelny "has been a godsend. He's a hard worker, musical sponge and always practicing, checking out different types of music and trying to expand his musical palate. I think now we just need him to let loose a bit more so he can find his own voice in the band. We're lucky to have found him."[10] Finally having a full lineup again was a relief for Salmon after being in transition and in so much pain for the past year. "It was like climbing out of a hole," said Emmitt. "We [could] start feeling like a band again."[11]

Having a complete band again, combined with Pikelny's enthusiasm, reinvigorated everyone after the uncertainty of the previous year. "We're probably more psyched now than we have been in a while," said Herman at the time. "Initially, it was tough to tour without Mark. And it was hard not having a cohesive group. After Mark passed away, it was hard to go out on tour. It was one of the hardest things I have had to do in my life. But I think we have found new life with Noam."[12] Tour manager Pfarr summed up the young banjo picker's addition to the band: "His playing spoke for itself and his youthfulness was a joy to have

Feeling like a band again with a full lineup (from left): Drew Emmitt, Vince Herman, Jose Martinez, Greg Garrison, Noam Pikelny, and Bill McKay. Courtesy of John Joy.

around." While his youthfulness was a breath of fresh air for the band, there was some concern over his age and lack of experience. His quick wit proved to be the perfect fit for a band who was known for their humorous antics, though his college years did nothing to prepare him for the eye-opening indulgences of the hard-living ways of Salmon on the road.

With Pikelny in the band, Salmon did what they had always done, they boarded their bus and hit the road, including a monumental tour called "Under the Influence" with bluegrass legend Del McCoury. The tour further deepened the friendship between Salmon and the McCourys that began a few years prior during the recording of *The Nashville Sessions* with Ronnie McCoury declaring, "Leftover Salmon are friends for life."[13] The tour was a typically wild affair that was the norm for Salmon. It got off to an auspicious start when Herman missed Salmon's bus the morning following the first night of tour. Thankfully he ran into the McCourys in the hotel lobby and was able to catch a ride with them to the next show. Each show featured three sets that began with a traditional bluegrass pick from Salmon, followed by a set from McCoury, before closing out with a full-on electric set from Salmon. Sit-ins each night seemed mandatory. "It was huge honor to do some shows with those guys," says Herman. "It was a great blessing, especially since we have done such godawful things to bluegrass music over the years. It was great to have someone carrying that torch understand what we're doing."[14]

The turmoil of the lineup changes, followed by the emotional drain of Vann's illness, combined with their nonstop touring ways, kept the band out of the studio since releasing their celebrated masterpiece, *The Nashville Sessions*. Since then, they had only released the live collection, *Live*, Vann's final album, shortly after his death, in May of 2002. The same year, Emmitt released his first solo album, *Freedom Ride*, a slick collection of newly penned songs paired alongside some of his classic tunes that were recast from Salmon's rocking energy to a more straight-ahead bluegrass/country tempo. The album was recorded while Vann was going through chemo treatments and was dedicated to his memory. *Freedom Rides* sounds like a long-lost New Grass Revival album and raises the question of what might have been if Emmitt had cut his hair, cleaned up his image, and made a go of being a songwriter in Nashville. In those years following Vann's passing, they were understandably unable to focus their attention on writing and studio work and it was not until an opportunity fell into their lap that they would enter the studio as a band again.

During the time following the passing of Vann, when they were using the rotating cast of players, they played a pair of shows in Richmond, Virginia, at the Canal Club, May 20 and 21, 2002, with Tony Furtado on banjo. Furtado was good friends with David Lowery from Camper Van Beethoven and Cracker, as they shared the same management. Furtado invited Lowery, who lived in Richmond, to come to Salmon's show at the Canal Club. "I'd seen them a couple of times before and I went there and started talking to the guys," says Lowery, "and it turns out they knew 'Eurotrash Girl' and they knew some of our [Cracker] songs and they got me onstage to do a couple of them."[15] Lowery joined the band backstage after the show, where the excitement of their collaboration continued. Emmitt says, "He was just so excited about the band. He loved it and was just gushing about us and jumping up and down saying 'I want to make a record with you guys.'" In the haze of the good times being had backstage, Emmitt says he took what Lowery said with a grain of salt: "You know how those things are when you are partying after a show, you are like yeah, sure, that sounds cool. He actually called us and said, 'Let's do this.'" Lowery had been on the lookout for potential collaborations for Cracker when he sat in with Salmon, and the highly combustible energy they created together made them seem like the perfect choice. For Salmon, who did not make the time they should have for the studio, they wanted to get something out with the new lineup, and this seemed to be a good, low-hassle opportunity.

Emmitt admits while he was familiar with Cracker due to the huge radio hits they had in the nineties, when "Low" was a ubiquitous presence on MTV and radio, he was not as familiar with Camper Van Beethoven, Lowery's first band. Camper Van Beethoven, while stylistically worlds apart from Salmon, was similar in their nontraditional approach to music. Camper was a punk band with a fiddle, while Salmon was a bluegrass band with drums. Both ideas went against accepted norms, but both bands made it work effortlessly. The similarities between Salmon and Lowery and his bands, while not readily obvious, run deep. They are both bands who are dominated by two longtime friends and songwriters, Lowery and Johnny Hickman in Cracker, Emmitt and

Herman in Salmon. Both bands had long been messing with the DNA of Americana music and delivering it with a mischievous laugh each night. The two bands were like long-lost soul mates.

Later in the year, the band had a couple of days off and went into Lowery's Richmond studio to work on the album. Lowery's studio had multiple floors with gear everywhere and bunks for the band to crash in after a long night. "It was a great place to hang out and play," says Herman. "It was the ultimate sandbox for musicians." Lowery's idea was to recast some of Cracker's more well-known songs in a stripped-down, partially acoustic arrangement. To help prepare for the recording session, Lowery sent Salmon a stack of Cracker's CDs so they could familiarize themselves with the music. In the typical Salmon nonchalant, "why worry" approach, some of the band listened to the albums, some did not. Instead they waited until they entered the studio to learn all the songs. "We were very much flying by the seat of our pants," says Emmitt. With Lowery and Hickman singing, and Salmon acting as their band, they completed the album in only two days. The idea of days was subjective as much of the album was completed at night after they had fully prepared themselves after a long day of partying. "Once the beer came out, it started flowing," admits Lowery. "It's true. I made everybody this drink I am fond of. It's sort of a combination of an Appalachian hillbilly drink and a rave drink. It's a Red Bull and bourbon, so we call it a young coot, not an old coot. Anyway, we drank beer and started playing and that's really what it is."[16]

Lowery says it was a combination of out-there ideas from Salmon and the bacchanalian atmosphere of the sessions that helped set the tone of the album, "They came in and said, 'We want to do this one this way, this one that way.' Like 'Eurotrash Girl' was a country waltz. It was pretty ingenious actually. It was so different that it worked. There were a few things I suggested, but the general sort of vibe and the groove of how to do it, they came in with."[17] After the crew and engineer had gotten everything set up in the studio, Lowery says, "It became more about drinking, smoking cigars, or whatever else. There was a nice restaurant across the street from my studio they completely fell in love with and we were constantly just eating, drinking, smoking, and occasionally playing a song. And there was like forty-eight hours of this."[18] For a band as loose and who liked to party as much as Salmon, the session was an almost dream way to work, though not everyone was entirely happy with the results. Garrison felt the recent addition of Pikelny, who had only been in the band a few weeks when they began work on the album, and the short turnaround time in the studio limited the band's ability to get completely comfortable. "I don't think the playing from our end quite found the pocket it needed. Noam had literally just started full-time with us, so we were still integrating his sound, and at the same time learning all the Cracker tunes on the fly."

The resulting album, jokingly named, *O Cracker, Where Art Thou?* in mock jest of the mega-selling *O Brother, Where Art Thou?* reimagined the familiar Cracker catalog into a whole new Americana vein. The album was mostly recorded live, with only a few vocal overdubs and guitar additions from Hickman. Lowery's sardonic voice was given a new edge with the backing of an "organ, all kinds of banjos and mandolins, pedal-steel, electric, and acoustic guitars." Emmitt's trademark slide mandolin and Hickman's pedal steel turns the familiar "Low" into a spooky, haunting hymn. Herman says, "The pedal steel solo on 'Low' was just the most sublime musical moment I was involved with up to that point. The vibe in it I just love." Pikelny's banjo shines throughout the whole album. Perhaps it is noticeable as it was such a foreign sound on Cracker albums. Maybe it was just the young picker asserting himself like the rest of the band hoped he would. Emmitt says, "He had quite the spotlight on that record."

The beauty of *O Cracker* is the simplicity of the songs. Leftover Salmon came up with the bulk of the arrangements as they partied in the studio and turned some of Cracker's better-known songs into bluegrass tunes and had a good time while doing it. "When we got there to do it, we just pounded it out," says Emmitt. "It's not a real polished record. There are even sometimes when you can hear David calling out solos, like 'Okay now piano! Okay now bring in some guitar!'"[19] The freewheeling attitude that started early in the day with Lowery's young coot was the perfect way to craft an album built on shared admiration and an idea born from a drunken conversation late-night backstage. But don't many great ideas start late night from a drunken conversation? "The record is loose," says Garrison, "but that's what those sessions were all about—lots of beer, whiskey, pot, good food, and good tunes."[20] The sessions bonded the two bands and helped introduce their audiences to each other. Lowery says they felt a kinship due to their shared odd approach to music that often found them on the outside of normal looking in. "You know, they're kind of like 'our guys,'" he says. "In some ways, they don't exactly fit. They're a little bit the odd man out in the jam world, because they lean a little more bluegrass, more traditional than most, and Cracker is sort of the odd man out in the alternative world because we do lean toward country and the more jammy stuff. So, we are sort of the odd man out in that world. So, there's a kindred-spirit connection there."[21]

When the album was released, it might have not been a huge commercial hit, but it was a critical one, making many publications year-end best-of lists. *Relix* magazine called it, "A near perfect marriage of exuberance."[22] Even with this positive reception, Salmon knew after going nearly four years in between studio albums, *The Nashville Sessions* in 1999 and *O Cracker* in 2003, it might be time to get back into the studio with an album focused on their own material. "We have been such a touring band," says Emmitt, "we probably could have made twice as many records as we have made, but we are always so busy touring it is hard to find time to get in the studio. It was always about getting back on the road for Leftover Salmon." The lack of studio work during this time was understandable. They were dealing with an entire turnover of their rhythm section, working a new keyboardist into their lineup, and Vann's illness and tragic passing. Salmon, as they have done since the beginning, continued to tour relentlessly, leaving precious few days available to spend time in the studio.

The touring served as an essential time for the new lineup to come together and gel as a band, though this was often met with mixed results. With Pikelny the band spent more time than they had in the past as a unit trying to tighten the band's sound. With the jazz backgrounds of Garrison, Martinez, and Pikelny straining to be heard, the band sometimes pushed in a more progressive direction than they had been comfortable with in the past. "Some were on board," says Garrison, "Some weren't. Some nights it could feel like two bands, Noam, Jose, and I on one side and Bill, Vince, and Drew on the other." The constant touring was a double-edged sword. For all the benefits they found musically and financially on the road, it was physically and emotionally draining. But touring was their primary source of income, meaning the band had to be on the road. "It was a big machine," says Herman. "We had a publicist, we had road managers, we had crew, we had all this thing. It was like the Grateful Dead were toward the end.

We had this big thing to support and even if we didn't want to do it we had a lot of people counting on us. That responsibility always weighed pretty heavily on me." This "machine" made it almost impossible for the band to spend any quality time off the road without sacrificing substantial income. "The band's overhead out balanced a healthy workload," says Joy. "To keep up with the large overhead they had taken on, they had to do an unhealthy amount of touring to make ends meet. We were chasing small paydays in east bumble fuck just to make our quota, but at the same time the cost to get there did not make it worthwhile. We were just chasing our tail." As much as they loved being onstage and the good times that comes with being on the road, it was a long, hard grind and more time away from families and loved ones, and they were not as young and resilient as they once were. "It wasn't doing anybody any good the amount we were still touring," admits Emmitt. "We needed to stop touring after Mark passed away. It never happened because everyone needed us to be out on the road. We had this business model set up where were we had to be touring all the time to make it work."

Even though the band did not always make time to get into the studio, they continued to regularly write and were beginning to develop a backlog of material. They also were trying to discover who they were going to be musically with Pikelny. With the positive experience of their time in the studio with Lowery and Hickman, the band was finally charged up to get after making a new album. Emmitt says, "It was toward the end of the old era in which we were touring our assess off and just trying to get through Mark's passing. I think we just felt it was time to make a record. We were trying to revitalize the band at that point. We kept it together through Mark's death and we felt we finally solidified again with Noam on banjo." Shortly after working on *O Cracker*, and a month before it was released in May of 2003, Salmon entered Mighty Fine Sound in Denver to start work on their first studio album since 1997's *Euphoria* that was not a collaborative effort as *The Nashville Sessions* and *O Cracker* were.

The problem the band was encountering was their large overhead left little money for them to use for a new album. Every bit of money went to pay bills and salaries. They had offers from several labels but could not agree on what they wanted. They were also protective of losing the rights to their master tapes. As they were negotiating with the different labels and debating among themselves what to do, manager

Joy decided it was best to get into the studio sooner rather than later and agreed to pay for the sessions himself with his own personal money and recoup it after they were done recording and figured out the record label issues. After months of negotiating, they eventually signed with Nashville-based Compendia.

The band found over the years they worked better when they had a strong personality on board as producer to help mediate the differences and strong opinions that followed the band into the studio. "It can be a touchy situation," says Emmitt, "which is why we always need a producer with us so we don't get at odds with each other. A lot of times I hear things I feel should be a certain way and I have to catch myself and not always be the person saying how it should be and let everyone have their say. Over the years Vince and I have gotten better working with each other in the studio and listening to each other's ideas." Joy knew this and suggested Little Feat's Bill Payne to produce. Payne is recognized as one of rock's preeminent keyboardists. In addition to his seminal work with Little Feat, he has played with a roster of rock legends including the Doobie Brothers, Carly Simon, Jackson Browne, Robert Palmer, Art Garfunkel, Gregg Allman, Bob Seger, James Taylor, Stevie Nicks, Jimmy Buffett, Pink Floyd, and countless others. He also had a lengthy rèsumè as a producer working on albums by Little Feat, Bonnie Raitt, Carly Simon, Toto, Chris Daniels & the Kings, and others. Payne and Salmon had come to know each other over the years, sharing the stage several times. Their friendship was cemented over a couple of sit-ins. First, when Payne and Little Feat bandmate Paul Barrere were invited to play at the benefit shows for Vann. The following year, Emmitt and Herman had participated in Little Feat's twenty-fifth-anniversary concert celebrating the release of their historic live album, *Waiting for Columbus*.

Leftover Salmon moved on the same thinly traveled paths Little Feat used. Salmon is a band whose music could often confound because of its far-flung influences, much the same way Little Feat confounded critics nearly three decades prior. They both tiptoed around mainstream success, but still found greatness. Both bands skirted the fringes of Americana, bastardizing it, and making it into their own special, one-of-a-kind sound. They also both suffered great losses. Little Feat with the untimely death of founder Lowell George and Salmon with the passing of Vann. Like Salmon, Little Feat were criticized for having studio albums that did not live up to their fiery live performances. Payne recognized these similarities between the two bands and, with his years of experience with Little Feat, felt, "Maybe I could help them out a little bit in the studio." He knew he just need to "get them away from thinking about the red light being on and come up with performances." Any band can find it difficult to translate the energy of the stage to the studio, and this was made even more difficult by Salmon's already frayed emotions and road weariness. These emotions led to what Emmitt describes as, "An interesting time for us in the studio. We were touring so hard and been through so much. I feel like it was a challenging record to make." There were a lot of tough internal band dynamics happening at the time. The stress of the constant touring led Martinez, who was not cut out for the road and usually unhappy with the lengthy amount of time they toured, to almost quit shortly before entering the studio. Garrison bluntly says, "With that lineup, we never found the chemistry and balance as far as whose songs needed to be represented, who was leading the musical charge, or even who really wanted to be there."

Thankfully the band had Payne on board, who experienced his fair share of challenging times and band dissension in the studio with Little Feat. Payne knew the key to making a good album was getting the band to forget about all the tensions and conflicts and just have them focus on the performance. One morning after a particularly difficult evening in the studio, when it felt as if they could not get anything right, Payne reassured the band in a roundabout way what they were doing was working. Herman says, "Bill came in and said, 'I listened to a John Lee Hooker record this morning, and man, it was so cool. It had a great feel and texture.'" To Herman the message was clear, "It made me realize if [Hooker] recorded that album today there would be some guy pushing the button saying, 'Umm, Mr. Hooker you are a little pitchy. And in the third verse you are speeding up.' Bill made it clear, it's the feel in the music that counts." One thing Salmon has always had, no matter how difficult the times got for them, was feel.

Payne knew the band would have great material to work with, but in his experience, it was the ability to play like you do live that makes a great album. "My main advice was for them to play to someone," says Payne. "Just like they do when they are onstage. When I am in the studio I play to the producer, or the janitor, or some guests who have come in. That is my audience. That puts me in the performance mode, which is what you have to be thinking about." Payne also had the band focus on just being themselves, instead of inviting in guests as they so often did on their studio albums. Except for some piano from Payne and some harmony vocals from fellow Colorado bluegrasser K. C. Groves, the new album was Leftover Salmon from start to finish.

While the current lineup had the experience from the previous year of working in the studio together, this was an entirely different situation altogether. During the party-filled sessions for *O Cracker*, the band was essentially acting as Lowery's backing band. There was no pressure to write. They simply had to do what they always did, play their asses off. Over the years, Salmon usually never had trouble writing and creating new material. The difference now was whereas the band usually only had Emmitt and Herman's songs, with occasional contributions from Vann, they now had five legitimate songwriters in the band with Emmitt, Herman, McKay, Garrison, and Pikelny, who all wanted their space on the album. The addition of so many new voices in the band also resulted in subtle changes in the band's sound. McKay's keys especially seemed to push the band from a more roots-based sound to a more rock-based sound. They had spent the previous two years on the road discovering who they were going to be now with Pikelny filling the hole Vann's passing left. "It's a challenge," explains Garrison, "to just let go of the way the band has always done things, but as we've (Garrison, Gonzalez, McKay, and Pikelny) been in the group longer, we've opened up a little bit more and have pushed the band in new directions. The only way a band like this works is if everybody can bring their own influences and keep it in the structure the band set up through the years."23

Emmitt and Herman struggled to find footing after Vann's death. They were also dealing with the simple reality they were no longer the same twenty-somethings who first started the band fifteen years prior. The loss of Vann was a daily reminder of their own mortality, a mortality they had not had to face as they could live a life of excess as they toured across the country for the previous fifteen years. They still brought the party and could rage every night onstage, but life did not seem so eternal now. They knew tomorrow might not be a given. They had grown, matured, and had families. It was this new dynamic that was adding to the growing tensions in the band. "I had two kids at the time and a somewhat difficult marriage," says Herman. "The price it was taking being gone all the time was high. We were on the road so much and the less joy I had going out on the road, which was becoming less and less all time, made me think this is a crazy way to make a living."

Emmitt and Herman were still the dominant personalities and voices in the band but were always open to incorporating everyone's influence on albums. Garrison, McKay, and Pikelny all contributed tracks to the final album, though McKay's insistence on having more of his songs on the album led to further stress as everyone was not that into the material he had written. This just added to the underlying tensions which surrounded the band. Often these tensions and disagreements were left to simmer and fester as Salmon is a "band that has never really been about the big, open arguments." In the end, each of the new additions contributed one song to the final album. McKay with the bluesy rocker, "Just Keep Walking," which was becoming a live staple. Pikelny added the banjo instrumental, "Lincoln at Nevada," which helped maintain the band's bluegrass roots. Bassist Garrison contributed perhaps the most poignant song on the album in "Fayetteville Line," a heartbreaking ode to Vann. Garrison said it was a song that needed to be written and "no one had put any thoughts about Mark down on paper at that point." The name came from a story their lighting director Tom Konicke told Garrison about taking banjo lessons from Vann. He told him of a time when he and Vann were practicing as they sat on train tracks that ran behind Dave's on Dickson in Fayetteville, Arkansas. Garrison's lyrics reflect this simple sentiment and a wishful longing to hear Vann's banjo again.

Emmitt, again, contributed the most songs to the album despite the addition of new songwriters into the band. He also sang lead on a cover of Jim Messina's "Whispering Waters." It was a song that had struck a chord with Emmitt when he first heard it on the radio in Boulder years before. It instantly found a regular spot in Salmon's live repertoire, establishing itself as a centerpiece of any show at which they played it. When Salmon performed "Whispering Waters," it revealed a subtle streak of classic seventies rock that lived in Emmitt's voice. To witness proof of how Emmitt melds the seventies rock of his childhood and the bluegrass in his soul, one simply needs to listen to his cover of the Supertramp classic, "Long Way Home," that sounds as if it was ripped from its bell-bottomed past and deposited on a mountainside porch.

The song, which was long part of his repertoire, would appear on his 2008 solo album, *Long Road*. Salmon tried to record "Whispering Waters," for *Euphoria*, but they could not seem to get a take that fully captured the beauty of the song. This time around in the studio, Payne added some of his one-of-kind piano to it and they were able to finally capture the essence of the song. The finished song clocked in at over eight minutes and did not lose any of the adventurous spirit it had developed over the years onstage. Emmitt says, "Having Bill Payne on piano was magical. That version is really, really cool."

Emmitt's original contributions were a pure reflection of the state of mind he was in. "Last Days of Autumn," is a contemplative meditation he wrote shortly after the birth of his son. He explains, "It was before Mark got sick and the whole world got turned upside down. I wrote it after our son was born. It was fall on the Front Range. The wind was blowing through the aspens and I was feeling a little nostalgic. Fall's a time of change and introspection for me anyway and that is what came out in the song."[24] Another of Emmitt's contributions, "Weary Traveler," highlighted the direction band seemed to be heading. For Emmitt, the time off the road exacerbated the feelings he and the rest of the band were beginning to feel about the constant touring and the emotional drain and stress of being away from home. Being on the road was starting to become less fun. He says, "We toured so much things didn't feel like they were growing, it felt like they were declining. We lost some of our excitement. People were still coming to see us, but we were going back to the same well far too many times." Emmitt had begun working on the song following Vann's passing and over the past year those thoughts began to crystallize every long day spent on the road. Emmitt would admit the band still had moments of fun and for the most part enjoyed their time together, but hard touring had taken its toll. The band was strung out from the road. "After traveling for fifteen years and then losing Mark it had gotten pretty difficult," he says. "We all felt like we needed to stop and take a break." Upon entering the studio, all those feelings came tumbling out and the song about a road-weary traveler finally was completed. Emmitt's lyrics perfectly encapsulated the endless feeling of constantly traveling, but never getting anywhere, as he sang, "I've been so many places/ It all beings to look the same/ Chasing the illusion/ of the fortune and fame/ As the miles roll by, I think about/ the life I left behind/ Searching for an answer/ Trying to find a sign."

Even the pied piper of partying, Herman, seemed to be more thoughtful and introspective, with both his contributions being contemplative, reflections of the changing times. "Woody Guthrie" was a plaintive plea from the current generation longing for the guidance of the legendary songwriter. "Mountain Top" could have just as easily been written about his home in Nederland as about West Virginia, a land that so inspired Herman during his college years and continued to exhibit a strong influence over him and his music. Herman also covered "Everything Is Round," by legendary folk singer Jim Page. Page had written the tune with Salmon in mind when he was preparing to go on tour with them a few years prior. "Before I went on tour with them," says Page, "I thought this is going to be challenging because those guys play so fast all time. I thought I am going to do two things. I am going to slow them down by playing ballads and I am going to write a song for them to play." Page wrote, "Everything Is Round," but says once the tour got going two things happened, "The slowing of Salmon down didn't happen and I never go around to trying 'Everything Is Round' with them." Instead he recorded the song and put it on his 2001 album, *Music from Big Red*. Unbeknownst to Page, Herman heard the album and latched on to the song and decided to record it for the new album. "It's crazy," says Page. "I wrote that for them, but never told them about it, and they chose that song of mine to record. I thought it was great. They reworked it and made it a calypso thing. I like it better. It had more balance."

The time in the studio was difficult for Herman. With the addition of Garrison, Martinez, and Pikelny, who were all highly technical musicians and all well versed in jazz, Herman admits to feeling he was at times no longer part of the musical conversation in his own band. "My playing at times didn't feel up to par," he says. This feeling would come to a head when Pikelny ended up playing some of Herman's guitar parts on the album. "I was definitely bothered by it," says Herman. "I was definitely emotionally butt-hurt. It is something I always struggle with. My approach my whole career has always been be the worst player in your band. But that has a price you pay within your own personal confidence, and my confidence was at a serious low at that time. Now that I have produced some records I can understand the decision, but as one of the guys who started the band it was pretty hard to be kicked off some tracks."

For a band not known for their introspective side, the material on the new album was highly reflective and thoughtful. There were still those classic, high-energy Salmon songs that took the best of the blue-grass world and deposited it into a rock 'n' roll landscape, best encapsu-lated by the album opening "Down in the Hollow." But it was the more poignant tracks on the album that truly reflected the state of the band. The *Chicago Tribune* noted this change in mood in their review of the album, "In the past, the group's self-conscious mix of other musical styles with a core bluegrass sound and tendency toward comically exag-gerated singing have detracted from the band's strengths as musicians. On *Leftover Salmon*, there is a newfound seriousness in the wake of Vann's death as the band plays songs that range across bluesy Southern rock, no-nonsense bluegrass and earnest folk balladry."[25]

The finished album, released March 23, 2004, was self-titled, after almost being called *Hollerwood* or *Everything Is Round*. It was a ma-ture, thoughtful album, and with the help of Payne, well-crafted and produced, but perhaps less fun than previous albums. Though given what they went through and where they were mentally, that was to be expected. The *Anchorage Daily News* called the album, "Introspective, revealing, painful and private."[26] The *Washington Post* elaborated on this even further in their positive review of the album. "When a band heading into its 14th year puts out a self-titled album, it's not a good sign. Either the musicians are so creatively tapped out that they can't conjure up another CD title, or they're pretending—usually ridiculous-ly—that they're beginning anew. Leftover Salmon is simply coping; banjo player Mark Vann succumbed to cancer in early 2002, devastating the group's remaining founders, Drew Emmitt and Vince Herman. With four 'brand new Leftovers' added to the Colorado group since the last proper studio album, Salmon's lineup isn't just revived. It's re-spawned. These songs are more mature, more rounded and less . . . fun."[27]

While everyone connected with the band was beginning to feel burned out from long years of hard living and endless touring, no one was willing or able to say out loud maybe the band needed a break. "It was never really about us being sick of being around each other," says Emmitt. "There are ways we get annoyed with each other, but it was never about that. It was about the situation and the constant touring and everything that came with that. As a band, we still had a pretty good connection as friends. Vince and I have always seen eye to eye on things. Mostly. There can be little disagreements but we always gotten along incredibly well considering how long we have been together." Still, the times Emmitt and Herman agreed was becoming less and less, often leading to personal and creative tensions between the two. These tensions were exacerbated by the loss of Vann, who was the mediator between them and settled differences. But as a band who often avoided confrontation with each other, their feelings toward the constant touring and their true mental state were for the most part left unsaid. Herman chose to deal with his unhappiness by simply removing himself from the situation as much as possible. He says he began to isolate himself from the band. First thing in the morning he would get off the bus and go walk around for hours or hang out by himself in his room for hours. "I had a kind of separate existence," he says. "Whenever I could get off the bus, I did." For Herman, who believes, "Your happiness is dependent on what you do when you get up in the morning and who you are hanging with," he found he was not happy. "That is how my world works," he says. "I found I wasn't happy with what I was doing when I got up in the morning and who I was spending the majority of my time with. I hate to say this, but it just wasn't a group of people I wanted to spend my time with at the time. I love them all deeply, so it is hard for me to say. Some of it might have been me, but at the time it was not where I wanted to be." Garrison recognized Herman's mounting misery: "I felt we were pushing Vince out of his comfort zone by wanting to rehearse more and kind of holding him more musically accountable than he was used to. He never said anything, but we felt his resistance and unhappiness. And I'm sure he felt our frustration." No one in the band was willing to admit they felt the end was near, or they were unwilling to see that it might be. They instead all found their own ways to cope with the unhappiness enveloping them all. It was clear they were reaching a breaking point. Emmitt admits, "I was personally toast at the time." Instead, the band did what they had always done— they hit the road again.

Even with the tensions present before heading into the studio and the struggles they had working on the album, the band was able to cobble together a strong, cohesive album that sounds better the further away from those troubled times the band gets. "When I listen to the record," says Garrison, "all the emotions from that time come flooding back; the band still reeling from losing Mark, the excitement of being in the studio, the tension between the songwriters lobbying to get material on the record, the thrill of working with Bill Payne, and quite honestly, the frustration related to some of the musical decision making. There is a lot of pretty loose playing just overlooked and accepted to the detriment of the record in my opinion. Somehow we did wind up with a pretty great collection of material despite everything going on."

Despite the reservations Garrison had about the album, it garnered positive attention when it was released, much of it due to the more serious tone of the album. It quickly shot to number six on the Americana music charts. Payne's strong producing hand and the addition of McKay on keys had the band sounding more like a rock band than ever before, but it seemed a comfortable evolution. This lean toward a more rock sound was balanced by Pikelny's prodigious banjo skills that made sure the band was still rooted in the bluegrass at their core. Jambase.com said the album was, "Mature yet playful, graceful yet dirty, it [is] apparent Leftover Salmon [is] poised for out-and-out domination."[28]

For Salmon, the positive response the album was receiving could not mask the rising tension and uncertainty the band was beginning to feel with Pikelny itching to move on and everyone else experiencing a serious case of fatigue and burnout. "I think Noam, like myself, was frustrated with the lack of musical direction and dedication happening in the band. But that's the thing about a band, everyone must be on the same page for it to work," says Garrison. It was starting to become clear Pikelny wanted something musically different than what Salmon could offer. He is a very cerebral, articulate, amazing player and Salmon was a little looser, a little more rock than the musical direction in which he was headed. "We are a little more ragtag than what he wanted," says Emmitt. "I think we were a little at odds with Noam because it was clear he really wanted to go in a different direction. I think there was a feeling of disconnectedness in the band."

The loss of Vann was still being felt and not just musically. He was long the dominant voice and driving force when it came to business decisions. His loss left a void in management the band was struggling to fill. No one else in the band expressed an interest in taking over that role. Emmitt and Herman had always been willing to let Vann take the lead. The usual solution to difficult conversations was to simply avoid them. Communication was minimal and lacking, often only in small groups, but never addressed to the whole band. This was an easy way to avoid conflict as the unhappiness everyone was feeling was simmering below the surface, with no one willing to deal with it head-on. Those conflicts and differences had been kept tucked away for most of the life of the band, but now with the absence of Vann's authoritative presence to buffer, the differing opinions started to collide. "He was the one who told everyone to shut up," says Joy. "He made a lot of decisions, and everyone went along with what he said." Salmon is a band that does not like conflict. Issues and disagreements often go unsaid. The strong personality of Vann was regularly the arbiter of these differences, taking charge and making decisions when no one else would. This allowed everyone else to pass the blame or not feel responsible when things went bad. With Vann gone, everyone had to face their own decisions and the consequences that came with them. Herman says, "Drew and I are different people with different wants and expectations and the tensions arising from that without Mark became more unmediated." Joy noticed with the loss of Vann and his peacekeeper role, the band now kept those issues pent up until they returned home from tour and then unleashed their unhappiness on him. "As soon as they got home my phone would blow up," he laments. "Everyone would be complaining about everyone else, saying so and so did this, so and so did that. I would spend days calling to try and deliver all the messages everyone was upset about."

There was a sadness beginning to envelop the band. It was not always visible to the crowd every night when Salmon took the stage in their usual happy-go-lucky way. But it was affecting everyone and leading to emotions that were pulled in every direction. There were often threats of "I quit" from Herman and Emmitt. Manager Joy often received phone calls from the two and had to act as an amateur psychologist convincing them not to leave. It became a running joke between Emmitt and Herman, with them remarking to each other, "You can't quit now, it's my turn." It was the same old story for the band that had been repeated before. When it seemed they finally succeeded in climbing to the top, of finding success, of creating a truly great album, there was something there to knock them back down. Pikelny would soon receive an offer to join John Cowan's band and it became clear his days with Salmon might be coming to an end. At the same time, the band's numbers each night were going down because they were always on the road so there was less demand. The band was touring three weeks of every month, were never home, and not making any more money than they had years before. They were simply playing dates to meet their minimum payroll. It was a stagnant situation with the same results and no growth. The wheels were always spinning, but they were never getting anywhere, and it finally was too much for Emmitt. After a show for Boulder radio station KBCO, May 1, 2004, with the Los Lonely Boys, Emmitt exploded backstage. It was an odd gig, as it was moved indoors at the last minute due to the weather. Salmon was the headliner, but the crowd was clearly there for the Los Lonely Boys, who had just released the hit song, "Heaven." The venue changes and the unenthused crowd led to a show the band felt was "pretty terrible." The band was also dealing with McKay's increasing heavy drinking, which was proving destructive to not only him, but the rest of the band as well, and adding to the friction growing between everyone. All this combined was too much for Emmitt. He was tired, fed up, and frustrated at the lack of direction. "I just blew up and quit," says Emmitt. "I knew I couldn't physically tour this hard and be away from home and my family. I just had it. I couldn't tour anymore. It just seemed hopeless. We were just beating a dead horse. There was no creativity because there was no energy. I just kept begging everyone to do it differently. There had to be another way." As was the norm, Joy received an unpleasant call from an unhappy Emmitt. Joy, who was in New Orleans when he received Emmitt's call, says, "It wasn't the first time I had gotten that call. I was thinking I just need to get home and navigate these waters as I have done in the past." By the time Joy got back home, Emmitt had calmed down. He had spoken with Herman and changed his mind and wanted to keep it going.

In the end, neither Emmitt or Herman could leave what they had worked so hard to create as Pikelny beat them both out the door. A few days after the KBCO show, following a gig in Laramie, Wyoming, on May 5, Pikelny announced he decided to accept the offer from Cowan and join his band. While the band could recognize the opportunity being presented to Pikelny, they knew what his leaving meant. Emmitt and Herman invested a ton of energy and time into Pikelny and rebuilding the band and were devastated by his decision. "It was hard to carry on without Mark," says Herman. "I guess we kind of thought we had that problem licked when we got Noam. Thinking of finding another banjo player was the straw that broke the camel's back."[29] The irony of Emmitt's decision is while he decided to stay with the band and continue forward after threatening to quit, the uncertainty it created helped push Pikelny out the door. Emmitt says, "I think my quitting had an influence on Noam because he had the John Cowan offer and I think he thought maybe things were falling apart for Salmon. Which they were." Pikelny's announcement was documented in Herman's personal daily calendar with the blunt entry, "Noam drops the bomb." Shortly after Pikelny's announcement, Emmitt and Herman made the decision to bring the band to an end over a short phone call. The two bandmates recognized they could no longer continue. "I think we both felt it was time," says Emmitt. "Basically, in that phone conversation we decided to stop it." Herman says in the end it was a "short conversation and an easy decision. Spiritually we were all struggling in the wake of Mark's passing. Looking back, we should have taken a pause right after his death, but he insisted and made us promise to continue without him. The pressure of it all was beginning to mount and the tensions were cranking up a bit when Noam decided to leave. The thought of rebuilding again was just too much to contemplate. We all needed a break and Noam offered us that chance." Joy found out of their decision a few days later. He had gone to a local solo show Herman was playing. The two were outside smoking a joint and Joy asked Herman about upcoming plans for the band. Joy says, "He looked at me and said, 'It ain't like it use to was.' Right when I heard those words, I knew that was it."

Besides hastening the end of the band, Pikelny's leaving was also bittersweet as the band had released a studio album that should have been hailed as another masterpiece but was now simply seen as the band's swan song. Because the album never got to live and breathe as it should, it is an often overlooked part of the band's catalog. Instead it should be viewed as a mature step forward for the band with some of the strongest songwriting of their careers.

For the band, there was relief as this thing that had been draining them spiritually, emotionally, and physically for so long was coming to an end. Garrison said Pikelny's departure signaled it was "time to step back and assess the situation," and called the decision to disband "a delayed reaction to Mark Vann's passing."[30] It was clear to all involved, not just the band, but their crew, managers, and families they all needed to get away. "We were all ready to do something different honestly," says Emmitt. "I was feeling I needed to get off the road all the freaking time. I felt I was starting to lose it a bit. There was tension. I think I was just waiting for something to give so we could stop. Somewhere internally I just needed the right reason to stop."

Salmon's decision to end things seemed to be an echo of what was happening to so many of their peers in the original jamband scene. A few months after Pikelny's announcement, Phish played what they called their last show at a mud-soaked, disaster-filled weekend in Coventry, Vermont. Widespread Panic was scaling back their time on the road due to the death of their own founding member Mikey Houser in 2002. Blues Traveler had not been relevant in some time, the Spin Doctors had hung it up years prior, and the Aquarium Rescue Unit had splintered into several different projects. Many of the bands that helped pioneer the jamband scene were starting to call it quits. Years of hard living, drug abuse, and untimely deaths pushed them all to the edge of breaking. Given all Salmon had been through over the previous fifteen years, it was excusable Emmitt and Herman wanted to call it quits. The emotional toll and financial strain were beginning to catch up with everyone. "The pain of losing Mark, who was a key contributor to the music creativity and the constant touring for fifteen years pointed toward everyone needing some time away," says Pfarr.

With the impending departure of Pikelny, the pressure of having to again find a new replacement, and the growing tensions and divisions in the band, it all seemed too much and the decision was made to pull the plug and bring the band to an end. No one knew exactly what that meant. Was this the end for good? Was it a hiatus? No one knew for sure, but the general feeling was this was not a break, but a breakup. It was the end. There were differing opinions on what to announce and how to say it. Joy ended up drafting an announcement of the breakup because he says, "No one else would do it." He crafted a statement ambiguous in its finality. "I wrote this letter to the fans," Joy says, "I was still refusing to say we were broken up and it was done, so I said we are not breaking up, we are taking a break, and everyone let me leave it at that." In interviews the band gave at the time, they only spoke of a hiatus and time away. Emmitt was quoted as saying, "I'm not going to say never, but I'm personally not really planning to do it again."[31] Salmon believed this was the end. "I think we were like a three-legged beast walking on two," said Herman. "We had never quite gotten that balance back and it was a struggle just changing personnel. We had never taken a break after Mark passed and we just said at one point it was time to give it a rest. It was too spiritually taxing. It had run its course."[32]

As the band prepared to release the statement announcing the future of the band, they were, as so often before, the victim of bad timing. The same week Joy was finishing the letter to fans, Phish's Trey Anastasio released his own statement announcing Phish breaking up at the end of the summer. "Suddenly it's an uproar," says Joy, "and I was thought I can't do this same thing, the same week as Phish. So, we sat on it for a couple of weeks." As rumors began to swirl on the internet about Leftover Salmon, the band finally released their press release on June 15, 2004. It stated in part, "After years of touring everyone is ready for some time off to spend with their families and to pursue solo projects that Salmon's busy schedule has not permitted. As of right now the future of Leftover Salmon is uncertain but the band is not breaking up, just taking a break. Mark wanted us to continue after he left the band and that's what we did. We have toured just as hard, rebuilt the band and put out a new record. Now we feel we can take a break without letting him down." Following the announcement, Jambase.com declared, "For fifteen strong, energetic, and eclectic years, no band ruled the underground roots-music stage like Leftover Salmon. They traversed the North American highways all in the name of music—using fun as a guiding principle and festival as religion."[33]

Salmon closed out the year and their time together with a four-night run at their home base of the Fox Theatre in Boulder. The first night they proved despite all the ill feelings and differences among them, they still were something special together as they made magic from a near catastrophe. A transformer blew in Boulder that evening and the venue lost power. With only the emergency lights working, Salmon took the stage and played a full acoustic set with no amplification. As they had done so many times over the previous fifteen years, Salmon showed how it is a high level of art every time they made something out of nothing. The power later returned and the band would play two more electric sets. The following nights leading up to New Year's were more of the same. For the final night, manager Joy, who also has his birthday on New Year's Eve, refused to acknowledge it being the final show. "I was not going to make it about the breakup," says Joy. "So, I turned it into the fifteenth-anniversary show. I went and got a big cake that said Happy Anniversary." Still, there was no hiding what was going on. Band archivist Staehly says, "Those shows were so emotional. It felt like a funeral, but a New Orleans–style funeral. There was plenty of festivating, but everyone had a giant pit in their stomachs." Everyone remembers the final show was good and the band played with a lot of energy, but there was still the weird lingering feeling in the air knowing it was the last one. "It was emotional for sure," says Joy. "When everyone came offstage Vince was in tears. Both of us were." Following the show, everyone shared New Year's wishes and a few beers backstage, but unlike New Year's past, the after-party did not go until the wee hours of the morning with everyone hanging together. Instead everyone gathered their stuff and left quickly.

Early in the morning of January 1, 2005, fifteen years after Emmitt and Herman shared a long ride from Boulder to Crested Butte, where they were excited about the possibilities of the great unknown that lay ahead of them, the twists and turns, the highs and crushing lows, the two men who had shared so much over that time together, who crafted Leftover Salmon into a true giant of American roots music, pulled the plug on it all and walked away. What this decision meant was unclear. There might not ever be Leftover Salmon again. In an interview at the time, Emmitt addressed this uncertainty:

> It seems a good time to stop and reassess where the band is going. So, it's definitely a hiatus. We don't know for how long. It could be a year, it could be two years, it could be forever, we don't know. We'd like to leave it open ended and we'd like to think we would get back together and play more shows at some point. But I think what we need is to stop the touring machine as it exists. I think once we do that and the dust settles and the smoke clears, we can get a better idea of what we want to do with the band in the future.[34]

As 2005 dawned, Leftover Salmon was no more.

Chapter 10

ANDY THORN

He is just one of those guys. Music flows through him on an incredible level. There is no impediment between his brain and his banjo. Whatever he thinks, he can play. That is the sign of a great musician. A lot of people can have a great idea, but it is hard for them to get it to translate 100 percent right to their instrument, through their synapses and fingers to their instrument. Andy never has that problem.—*Anders Beck (Greensky Bluegrass)*

"The first time I saw Leftover Salmon play with Andy Thorn I didn't spend the night watching him," explains Jeff Austin, "I instead spent the night watching Drew and Vince and their faces and the huge shit-eating grins they had and their sheer joy. All I keep thinking was my friends are so happy." Austin was seeing Leftover Salmon in the summer of 2011, for the countless time at another summer festival as he had done so many times before. Only this time it was different. After a decade of emotional loss and band upheaval—including a two-year hiatus—the band was back and playing with a joy Austin had not seen since the death of Mark Vann. For Salmon, it had been a hard run following the loss of Vann and the devastating effect it had on the emotional well-being of everyone involved with the band. But with the addition of the young, supremely skilled Thorn, it seemed brighter days were ahead and there was an enthusiasm surrounding the band that had been absent for too long. Austin was overwhelmed to finally see his friends seem whole again: "To see them playing with Andy and see not just a smile because they are onstage playing music, but real joy. I wanted to see them that happy. They were onstage looking over at this dude who is tapping into that weird vein that Mark could tap into, it was like they had taken a breath for the first time in a long time. It was amazing to see. I walked away and cried in a port-a-john for ten minutes because my friends were so happy."

Unfortunately, that moment of elation and rebirth was still years away when Leftover Salmon walked offstage in the early morning of January 1, 2005, as they finished what they said was their last show. The band scattered their separate ways after the show and it seemed Leftover Salmon was no more. In the intervening years between the last show and when Austin saw them with Thorn, much had changed for the band. Everyone had moved on, started new projects, and joined other bands. When asked if he thought he had played his last shows with Salmon, Emmitt answers flatly, "I did. Everyone started anew and had their own lives. It didn't seem it would happen again or was even worth doing again."

As the winds of change blew Leftover Salmon apart after the tense years following Vann's tragic death, Emmitt was the first to move on. He started a solo band, simply called the Drew Emmitt Band, in 2002 when he released his first solo album. Toward the end, Emmitt began seeing some interest from various booking agents who thought he had the potential to break out as a solo artist. He signed a deal with Compass records. Emmitt had never been frustrated with the music, he was frustrated with the endless cycle of touring the band was stuck in and happy to now be controlling his own schedule. "I was just tired of the whole machine and having to tour regardless of how anyone was feeling or regardless if there was a plan or if things were progressing. It wasn't a good feeling. It didn't feel like we were moving forward. We were just burnt."

For Emmitt, it was a liberating moment. While he admits he never felt constrained or limited musically in Salmon, the chance to be in complete control and making all the decisions was something he never experienced in Salmon. He says, "Going out on my own and overseeing the band and being in charge of making my own records. It was empowering to find out, yeah I can do this thing on my own if I have to." Emmitt still wanted to be able to make music, but to do it in his own way and without the stress of the schedule Salmon had taken on. "I was poised," he says. "When Salmon quit, I jumped right out on my own.

Somehow I was able to keep the family fed and the bills paid." Emmitt assembled a band that included Greg Garrison on bass, Matt Flinner on banjo, and Ross Martin on guitar and hit the road in 2005. Over the course of the year, the band went through some changes as Martin left and was replaced by Tyler Grant. In April, Emmitt was invited to come on the road as a special guest with The String Cheese Incident for three shows. Traveling between gigs, Emmitt and String Cheese Incident guitarist Bill Nershi spent time in the back of the bus picking bluegrass tunes and talking about how cool it would be to get out and play some bluegrass like in the old days when Nershi sat in with Leftover Salmon before String Cheese started. Following Emmitt's brief tour with String Cheese, they went their separate ways as Cheese's hectic touring schedule keep Nershi occupied for most of the rest of the year. Toward the end of the year, Nershi had time off and joined Emmitt's band on the road for a run of shows as a special guest. "It went really well," says Emmitt. "Every show sold out and we thought this could be good to keep doing this." At the same time, tension was rising in String Cheese due to what Nershi felt was his shrinking role in the band and the overreliance on electronica in their music. Much like with Salmon, years of hard touring and simmer personal tensions resulted in String Cheese drastically scaling back their touring schedule, leading to the band taking an extended hiatus. As things were winding down for String Cheese, Emmitt and Nershi, excited by the possibility of the energy they felt during the run of shows they had done together and the thought of getting back to basics playing more straight-ahead bluegrass, decided to have Nershi join Emmitt's band, renaming it the Emmitt–Nershi Band.

Meanwhile Herman was also starting to find his own footing outside of Salmon. He struggled with the tensions pulling apart the band and he knew personally a change needed to be made for him to be happy. He admits the prospect of bringing Salmon to end, while a relief to be away from a situation he viewed as negative, was also frightening, explaining, "Being that is how I made my living for all those years it was a challenge. I had no other tricks up my sleeve, nothing to fall back on. I didn't know what I was going to do, but I knew I couldn't do what I had been doing." Herman had grown tired of the all-consuming "machine" of touring. To ensure he was making a change, he went in the complete opposite direction of the large-scale operation Salmon had become and

Drew Emmitt (left) and Bill Nershi play DelFest in May 2012 as the Emmitt–Nershi Band. Photograph by the author.

set out on a series of solo tours that was nothing more than him and his guitar. It was his way of guaranteeing what he was doing would be different than what had grown so wearisome doing with Salmon.

Much like Emmitt, Herman had already found other ways to satisfy his musical needs and curiosity before the decision to end Salmon was made. In the fall of 2004, before Salmon's final shows, he crossed paths with bassist extraordinaire Rob Wasserman. Wasserman was working on a new project called the Spirit of Guthrie, where he used old lyrics and words from legendary folk singer Woody Guthrie to craft an album of new songs. This meeting led to a brief tour with the trio of Herman, Wasserman, and folk singer Jim Page, whom Herman calls the modern-day version of Woody Guthrie.

Shortly after the band called it quits, Herman broke his neck when he slipped on ice near his house in Eldora, Colorado. He was holding guitars in both of his hands when he slipped and was unable to catch himself as he fell backward. The fall busted a vertebrae and disk in his back. He ignored the pain and tried to continue working as he was feeling the financial pinch of no longer having the steady paycheck from Salmon. As the pain increased and began to affect his daily life, Herman says, "I thought I was developing MS or something. I was having trouble walking." After six months, he finally got an MRI. As he was preparing to leave for another solo tour, he got a call from his doctor who told him he needed surgery immediately. His spine was 50 percent compressed and was having trouble communicating with the rest of his body. The surgery took Herman off the road and that, combined with mounting medical bills, put him in a "difficult financial situation." So, twelve days after surgery he was back onstage with the New Riders of the Purple Sage with a neck brace he would wear for the next five months.

Herman also began playing with Chad Staehly, Salmon's archivist, who was a talented keyboard player. The two played together locally and were often asked to put together various bands for different local fund-raising events. Staehly asked Herman and Bill McKay to join him for a couple of shows with a local band he was in called the Canine Unit. Out of these shows, the first annual Mark Vann Foundation Holiday show was born. The Mark Vann Foundation was started in the wake of his passing and strived to live up to his motto to always, "Go Big!" The Foundation raised money to help community-based nonprofit organizations with their music and arts programs. Its stated goal was, "Bringing light, love and laughter into the lives of those in need through nature, music and the arts; and to provide a conduit for kindhearted people with similar values to nurture impactful positive change within their own communities."[1] Over the years, it would hold all-star benefit shows to help further this cause and these ideals. "It is one of the best things I have ever been a part of," says Staehly. "I was happy we could do so much good in Mark's name for a solid ten years after we lost him."

Herman and Staehly played together sporadically over the years whenever Herman had time away from Salmon. In 2005, following Salmon's final show, Herman and Staehly were asked to put together a band for the Rainforest Action Group benefit show in Boulder. They recruited an all-star roster from the wealth of musicians in the Boulder area. During rehearsals as they were thinking of what to call the band, Staehly recalled a story Herman told him a few months before as they were having some beers following a duo show they played in Vail. "Vince was talking about skiing," says Staehly, "and mentioned the term great American taxi, and how one of his friends described his skiing style as that of a great American taxi rumbling down the hill. I stopped him and said, 'That's it.' He asked what I meant, and I said that's what we should call the band for the show." From that show and conversation, Great American Taxi was born. Staehly said over the years he felt Herman should have a country outlet, like Jerry Garcia had with the New Riders of the Purple Sage, a place and a band where Herman could try out songs that might not have necessarily have found a home with Salmon. This idea of a separate band was soon for naught when Salmon ended. Still, the chemistry and the fun the pair felt from playing together was undeniable, and Staehly says, "The music was feeling so good we knew it wasn't going to be for just one show." The two decided to make Great American Taxi a full-time band and "set a course to bring the hippies back to country music." Herman greatly enjoyed playing with Great American Taxi, "I was happy with them. It wasn't like Taxi was playing the level of gigs Salmon was when we quit. It was back to the Suburban instead of a bus, but they were good guys and it was a fun band."

The rest of Salmon was similarly busy, finding new musical paths. Keyboardist McKay fell back into the local scene and busied himself playing with a few different bands. Drummer Jose Martinez, who had long been unhappy on the road, moved back to Seattle, got married, and began playing local jazz gigs in the area. Bassist Greg Garrison would reunite with Noam Pikelny in a new project. Over their short time together in Salmon, the two had grown close. They were scheduled to play a set together at the RockyGrass Bluegrass Festival the summer after the band called it quits. While in Nashville rehearsing for the set, they got together with mandolinist Chris Thile, fiddler Gabe Witcher, and guitarist Chris Eldridge for an all-night jam session. The chemistry that night was something special, and the idea for a new band was born. The band was at first called How to Grow a Woman but soon became known as the Punch Brothers.

Over the ensuing years, everyone associated with the band gained experience from having solo careers, playing with different bands, and being apart from Leftover Salmon. For Emmitt and Herman, it was freeing to be on their own, without the constraints of Salmon and opinions of the others impacting what they did. At the same time, it was a scary proposition to be without the safety net they performed with for the past fifteen years. They were truly stepping out into the great wide open. It was a huge change not only musically, but personally for the two. "We didn't see each other much," says Emmitt. "We didn't talk. We both went into our own worlds and started touring on our own." The two crossed paths occasionally when their bands were booked to play the same festival. Even then there was no guarantee the two would hang out or talk. "It seemed Salmon was not going to get back together. It just felt like it was over," says Emmitt.

All their respective new groups were working to establish new identities apart from Leftover Salmon. Emmitt was pushing forward with the Emmitt–Nershi Band and recently added a new member to the band in banjo picker Andy Thorn. Thorn was recommended to Emmitt by the Emmitt–Nershi Band's outgoing banjo player, Chris Pandolfi, who first met Thorn in his sophomore year of college at the Joe Val Bluegrass Festival in Boston. Thorn laughs, "It's funny because I didn't know Chris, but he was another young progressive bluegrass banjo player like me at the time. I was all clean cut at the time and everyone thought I was him all weekend." The pair eventually met and became good friends that weekend. When Pandolfi was preparing to leave the Emmitt–Nershi Band, the first person he thought would be a good replacement was his friend Thorn and suggested him to Emmitt. Emmitt called Thorn and based on their brief conversation and Pandolfi's recommendation, asked him if he wanted to join the band. "I got hired without an audition or anything," says Thorn.

Despite his young age, Thorn was already a well-seasoned musician. Hailing from North Carolina, he first discovered the banjo as a twelve-year-old when he bought one at a neighbor's yard sale. The neighbor threw in the Earl Scruggs instructional book with his purchase and Thorn's exploration of the banjo was underway. His parents were into bluegrass, and Thorn was musically inclined as he had taken guitar and piano lessons. He says, much like Vann had upon his discovery of the instrument nearly twenty years prior, "I sort of started exploring banjo music because I got one, not the other way around." Over the next couple of years, he got deeply into banjo music. He was a voracious reader of the *Banjo Newsletter* which featured regular columns with new things to try and new songs to learn. He even attended the Maryland Banjo Academy when he was fifteen. He was a self-described "banjo nerd." In 1998, when he was sixteen, his parents took him to

MerleFest, which was nearby. It was his first exposure to Leftover Salmon. "That is when I discovered a lot of new bands," says Thorn. "Sam Bush, The String Cheese Incident, Salmon, and a lot of other jambands were there that year." Impressed by what he heard, Thorn picked up a copy of *Ask the Fish* at Salmon's merch table. Shortly after, he saw Salmon again at the Cat's Cradle in Chapel Hill. Thorn was still too young to drive to the show, so his mom drove him and a friend to the show, where his friend proceeded to get blackout drunk and had to be taken care of by Thorn's mom the whole show.

In high school, Thorn began to hang out and play with some similarly musically inclined friends, brothers Jon and Jeff Stickley, and Ian Thompson. They started a bluegrass band Crawdad PA, that featured Thorn on banjo, Jon on mandolin, Jeff on guitar, and Thompson on bass. The band's name came from Thorn's nickname at the time, "Crawdad." For the teenage band that was just beginning to become immersed in bluegrass music, they fleshed out their sets with such non-bluegrass material as the Dead Milkmen's "Dean's Dream." The band developed a pretty good local following and recorded one album while still in high school.

After graduation, Thorn headed to the University of North Carolina to begin work on a degree in jazz guitar. While in college he fell in with a crowd of older, established bluegrass pickers that would evolve into Big Fat Gap. Big Fat Gap became a long-running bluegrass band, based in Chapel Hill. The band became a hub that attracted some of the area's best pickers and musicians. Its lineup changes and fluctuates every couple of years as new students and musicians moved in and out of the area. Big Fat Gap was mostly a traditional style band that played old-school style around a single condenser microphone, but as different members came and went, the band's sound and style changed. Thorn was a freshman in college when he first joined Big Fat Gap, while the rest of the band was all a few years older. This was fine by Thorn, as he says, "They had me going into the bars when I was eighteen. They never ID'd me because I was the band. When I turned twenty-one and was out celebrating my birthday and I had been at all these bars for three years all the bartenders looked at me funny."

Big Fat Gap featured a rotating roster of stellar musicians over the years in its lineup. Many of the musicians from the band would move onto bigger, national bands like the Jeff Austin Band, Steep Canyon

Rangers, Mandolin Orange, Kripplekrunk, and Town Mountain. Over
Thorn's time in college the lineup for Big Fat Gap featured fiddler
Bobby Britt, who later joined Town Mountain; mandolinist Andrew
Marlin, who formed Mandolin Orange; bassist Miles Andrew, the long-
running leader of the band; and Thorn's high school friend Jon Stickley,
who was attending nearby North Carolina State, on guitar. Despite
Thorn's young age, his easygoing personality made other musicians
gravitate to him. This combined with his advanced knowledge of music
theory provided an inspiration to the younger Britt and Marlin. "Andy
has always been an amazing player and leader," says Britt. "Not only
that, but he has always had this humble, inclusive musical confidence. It
makes it a joy to play with him and he brings people together with his
presence, on and offstage. He is also a couple of years older than me
and at the time I looked up to him a lot. He was a musical mentor to
me. Andy also saw Andrew's talent early on and was a mentor to him as
well."

For Thorn, his experience with Big Fat Gap was one of the high
points of his time at UNC, as he almost backed out of finishing his
degree a few times. He would stick it out though and finish his degree
in 2005. The one constant during his time at Chapel Hill was Big Fat
Gap, which became the center of what he did and established many
connections he carried well beyond college. Britt says, "There were too
many wild nights with Big Fat Gap to keep track of. We were in a
strange situation where bluegrass was starting to be cool and we were
playing a lot of rowdy bars and living a small-town rock-star lifestyle.
We would stay up 'til sunrise picking and singing at least a couple of
nights a week. This produced a strong musical bond between all involved. It is easy to say we are friends and collaborating musicians for
life." Thorn's time with Big Fat Gap also made him think music might
be his career path, "It was a fun band. We did a lot of frat parties and
college events at UNC. We stayed busy. First time I played a wedding
was with those guys. I got to hang out and drink free beer all day and
make $200. That was when I thought, 'I could do this for a living.'"

During the winter of Thorn's sophomore year, he and a friend, Rick
Hauchman, who also played guitar with Big Fat Gap, went to Durango,
Colorado, on a ski trip. One afternoon while in Durango they wandered
into a local music store, Canyon Music Woodworks, to kill some time.
One of the store employees, Anders Beck, says, "They picked up some

instruments and just proceeded to shred the shit out of them. My immediate reaction was who the hell are these guys?" Beck was a local musician and blown away by what he heard from Thorn and Hauchman. He introduced himself to the two and invited them to a party later that night where his band the Salty Dogs would be. "That night we went to my friend Robin Davis's house and played some music," says Beck. "It was me, Robin, Travis Book, Andy, and Rick. We played tons of music into the wee hours of the morning, which became a major theme in our lives. We went skiing the next day and played more music the next night and then Andy and Rick had to go back to North Carolina." They all agreed the vibe of their two jam sessions was pretty great, and Beck and Book hatched a plan to get Thorn and Hauchman to come back out to Colorado for the summer.

In the summer of 2003, Hauchman and Thorn returned to Durango to pick up the musical conversation they had started with Beck, Book, and Davis on their ski trip a few months before. The chemistry was still there, and the five musicians started a band, the Broke Mountain Bluegrass Band, with Beck on dobro, Book on bass, Davis on mandolin, Hauchman on guitar, and Thorn on banjo. Their name came from an afternoon playing Frisbee golf, when Hauchman remarked how much money they did not have at the time, saying, "We are just a broke mountain band."[2] Beck jokes that he was the worst musician in the band, so it became his job to act as manager. He booked a bunch of gigs all over Colorado and the band spent the summer traveling around in Book's 1987 Toyota 4Runner, swimming during the day, camping at night, and playing to twenty or so people whenever they had a gig. Beck says the couple of months they traveled around gave him a new appreciation for Thorn's talent. "Traveling around, I got to see a lot of other banjo players play. I knew Andy was good, but I didn't know how good, then I see all these other banjo players and I realize holy shit this guy is ridiculous." Yonder Mountain String Band guitarist Adam Aijala had the same reaction the first time he met Thorn when Broke Mountain stayed at his house in Nederland while they were driving around Colorado for the summer. "He was playing one of my guitars and I was like holy crap this guy is good at everything. He plays fiddle, he plays mandolin. He is an awesome dude."

Toward the end of the summer, they worked their way toward the town of Lyons and secured a spot in the RockyGrass Bluegrass Festival band contest. In addition to the band contest, they all entered the individual instrument contests. Thorn easily won the banjo contest, and Davis was winner on the mandolin. Beck says he had to keep the uber-talented Thorn from also entering the Dobro contest. "When we started the band, he would pick up my Dobro and be better than me," laughs Beck. "The only way to stop it was to not let him play my Dobro anymore. Andy said he wanted to enter the Dobro contest and I said to him, 'No dude, not cool. Not cool at all.' I wouldn't let him do that." Following the individual contests was the band contest, which Broke Mountain won. No small achievement for a band that had been around for less than two months and whose entire experience was driving around the Colorado mountains for the summer partying and playing whatever gigs they could find. Winning meant that Hauchman and Thorn had to return to Colorado to continue to play with the band the next summer. "When you walk offstage after winning," says Beck, "you have all these festival promoters saying, 'Hey, come play our event.' You immediately start getting paid real money. It is a big deal for all the smaller bands in Colorado, so Andy and Rick had to come back." Over the next couple of winters and the following summer, Thorn returned to Colorado to play with Broke Mountain. The following summer, he brought longtime friend Stickley to replace Hauchman, who was unable to make the trip.

Broke Mountain fit perfectly into the Colorado bluegrass scene born in the mountain towns and the campgrounds of Telluride, first with Hot Rize and continued over the years with Leftover Salmon, The String Cheese Incident, and Yonder Mountain String Band. They were part of the next generation of bluegrass bands who were just as equally into traditional music as they were jambands like Phish and Widespread Panic. They used bluegrass instrumentation, but like Salmon they im-provised and jammed onstage each night. It was an atmosphere where it was completely comfortable to have a traditional Jimmy Martin tune existing next to a rip-roaring sixteen-minute jam, next to a familiar rock tune. It was a world Salmon helped create.

As the band continued to build up a head of momentum, Stickley says, "The Durango dudes in the band, Travis, Anders, and Robin, wanted to come to the bluegrass mecca of North Carolina to record an album." So, they drove out and convened in the basement studio of Dewey Brown, a friend of Stickley's. Brown was the fiddler for Ralph

Broke Mountain Bluegrass Band, "a pretty amazing farm team," in 2004 (from left): Rick Hauchman, Travis Book, Andy Thorn, Robin Davis, and Anders Beck. Courtesy of Andy Thorn.

Stanley and the Clinch Mountain Boys and lent his considerable talents to two tracks on the album. The album *Cabin in the Hills* perfectly captures the vibe of the band with Stickley and Thorn's obsession with hard-driving, contemporary bands like Doyle Lawson & Quicksilver and the Lonesome River Band, meshing seamlessly with the Colorado contingent's love of Hot Rize and the songwriting of Benny Galloway. It was what Stickley called, "A pretty rippin' hybrid of east meets west bluegrass picking and singing." Unfortunately, just as the band seemed poised to take the jamgrass world by storm, they would be gone, with everyone having scattered to bigger projects. In hindsight, the immediate success of Broke Mountain is not surprising. Yes, they were a band that only formed a few months prior to taking the stage at the Rocky-Grass Bluegrass Festival and the success they started finding immediately after their win was extraordinary, but they featured an absurd amount of untapped talented musicians who were just starting to discover how great they could be. That greatness would be fully revealed after they all left Broke Mountain.

After two summers and a couple of winters of touring around Colorado, Broke Mountain was ready to make a go of it full-time, but Thorn was hesitant. He was still in college and not ready to move to Colorado. "I was definitely a little scared of fully moving at the time," says Thorn. At the same time, he received an offer to join Larry Keel's band. Thorn spent some time at the Galax Fiddler Convention and played with a pair of musicians, Dave VanDeventer and Mark Schimick, who were members of Keel's band. They told Keel about the talented young banjo picker they had played with, and Keel, who was thinking of adding a banjo to the band, asked Thorn to come to his house to play and see how they got along. "I instantly loved Andy's playing," says Keel. "He is excellent with all the traditional styles, but he's also very improvisational and a total free spirit. That's a winning combination." Keel invited Thorn to join the band. The opportunity was perfect for Thorn as he "was totally into Larry Keel & Natural Bridge at the time," and allowed him to stay in North Carolina and finish his final year of school.

Broke Mountain carried on for a few more months after Thorn's exit from the band, until Book was invited to join another upcoming band, the Infamous Stringdusters, to replace their outgoing bassist Alan Bartram. Book had met the band at the International Bluegrass Music Association's annual festival, when the Stringdusters needed a bass player to fill in for a set they had scheduled and asked Book to fill in. A few weeks later he got a call asking if wanted to join the band. Despite knowing what it meant for Broke Mountain, Beck told him, "You have to do it."

After losing Book and Thorn, Broke Mountain knew they were done as a band and played their last show September 4, 2005, at the Four Corners Folk Festival in Pagosa Springs, Colorado. Following the last show, Beck and Davis joined Benny Galloway in the Wayward Sons. Beck soon received an invite to join another young, upcoming band, Greensky Bluegrass. Stickley joined the Biscuit Burners for a short time before leaving to start his own band, the Jon Stickley Trio. For all of them, their time in Broke Mountain was a special time. "It makes me happy to look back on that period," says Stickley. "None of us had commitments, bills, wives, or any of the other stuff that can add pressure to a situation. It was just five dudes rolling around Colorado picking, camping, hiking, and enjoying the hell out of life. We didn't make any money at the time so we didn't even have that to worry about. We knew we sounded good, but I don't think we realized exactly how talented we were at the time." Their time together in Broke Mountain was a crucial learning experience they took with them when they moved onto bands that would find national success. For Beck, he says he learned a lot from Thorn, who he felt understood the traditional side of bluegrass much better than he because of his North Carolina roots. "He taught me how to play bluegrass right," says Beck. "You can't bastardize it until you learn to do it right, in my opinion. Those were formative years because we were playing pretty traditional bluegrass. We were writing songs, but still playing pretty traditional-style bluegrass." Some of those songs, including Thorn's "Thornpipe," Book's "Long Lonesome Day," and "How Far I'd Fall for You," and Beck's "Broke Mountain Breakdown," came to find new homes among the bands they moved on to. Despite the all-too-short existence of the Broke Mountain Bluegrass Band that streaked across the sky for a moment like a comet, their legacy was secure with all its former members finding wider fame than they ever thought possible. "As time goes on," says Beck, "it turns out Broke Mountain was a pretty amazing farm team for lot of bluegrass bands out there now." Beck's statement is wholly accurate, as all Broke Mountain has established themselves in bands that were the next generation of jamgrass bands. Beck says, "It was just the five of us hippies picking music and sitting around a living room and now those hippies have gone onto do some pretty cool shit."

Following his time with Broke Mountain, Thorn jumped right on tour with Keel. His whole last semester of college he was on the road touring every weekend. He would leave Chapel Hill each week for the three-hour drive to Keel's home in Virginia to meet up with the band and get in the van to hit the road. Keel's band toured hard at the time, and for Thorn it was his first real road experience and an eye-opener. Still, he values the time for how much he learned from Keel. His time with Keel came with the bonus of being introduced to so many of Keel's musician friends, whom Thorn looked up to. He says, "That was an amazing time of learning for me. That was the real reason I wanted to play with Larry, because he was one of my favorite artists. I learned so much from him." Keel knew Thorn was a big Leftover Salmon fan and shared many stories of his and Vann's time playing together. Keel recognized a similar, shared musical spirit between the two. "Andy has taken on the spirit of Mark to the highest degree. He is like Mark reincarnated, but with his own style."

During his tenure with Keel, Thorn found time to record his first solo album, *Bolin Creek*. Thorn had a backlog of songs he accumulated over the years and felt it was time to record them. Thorn recruited all his music-playing friends from over the years, including Keel, Book, Stickley, Schimick, and many of his bandmates from Big Fat Gap, for the album. The resulting album was well received, with *Bluegrass Un-limited* saying, "*Bolin Creek* is a totally delightful production and establishes Andy Thorn as a rising star in bluegrass music."

Despite the positive experience Thorn was having learning and playing with Keel, he admits, "I got burnt out kind of fast. They were on the road a lot in a van. I got a little road weary." He left after spending about a year and half with Keel and returned to playing with Big Fat Gap. The idea of being home and not having to travel to make money playing music was appealing at the time. Big Fat Gap was well established and could make a good income without the grind of touring in a van. Thorn taught the occasional music lesson to help make a few bucks, but mostly relied on his income from Big Fat Gap. "I didn't need a lot to get by, I was just having fun," says Thorn. He stayed with Big Fat Gap for the next two years until he finally felt he was ready to get back out on the road. He let some friends know he was on the lookout for a new road gig, when his friend, Pandolfi, told him he was going to be leaving his current spot as the banjo player for the Emmitt–Nershi Band and recommended Thorn to take his spot. Pandolfi was leaving to join Thorn's former Broke Mountain bandmate, Book, in the Infamous Stringdusters.

The timing was perfect for Thorn, who after two years with Big Fat Gap was ready to get on the road again. He packed up his station wagon and drove out to Colorado. The Emmitt–Nershi Band had a full slate of tour dates and festival spots already lined up for the summer. Thorn says, "I drove straight out there and stashed all my big shit in Nershi's closet. I love to camp and hike and I did that all summer in between gigs. I would show up at the airport when I needed to be there or at the van when we were going somewhere. I probably didn't live anywhere for almost a year."

In between Salmon's last show and Thorn joining Emmitt–Nershi, there was little contact between Herman and Emmitt. They rarely saw each other and spoke even less. They played together a handful of times when their paths crossed at a festival, but for all concerned, Leftover Salmon was done. Everything related to the band was dormant. Manager John Joy had closed his offices and moved to Hawaii. He stayed vaguely in touch by helping book some solo shows for Herman, but says, "It got to the point where I was just burnt. I told Vince I was going to back out and took a break from working with him."

One day, early in 2007, Emmitt felt he should call Joy. Everyone's various side projects were starting to see modest success. Emmitt had played High Sierra Music Festival and Telluride, as well as headlining some smaller festivals with his own band. "I was starting to see numbers coming up," says Emmitt. "I was selling records and good things were happening, but I definitely missed Salmon in a lot of ways. I began thinking about how we could get back together, but it seemed unlikely. It didn't seem it was going to happen." Some of the tension between Emmitt and Herman had begun to thaw a few months prior at a show Emmitt played in Springfield, Illinois with Garrison, Jeff Sipe, Matt Flinner, and Tyler Grant. Herman was booked to play a solo show across the street, with his show starting after Emmitt's ended. Emmitt made his way across the street after his show, and joined his longtime bandmate Herman for a lengthy portion of his set. The evening helped mend some of the tensions between the two and pointed to brighter days. With that in mind, Emmitt woke up one morning and "just had this idea in my head I should call John, not Vince, not Greg and ask if there is any interest in people hiring Salmon because I think we should consider it if they are." It had been nearly three years since Salmon played together, and absence had made the heart grow fond, as Joy informed Emmitt that he had received substantial offers for the upcoming summer. He said they had offers to play AllGood Festival, High Sierra Music Festival, Snowmass, and a Red Rocks date with moe. for "really good money." Emmitt and Joy agreed they should pursue these opportunities. They were hesitant to tell Herman, as they were unsure if he would do it. He had long opposed getting the machine going again. They knew without Herman there would be no Leftover Salmon shows. "Initially it was just John and I cooking it up," says Emmitt. "We weren't sure what Vince would say. We weren't sure if we should tell him about it or just go ahead and book the shows and then tell him. That is what we did. We just took the offers and then called Vince and said here is what we are doing. It was a little risky. I didn't know how he was going to react." Joy said if Herman was reluctant he had a way to help convince him. Since the band had called it quits, Herman had run up a substantial amount of debt on the band's credit cards. Joy says he pitched it to Herman as a way to get his debt cleared. Herman was agreeable to do the shows for both financial and personal reasons, saying, "It had been like two-and-half years and I thought, 'I miss that pile of songs. It would be fun to play them again.'" The band slowly started the ball rolling for those shows. They kept everything stripped down to a bare-bones minimum. They would hire the band for the shows, fly in, play, fly out. One show at a time. Simple, with minimal hassle.

Shortly after Emmitt and Joy talked, Emmitt received a call from Craig Ferguson, the director of Telluride Bluegrass Festival, asking if he was interested in doing a special set at Telluride that year with Herman. He suggested they could call it Drew & Vince and Friends. Emmitt and Herman agreed. The show would take place before their other reunion shows, which they felt was appropriate, as Telluride was where it all started for them. For their "Friends" they had Garrison, Martinez, and Pikelny join them. It was the last version of Salmon, minus McKay. They also invited several other friends, including Sam Bush, John Cowan, Jeff Coffin, Andy Hall, Tyler Grant, and Jeff Austin to join them throughout their set. Even with the absence of McKay, it was clear who Drew & Vince and Friends really was. Yonder Mountain String Band was asked to introduce them onstage before their set. For mandolinist Austin, it was a special moment seeing Emmitt and Herman onstage together again. He says, "For some people Telluride is Sam Bush or Emmylou Harris, but for a lot of people Telluride is Leftover Salmon, and for me Telluride is Leftover Salmon. If they are not there it is just not as fun." Those emotions carried over to the stage for Austin. He says having Emmitt and Herman together meant only one thing and it was not a Drew & Vince show. He asked Emmitt and Herman if they minded if he introduced them as Leftover Salmon, but adds, "Truth be told, I was going to do it anyway, no matter what they said. Vince always told me sometimes you just have to say, 'Fuck it,' and do what you know is right. I thought, 'Fuck it,' this is Leftover Salmon onstage at Telluride for the first time in a long time and it just sounds better when you say it like that." He took the stage with his bandmates to introduce a group who was so key in the development of Yonder.

"We are Yonder Mountain String Band and we get the great privilege of introducing this great group of musicians," said Austin from stage. "The importance of what they have done for music can never be overstated. We know what it might say in the program, but I think we all know what is really going on here. Ladies and gentlemen, Leftover Salmon!"[3] When Salmon launched into their opening tune, "Let's Give a Party," with the opening line, "Let's give a party, give it right here. You buy the whiskey. I'll buy the beer," everything seemed to get just a little better in the world. After the opening song, the emotion was clear in Emmitt's voice as he announced, "It feels good, don't it. It's great to see all of you. It's been a long time."[4]

Emmitt liked the feeling he found onstage that day at Telluride. It was a feeling that was absent in the years leading up to Salmon calling it quits in 2004. "It felt great. We had a great set," says Emmitt. "It was interesting because we played without keys. Initially we thought we were going to put the band back together without Bill. We were just going to be the five-piece, but John felt we needed some continuity and we needed Bill. So, we brought him on for next shows." The following reunion shows over the rest of the year in 2007 were also a huge hit and a reminder of the special power that was Leftover Salmon and why they were missed so much in the years they were gone. While the Emmitt–Nershi Band and Great American Taxi are both quality, enjoyable bands, there was something about the combined might of Emmitt and Herman that could not quite be replicated with their other bands.

In 2008, the year following the first reunion shows, Yonder Mountain String Band was hosting their annual String Summit Festival at Horning's Hideout in North Plains, Oregon. Emmitt and Herman were both playing the festival with their respective bands. Their individual bands were still their focus, as they were only doing a handful of reunion shows a year. Former members bassist Tye North and drummer Jeff Sipe were also playing the festival. From the stage, Austin remarked how it was a family reunion backstage with all the Colorado bands he looked up to as young musician, as he had seen members of The String Cheese Incident, the Left Hand String Band, and the Salmon Heads hanging out, saying it was like seeing his whole family tree. He joked about Salmon's huge influence saying, "We have been backstage writing them checks and stealing licks from them all day."[5] On the second day of the festival, all the past and present members of Salmon in attendance were off and hanging out. Yonder was playing two sets, and Austin had an idea to bring all the Salmon guys onstage during their closing set. When it came time for set break, all of Yonder would leave the stage, leaving Salmon and the band's longtime friend, banjo-picker Danny Barnes, onstage to continue to play.

One by one Austin invited them all onstage to play. The last invite was for Mark Vann's banjo, the Stump, which was now owned by Yonder banjo-picker Dave Johnston and was going to be played by Barnes. As they all gathered onstage and tuned up, Austin joked, "I don't know what's going on here. It looks funny to me. I don't know about you guys, but I have seen these guys somewhere before."[6] The assembled musicians launched into a fiery cover of the Dillards' "Two Hits and the Joint Turned Brown," before shredding through the rest of Yonder's first set. As they neared the end of the set, Yonder started their own "Raleigh and Spencer." Midway through the song, Yonder left the stage. Salmon and Barnes did not miss a beat, seamlessly segueing "Raleigh and Spencer" into "Fixin' to Die." For Emmitt, Herman, North, and Sipe, it would be the first time the four of them were onstage together since North and Sipe's last shows with the band eight years prior. Austin says, "When Yonder left the stage and people realized what was happening, the crowd made a sound that was guttural. It wasn't a scream. It was joy. It was like wait a fucking second, this is happening." In typical Salmon fashion, they only had a loose plan of what they were going to do, thinking maybe they would play a song or two. Yonder informed them they should play the entire set break. During their second song, "Carnival Time," Emmitt broke a string. He looked over as if to say, "I guess we are done." Austin rushed out and handed him his own mandolin, a mandolin Emmitt sold Austin years before, to continue playing. "I told him, 'No, you keep playing. We need you. We need this band. We all need you."

Despite the excitement they felt playing together again, Salmon continued to play only select dates that were low stress and nice for the wallet. "We were a full-on reunion band and loving that people were paying us a lot of money to come in and play their festivals," says Emmitt. "All we had to do was fly in for the weekend, play a show, and go home." No one in the band was seriously considering putting the band on the road full time or making a record. They all had their own projects going, Herman with Great American Taxi, Emmitt with the

Emmitt–Nershi Band, and Garrison and Pikelny with the Punch Brothers. When asked about the future of Salmon in an interview for *Relix*, Emmitt said, "We're definitely going to keep doing our side projects, which aren't even side projects at this point—they're probably the main projects. Our plan is to do two or three tours a year with Salmon. We're going to keep touring, but not like before. We're going to keep the other bands alive. It's nice to have some different things going on and not be pigeonholed into doing the same thing all the time."[7]

Pikelny, after playing the first summer of reunion shows with the band, again left the band and was replaced by Matt Flinner. While the excitement level was always there for the reunion shows, Garrison says musically they were hit or miss: "It was usually kind of a mess. We never knew who would be on drums. Jeff Sipe had a different repertoire for the band in his head than Jose did, which led to the occasional train wreck."

Despite the "occasional train wreck," the shows began to serve an important role for Herman. When the band called it quits, he was perfectly content to walk away. He had long said, "Music is something that has to feed the soul," but felt Salmon's music was not feeding him toward the end before they called it quits. "I was done," he says. "I really didn't want to get back into a situation that wasn't feeding me. I just did not think Salmon was going to ever get back together and I was fine with that." He had found new music to feed his soul, first his collaboration with Page and Wasserman, and then Great American Taxi. For the first time in a long time he was happy, having fun making music, and getting to express himself in a what he called, "A comfortable musical setting." But then Salmon got together and played at Telluride, things changed and old feelings were awoken. He says, "At one point I said I had no interest in going back to Salmon, but that first gig back at Telluride was just a pile of fun. It was great to get back into those old tunes and Salmon did feed my soul from the very first time back." Even though musically Salmon was satisfying Herman, he was unwilling to commit to the band full-time as he made clear Great American Taxi was his primary gig now. He was also reluctant to see the band restart any of the machinery associated with the band. He even chafed when Joy restarted the band's dormant website to help promote upcoming shows. "I was adamant we cannot build this machine again," says Herman, "and get back into the complexity of what we had been doing. That was the idea at first. Just hire the band for each show and take it as it comes, one show at a time."

Even with positive feelings starting to resurface about Salmon, no one thought they were getting the band back together full-time. They were all still occupied with their various bands and projects. Salmon, which for a long time had been the source of so much stress, tension, and hard feelings, was now a fun, low-pressure way to get out and play some tunes and make some good, easy money. They were a full-on reunion band. "It was good to hang with old friends," says Herman. "A lot of the tension was in the water under the bridge. Getting to do more things and have more time with my family and being able to do the things I need to do and wasn't able to do in the absolute chaos of Salmon touring, made getting together for those reunion shows much more enjoyable."

Over the next few years, Salmon continued as a pure reunion band, never interfering with the various other bands and projects everyone had going on. Emmitt and Herman hired the rest of the band for gigs. Beyond that there was never any real thought about doing anything more or making it a permanent band again. Garrison says, "It was a fun side thing to my work with Thile and the Punch Brothers at the time. I didn't really expect for things to ramp back up. It was just kind of pickup gigs that pleased our fans. The more we played, though, the more our lack of rehearsal, lack of new material, lack of general cohesion started to show, I think."

Meanwhile Emmitt and Thorn were developing a close friendship from their time together in the Emmitt–Nershi Band.

Emmitt was starting to realize how rare a talent Thorn was and invited him to sit in at the occasional Salmon reunion show. Flinner was going to have to miss an upcoming gig, and, instead of having to cancel, the band asked Thorn if he would take Flinner's spot. The show was at a poorly run festival in 2009 in Baltimore named the Traffic Jam. What was originally supposed to be an outdoor festival was moved inside to the Sonar Lounge due to lack of planning on the promoter's part. As the day wore on, it became clear getting paid might prove to be difficult as the promoters were not seeing the turnout they hoped for and were starting to avoid the bands. Joy cornered one of the promoters and told him Salmon would not be taking the stage unless they were paid in cash first. The promoter, with Joy following him, began going from bar regis-

Andy Thorn (left) and Drew Emmitt with the Emmitt–Nershi Band at DelFest in 2012. Photograph by the author.

ter to bar register gathering cash until he had $40,000 in mostly fives and tens, which Joy stuffed into his pockets. The band followed this show with a stop at ekoostik hookah's annual Hookahville Festival before heading home. Flinner could make the Hookahville show and had flown in to replace Thorn. Playing with Flinner made the band realize how well they meshed with Thorn musically, and a seed of change was planted in everyone's mind.

Over the following year, Thorn continued to sit in or replace Flinner whenever he was unable to make a show. It was becoming clear Thorn was uncommonly talented and filled a hole missing since Vann passed away. Garrison remembers a run of shows with Thorn where everything just "clicked." As the band was beginning to think more and more about moving forward full-time again, it was clear the future had to be with Thorn, who was revitalizing the band with his infectious, youthful spirit, and inventive playing. "Andy really helped tie the room together," says Herman. "It was like the tripod we had with Mark. It felt we had three legs on the frontline again. It felt really good. Andy was definitely the key to wanting to get after it again." Salmon realized the answers they had been looking for were there all along. The feeling was so reminiscent of what they had with Vann that Thorn says Herman even accidentally called him Mark one night during a show. While Flinner was an exceptional talent, it was obvious after playing with Thorn who the band needed with them. "I had the unpleasant job of calling up Matt and telling him we were hiring Andy," says Emmitt, "which was difficult, because I admire Matt quite a bit. He is a great banjo and mandolin player. He was awesome, but he didn't fit the chemistry of the band. The more I played with Andy, the more I realized he was the one."

One of the contributing factors that led to the eventual hiatus was continually trying to find a replacement for Mark. The constant turnover began to wear on the band. With the addition of Thorn, worry over who would be with the band tomorrow evaporated. While they had played with an array of ultra-talented banjo players since the passing of Vann, something was still missing and it was the something that made Salmon uniquely Salmon. Thorn was the missing something. Like Vann, Thorn plays the banjo in a most un-banjo way and it is that uniqueness that is at the heart of Salmon's music. Still, Thorn, as Vann had done nearly two decades prior, at first struggled with how to create the volume needed from his banjo to be able to play with electric instruments. "I wasn't used to playing that loud," he says. "I didn't have my banjo rigged up properly. It was so much to figure out. Emmitt–Nershi was a jammy band, but we didn't have drums. On the banjo, there are certain things you have to do to be that loud and still sound good and I didn't figure that out for a while." Thorn was eventually able to find the space Vann inhabited in Salmon's music and make it his own. Still, he admits at times he struggled to fully comprehend all Vann did on the banjo, saying, "I can't figure out a lot of the stuff he does. It is so weird and awesome. It is different and cool. I was trying to learn 'Funky Mountain Fogdown,' and I don't think I ever really got it right. The picking part is so strange. I love it." Thorn avoided playing it for a long time out of respect for Vann, whom he held in such high regard. Even after he got to a point where he felt he was playing "Funky Mountain Fogdown" in a way that did justice to what Vann originally created, he delivered it as a tribute to Vann's memory and legacy.

The importance of the addition of Thorn was apparent, not just to Salmon, but also to their friends and family, who had struggled along with them at the immeasurable loss of Vann. "Even though they had tremendous players like Noam and Matt Flinner, it was just different," says Sam Bush. "Thank goodness for Andy. He is just the right personality for them. He is the best guy in the world to get along with." For Emmitt and Herman, he filled more than just a musical role. The trio of Emmitt, Herman, and Vann was looked at as a tripod that helped support the rest of the band. With the loss of Vann, the tripod was missing a leg and no longer able to provide the support it used to. All the banjo players they had since Vann were amazing and talented, but none clicked with the pair like Thorn did. Thorn would prove to be the key to the band's rebirth, not only musically but personally. Upon joining the band, he already had personal connections with both Emmitt from his time with the Emmitt–Nershi Band, and Herman, whom he had recently come to know through his sons Silas and Colin, who were friends of Thorn. This allowed him to be a buffer to the two as they slowly reconnected their friendship that had become strained over the previous years. "We all like to do the same things," says Thorn. "Drew and I love to ski and mountain bike, and Vince just loves to pick, and I will pick all day. So, we became good friends and I think that was the difference. They had that friendship with Mark and they needed that third personality in there." With Thorn, they were a complete band again. They felt the energy they had been missing was back. Their future seemed secure and the band could go back to simply worrying about the music. Emmitt states, "When Andy joined, that's when things took off. When we got the chemistry back. After all these years he was one who made it a band."

With Thorn on board it was becoming real again and they knew they needed a plan going forward. "We were starting to play with the idea of doing more shows, jumping back into the rat race a bit," says Garrison. "We knew we needed to produce something to sell ourselves and especially needed to feature Andy's contributions to the band." Salmon could no longer just play a handful of reunion-type shows a year with nothing new to show for it. If they did, they risked becoming a novelty nostalgic act. "We came to the realization we needed to shit or get off the pot with the Salmon thing," says Herman, "and we knew Andy was the guy to help us do that." With this realization, Salmon wanted to push forward and record an album, but they had no money. Or so they thought. Since reuniting, the band had been collecting paychecks, making sure expenses were covered and pocketing the rest. As they began to build some momentum and play more and more reunion-type shows, Joy helped the band remove any prior debts they had and restart the business side of things, giving them "a clean slate moving forward." Joy, who was always looking forward to tomorrow even when the band was not, had been preparing for the band's future. He says, "I knew we needed capital to run this business again. I was stashing away some money in the bank. It's their money, they just never looked at the account. They were happy with what they were getting." At dinner one night while on tour, Joy, Emmitt, and Herman began discussing the possibility of recording a new album. Joy told the pair, "If we are going to do this, let's go for it." They agreed but asked how they could afford it, thinking they had no money. Joy told them he had that covered, "That was when I revealed I had stashed away enough money to record the album. They were floored they had all this money saved up and could do the record."

With the issue of how to pay for a new album taken care of, the band prepared to start work on it. They had a short run of shows coming up at the Mishawaka Amphitheatre in Bellevue, Colorado, at the start of the summer in 2011 and thought it was an ideal time to get some pre-production work in together. They convened a few days before the shows in some cabins they had rented along the river. Their time on the river showed how far they had come since ending the band nearly eight years prior. "Everyone had grown quite a bit musically," says Garrison. Salmon found they approached the writing process with a fresh perspective after time spent collaborating with other musicians. Herman says their time apart allowed for them to grow individually and as a band. "I think all the side projects we've done have brought us into the studio with kind of bigger ears and a real more comfortable, less deer-in-the-headlights kind of feeling."[8] The writing session was an eye-opening moment for the band, as it was the first time they all heard the new material everyone was working on. One of the first songs they tackled was one Herman had been writing called "Liza." The tune was a simple love song with a welcoming Caribbean flow everyone immediately latched on to. "We all thought, 'Wow, this is a great tune,'" says Thorn. The positive feelings the song created was palpable. Whereas in the past, it was often a struggle to work together on new songs, now with the tensions and bad blood from the prior years starting to recede further and further in the rearview mirror, the band found they enjoyed working together. During their writing retreat, they also worked out arrangements for an Emmitt tune, "Gulf of Mexico," and a Thorn instrumental with no name at the time, but that would come to be called "Aquatic Hitchhiker," after a sign Emmitt saw in Montana that said, "Stop Aquatic Hitchhiking." "Aquatic Hitchhiker," was based on a warm-up roll Thorn did on his banjo. "It's a right-hand pattern I do a lot," explains Thorn. "You can do it on a lot of different chord shapes. I showed it to the guys and said play some chords over this and it sounded really cool. Greg thought of the weird rhythmic thing for the opening and it made it sound so trippy. I was like let's slow it down and that became the intro and then bam, it was a whole song. That song is so cool because everyone contributes to it." The simple warm-up roll, with the help of the rest of the band, was transformed into an epic acoustic journey. This collaborative effort pointed the band in a new direction, who in the past usually worked separately on new songs. The ease with which everyone was working and collaborating was a refreshing change from the struggles and tense times they had experienced working on their last album nearly eight years prior. "That is when it hit me, this is going to go somewhere," says Thorn.

The band hit a snag a few months later following their annual Thanksgiving shows. Herman discovered he could not find his iPad and thought he might have left it at the hotel they stayed at after the shows. The iPad had all the music he had been writing for the new album. For Herman, who did not often prepare so extensively for work on their albums, it was a potentially devastating loss. Joy set out to see if he could track it down. Using Herman's Apple login, he could see the iPad was still at the hotel using the Find Your Phone App. He called the hotel to let them know it was still on the premises. The hotel said they had not found it. Joy went down to the hotel to talk with them. When he arrived, he noticed on the App the iPad moved from the hotel to a nearby house in a not so nice part of town. He headed to the house and started banging on the door. While at the house he noticed the iPad moved again and was now back at the hotel. Whoever had the iPad knew that Joy was hot on their trail. Joy went back to the hotel and confronted them. "I said where is it, I know it's here," says Joy. "Suddenly someone said, 'Oh, here it is.' It was so fucking funny. It wasn't, but it was. A lot of the music from Vince that went on *Aquatic Hitchhik-*

er was on that iPad." With the iPad and all its contents safely back in Herman's hands, Salmon set out to start recording for the new album.

For the new album, Los Lobos' Steve Berlin was brought on board to produce. Berlin has long been recognized as one of the premier producers in the country and the band was excited to have him as part of the project. To help Salmon and Berlin get acquainted, they decided to spend a couple of days working in Herman's home studio. "We kicked each other's tires," says Berlin. "We spent some time messing around with the songs and they got a glimpse of my process and vice versa." Their initial sessions proved Berlin and Salmon had chemistry as they completed a couple more songs, "Bayou Town," and "Sing Up to the Moon." Berlin says working with Salmon was a comfortable experience that felt familiar to what he did in Los Lobos. "In an odd kind of way, they resemble my band," he explains. "There are two main songwriters with two totally different styles. They have the capability of playing many different styles of music authoritatively. It was like hanging with my own guys. On my end, it felt like a seamless fit." Following their time in Herman's home studio, they followed up with another session at Denver's Mighty Fine Studios, the same place they had worked on their previous album.

While the band was flying high from the good feelings and success from the recent recording sessions, it was becoming clear they had a serious issue in the band becoming harder and harder to ignore. "We had a full-blown alcoholic we were dealing with," says Joy about McKay. Over the years, the band watched as his drinking increased to the point where it was becoming detrimental to not just himself, but to everyone in the band as his destructive choices were getting more and more out of control. In the years before the band broke up, McKay's drinking, while always a source of tension among the band, was just one of many issues the band was dealing with and often easier to ignore with everything engulfing them at the time. Since the band's return, McKay's drinking and the negative behaviors that came along with it became more noticeable and harder to ignore. Garrison says, "The Bill situation was becoming tough on everyone." There had been some shows where Joy says, "It was really bad and he was a drunken embarrassment."

Shortly after New Year's Eve in 2008, a story broke that McKay was being accused of sexual assault following a party. While the charges would eventually be dropped, the chaos and drama that seemed to be following McKay was swallowing up the whole band and threatening to blow up all they had worked for since returning. When the story first broke, conflicting statements from the band about the situation began to emerge into the press. A local writer in Boulder arranged an interview with Emmitt under the pretense of chatting about some upcoming solo shows he was promoting. As soon as the writer got Emmitt on the phone, she cornered him with questions about what was going on with McKay. The story was still breaking and fresh and no one in the band knew the full story yet or had got together discuss what they were going to do. Under pressure from the writer, Emmitt said, "We have been aware of Bill's drinking problem for a long time. We've been trying to help him, but we knew he was going down this path." Then blurted out, "He is no longer with this band."[9] As facts started to come out about what happened and exonerating McKay, Emmitt's comments started to create a "shit-storm" within the band, with everyone wanting to know why Emmitt was making pronouncements without talking with the rest of the band or knowing all the facts. Joy released an official statement contradicting Emmitt's initial statement. "Drew told me he didn't know what to say when asked," recalls Joy. "He was torn up about it. It was our first real conflict since the band came back." Emmitt released another statement a short time later that in part read:

> With a level head and a heavy heart, I appreciate this opportunity to respond to the recent article in the *Colorado Daily* . . . In retrospect and having more time to better understand the situation, I realize I was reacting from a place of confusion and hurt, troubled by even the thought Bill could or would do something like he's being accused of. The truth is, the dynamic between members of any band is very difficult at times. Bill is a brother to me, and a best friend. It was unfair of me to air any personal gripes between Bill and myself publicly. I can only hope people understand my comments came from a place of personal turmoil and not as an official statement from the band on Bill's innocence or guilt or on the status of him as a member of Leftover Salmon.[10]

A few weeks later, McKay was cleared of all charges.

Even though the horrible allegations against McKay had proven to be untrue, the band all still sensed there was a problem with McKay and his drinking. Salmon had demonstrated over the years they were a band that did not like conflict. They found it easier to look the other way and not confront McKay. Being an alcoholic in a band like Salmon was tough. They are a band that likes to party and their backstage is always awash with good times. It was hard for McKay to avoid being around the temptations that can lead one to drink. It became apparent he was either on or he was off the wagon, there was no middle ground, and in the environment where Salmon exists, it was hard to be on. Joy had a few conversations with McKay about his behavior and noticed a change for the better. The two went out for lunch right before the band's Thanksgiving shows. Joy wanted to let McKay know how proud he was of the effort McKay was making with his drinking and to give him a little pep talk to keep it up, knowing the band was about to get busy and hectic as they entered the studio to work on the new album and prepared for the New Year's Eve run. "I told him how much we needed him," says Joy, "I told him how much we loved him and reminded him he is a part of this. I told him we are going for it with this new record and we needed him there 100 percent."

Salmon was going to close out the year with a short West Coast tour ending in Portland, Oregon, for two shows December 30 and 31. They would stay in Portland to head into the studio to complete work on the album with Berlin. The tour started in San Diego and Joy noticed McKay seemed to be keeping to himself, which was a good thing, "Because if he was around us he wound be drinking and everything." The next day in San Francisco, Joy had lunch with McKay to let him know again how proud he was of how McKay was handling everything and to encourage him to continue doing what he was doing. Later in the day, Joy arrived at the venue, the Great American Music Hall. While eating dinner backstage, Garrison came over and informed him, "Bill is fucking wasted." At showtime as the band prepared to hit the stage, Joy noticed McKay was not around. In the chaotic, crowded atmosphere backstage the rest of the band, besides Garrison and Joy, had not even noticed McKay's absence. As the band prepared to take the stage, Joy tracked down McKay in another dressing room passed out on the couch. After some effort, he was finally able to wake McKay and get him to the stage. McKay spent much of the set barely playing as he struggled to stay awake at his keys. For a band who had often taken the stage in various altered states of mind and never let it impact their performance in a noticeable way, McKay crossed a line by allowing it to impact and ruin a show. At set break, the band cleared their friends and family out of their normally wide open and welcoming dressing room to address McKay. According to Joy, it was "high tension." Though the tension was slightly broken by the presence of legendary activist and icon Wavy Gravy, who is a good friend of the band and happened to still be in the dressing room. As things began escalating among the band and McKay, Wavy Gravy tried to excuse himself and leave the room. Joy stopped him and told him to sit back down, informing him, "It's just rock 'n' roll, it's nothing you haven't seen before." Still, even though it was rock 'n' roll, the band felt it was "an embarrassment to have him onstage." McKay seemed to get coherent enough to get through the rest of the show, but to the band it was clear this was a situation that could not continue.

Back at the hotel after the show, Emmitt, Herman, and Joy met to discuss what to do about McKay. Their initial reaction was to send him home. But on their minds was their friend, "Michigan" Mike Torpie, who had committed suicide a few weeks before. "A lot of how we handled things that night came back to Michigan Mike. We recognized Bill was in a dark place and we needed to watch over him a bit," says Joy. "We couldn't just send him home. We needed to get him to Portland with us and try and get through the weekend as best we could."

The band headed north to Portland, Oregon, for the final two nights of the run. Emmitt and Joy stopped by McKay's room to talk with him and to try to encourage him through the final two shows. Following soundcheck everyone scattered to get dinner and headed back to the hotel to rest up for the show. Their first set that night was going to be a combined one with Cracker performing the *O Cracker, Where Art Thou?* album in its entirety. As showtime approached and the band headed onstage, they noticed McKay was not around. They started to turn around, but the crowd had already seen them and Joy told them to just head on stage and play. He called McKay's hotel and got a groggy sounding McKay, who was clearly just waking up when Joy called. McKay made it to the venue mid-set. Joy told him to stay away from the stage, as there were already stories spinning around the internet about McKay being passed out onstage in San Francisco. Joy reasoned McKay strolling on stage late, halfway through the set, would only add to the drama and rumors. He figured it was easier to explain McKay's absence from the first set as a planned thing, saying the band decided to not use keys onstage with Cracker. The band came offstage and there was further confusion and building tension as the rest of the band confronted McKay. "Still, they played the second set with Bill," says Joy, "and it was awesome. He was sobered up enough. If anything, he was just waking up from the night before because he was so banged up then."

Back at the hotel, Emmitt, Herman, and Joy again reconvened to figure out what to do. While the second set showed how great McKay could be, his inability to play the night before and missing the first set was just too much for Joy who told the other two, "We are going to record a new record and this guy is going to ruin your career. The best thing for the band and Bill is to be done with him. It's him or me. I can't work with him anymore. If we are going to go for it again this guy is way too much of a wild card to gamble on. If this happens on a little run, what is going to happen when we start do some real dates and are banging after it on the road?" Emmitt and Herman agreed it was best for the band and for the health of McKay for him to be out of Salmon. As was usual for the band, they agreed what should be done, but did not commit to any action or how they would go about it.

The next day as they started to prepare for the evening's show, word started to trickle in McKay was not answering his phone or coming to the door of his hotel room. Finally, someone saw him, but said he "Reeks like booze." The band continued to try to get ahold of him throughout the day. Right before the show was supposed to start, they still had not heard from McKay and finally had enough. They made the decision to get the keys off the stage. That was it. They were done with him. They were going to go on as a five-piece without him. Joy says, "It had been a long time since they played as five-piece and I remember them walking onstage and they were definitely a little nervous. But they went up and slayed it and it turned into one of the most fantastic New Year's Eve shows." After everything they had been dealing with and the stress from McKay, it was a relief to not be worrying about him onstage. "We never had to talk about it again," says Joy. "After that night, there didn't need to be any more discussion. Throughout the night we kept having people making sure he was safe in his room. The next day we called him a cab and changed his plane ticket. He went to the airport and we changed hotels and got into the studio."

Shortly after New Year's Eve, McKay sent a letter to Joy apologizing for everything and Joy returned one reinforcing how much the band loved him, but that this was clearly the best for him. "I don't think the road was the best place for him," says Emmitt. "We all realized that and made the choice to let him go. For us it was a relief. It felt like getting us getting back to what the band was about and has always been about. It was a lightening of sorts. For Bill, it was too." It was a turning point for McKay as he has been sober since shortly after he returned home from Portland and has remained a vital part of the Colorado music scene. "I thought it was the best thing for him to not bring everyone's career's down and for him to get the help he needed," says Joy. "As unfortunate as it is, it seemed everyone ended up where they needed to end up."

With the weight of the McKay situation now removed, Salmon breathed a sigh of relief and entered Cloud City Studios in Portland to finish work on the new album. "The band was really focused in Portland," says Garrison, "and I think we all started to feel the collective energy we could generate as a five-piece." With Berlin's help, the band picked up right where they had left off a few weeks prior at Herman's house and Mighty Fine Studios. "He understands what we are going for as a band better than any producer we have ever worked with," says Emmitt. "He has some creative ways of thinking and doing things and is so good with different guitar tones. He has such cool ways of producing." Starting with the session at Herman's house when everyone in the band "laid all [their] songs on the table," through the time in Mighty Fine and Cloud City, the band collaborated like never before. Many of the songs brought into the sessions were just ideas or outlines and the band worked together to flesh them out. Berlin was integral to this process, helping to arrange lyrics and melodies for the in-progress tunes. He says, "I wasn't coming up with the songs, I just thought about them in a different way. I made them less jammy I guess. They are still jammy, I just cut out the stuff I thought made for a long record. I wanted it to be a streamlined, concise record. Whatever experiments we did seem to work. They were so receptive and excited about the changes, which was gratifying for me." The resulting album, named *Aquatic Hitchhiker* after Thorn's instrumental track, would be the first album of all-original material the band ever completed. On past albums, they always included some obscure cover or added a song written by one of their friends, but the positive collaborative energy surrounding the band had them focusing on what the five of them could do. "It felt a lot easier and streamlined to go at it again as the five-piece. There were definitely certain songs we missed the keyboards," says Emmitt, "but we all felt we could just play a little more and cover it and it was great." *Aquatic Hitchhiker* was a renaissance release, harkening back to the best days of the band. It is a reminder of all they have accomplished and serves to introduce the greatness that is still to come. Herman says *Aquatic Hitchhiker* "Showed the evolution of the band, both in playing and songwriting. It felt good, comfortable, and went to some new places. We were happy with the results." *Relix* magazine recognized all of this in its review of the album, declaring the band has "picked up where they left off," and that they "sound revitalized."[11]

Aquatic Hitchhiker was released in May 2012 with a free street show in downtown Denver. The band shut down the streets in front of Joy's office and had 8,000 people show up on a sunny afternoon. "That served to put us back on the map," says Garrison. "It was incredible." It was a moment that proved how far the band had come since they first decided to test the waters and play a few shows together to see if their music did as Herman said it once had, and "fed his soul." From the first time, back onstage together at Telluride, Leftover Salmon found the music they created together fed not their only souls, but those of countless others as well. As Jeff Austin told the band years before onstage at String Summit, "We need this band." Now after years of trying to find themselves again, Salmon was finally beginning to understand what Austin meant. After being lost for so long since the passing of Vann, they felt whole. "It felt like we were back," says Emmitt. "We were pretty excited about being a band again. It made us feel we were finally moving forward again."

Chapter 11

ALWYN ROBINSON

Alwyn is a standout guy and a stellar musician. When I first met him I just knew him as the hotshot drummer Greg brought in. I appreciate how he has remained himself musically in the Leftover Salmon mix, and it's appropriate they feature him during shows these days. He has brought the band to a different level with his approach to drums.—*Tyler Grant (Grant Farm)*

"**L**uckily enough we got Alwyn," says Andy Thorn, recalling the addition of drummer Alwyn Robinson to replace the departing Jose Martinez. "Alwyn is just the best. Since he has joined he has taken the band to a higher level. He has taken it completely over the top. He is such a good player and a great guy to be around." While Robinson, who exudes a cool, old-school jazz soul, seemed on paper an odd fit for Salmon, a jazz-inspired drummer with no connection to them or their world, he proved to be a masterful addition as his youthful energy and inventive drumming helped propel the band into their third decade. Much like his predecessors Jeff Sipe and Martinez, Robinson's jazz background, while a seemingly unlikely starting point for a drummer in a band born from bluegrass roots, was an absolutely splendid fit for Salmon. "For some reason—Jeff Sipe was a jazz drummer, Jose was a jazz drummer, and now Alwyn is also a jazz drummer—it seems jazz drummers are a good fit for this band," says Emmitt. "You have to have a lot of chops to play jazz and you have to have a lot of chops to play in this band because of all the different styles. You have to be able to play really fast two-beat, which is difficult for a drummer."

Martinez was with the band for over a decade since joining in 2000 and helped them weather some tumultuous years as they worked through the passing of Vann, the hiatus, and the slow reunion of the band. Despite his aversion to being on the road, his calm, steady presence was a rock of reliability for the band during those difficult years. But Martinez wanted to be home full time and decided to leave the band. "That was kind of scary because he was great," Thorn says, "but you could sense he had one foot out the door and wasn't loving the road. It's difficult to have someone like that around because it is already tough to be on the road. When people are unhappy it just makes it harder."

Prior to Martinez leaving, Salmon was swimming closer to the mainstream then they had in quite some time. Their latest album *Aquatic Hitchhiker* was receiving rave reviews and touting the band's triumphant return. *Bluegrass Unlimited* called *Aquatic Hitchhiker* a "wonderful comeback album that is full of fun and verve,"[1] while *Cincy Groove* hailed the album as a "Masterwork."[2] Thorn's addition and large role in the rebirth of the band was also getting much attention. *Blurt Magazine* stated, "Salmon founders and principal songwriters Drew Emmitt and Vince Herman have found a foil to match their energy in young banjo upstart Andy Thorn and the revitalized spirit is palpable on *Aquatic Hitchhiker*."[3]

Since the release of *Aquatic Hitchhiker*, the band had also gotten offers to be part of some higher-profile projects. They were asked to appear as the house band for the Discovery Channel's *After the Catch*, a weekly wrap-up show for the hit reality show *Deadliest Catch*. Salmon served as the house band for six shows, playing songs in and out of commercials and at times bantering back and forth with the crab boat captains who were the stars of the show. In seasons past, the show had been filmed with a different band serving as the house band for each episode. When the show moved to Breckenridge, Colorado, for the 2012 season, Leftover Salmon was the obvious choice to be the band. Things clicked so well it was decided they would remain the band for the entire season. For the band, it was a low-stress gig. They taped six shows over four days, hung out and partied with the captains from the show, and got to do it all without having to leave their home base of Colorado. The other high-profile spot was an appearance on the comedy show *Your Pretty Face Is Going to Hell* on the Adult Swim network.

The episode titled "Schmickler83," featured the lead character, Gary, an associate demon, attempting to capture the soul of Vince Herman so he can climb the corporate ladder of the demonic underworld. Throughout the episode, Gary refers to Salmon as the "premier prog-fusion washboard band," and one of the two greatest hippie jambands named after fish. The band flew down to Atlanta and filmed a live segment at the Amphitheatre in Alpharetta Park. In the end, their live performance was cut from the final edit, but the episode did include a brief appearance of them playing at the *Aquatic Hitchhiker* release party show manager John Joy arranged on the streets of Denver. It also featured snippets of three tracks from the album, "Aquatic Hitchhiker," "Sing up to the Moon," and "Stop All Your Worrying."

In the spring of 2013, the band headed into the studio to begin working on the follow-up to *Aquatic Hitchhiker*. As smooth and painless a process as the recording for the previous album was, this time was not as smooth. Again recording at Denver's Mighty Fine Audio studios, bassist Greg Garrison felt the sessions were a struggle right from the start, as "we didn't have quite enough quality material floating around" to make it work. Whereas *Aquatic Hitchhiker* was built from collaborations and band writing sessions, *High Country* featured songs mostly written individually. Even though it was the band's eighth album, it was only their second since the band reunited, and it almost fell into the classic second album trap that plagues bands where they are rushed to come up with material to complete an album and do not have time to put the same effort and care they did for the prior album.

When they first entered the studio, it was not necessarily to record a full album. They knew they eventually wanted to finish a follow-up for *Aquatic Hitchhiker*, but their first goal was to get a couple of songs ready for a special release Joy arranged. In conjunction with Colorado Brewery, Breckenridge, the band was going to release four original songs exclusively through the brewery's sampler packs on limited edition coasters. With some of the struggles they were experiencing in the studio, they chose the four tunes they felt were the most polished at the time: "High Country," "Get Up and Go," "Thornpipe," and "Two Highways." While the collaboration with Breckenridge Brewery was further proof of Joy's outside-of-the-box thinking, the idea did not quite take off the way everyone hoped. Still, it was the start of a long-lasting relationship between Salmon and Breckenridge that has found them collaborating on many ideas and events over the ensuing years. In 2015, they collaborated again, releasing a limited-edition beer, the Silver Salmon, to celebrate both of their twenty-fifth anniversaries. Salmon also marked this milestone with the release of a live album appropriately enough named 25, which gathered twenty-five live tracks from the previous two years to highlight their long career.

As they had with *Aquatic Hitchhiker*, the band enlisted Steve Berlin to produce the new album. Following the release of the four Breckenridge songs, they began to focus on cobbling a complete album into shape. With Berlin's help, they finished, "Western Skies," "Better Day," "So Lonesome," "Home Cooking," "Light in the Woods," and "Finish Your Beer." Emmitt admits there was some hesitation about the new material before they entered the studio, as everything came into the studio in various stages of completion. "The studio time was booked and we had no freakin' idea what we were going to do with it," says Emmitt, "but somehow, we managed to scare up ten original tunes. It just all kind of came out of the ether."[4] Even with Berlin's expert help and ability to pull something out of nothing, something did not quite gel in the studio, and Garrison says, "We weren't super stoked with the tracks after they were done. They were unsatisfying as a collection when we finished."

The tracks were set aside as the band took a break from work on the new album. They hit the road for a swing through the South, including a tour-ending stop at the New Orleans Jazz Festival. Their world would be thrown upside down following a show at the Howlin' Wolf in New Orleans April 27, 2013. As it was New Orleans and Jazz Fest, the show did not end until 4 a.m. Following the show and after getting all the gear broken down, the band and crew headed to a nearby bar to continue the after-party. Things began to wind down around 10 a.m. as most everyone began heading to the airport. As the party began to break up, the band's lighting technician Joe Cahill, who had plans to stay in New Orleans for a few days, left to meet up with some friends. Cahill had joined the band in the spring of the previous year and was a skilled lighting technician, who, Joy says, "was really good and a hard worker who got along with everyone." While in a cab heading to the Jazz Festival fairgrounds, Cahill's friends say, "His laughter turned into anger and rage, at which time he began to yell and trash the interior of the vehicle."[5] In his fit of rage, he also began to bite the side and top of the car while yelling at pedestrians. His friends say he threw his sunglasses out the window of the moving cab and "pulled his chain from his neck, which caused him to bleed and then tried to jump out of the window."[6] As the cab pulled to a stop near the festival grounds, Cahill leaped out of the cab. His friends tried to restrain him, but he pushed them away and ran down the street with his friends losing sight of him. He was spotted in a nearby neighborhood by two men who noticed the bloody, disheveled, and intoxicated Cahill. They described his appearance: "He may have fallen and hurt his face. He did not look like he had been beat up. But that man was bloody and that man was drunk."[7] Cahill, who was now shirtless, got into an argument with another neighbor that drew the attention of the police who were in the area for Jazz Fest. The police approached Cahill. He pushed one officer off his bike, before throwing his belt at the other. He took off running. Witnesses say it was clear "he was on a little something extra." The officers lost sight of Cahill as he ran away from him. Neighbors recall him running into the road and forcing cars to stop to avoid hitting him. They said it "looked like his mind was not right. He was drunk or high or might have taken something."[8] Cahill was eventually spotted barging into a house. The officers in pursuit heard gunshots as they approached the house. Moments later a young man came out of the house and told police he had shot Cahill, who barged into the house and began fighting with people inside. Cahill later died at the hospital. It has never been clear what caused Cahill to act the way he did the morning he was tragically killed. Was he drunk? Were there larger emotional or mental issues at play unknown to everyone? Was he on some other drugs? What could cause him to act in the completely irrational way he did that morning? These questions have never been fully answered, and it is still not known what led to Cahill acting in such an out-of-control, unpredictable manner. The violence and uncertainty of what caused Cahill to act the way he did would shake Salmon. "It was more tragedy in the Salmon family," says Joy, "as if we haven't had enough." As Salmon had done so many times before when tragedy and misfortune struck, they relied on each other and the family bonds of the band to get through yet another challenging situation.

As they had done before, Salmon did what they do best and what had gotten them through so many troubled times before—they played music. Musically, their most pressing need was to find a drummer to replace the departing Martinez. After years of turnover and turmoil, the band seemed to be in a period of relative peace and ease. That was shattered with the senseless death of Cahill and continued with the departure of Martinez. Martinez's steady drumming and easygoing personality had been central to Salmon's newfound stability, but he had long been unhappy on the road, and that unhappiness was only growing with each passing tour. "I think Jose had been worn out for a while," says Emmitt. "He was great and he was with us for a long time, but he just wasn't a fan of the road."[9] Their search for a drummer was a short one. They auditioned a few drummers and even offered the spot to drum legend Wally Ingram, who filled in for a few shows, but it was a young drummer, Alwyn Robinson, who Garrison knew, who had ended up in the drum chair. Since joining the band in 2000, Garrison, since the passing of Vann, had seen his role continue to expand with more and more involvement in business and band decisions, becoming a highly influential voice in the group over the years.

Robinson, from Marshall, Texas, had been playing drums as long as he could remember. He was born into a musical household as his father was a music teacher and both of his older brothers played drums. He was exposed to a wide range of musical styles at a young age, which would prove beneficial as by age twelve he was already playing in a local rock band, the Knowmads. They played their first paying show for fifty dollars. Shortly after, they were regularly getting booked to play around town. This led to more and more opportunities for the young drummer. Robinson was a musical sponge and says he was listening to everything he could. "The influence of my brother brought me Nirvana, the Smashing Pumpkins, A Tribe Called Quest, and De La Soul. My dad got me into Bach, Chopin, Tchaikovsky, Beethoven, and Mozart. Hanging around my friends I was listening to a lot of hardcore rap. And of course, the jazz was always there. Coltrane when I was younger and a lot of Miles, of course." In high school, Robinson was a highly decorated musician, being selected for numerous All-State and All-Region bands and orchestras. Following high school graduation, Robinson received a music scholarship at Texas Tech University, where he received a degree in classical music education and music performance. While in college, Robinson played with several groups across a wide range of musical styles. "I did it all," says Robinson. "I was in rock bands and played in the bars. I played in a steel drum ensemble. I did a lot of jazz. It was great exposure to playing in front of people. I was working four or five nights a week while in college. It was great to play in all these ensembles and get comfortable playing in front of people and to have to get comfortable playing in front of no one, because a lot of times at jazz gigs no one is there. It was cool. I got to play a lot of top-notch gigs."

Following his graduation from Texas Tech, Robinson enrolled at the University of Colorado to start work on a graduate degree in music. While pursuing his graduate degree, Robinson continued to steadily perform, but was mostly focused on jazz. While in grad school, he received a call to be part of a faculty recital. The program was focused on American and folk music. "I can't say that style was completely foreign to me as I played in some country bands growing up in Texas," says Robinson. The program was for Garrison's thesis for his doctorate, which focused on the historical connections between American jazz and roots music forms to form an argument that roots music (bluegrass, folk, etc.) should be accepted and studied at the college and university level in much the same way jazz is. Following the gig, Robinson thought nothing more of it, but it clearly resonated with Garrison, as he reached out to Robinson to see if he was interested in auditioning for the open spot in Salmon. Six months after his one and only gig with Garrison, Robinson was on his way to Fort Collins for a Leftover Salmon gig at the Aggie Theatre to audition for the band. Robinson had no awareness or concept of Salmon or what it is they did and says, "I was taking a bold leap into the unknown. I never heard of them. The only jamband I had ever listened to is the Dave Matthews Band and that is because Carter Beauford is my favorite drummer. I had never listened to Widespread Panic or Phish. I had no knowledge at all of what I was getting into. I can say it was the first time musically I stepped into something with no prior knowledge of what I was getting myself into. I had never been to a music festival. I had never done any of that stuff. It was a first for me." For Robinson, his uncertainty was balanced by his faith and belief in Garrison, whom he had admired since their gig together the previous August. "Anything Greg asks me to do," says Robinson, "I trust him. If he is asking me to participate in something, then it must be something worth checking out. He cares a lot about what he's listening to and what he is doing. I thought if he is part of something I should take advantage of this opportunity and become a part of it too, because I respect Greg so much. He is a killer musician and I trust what he hears and I trust his musical intelligence. Anything he is part of must be great."

Garrison sent Robinson a couple of tunes from *Aquatic Hitchhiker* to learn for the audition. Robinson says beyond that he did not do much research prior to trying out. At his audition, Emmitt says, "As soon as he sat down behind the drums we were amazed by his pocket and feel. We were pretty sold on him right away." They immediately asked him if he wanted the spot. He was and set out to get up to speed on what Salmon does. Joy gave him the band's albums to help him prepare. "I listened to them all," says Robinson, "and the way I learned from the record was completely different than the way they played it. After that I was like I am never listening to another record again. I am just going to learn this on the spot. Trial and error. That is how I learned it, listening to how they play it onstage. They do it so differently each time. You have to dig in and learn how they do it live."

Upon joining, Robinson, who was still in grad school at the time and a year away from graduation, informed his adviser he was joining Left-over Salmon. Robinson says the conversation with his adviser was something he will never forget. He told his adviser he had an opportunity to join Leftover Salmon and was excited about the possibilities of joining them. There were tour dates in the fall and he had to miss one class as he would be on the road. Robinson asked if it was all right to miss one day. His adviser told him, 'No, it's probably not a good idea. It does not sound like the right direction you need to be heading. If you were touring with Wayne Shorter we would let you do it." Robinson asked, "What is the difference between touring with Shorter and Leftover Salmon?" He says his adviser could not give him a good answer. "That kind of motivated me," says Robinson. "Him telling me I was doing the wrong thing and how he segregated the genres of music and telling me I joined the wrong thing because I was not playing jazz."

A few weeks after his audition, Robinson played his first gig with the band at the annual DelFest in Cumberland, Maryland, May 23, 2013. To help ease Robinson into the band, Salmon had percussionist Wally Ingram along to play with them. Ingram was a highly experienced drummer who played with everyone from Sheryl Crow to Eric Burdon to Jackson Browne to Warren Zevon to Bruce Hornsby and countless others. Over the years, Ingram had played the occasional gig with Salmon, subbing for Martinez when he could not make a gig. That first gig at DelFest was an eye-opening experience for Robinson. Not only was his first show with the band a headlining gig at a major festival, he was also to learn about the festival life that was such a part of who Salmon is. After their set, Herman asked Robinson if he wanted to hang out and have a drink. "I thought we were going to go to a local bar or something," says Robinson. Herman laughed at the idea and led Robinson into the campground where the two hung out until 7 a.m., mixing it up and partying with fans.

Robinson followed up his first show with a run of high-profile festival gigs throughout the summer, with dates at the Telluride Bluegrass Festival (featuring a sit-in from Jackson Browne), High Sierra Music Festival, AllGood Music Festival, and the Northwest String Summit. That summer as he learned the band's songs, Robinson witnessed what it was that made Salmon so special. From his drum seat each night, he watched Emmitt and Herman, and noticed the qualities the two possessed that helped make Salmon such an engaging act. "He is the man," says Robinson about Herman. "There is nobody like him. His persona onstage. His ability to get a crowd into something. His ability to read audiences. He is an entertainer. I have been onstage with some badass musicians, but I have rarely been onstage with someone who knows how to work an audience like he does. My first impression of him is the same it has always been, he is the coolest guy." Robinson continues, "Drew is a killer musician. He is playing four different instruments and is just killing it. And he is such a nice guy. Anyone that is going to allow a twenty-three-year-old to be part of their organization they have had for twenty-three years, I respect the hell out of."

As much as Robinson was in awe of his new bandmates, they were equally in awe of his raw talent that allowed him to play as a seasoned professional well beyond his twenty-three years. Much like his predecessors Sipe and Martinez, Robinson's extensive jazz background allowed him to play with an intuitive touch that gave the bluegrass heartbeat of Salmon a dynamic, engaging drive that created a wide canvas for the rest of the band to work over. "He's young, he's got great energy, he's got great chops," says Emmitt, "and the other thing is he doesn't play too loud. So, it's really created a lot more space in the music, instead of just balls-to-the-wall, all the time."[10] Robinson quickly grew comfortable with this new style of music he was playing. He admits he is always still learning new things, but that his approach to understanding Salmon's music was for him in finding the commonalities he could relate to and work from there. "Bluegrass music structure is the same as

From his seat each night, drummer Alwyn Robinson gets to watch Drew Emmitt, whom he calls a "Killer musician." Pictured here at Red Rocks Amphitheatre July 23, 2016. Photograph by the author.

jazz," he explains, "where you solo over the head. The groove is almost a train beat, which is equivalent to what I did when I was playing in country bands in Texas. The jamband elements are a lot of funk and rock, which I have done a lot of before. So, for me it was just figuring out how to put it all together with their music. I just had to put it into the context of Leftover Salmon's style."

Much like when Thorn joined two years prior, Robinson's addition pushed Salmon to uncharted directions every night. At one of Robinson's early shows, producer Berlin was sitting in with the band and was captivated by what the young drummer was capable of. "I just kept thinking, 'Wow, the sky's the limit with this guy. It is just so cool to have the bluegrass and Cajun slamgrass thing and to add this modern freeform jazz thing to it with Alwyn." Robinson and Garrison discovered a musical chemistry between them that propelled the band with a ferocity not seen since Tye North and Sipe powered the rhythm section. Dave Watts, drummer for the Motet, noticed this powerful chemistry:

"Leftover Salmon always seem to push the sonic envelope and now with Greg and Alwyn driving the train the band's sound is unstoppable." Longtime friend of the band Sam Bush also noticed the way this new rhythm section was energizing Salmon: "It seemed to me when Andy and Alwyn joined, and with Greg on bass—his playing is so solid, I just love it—it became a coherent unit that communicated and worked so well." Musically it was clear Robinson was a powerhouse and perfect for the band. It truly registered they had chosen the right guy when they went down to Mexico for the Strings & Sol Music Festival held right beside the sea, and he donned a Mexican wrestling outfit and played the entire show in costume. Yonder Mountain String Band guitarist Adam Aijala says the first time he really had a chance to listen to Robinson was at that Strings & Sol, "I always thought Jeff Sipe was the best drummer they ever had, but Alwyn is equally amazing. There is nothing he can't do. First time I listened to him I remember thinking this guy is something else."

As Salmon seemed to be hitting their stride as a reborn five-piece following the dismissal of Bill McKay and the addition of Robinson, the idea of bringing in keys again, and more specifically Little Feat's Bill Payne, started to get kicked around. Payne was a longtime friend of the band. He was one of the first people to jump onboard in 2001 when Salmon was looking for helping in organizing the benefit shows for Vann following his cancer diagnosis. He also produced the band's self-titled effort in 2004 and they had shared the stage many times over the years. As they prepared for their annual Thanksgiving shows in 2013, Salmon reached out to see if he was interested in playing with them as a guest throughout the weekend. "We hit it off there," says Payne. "From there it just blossomed. After the two nights in Boulder, they asked if I wanted to go to Mexico for the Strings & Sol Festival to play with them." Strings & Sol provided the perfect environment for Salmon and Payne to test out their developing relationship onstage in a front of a friendly, welcoming crowd. Salmon was excited when he agreed to join them, because, as Herman says, "He is Bill frickin' Payne." For Payne, who found himself with time on his hands, as Little Feat had taken time off due to Paul Barrere's diagnosis of liver cancer, it was the perfect chance to get out and play with some friends. Their couple of gigs together and time in Mexico highlighted what it is Payne found so compelling about Salmon. He says the way they played onstage togeth-

Alwyn Robinson (drums) and Greg Garrison (back right) driving the Leftover Salmon train at String & Sol 2013 with Drew Emmitt (left) and Vince Herman. Photograph by the author.

er spoke to him about the importance of being in a band. "They always bring a sense of what it is to be a band," says Payne. "A band is not an artist like James Taylor or Bruce Springsteen. Bands are reliant on each other in a way James and Bruce are not. It is a deeper commitment when you are a part of a band." For Payne, who has been playing in bands since he was fifteen, it's that shared connection between bandmates that has always inspired him. He found countless similarities between Little Feat and Leftover Salmon and it was these shared qualities that made it clear to Payne why Salmon was a band he wanted to part of. "It's the dichotomy of feeling comfort and going to comfort zones," says Payne, "but still challenging each other. That is what keeps bands together for a long time. It is what keeps bands and their audience on a level where they keep progressing together. Being able to see it grow makes it exciting for everyone. Salmon and Little Feat does this. It is infused in the material you play and the audiences your reach." It was this idea that spoke to the reason why Salmon had stayed together through so many hard times. It is a deeper commitment when you are part of a band, but the payoff and results can be more rewarding.

Payne loved the excitement he found playing with Salmon. "I liken playing with these guys to being in the middle of lake on water skis and you are going to be pulled out of the water at moment's notice by the world's fastest boat so you better just hang on. That is how it is playing with these cats." Much of Payne's excitement about playing with Salmon was with the parallels he found between them and Little Feat. They are both bands that use a recognizable palette to color outside of the lines, creating music that is all together at the same time cutting edge and comfortable. They are unafraid to take chances and expose their musical souls to their audience each night. Payne calls this willingness to take chances "An experiment in terror." The idea a band is doing something onstage "on an intimate level, where they bare their souls regarding their music." The musicality of everyone in Salmon also struck a chord with Payne. "They can all play just about anything. Alwyn and Greg—those two cats as far as their musicianship and their ability to take the music to different places is just amazing. Each one of them on their own is so strong. It reminds me of Little Feat in that regard because that is how it was with that band. We were all strong in our respective areas as well. That is what makes a really great group and allows you to generate a lot of momentum." The connections Payne sensed were not unmerited as Emmitt readily admits to the importance of Feat's music on the evolution of Salmon, saying, "Little Feat is one of our biggest influences. You could almost break it down to New Grass Revival and Little Feat. That is what created this band's sound."

The thought of having Payne join the band full time crossed everyone's mind, but they decided to take it slow. "I said why don't we just consider to be dating," laughs Payne. Herman agreed, stating in an interview at the time, "It's open-ended. We want him for every gig he's available for. We're not putting a wedding ring on it or anything, but we're already starting to write with him for the next record. He's very much involved in all the things we do."[11] They would finally put a ring on it the next year, following a special show at the Ryman Auditorium Joy had arranged to celebrate the fifteenth anniversary of the release of their masterpiece, *The Nashville Sessions*. While the show was a chance to celebrate the greatness of the album, Herman says it was also a chance to remember those who were part of the album and no longer around. "That was a pretty special time for the band. Fifteen years on we've lost Mark, Earl Scruggs, and Waylon Jennings from that album. It just makes you think, God, we have to celebrate what time we have with people." The band played the entire album with all the original guests minus Jennings, who passed away in 2002, and Lucinda Williams, who was unable to make it. Payne, who had been playing with the band regularly for the previous year, was also there. Early in the night, Herman announced from stage they were finally putting a ring on Payne's finger as he officially joined the band, saying, "This is an incredibly special night for us as you can imagine and this is one of the reasons why. Make this guy back here on the piano feel welcome as we are here to tell you Bill Payne is the newest member of Leftover Salmon."

Payne was embracing the musical freedom he found in Salmon. "I realized I was playing more, singing more, and doing more adventurous things with Salmon than I had in the last few years with Little Feat." The overriding difference for Payne between Little Feat and Salmon was how far Salmon was willing to go each night and "stray from the

Bill Payne plays with Leftover Salmon at Strings & Sol 2013 prior to joining the band full time. Photograph by the author.

script." That difference was noticeable not just from a musical stand-point, where Payne says he felt he was in the unusual position of playing bluegrass piano, "Because there is really no such thing as bluegrass piano," but also in the atmosphere of freedom the band cultivated in their performances each night. Early in Payne's tenure with Salmon at a show at the Hamilton in Washington, DC, Payne fully embraced this ideal. During their set, they ratcheted the tempo up and got to a point where Payne was supposed to drop in and play. He says, "I lifted up my hands like are you fucking kidding me, no fucking way. I jumped off the stage and started dancing with a group of friends who were up front. They pushed me back onstage right when it came back around to me again. This time I hit it on all cylinders. I could have played it the first time, but the idea of the theatre of the absurd, that I know the band embraces, made it possible and much cooler to do it this way."

The addition of Payne to the band, while fulfilling a musical need, also was a boon to new drummer Robinson, who had to give up gradu-ate school when he joined Salmon. "Bill changed my whole mental process on what it means to have a career," says Robinson. "It is not about being the best on your instrument. It is about being a musician and playing the right way in every setting of being a professional. I came to be exposed to all these little details many musicians don't pay atten-tion to that Bill has such a strong grasp of. That changed everything for me. Everything I missed in grad school I have learned in more detail being on the road with Bill. And not just from Bill, all of them, Andy, Greg, Vince, and Drew. I have learned what it takes to be a musician. To be a professional musician." For Robinson, it was the things they do not teach you in school, or that you cannot understand until you have lived it, that made his decision to leave grad school sit as the correct one with him.

With Robinson and Payne reinvigorating the band, Salmon decided to head back into the studio and revisit the tracks they previously worked on with Martinez that just never seemed to fully click. "With those two in the fold," says Garrison, "we felt it was a good idea to finish the tracks we started and record a couple of new things." The two new songs were both connected to the addition of Payne. The first, "Six Feet of Snow," was a Little Feat tune that further highlighted the similarities between Feat and Salmon. Salmon had dabbled with the tune over the years and with its subtle bluegrass feel and the addition of Payne it seemed a perfect choice for the band. They recorded it live and captured the loose, fun spirit of both bands. The other track, "Bluegrass Pines," Payne had written with Grateful Dead lyricist Robert Hunter. Payne had recently written several songs with Hunter. When he joined the band, he shared them with everyone. "Bluegrass Pines," was the one they all agreed grabbed them. Payne felt it was the kind of song he would have written with Little Feat. "It's a kind of haunting and a really cool song," says Emmitt. "We were fortunate enough to be able to record it and I was honored to be the one to sing it."[12] Payne also overdubbed new piano and keyboard parts to the tracks they previously worked on. While the band did not feel as strongly about the results as they did with the highly collaborative *Aquatic Hitchhiker*, the addition of Payne and the inclusion of the two tracks with Robinson gave this batch of songs, that had been so troubling for the band to finish, a cohesive feel not there when they worked on them earlier in the year. The resulting album was titled *High Country*, and while not as strong as *Aquatic Hitchhiker*, it eventually came together as a solid album. Herman says, "It was not a real organic process, but for some weird reason it worked out in the end." The album was dedicated to the memory of Mark Vann and Joe Cahill, whose losses both shaped the making of the album and proved to be another example of the band overcoming adversity. The liner notes also recognized the importance of Joy to the band and his vital role in helping them continue on in the years following the hiatus, saying "Big thanks to John Joy for doing it all. We wouldn't be here without you."

As with *Aquatic Hitchhiker*, *High Country* found the band evolving in a more Americana direction, that while still having traces of their bluegrass roots, finds the band sounding more akin to the Band or Little Feat than ever before. *Relix* called the album, "As eclectic a collection of Americana tunes as any."[13] This evolution begs to ask the question, as Leftover Salmon enters their third decade, who are they? Are they the next generation of progressive bluegrass, following their predecessors like Hot Rize, the Dillards, John Hartford, and New Grass Revival? Are they a key figure of the H.O.R.D.E. and jamband scene, who along with their peers Phish, Widespread Panic, Aquarium Rescue Unit, helped establish a new standard for live, improvisational music and created a blueprint for touring bands to follow? Or are they the fathers of the jamgrass movement, helping to spawn such bands as Railroad Earth,

Yonder Mountain String Band, The String Cheese Incident, Blueground Undergrass, Greensky Bluegrass, the Infamous Stringdusters, Horseshoes & Hand Grenades, Billy Strings, and the Sweet Lillies, who dwell in a landscape created by Leftover Salmon where bands schooled in the traditional rules of bluegrass break free of those bonds through nontraditional instrumentation and an innate ability to push songs in new psychedelic directions live? Or are they all three? Either way, they are a band who over their thirty-year career has never stood still; they are constantly changing, evolving, and inspiring. If someone wanted to understand what Americana music is, they could do no better than to go to a Leftover Salmon show, where they effortlessly glide from a bluegrass number born on the front porch, to the down-and-dirty Cajun swamps with a stop on Bourbon Street in New Orleans, to the hallowed halls of the Ryman in Nashville, before firing one up in the mountains of Colorado. This subtle evolution toward a more Americana-based sound has not detracted from who Salmon is and has always been: one of the great purveyors of American music. *Marquee Magazine* noted this, writing, "*High Country* doesn't break any new ground for Leftover Salmon. The album won't go down as a turning point for the band—even considering recent changes to the group's lineup. And that's a damn good thing."[14]

In quintessential Salmon fashion, when things seemed to be rolling, something came by to knock them back down. Just as the band was finding its groove with Payne, he received an offer to join the Doobie Brothers. Payne had a long history with the band. He had become friends with them in the early seventies as they and Little Feat were first starting. Over the years, he played on many of their albums and is even given credit for coming up with the piano lick for one of the Doobies' signature songs, "China Groove." There was always speculation he might join the band, as he had toured with them occasionally when Little Feat was not busy. He had been asked two previous times if he wanted to join and turned them down both times. Now with Little Feat on an indefinite hiatus due to Barrere's health issues, he felt it was the right time to join when they asked him again. "It was a little awkward, actually probably a lot awkward to leave Salmon when I did," says Payne. "I had just joined the year before." For Salmon, there was some hard feelings, but it was more disappointment than anything else. "You are not going to turn down the Doobie Brothers to play in Leftover

Salmon," says Emmitt with a laugh, "As great as our band is, that is a
tough one." With Payne, they released *High Country* and the live al-
bum, *25*, that showcased his additions to the band. The band was starting to look forward and write songs for a potential new album which
Payne was heavily involved with when he decided to leave to join the
Doobies. The new album was a planned follow-up to the *Nashville
Sessions*, this time with Salmon decamping to New Orleans and recording with some of their friends and favorite musicians from the Crescent
City. As much as the music on the *Nashville Sessions* helped define who
Salmon is, the gumbo-mix of styles from New Orleans has also long
been a key ingredient in their sound. Several writing sessions were
arranged with Payne heavily involved in helping to craft the new album.
As the writing sessions for the new album were getting underway, Emmitt's wife, Renee, was diagnosed with cancer. "I said there is no way I
can do a record right now," says Emmitt. "I told everyone I can't be
gone for a month as she was in heavy chemotherapy every other week."
They put a hold on the preparation for the new album as Emmitt stayed
home to help take care of his wife, who would make a full recovery. "It
was a big thing and quite a deal to go through," he says. "She is great
now, but it definitely affected the whole band and our plans."

The time away from working on the New Orleans album made some
in the band question if that was the direction they should be heading in,
with another genre-themed album. When Payne—who was a driving
force for the New Orleans album—quit, the loss of his enthusiasm for
the project and others' disinterest in pursuing it caused the project to
crumble. Emmitt says:

> Who knows what would have happened had we not canceled that
> project. We were starting to come up with new material. We were
> writing new songs and felt we were killing it. Of course, we were
> disappointed when Bill told us he was joining the Doobies. We were
> just getting this going with him and then he is leaving. But we have
> been through a lot of disappointment in this band. We have had lot
> of near misses and brushes with greatness. We are no strangers to
> disappointment, losing Mark, Noam, and breaking up. It's no new
> thing for us. We have been through a lot. It was definitely a hard
> thing to deal with, but we still had Andy and Alwyn and we felt like
> we had a strong new band. We knew we were going to keep this
> going.

While disappointed, Salmon was not surprised in Payne's decision to leave and were able to find solace in the time they got to play with the legendary musician. "It was a great experience playing with him," says Herman. "He is a brilliant musician, historian, and storyteller. Really stimulating intellectually and musically. But shit, he is Bill Payne, we never thought he would be in the band long." Payne also appreciated his time with the band and the freedom with which they play. As he prepared to join the Doobies, he remarked on the contrast between the two bands: "The Doobies are very structured, but what Salmon provides is that feeling of just hanging onto your seat and hoping you don't spin off and fall into the audience. That freedom is something I will always treasure from playing with them."

Despite leaving the band, Payne left a legacy and something that ensured the band would be even better going forward. A couple of months after joining, he forced an uncomfortable meeting, questioning everyone's financial stake and how things were divided. Since the hiatus, Emmitt and Herman had received a much larger share than everyone else. When they first returned from the hiatus, it made sense. The band was influx from show to show. Emmitt and Herman were the constants, the decision makers, and carried more pressure. But over the years as they became settled as a regular working band again, the rest of the band, while well compensated, was still on some level treated as hired guns, not equal members. "We knew it had to happen at some point," says Herman. "At that point, we restructured the financial way the band worked. Bill stirred the waters on that front. Finances are difficult to talk about. It went pretty well for such a difficult conversation." Payne pushed the issue and Emmitt and Herman recognized they needed to change how they ran things if they were to continue as a viable, permanent band. The decision to make this change made Garrison, Robinson, and Thorn feel they had more of a stake in the band and more ownership in what happened moving forward. "The current setup of the band is so good," says Herman, "and going to move us into our third decade. There is a feeling of being revived and we feel so strongly about everyone in the band. Having everyone on board and having a vision and feeling like we are all in the boat together is great. We wanted to stick together." These changes would be felt not just financially, but also musically as the band has come together over the ensuing years and started crafting some of their strongest material ever. "I tried to push them out of their comfort zone," says Payne.

"Thank God for Bill Payne, I tell you," proclaims Garrison. "He was only with us for a short while, but he left lasting influences that helped the band become a more functional unit in so many ways."

Chapter 12

ERIK DEUTSCH

> Erik is one of the nicest, most sincere people I've had the pleasure of sharing a stage with. From the first time, I heard him play it was clear he had a unique approach to his instrument. He's a great friend and honestly has one of the biggest hearts in the business.—*Dave Watts (The Motet)*

Leftover Salmon was onstage at the Red Rocks Amphitheatre in the summer of 2016. It is a venue they have played countless times before. This time, they were sharing the bill with Greensky Bluegrass, a band whose existence and style of music was only possible due to the influence and groundbreaking work of Salmon over the years. To be able to play bluegrass music with a rock edge, in a venue as legendary as Red Rocks, was at one time unheard of for bands of a similar ilk. Midway through their set, Greensky Bluegrass invited Drew Emmitt and Vince Herman to come share the stage for a couple of tunes, Salmon's "Woody Guthrie," and the Jimmy Martin classic, "Hit Parade of Love." For Greensky's Anders Beck, it was an almost surreal moment. "Having Leftover Salmon here with us is about the coolest thing that could happen," proclaimed an emotional Beck as Emmitt and Herman strode onstage. "It's cool when your heroes become your friends. The reason we are allowed to do what we do with music is because of the guys in Leftover Salmon. That is the damn truth. We learned it from them and it's all their fault."[1]

It was a real link in the chain moment as Salmon experienced the same thing when they were a young band like Greensky and first had the opportunity to share the stage with their heroes in Hot Rize and New Grass Revival. Now Greensky Bluegrass, a band that did not even start until Salmon was already in their second decade, were sharing the stage with their heroes. "It was incredible to bring them onstage with us," Beck would say after the show, "and explain to that crowd of 10,000, who I am sure all who know Leftover Salmon is, that they are the jamgrass forefathers and the reason we can do what we do is because of Vince and Drew. I got a little choked up trying to explain that to the crowd. It was heavy shit." As much as it was a dream for Greensky to share their stage with their heroes in Salmon, it was even more of a dream for Salmon to be onstage nearly thirty years after first playing together in the campground of Telluride. The previous three decades had seen tragedy, loss, turmoil, and hard times, but like their namesake they forged ahead, swimming upstream in the face of unrelenting adversity and emerged a stronger, more focused band, who was playing at a level not seen from them in years. It is unfair and maybe impossible to say when Salmon was at their best—the early carefree days, the tight five-piece with Tye North and Jeff Sipe, the expanded six-piece with Noam Pikelny, or the current version—but that is exactly where the band found themselves at Red Rocks. They were the topic of debate among fans and peers as to just how great they currently are, as they play with a hardened confidence that is only matched by the magic they bring each night. "It took that first iteration of Salmon to change my life," says Yonder Mountain String Band's Ben Kaufmann. "But now they are a band that is as good, if not better than they have ever been." It was a long time for Salmon to get to this point, but the smiles onstage were real, the feeling of relief palpable. After years of struggle, heartache, and adversity, they were a band again. A real band. Not just a collection of musicians, playing the same song, but a group who lived and breathed as one, who created new experiences every night onstage. "It's hard to compare to the days with Mark, Sipe, and Tye, that band is one of the best incarnations. But I feel right now the way everyone is playing and contributing, this is the best," says Emmitt. Los Lobos' Steve Berlin is clear on how good he thinks the band is in 2017, "They have gone up a magnitude in terms of everything. Everything is just so excitedly solid now. It is almost like a different band. At the same time, there is still Drew being Drew and Vince being Vince. The voices are still there, the music has just taken on a more colorful palette."

When talking about Salmon, it must always come back to Emmitt and Herman. As they go, so goes Salmon, when they are great, Salmon is great. Following the band's rebirth in 2007 after a nearly three-year hiatus, the two longtime bandmates, after finding out what they were capable of on their own, now fully recognized the power of being together. They found they were playing with the energy of their twenty-something selves like they did at the Roma or the Fox Theatre or the Stage Stop, when all-night shows were the norm and endless parties were habit. For anyone who forgot about the extraordinary qualities of the two, they were being reminded of it on a nightly basis. Elephant Revival's Dango Rose asserts, "There is pure heart translated through the songwriting of Drew and Vince. It boils down to authenticity and an ever-evolving process of musical creation for those two."

The current lineup is not just about Emmitt and Herman though. Salmon has a lineup playing with unrestrained excitement that is only matched by their limitless talents. Bassist Greg Garrison has for the past

Leftover Salmon onstage at Red Rocks Amphitheatre in the summer of 2016 (from left): Drew Emmitt, Alwyn Robinson (partially obscured), Vince Herman, Andy Thorn, and Greg Garrison. Photograph by the author.

fifteen years been the rock of the band, serving as a grounding force both onstage and off-. "He is everything to the band," says drummer Alwyn Robinson. "He holds everything together. His knowledge of touring and logistics is ridiculous. He is the glue to the band. He is the real deal." String Cheese Incident bassist Keith Moseley agrees, "He is a perfect fit vibe wise and playing wise. He is an incredible player. He understands what they do and knows how to do it just right." To Garrison's steadiness is combined the Vann-like qualities of banjoist Andy Thorn, whose addition signaled a return to the special Salmon chemistry absent since the passing of Vann. Thorn helped the band realize how far they could go and who they could be after the hiatus when it was easy enough to just be a reunion band. The addition of uber-talented drummer Robinson pushed their rhythm section into directions they never thought possible and cemented their comeback.

This rebirth started to take flight with the addition of legendary keyboardist Bill Payne, but his tenure with Salmon proved short-lived as he accepted an offer to join the Doobie Brothers. Upon his departure, the band debated what to do. Find another keyboardist? Add a more bluegrass-centric instrument? Revert to the five-piece? "We were thinking about a few different options," says Emmitt, "and different directions for the band and thought maybe we should get a string player." For Thorn, he enjoyed the freedom he found in the five-piece but felt if they were going to add another instrument they should add another bluegrass-type instrument. He admits he was, "Kind of anti-keyboards at that point." In standard Salmon fashion, there was much discussion on what to do about adding another instrument, but very little action. At the same time, they were preparing for their annual Stanley Hotel event that was set for March of 2016. Since its first year, the Stanley Hotel has grown into an annual spectacle that is a yearly high point for band and fan alike. It is chance for them to play with no boundaries for their most devoted fans. Each year, they toy with different themes and incorporate special covers. As they prepared for the Stanley show, Garrison lobbied hard to bring Erik Deutsch on board. Deutsch was a keyboardist whom he first met when he moved to Colorado in 1998. They had studied under the same teacher for a stretch and did a few gigs together, playing in a short-lived band called Commander Robot. Garrison felt Deutsch was perfect for what they do at the Stanley Hotel shows. Emmitt agreed, "I pushed hard for Erik. I had known him for years. Greg played with him. We all knew about him."

Deutsch, originally from the Washington, DC, area, had been around the same scene as Leftover Salmon for years since enrolling at the University of Colorado in 1995 on a scholarship for jazz piano. His first week in Colorado a friend invited him to party where she knew there were going to be some people jamming. Deutsch connected with the musicians at the party, and they soon coalesced under the name Fat Mama, which they took from a Herbie Hancock song. "We debuted Halloween of my freshman year," says Deutsch. "By January we were the biggest band on campus." The lineup fluctuated over the first year, before settling on Deutsch on keys, Jonathan Goldberger on guitar, Kevin Kendrick on percussion, Brett Joseph and Jon Gray on horns, and Jonti Simmian on bass. The band's first drummer was a senior and graduated the following year. He was replaced by an incoming freshman from New Jersey who they heard was a powerhouse drummer, Joe Russo.

Fat Mama, who incorporated a wide range of influences and liked to jam and get experimental onstage, found a home in the jamband scene in Boulder that besides Leftover Salmon also featured Big Head Todd & the Monsters, Zuba, and Chief Broom among many others. They were one of the earliest jambands, along with the Disco Biscuits, Lake Trout, and the New Deal, to start incorporating electronic influences into their sound. "We were on that early wave of nineties jambands doing the jazz thing which was different from what a lot of other bands were doing at the time," says Deutsch. While Fat Mama was a key part of the Boulder scene, Deutsch, who was only eighteen at the time, says he was aware of Salmon because they were one of the most popular bands in the area, only saw them once or twice as he was not old enough to into any of the venues Salmon was playing. He also admits, "I was more opinionated then about what music I was into and I was into jazz and funk," before adding, "I probably also never made it into a Salmon show because they were always sold out."

After a few years in Boulder, Fat Mama relocated to the East Coast in 1999. Much of the band had roots there and Deutsch says, "Even though we formed in Boulder we had an East Coast sound." They began to find success and took part in many of the earliest festivals of the jam scene, including Gathering of the Vibes, Camp Bisco, and All-

Erik Deutsch's college band, Fat Mama, became a key part of the "early wave of nineties jambands doing the jazz thing" (from left): Jon Marvin Garrett (bass), Mike Rhode (percussion), Erik Deutsch (keys), Brett Joseph (saxophone), Joe Russo (drums), Jon Gray (trumpet), and Jonathan Goldberger (guitar). Courtesy of Erik Deutsch.

Good Fest. Fat Mama broke up a few years after moving to the East Coast. Drummer Russo would go onto find even greater fame over the ensuing years with several bands including the Benevento/Russo Duo, Joe Russo's Almost Dead, Furthur, and American Babies, while Deutsch would relocate back to Boulder. Upon his return to Boulder, he started playing with several bands including the Motet, Liza Oxnard, and Billy Nerhsi's Blue Planet. He became an in-demand player both on the road and in the studio working with a wide range of artists including Devotchka, Norah Jones, Charlie Hunter, Roseanne Cash, and Shooter Jennings. In 2016, when he was first approached about possibly joining Salmon for their Stanley Hotel shows, he was working with Citizen Cope, but says, while "it was fun and we had big gigs, we only occasionally played and I do like being on the road playing shows."

In addition to Garrison, Deutsch, was also friends with Salmon manager John Joy, whom he knew since his earliest days in Colorado. Garrison was the first person to reach out to Deutsch about joining Salmon for the Stanley, but Deutsch says, "As you would expect in the music business I didn't hear anything back from him for two months." At that time, Joy reached out to find out if Deutsch was interested in not only the Stanley shows, but also a short tour of Colorado the band had booked immediately following the Stanley. Deutsch said he was interested and Joy said he would confirm with the band and get back to him. A month later, Joy and Deutsch spoke again. Joy said he grown tired of waiting for an answer waiting from everyone in the band if they wanted to bring Deutsch on for the Colorado tour, and said, "Fuck it, you do it."

Deutsch headed into the Stanley shows with a bit of trepidation as he was unsure of who knew he was joining for not only those shows, but the short tour following. "I don't know who knew, but I did, Greg did, and John did," says Deutsch, "but everyone seemed cool with it when I showed up." His worries soon faded as he found an immediate chemistry with the band during their first rehearsal and convinced them keys was what they needed. Even the skeptical Thorn was convinced: "After one weekend I said this guy needs to be in the band." Herman was a little less clear on Deutsch's role going forward following the Stanley shows. Deutsch says, "After the Stanley, Vince came up to me and said that fit like a glove, I look forward to the next time." After an awkward pause, Deutsch informed Herman, "I am actually going on the road for two weeks with you starting tomorrow."

The band headed out on their two-week run around Colorado and the chemistry they found at the Stanley was still there. "Once we got out on the road we were all in agreement," says Emmitt. "Erik seemed like the perfect person." Thorn concurs, "I had originally wanted to get another bluegrass instrument, but after the spending the month with him, he is such an amazing guy and so talented, it was pretty clear it was going to work." Near the end of the run the rest of the band wanted to officially invite Deutsch to join. "They asked me to come and sit on Uncle Vince's lap," laughs Deutsch. "They asked if I would like to stick around and join the band. I agreed, and here we are."

Deutsch did not have much of a background in bluegrass and took a little while to get fully immersed into all it is that Salmon does, but he, like Robinson, was a highly talented musician who played with a variety of bands over the years and quickly assimilated himself into Salmon's sound. He says his biggest difficulty was not so much finding his place in a band with bluegrass roots, but he had gotten out of the jam scene for a few years as he became involved with bands who existed in musical realms outside the jam scene. "The big change was being back in the jam scene," says Deutsch. "Salmon played a little longer and improvised more than what I was doing, which was great as improvising is my bread and butter. I was going back to taking twenty-five or thirty solos a night, which I had not done in a while. It was also coming back to a fan base who hangs on every note. But it was great to get back to it."

Musically he was a much different type player than Payne, and his sound seemed to find a more comfortable place in the band. "I'm not knocking Bill," says Berlin, "he is one of the finest musicians and people I have ever met, but having Erik's energy and being into the cutting edge of everything out there is amazingly powerful. It just frees up the rest of the band's imagination." Yonder Mountain String Band guitarist Adam Aijala says, "One of the things I love about Erik is he is very rhythmic. Less notey and more in the rhythmic sense." Not being a rock legend like Payne also proved to be a bonus. As much as Salmon loved playing with Payne, there was still the fact that at times he was the bigger name and unintentionally overshadowed his bandmates. "It always felt like it was Bill Payne and the band," says Emmitt. "Leftover Salmon featuring Bill Payne. It never felt like he could just be part of the band. It is not something he did, it is because he is Bill Payne. When Erik joined it felt like he is part of what we are doing."

The addition of Deutsch allowed Garrison and Robinson to pursue their jazz tendencies with the creation of their side-project Sockeye. Sockeye plays their own gigs as well as making appearances in Salmon shows, usually emerging out of a lengthy jam which finds Emmitt, Herman, and Thorn leaving the stage and allowing the rhythm section to improvise and the let the music go wherever it may in the moment. "The three of us speak the same language," says Garrison, "and there is a lot of conversation happening between us during every show that people in the crowd and onstage might not even be picking up on. Part of the reason we do the Sockeye thing is to give us an opportunity to let those conversation come to the forefront." Sockeye has helped influence the evolution of Salmon as they have been incorporating that sly, overlooked trait of jazz music, the ability to play with defined virtuosity but deliver it with the illusion of ease. It is an idea Salmon has long toyed with but refined over the years with the addition of Garrison, Robinson, and Deutsch. The trio has brought a fresh outlook and approach to Salmon with their skillful chops. Herman says, "Those guys' vocabularies are so intense and big. It definitely brings a lot of new energy to Drew and I."[2]

Prior to Deutsch joining, Salmon had been planning on heading to New Orleans to record a new album, but the exit of Payne and Em-

Producer Steve Berlin says the addition of Erik Deutsch, "Frees up the rest of the band's imagination." Pictured onstage at Red Rocks with Andy Thorn July 23, 2016. Photograph by the author.

mitt's wife's cancer scare brought an end to that plan. With Deutsch fully on board, the band wanted to get back into the studio. As they prepared for a new album, there was none of the uneasiness or tension Herman felt during other recording sessions. The days of feeling "emotionally butt-hurt," from having Pikelny replace his guitar parts on the *Leftover Salmon* album, when he says he felt he was not part of the musical conversation in his own band were long gone. His confidence was no longer an issue. He was secure in who he was as a musician. The days of worrying about being the least talented musician were gone. In fact, his true genius was beginning to be recognized. His role as a facilitator and onstage-mayhem conductor were brought further into focus. Even with the addition of Deutsch, who along with Robinson and Garrison now provided Salmon a jazz trio with some real credentials as their rhythm section, Herman has found a comfort level that was lacking for years. He says, "I guess it's the evolution of myself and my own musical confidence that I don't feel I am lost in the midst as everyone is going down the jazz road. There is a real sense of everyone contributing. My approach is as the guy who is standing in the middle to act as a somewhat leader to harvest the abilities and passions of the musicians I get to stand in front of. If they are not reaching every night and pushing and playing and going further and feeling this is something that captures all their intensity and all they can bring to a show, then it is not going to last because they are artists. They are not just people who do this for a living, they must be able to express themselves and follow that passion. If, I as the guy standing in the middle, don't harvest that from them, they will find someone where they can." Despite Herman's stated worry about finding his place among the band's jazz-loving rhythm section, Robinson sees it differently from his seat behind Herman onstage every night. "Honestly the biggest jazz cat onstage is Vince," he says. "As much as we studied it and listen to it and perform it, Vince whether he knows it or not is deep in the jazz realm. That cat improvises like no one I have ever seen in terms of stage demeanor and where he is going to take something and how he shifts the whole vibe of the sound based on the audience each night. He is probably the deepest jazz cat out of all of us. He gives us the freedom to explore onstage." Herman's musicianship is often overlooked due to his good-time attitude and the talented players he always surrounds himself with. Part of this is his own doing as his personal philosophy has always been to be the worst player in any band he is part of, proudly declaring, "That philosophy has always worked for me." But, upon closer listen, this philosophy does not always hold to be true, as Herman's skillfully guitar playing always shines through, serving to reinforce the idea of how talented he is, but proving he hides it well.

The rest of Salmon has also suffered from misconceptions about who they are. Even in the band's earliest years when they gave off the appearance of being stoned ski bums, in search of a good time, this perception was not true. While they have always enjoyed a good party and are not a band to say no to a good time, they have proven this misconception of them is false, with the advanced musical education and degrees of Garrison, Deutsch, Robinson, and Thorn, and the well-recognized notion that Emmitt is one of the most talented multi-instrumentalists of the last thirty years with his skill on mandolin, guitar, and fiddle. "It is some pretty good credentials that come along with this band," says Emmitt with a laugh. "We aren't just a bunch of hippies. We actually have some heady musical background."

With the band's heady musical background and Herman's newfound confidence they headed into Wavelab Studios in Tucson, Arizona, to start work on a new album. They choose the studio on the recommendation of Deutsch, who had recorded there previously. The band thought it would be good to get away from Colorado and the diversions that come from being at home. Garrison says, "We wanted to go somewhere we could hole up for a while to focus and allow things to develop organically. Being home is so convenient in some ways, but everyone is distracted by family, friends, going home, and other things to do. It was refreshing to just be in Tucson with one job, to make a fucking record."

After two albums working with producer Berlin, the band was thinking about changing up and using someone else. "I had to go and sell myself to them again," remembers Berlin, "They were thinking about using someone else, which frankly I understand. Doing three records with the same guy is a lot. I went to Denver and sat down with everyone one-on-one and asked what they wanted with new record. What were they expecting for it? What would they choose for it to be? This was before most of the songs were even written. I just had to get back in touch with everybody and let them know I was still interested and intrigued." After meeting with Berlin, they all agreed he understood the band like no other producer they every worked with and asked him to produce again. "I was nervous going into it," admits Berlin, "because they only sent me two or three songs in advance, and we had a whole album to make. That is not unlike my past experiences with the band, though. They wait to the last, last, last possible second to begin writing. Every record is just sweating bullets and then lo and behold there is a cool record that comes out on the other side." Berlin had no need to worry. The band was on a creative high the past few years and playing with an enthusiasm that belied their status as elder statesmen. Besides, Berlin, who would have preferred the band engage in some serious preproduction, had been down this road before the band. "I would rather have them rehearse before and know exactly what we are going to do when we get into the studio. But much like my band Los Lobos, they have been doing it for so long they don't need to do their homework. They can just show up, do it, and stuff happens. There is a certain thing that just clicks, where it just feels like it's going to be fine."

While the band entered the studio with few complete tracks, they had enough of a blueprint for the rest of the songs that with the creative roll they were on, everything would quickly "click," as Berlin said, and, "stuff," would happen. "We didn't have a ton of material that was polished going in to the session," says Garrison bluntly. "Seems like a familiar theme every time we go into the studio, but everyone brought at least some songwriting seeds to work with." They decided to record straight to analog tape to preserve that warm, live feeling, and because the band usually worked quickly and could knock out basic tracks in only a couple of takes. Garrison also jokes, "People lose focus and energy after a couple of takes." The band started in the studio working on a pair of Thorn's tunes, "Evermore," and "Winter's Gone," as they had been part of the band's live repertoire and were fully formed and required the least amount of work. After those two, the band started plowing through the pile of songs that were in various states of being.

Like they were with *Aquatic Hitchhiker*, everyone was in a contributing mood, and the vibe of the sessions was group centered. Berlin says, "A lot of the songs were effectively composed in the studio. They were very open to experimenting—not that they always weren't, they gave me free reign on *Aquatic Hitchhiker*—this time it just seemed everything came a lot easier on this one." The experience of the band shone through each day. They let the creative process move at its own pace, never forcing a song or idea to work that was not ready. They maintained their focus and flexibility as each song was crafted, allowing for changes to quickly be adapted. Whereas on previous albums it may have taken a couple of days to get comfortable with new ideas, with changing chords and structures, this time around everyone grasped onto changes immediately. While working on the track "Places," which for a while was going to be the name of the album, Berlin says after making several wholesale adjustments within the song, "It only took two takes and the song with the new changes was done. It didn't strike me as usual, because while they have always been open-minded about things, it never came together in two takes after changing the entire structure around. It used to take them a while to get comfortable, but now they are so professional they just adapted instantaneously. Seeing them work like that made think this is going to be fun."

The band was also heavily influenced by what was happening in the world with the 2016 presidential election, as they were glued to the news every night. Salmon was inspired by the idea music can affect positive change. Herman was especially influenced by the craziness of the 2016 election and came into the studio politically charged. There is often the misconception of Herman being a stoned, carefree jokester who just happily bounces along. There is some truth to this. To this day, he still trails pot smoke wherever he goes, lighting up a joint or smoking a bowl whenever he pleases. The world is still his party and festivals his home. Despite the gray in his hair, he still exudes the vitality of a man half his age. He is always on, and always on the go. "I don't know how he does what does," says Col. Bruce Hampton. "He is like a twenty-five-year-old. I don't know where he gets the energy. It is amazing." But Herman has always challenged this perception of ignorant, joyful bliss. He is highly intelligent and a voracious reader who can sit and discuss seemingly any topic in depth that arises in conversation. He has long been politically active since his college days when he partook in many protests and wanted to serve as a witness for peace in Nicaragua, to his days living in Nederland, when he got involved in several local issues. As the band prepared for the new album, he was disturbed by the election campaign of 2016 and took part in many protests and marches around the country. Herman is an improvisational lyrical master and draws naturally on the folk protest ways of old and this shone through on the new album. In response to the election of Donald Trump, he wrote "House of Cards," which reflects the turbulent times as seen by a man who cares deeply about the state of the world. It was the most overtly political song he had written since nearly thirty years prior when he took on the 1992 Los Angeles riots in "Head Bag." "House of Cards" was a reaction to the recent political climate and the direct impact of the nation's leaders and the way their actions left a mass of unsatisfied citizens. "The Trump song," says Emmitt with a knowing laugh as he reflects on the genesis of "House of Cards." "It kind of came together during this crazy year. There is a lot of hopefulness and introspection going on with what is happening in the world. I feel Vince's tune goes some cool places and captures some cool vibes." The powerful statement in the song and Herman's drive for change would have made his idol Hazel Dickens proud. Dickens, over the course of her legendary career, wrote many protest songs and was always an advocate for the working class and downtrodden and gave voice to those who had none with the way she not only sang of injustice, but also lived a life of positive action. The song was released as a single with an accompanying video in August of 2017 following the horrific terrorist attack during the protests in Charlottesville, Virginia. The video featured news footage from the previous several months of protests, interspersed with political figures such as Donald Trump and Bernie Sanders. Upon its release, Herman stated, "The revolution will not be televised. It will be streamed and forwarded. Now is the time to reject the hatred we see coming from so many and bring love and acceptance back into our national agenda. We hope this video can help nudge our country in that direction quickly. This is not normal and love must win again. Our world depends on it." Salmon hoped the song and video not only inspired people to strive for change, but also encouraged other artists to use their musical voice to write their own acts of musical protest.

The sessions were a departure from albums past where even if the band was collaborating and everyone was contributing, there was still a tendency for Emmitt and Herman to dominate the proceedings as the others deferred to them. This time around, Garrison says, "The band turned a corner and we became a six-piece unit, rather than Vince and Drew plus some other guys." Having everyone, with their own diverse styles, bringing songs into the studio was helping the band's sound grow in ways they never imagined. "Having everyone write has helped us to take it to other dimensions. It is atmospherically giving us new palettes to work with," says Herman. This change was not lost on Garrison, who deserves much of the credit for the renewed focused of Salmon as over the years he has become a musical director of sorts for the band, both onstage and in the studio. He says, "It was a big step in the evolution of the band as Vince and Drew weren't the primary drivers behind the bulk of the material. The things they did bring were often changed through the input from the rest of the band. It was lots of co-writes and lots of creative thinking going on. We also ignored the urge for, 'Yeah, but don't we need calypso tune on here to make it a Leftover Salmon record?'" Deutsch recognized this and felt much credit had to be given to Emmitt and Herman, who were so inviting to having everyone's voice in the process. "It is kind of crazy how open Vince and Drew are to the evolution of the band and how much of a blank canvas they give us all to utilize."

The stability of the lineup was another key factor in the evolution of the band. This album marked the first time since the return from hiatus that they entered the studio with a stable lineup. During *Aquatic Hitch-hiker*, Bill McKay was asked to leave the band after they started the recording process, forcing the band to rediscover who they were as a five-piece as at the same time they were integrating Thorn fully into his first studio experience with the band. On *High Country*, drummer Jose Martinez left the band after they started work on the album. This time they had a lineup, that, besides the exception of the newly added Deutsch, had been together for years. "This is definitely the best the band has ever been," declares Emmitt. "It is the first time in a long time where everyone is fully committed and not going to run off to join some other band. Everyone is so good, and I love everyone's contributions. Alwyn is so great and fits so well. Greg has always been a rock. Having Andy all these years, and now adding Erik, this band is so good right now."

Berlin, who had been with the band through the changes of their previous two albums, noticed the difference the stability brought to the band. "It made for a more pleasant recording experience. The energy the new guys brings is amazing. It is so revitalizing to have these young guys pushing them so hard and coming up with new ideas. I think the next phase of the band is going to be the best yet." He especially singled out Deutsch and Robinson's contributions as being key to the success of the new album. He mentions what he calls a "world-class hook" Deutsch came up with for "Southern Belle," as an example of how the keyboardist could inspire the band in bold, new directions. Berlin also heaps praise on Robinson and his song "Foreign Fields." For Robinson, it was his first time fully participating in the creation of a Salmon album, as previously he only overdubbed a few parts onto existing tracks for *High Country*. "I had the opportunity to fully contribute my sound from beginning to end so it felt so much more comfortable. I didn't feel like I was just filling a little hole. I was contributing creatively to the whole process." He says it was a "nerve-racking" experience when he brought "Foreign Fields" to the rest of the band: "It was more for a jazz ensemble. I was extremely nervous to bring it in. But you bring in what you bring in and the let the guys develop it. I was confident once they got their ears on it, they would turn it into something fitting for this band." "Foreign Fields" was the first song Robinson had ever written lyrics for. It was a deeply personal song as it dealt with the sudden death of a close friend of Robinson's. In the hands of Salmon, "Foreign

Fields" became an otherworldly, sonic exploration that created an emotional soundscape for Robinson's powerful words. "It is totally different from any Salmon song ever," says Berlin. "Foreign Fields" is powered along by Thorn's adventurous banjo, which roots the song in the bluegrass of Salmon's past. The song lives over a deep harmonic texture created by Garrison's bass and is decorated with flourishes of keyboards from Deutsch. Emmitt and Herman provide their classic sound of guitar and mandolin. Add to that Robinson's soulful singing and it became bluegrass for a new generation; sounds of the old living with sounds of the modern, coming together to create something new. That is what Salmon has done since their earliest days when they grew bluegrass into slamgrass. They take a sound we are familiar with and push it, pull it, and stretch it any number of directions, proving music is elastic and it can bend, but will not break. Salmon does this, yet at the same time, does it in such a way as to stay true to the music's roots. It is moving forward, while still looking back to where it came from. "On the record, there are some remarkable things that have never happened on a Salmon record before and I directly attribute that to both Alwyn and Erik," says Berlin. "It is so gratifying to have players like that on board." Yonder Mountain String Band guitarist Adam Aijala says, "I loved the original band I met them as, but I love the new lineup so much. Erik, Andy, and Alwyn are just ridiculous."

Despite the immense contributions from the new guys in the band, Berlin knew for it to be a Salmon record it still needed Emmitt and Herman to be at the top of their game. Much like the rest of the band, the pair were flying high from the creative winds blowing through the band. "Drew is remarkable," says Berlin. "It is always so exciting when he says he has a new song. He has never let me or the band down. His batting average as a songwriter is so extraordinarily high. Through the three records we've done together it is always so fun to hear what he is thinking about. What he contributes to a song is always going to be so useful and beautiful. I feel this is some of his best work on the new record. Both his playing and writing." Emmitt had long ago accomplished the rare feat of being recognized as a guitarist of the highest order and able to fit easily into the rock world, but also being a rare talent on mandolin and able to play with a skill reminiscent of the traditional bluegrass masters of the instrument.

Whereas Berlin knew he could always count on Emmitt's exceptional musical contributions in the studio, it was Herman's intangible qualities the producer relied on. "Whenever I get a chance I just look over at Vince," says Berlin. "He is smiling and I always think we got this. We will figure it out. People have strong opinions. Vince has strong opinions, but he administers it in such a way that he is helping everyone. It is a remarkable personality trait to have, to be able to calm a whole room like that."

The two longtime bandmates would shine together on "Show Me Something Higher," a track Emmitt had started writing on the drive home from Telluride. He says during the drive inspiration struck and he pulled off to the side of the road and began scribbling lyrics and ideas as he "received" the song. The song would be finished with an assist from Herman. "I had the idea I wanted Vince to write part of it," says Emmitt. "So, he wrote the second half of the verses." It was the first time the two had ever co-written a song. On the finished track, the two alternate singing verses bathed in splashes of blistering horns. Together they sing the chorus, "Show me something higher/ Show me a better way." An optimistic, hopeful wish.

In the sheltered confines of the studio it is sometimes easy to lose perspective while working on a project. The tendency to rerecord parts ad nauseam or not recognize how good something is can easily be lost in the haze of endless hours listening to the same part over and over. Garrison says the band always felt what they were capturing on tape was working: "I have to say externally there was quite a bit of skepticism we'd be able to get everything done. But internally we knew we were getting something special down on tape. It turned out better than any of us could have hoped. Sonically, I think it is special." This positive feeling was universal among the whole band, a rare feat in the Leftover Salmon universe. Thorn attributes much of the success of the album to the unified effort from the whole band. "It is a good record. It is really cohesive. It was done at one time, with one group. We all came together to arrange it. It is a true band record." Herman flatly states, "This is the best album we have ever done. Hopefully it will move us into our third decade feeling inspired to continue to do more like this." The album's eventual title, *Something Higher*, reflected this positive outlook, as well as serving as an optimistic counterpoint to the turmoil Herman documented in "House of Cards."

Berlin recognizes not only the unique beauty of *Something Higher*, but also what it is that makes Leftover Salmon so significant:

> There is something to say about a band that has been around as long as they have. It is not always one big happy family. There are lots of things daily pulling a band apart. People do stupid shit and you want to strangle them. There is something special about persevering and continuing to make modern, compelling records into your third decade, which they have done. It is a remarkable achievement when the road map for bands going into their third decade is not pretty. Look at the Rolling Stones. They just did a blues cover record, *Blue & Lonesome*. For the Stones, that is completely painless. They don't have to write or sweat or come up with cool ideas. It is easy and no one will give a shit about them doing it. For Salmon, it would be easy to just do a bluegrass album. But to keep trying as hard as they do is worthy of a self-administered pat on the back.

Something Higher was released the first week of May 2018. It was a powerful statement from a band who in their third decade could re-create themselves without changing who they were. It immediately garnered positive reviews that took note of the musical growth and recognized that in their thirtieth year, Salmon is playing perhaps the best they ever have with a mature sense of versatility. *Billboard Magazine* said, "By blending so many elements of two-step, rock 'n' roll, bluegrass and more, they're able to repeatedly maintain a fresh sound, no matter how many years pass."[3] *Marquee Magazine* noted, "There's a cohesiveness in this latest exploration that finds Leftover Salmon comfortably holding its place in the moving currents of cosmic-minded roots music. The band can still get as crazy as they did on their 1992 debut *Bridges to Bert* and they can still furiously pick with patented relaxed precision, but on *Something Higher* the legendary group reminds listeners we could all use some reflective thinking amidst it all."[4] Upon the release of *Something Higher*, *Relix* magazine had high praise for both Salmon and the album: "It's high time to acknowledge that Leftover Salmon is one of the best homegrown acts America has to offer. It's not just that they draw from so many homegrown sources—lots of bands do that these days—it's how they mingle those disparate elements into something uniquely theirs, how they turn out music with staying power . . . A tune as funky as the semi-title track, 'Show Me Something Higher,' probably never would have occurred to the original band, yet it doesn't seem that far removed from those days either."[5]

The album's release was celebrated with a trio of shows. First an intimate party at Etown Hall, in the band's original stomping grounds of Boulder. They followed this up the next day with a co-headlining sold-out show with Phil Lesh's Terrapin Family Band at legendary Red Rocks in Morrison, Colorado. Then, just to prove they had not lost their sense of fun, they played a pop-up show in downtown Denver, the day after Red Rocks, that was not announced until just a few days before.

Leftover Salmon's ability to always persevere and get stronger raises the question, how many bands have weathered the near misses, survived the tragedies, the gut punches, and the kicks to the balls to emerge stronger and better, and in year thirty craft an album that is possibly their best ever? Maybe it's the dogged determination and unyielding work ethic that have been trademarks of the band that have allowed them to find this success. Maybe it is how they are more comfortable as Leftover Salmon now than they have ever been. Or maybe it's simply the consistency they have finally found in their lineup. With the additions of Garrison, Thorn, Robinson, and Deutsch over the years to the core of Emmitt and Herman, Salmon realized the magic that they thought they lost had never really gone.

As they enter their third decade, they seem to be finally settling into their role as elder statesmen who have blazed the path for countless bands. "They have always influenced so many bands since their formation. The whole jamgrass scene. There are so many who owe their existence to Leftover Salmon," says Mark Mercier from Max Creek. Looking back, Emmitt says, "I think we paved the way for a lot of bands because we were crazy enough to get out there in a freaking school bus and tour all parts of the country, at all times of the year. We showed them how it could be done." This role of elder statesmen became more pronounced following the tragic passing of one of their mentors, Col. Bruce Hampton. Hampton passed away unexpectedly May 1, 2017, at "Hampton 70," a show held at the Fox Theatre in Atlanta, to celebrate his seventieth birthday. It featured a massive guest list of musicians, friends, and mentees who joined the legendary Colonel onstage during the four-hour spectacular that was a musical dream. The evening ended with Hampton onstage surrounded by his closest musical friends whom he mentored over the years including Emmitt, Herman, Jeff Sipe, Warren Haynes, Jimmy Herring, Peter Buck, Jon Fishman, Dave Schools, John Bell, John Popper, Jeff Mosier, Derek Trucks, Susan Tedeschi, and others. Hampton closed out the evening by leading the assembled musicians through his favorite song, the Bobby "Blue" Bland classic, "Turn on Your Lovelight." As the song neared its climatic conclusion, Hampton signaled for fourteen-year-old Brandon "Taz" Niederauer, another of his young protégées, to take a solo. As Niederauer began to solo, Hampton appeared to playfully lay down on the stage in honor of Niederaur's blistering guitar work. But the playfulness soon turned tragic, as it turned out Hampton had collapsed onstage. The show was quickly ended as Hampton started to receive medical attention. He regained a pulse backstage as EMTs worked on him, but he would depart the physical world a short time later at the hospital. The mystical magic and conflicting emotions that were so common in the presence of Hampton was not lost on Herman. "It was my favorite live music moment ever. Until the end."

Herman long looked to Hampton as a mentor. Hampton's gregarious personality and life-changing lessons about music have been a guiding factor in everything Herman has done since first crossing paths with him. Over the years he has taken on many of the legendary Colonel's best qualities. Herman humbly will say there is no way he could replace Hampton, but his presence onstage and off- speaks otherwise. Like Hampton, he believes in being "out," in being free on stage and off. When performing, Herman seems to channel the spiritual freedom and emotional, musical wanderlust Hampton embodied onstage. The Big Wu's Chris Castino noticed these similarities the first time he ever saw Leftover Salmon play. "When I did get to hear Salmon play for the first time, I was reminded of Col. Bruce in Vince Herman. Here was a similarly burly and beady-eyed preacher/singer who could spit lyrics with dizzying speed and venom." Herman, like Hampton, has an affinity for the absurd and for creative wordplay. When informed Hampton once called Leftover Salmon, "The Beatles of Puebla, Colorado," Herman's joyous laughter could not be contained as he continually repeated, "The Beatles of Puebla, Colorado," with a constant childish giggle and a huge smile plastered across his face. Also, much like Hampton, the number of bands Herman has helped mentor over the years is staggering. Salmon immortalized Hampton on *Something Higher* with the Emmitt-penned "Astral Traveler," in which he summed up the enigmatic presence of Hampton, singing, "Nowhere is no here no space without time, you came from a universe a million miles away, moonbeams and starlight couldn't make you stay."

For the uninitiated, it is easy to hear some of Leftover Salmon's more silly songs, see the costumes they have been known to wear onstage, witness the band lead the crowd in parade formation around the campgrounds, see them host a naked hippie race, or watch someone in the band get a haircut onstage and lose sight of how utterly important a band they are. Their genius lies in their ability to be all of that and still write socially, politically, and spiritually aware songs that resonate with the most powerful of all time, and still, their ability to write songs that document the reality we live in is but a small part of who Leftover Salmon is. They showed how you can take music seriously, but never lose sight of the fact it is supposed to be fun. They follow the ideal that if it is not fun, it is probably not worth doing, but at the same time they were always serious enough to put on an amazing show.

Leftover Salmon is the bridge from the roots of bluegrass to rock to jambands to jamgrass—a style of music they helped create by simply being themselves. Over their thirty years, they helped pioneer the jamband scene, practically invented the idea of the late-night tent at music festivals, and opened the door for an army of bands who looked up to what they did and followed in their footsteps. Over their thirty-year career, Leftover Salmon has helped keep alive one of the great American musical genres, bluegrass, in their own special way and help introduce it to a generation that was unfamiliar with it. Through their continued influence, Salmon has ensured that bluegrass music is in good hands as it heads into the future. "It is impossible to overstate the importance of them as a band and as people in my life," says Yonder Mountain String Band's Kaufmann. "They have affected every possible turning point in my career. You could not find a more important band or group of people who had an impact on my life musically and on my career." Kaufmann is not alone in his high praise of Salmon. Bluegrass guitarist Larry Keel calls them "heroes," explaining, "They always make me feel comfortable, inspired, fired-up, laid-back, free-spirited, ready to rock. Those guys are just super special."

One night while hanging out backstage after a Leftover Salmon show, Hard Working Americans' Chad Staehly remarked to Emmitt how much he loved what they did. With a laugh, Emmitt responded,

"What do we do? Because I have been trying to figure it out since we started." Staehly says he struggled to find the right words to explain to Emmitt what he meant that night. Later Staehly would explain, "They have always melded so many styles together. They are a true melting pot of American roots music, bluegrass, rock-'n'-roll, blues, jazz, folk, all of that. At the time, I didn't know the term 'Americana,' but looking back at it, that was what I was trying to describe when I started explaining it to him." Part of what was so appealing to Staehly about Salmon is how they have always been willing to letting everyone hear what they had for musical lunch that day. Of not being afraid to show their roots. Much as Hampton fully believed in the idea music should reflect life, that it should not always be the same, that if you had a good day or a bad one, it should be reflected when you play. Salmon have always let their daily lives, their travel, the scene at the show, the venue, and the crowd lead them to where they are going every night. It is this free approach to making music that has defined Salmon over their thirty-year career and made them such a forward-thinking, inspirational band as they toyed with the roots of traditional styles of music. "That is the magic in Leftover Salmon," says Staehly, "and what has kept people coming back through the years and what continues to bring new fans into the fold."

In an interview in December 2000, Mark Vann reflected on Salmon's ability to bring new fans into the fold. He more than anyone in the band came from a straight traditional bluegrass background and had been dragged into a brand-new world when he first met Emmitt and Herman. Once in that new world, he could not wait to introduce everyone to the traditional music he grew up with and was at the core of Salmon. He knew every night onstage he had a platform to expose fans to new music. He knew the way Salmon twisted bluegrass into something resembling rock was an original approach to a traditional genre and an avenue for people to start their discovery of the bluegrass and traditional music he loved so much. "It's satisfying seeing people find out, 'Hey this Leftover Salmon stuff is cool,'" explained Vann. "And telling them, 'If you think this is cool, you should hear the stuff we listened to that got us to play like this.'"[6]

While new to Salmon, Deutsch has been around the jamband scene long enough to fully comprehend the importance of what Salmon is achieving at this stage in their long career. "You would be hard pressed to find a band that has been around thirty years and are making better records now than in their first decade. It is really uncommon. Salmon is doing this. I think the new record, *Something Higher*, is the best one Salmon has ever done, and I think it is a testament to Drew and Vince continuing on their path." He continues, "When a band has been around this long you go from just being a band to being a national treasure."

Like Deutsch, Robinson is in awe of what Salmon is doing in their thirtieth year. "We are still packing the house and playing amazing venues," he says. "We are respected by everyone. For Drew and Vince to have been doing it for thirty years and to allow me to come in and be myself, that is unheard of. Many bands get new people, especially a younger cat like me who was twenty-three when he joined, but usually they tell them to play our music this way. These guys never did that. They said here is the music, you play how you feel, and if you play the music there is no restraint on what you do. They said, 'We are not hiring you to play everything another drummer did, we are hiring you to play and do your thing.' That is incredible. That is some Miles Davis shit."

Thorn, whom Herman calls, "The most positive expression of music you can ever run into on the planet," helped bridge the band from the hiatus to the present.[7] He has seen Salmon move from bad times to good and simply states, "Right now is an awesome time for us." For the banjo player who was long a fan of the band before he joined, he recognizes the qualities of Emmitt and Herman and how they have created an atmosphere so welcoming to the younger musicians in the band which has allowed Leftover Salmon to find new life in its third decade. "I always have loved this band," he says. "I loved those guys before I even knew them. I just thought they were so cool onstage and had so much fun. All the stuff I hoped they would be before I joined, they were. Vince is the most fun person to be around in the world. Everything is just more fun when he is there. And Drew has always been so good to me, he is like a big brother."

Since joining in 2000, Garrison has been the conscience and steadying influence of the band. He is a realist who is unafraid to tell it like he sees it, and often has the most straightforward impression of the band. In his nearly two decades with Salmon, he has seen it all, and is able to put it in all into to proper perspective:

The current lineup is the most productive I've been a part of. Everyone is happy to be here, understands what we are trying to do, and is
committed to being a part of Leftover Salmon. The willingness to
rehearse, to practice our craft, put time and energy into coming up
with creative ideas, is something that has developed with this lineup.
I credit Vince and Drew for seeing there are musicians now who
want to consistently do those things. Not that the band was bad in
the past, but there was a, "Well, we're Leftover Salmon, we don't
rehearse, it's all off the cuff. It's a party who cares if the music is bad
sometimes," kind of vibe that went on. The true legacy is really the
music you leave behind in the end and hopefully we can make a few
more good records to add to the pile.

Even thirty years on, there is still a family feel to Leftover Salmon
often not found in other bands who have been around that long. "Any
band who makes it through thirty years has done something special,"
reflects Garrison. "And it has always been a working band. It's not like
we make a record, do a big tour, collect our cash, and go live in Maui
until the next record. We spend pretty much half the year together,
every year. Truly a second family." They may not hang out every day or
live together on an old ranch as they did when they first started, but
Herman says even today he, "More than ever," enjoys the company of
his bandmates. This family quality is not lost on manager Joy. "This is a
real family band that has stuck around," he says. "They have been
through everything any other family goes through, all the ups and
downs. There are a lot of major hiccups that have kept us from getting
to the next level. But in the end, there is unconditional love with this
band that keeps us together. Even if we want to strangle each other
from time to time." For Herman, Joy is a huge part of that family and an
important reason why they are still going strong in their thirtieth year.
"The band would not be around without John's guidance. He made
getting back together happen. He really looks out for us."

The hiccups Joy spoke of are often personal regrets that weigh heavi-
est on Emmitt and Herman. Both men recognizing the time they lost
with family due to the nonstop touring of the band over the years. "My
regret is having less time with my kids," says Herman. "Those early days
of the band we were gone so much. That is my biggest regret of what
the band took away from me. I was missing a whole lot of family time."
At the same time, Herman expresses surprise he is still here today and

doing what he loves. "There have been so many different phases of this band. I started playing with Drew when I was just out of college. It was pretty footloose and hippie van when we first started. There was my first marriage and there was another marriage. I've gone through all these periods of change in my life and somehow Salmon has kept going constantly right through them all."

With thirty years together as band, an even longer partnership with Herman, and a new, bright future ahead, the always thoughtful Emmitt reflects on his life in Leftover Salmon. "There are always regrets," he says. "These people that say they have no regrets are completely full of shit. It's like fuck you, everyone has regrets. That's life. Things don't always go the way you want them to, and you have to live with it. I regret Mark didn't live to see the success of the band beyond when he

Since a chance meeting at the Walrus Saloon in October 1985, Drew Emmitt and Vince Herman have formed a partnership that has triumphed during the highs and weathered the lows of Leftover Salmon. During that time, they have left an indelible mark, influencing countless musicians and bringing untold joy to even countless more. The pair, pictured here backstage following a show in Ashland, Oregon, March 21, 2018, play with an energy and enthusiasm that belies their thirty-year career. Photograph by the author.

passed, because it got way better. I regret my parents never got to see this because they both passed." Emmitt also mentions *The Nashville Sessions* and his feeling the album never got the due it deserved. While the album has had a life, and is continually recognized as the band's undisputed masterpiece, Emmitt says, "I feel that is the one we got cheated on. I feel it should have gotten more accolades. It deserved it. It was a milestone for us. I am glad it has had such a long life. I am so proud of it." Even with those regrets, Emmitt is thankful for what Leftover Salmon has accomplished and the longevity and influence they have had. "It would have been nice to be bigger," he says, "but to be honest we have been playing in this band for thirty years and supporting our families and working steadily. What more can you ask for? There are a lot of bands that last two years and maybe get huge then are done. But to do this thirty years and still have people coming out to hear us and having people interested in what we are doing and loving it, you can't ask for more than that."

Herman is also thankful for Salmon's longevity and the influential role they have played in the lives of so many bands. "I guess we are proof that by showing up as a band consistently it is possible to make a living playing music," he says understating the true legacy of his band. Over their thirty years, Leftover Salmon has done more than simply show up. They have shown the importance and value of music and gathering with other people to listen to it live. They have shown how nothing beats standing in a field with no shoes on, with friends on a sunny day listening to music you love. Leftover Salmon has made it clear how the shared energy between fan and band is something we all can use to blow away the troubled times and enjoy even more in the good ones. "Getting out and playing music is important for the artist, but it is even more important to society," explains Herman. "In this world you have church, sports, and music to bring us together. That is how society works. To lose live music as a community glue would be tragic. It is important we have human interactions in a live setting. I'm glad we have been big promoters of that in an era when it seems valued less. It is what humans do. We are meant to make music. I am glad to say that is what Leftover Salmon has done for the past thirty years."

For Leftover Salmon, it has been a long journey, one long, hard climb. A journey that is still ongoing. "The way I feel about the band right now is we are growing," says Emmitt. "But I feel we have the best band we have ever had. I don't know if you could ask for more." It has been a journey that began from the humblest of beginnings and seen them break through and their dreams really come true somehow. "Going from the campground at Telluride to headlining the main stage," says Emmitt. "I never would have dreamed I would have been in a band that furthered tradition. To take the influences I had growing up and to take them further out with Leftover Salmon, making it more of rock 'n' roll thing, but still playing bluegrass. In a way, it was like a fairy tale. Along the way we got to play with all our heroes. I feel blessed to have spent over half my life playing in this band. I'm blessed for all the places we've gone, all the people we have played with, all the festivals, all the music we have got to make, and all the smiling faces out there we have gotten to light up."

Chapter 13

LEFTOVER SALMON

Leftover Salmon, one of the Great American Treasures.—*David Lowery (Camper Van Beethoven, Cracker)*[1]

Leftover Salmon is a band who has influenced many and is friends to all. Many of these musicians were fans long before they started their own bands. Salmon gave them license to start those bands and play music the way they wanted. All those friends and those influenced had much to say about their heroes and friends.

Reed Foehl (Acoustic Junction): I first met Leftover Salmon in 1990 in Boulder, Colorado, when they were playing every other Tuesday at a club called J.J. McCabes. Vince was the first one I met and we were fast friends and supporters of each other's music. Musically they were and are all about the spirit of fun and good times.

Mark Mercier (Max Creek): I was introduced to Leftover Salmon when we co-billed at the Hampton Beach, New Hampshire Casino (August 2, 1995). My impression was these guys were not only spectacular musicians, but they, shall we say, also loved to have a good time.

Dango Rose (Elephant Revival): I'll never forget the first show I saw in 1996 when I caught a hot dog launched from the stage.

Cris Jacobs (Cris Jacobs Band): I discovered Leftover Salmon when I was in college. They were my favorite band to see live during those years. Not only were they shredders, but they just knew how to have fun and make everyone in the room have fun. It was a revelation to see the genre bending they could pull off. As someone who loves so many different styles and never wanted to settle for just one, it was inspiring.

Dave Katz (ekoostik hookah): The first time I met them was at Hookahville in 1997. All I knew about them at the time was they were a great bluegrass band from Colorado. Of course, it didn't take long to realize they were much more than that. Bluegrass was just a platform they used to launch into a variety of genres, which made them more versatile than other bluegrass bands of that time. On a personal level, they were all extremely friendly and easy to be around. Vince, of course, is one of the most outgoing souls you could ever meet, and Drew, while quieter in nature, is also a blast to be around. If my memory serves me well, I believe there was some golf cart bowling going on that weekend.

James "Fuzz" Sangiovanni (Deep Banana Blackout, Caravan of Thieves): It was at a festival in Colorado in either 1998 or '99, when we first met Leftover Salmon and saw their spin on bluegrass, folk, and rock, which was yet another creative direction to take on this scene. I noticed Salmon had good songs, which is always important to me. The musicianship was solid and they were fun and lighthearted, which was infectious with the audience. I felt it, too. In addition, the fusion of the traditional styles and the unique spin on them set them apart from many of the other acts. On- and offstage, they were friendly, funny, and welcoming, which was further confirmation about the inviting nature of the jam scene we were still getting our feet wet in at the time.

Jon Stickley (Jon Stickley Trio): I heard of them in high school from Andy Thorn. We found out they were going to be playing at Duke University. We ended up going and had no idea what we were in for. It was an all-out rager. I remember being blown away by the energy those guys were putting out, and I'd venture to say they had a big impact on my future musicianship.

Andrew Altman (Railroad Earth): I had heard of Leftover Salmon back in the late nineties when I was college. I remember seeing their sticker behind the bar at Potbelly's in Tallahassee, Florida in 1999 and wondering what the music could possibly sound like with a name like Leftover Salmon. Once I heard them a few years later, it seemed fitting.

Adam Greuel (Horseshoes & Hand Grenades): I scored a bootleg of them when I was thirteen or fourteen years old and could just hear this sense of musical openness and feeling of anything goes, which created this idea of almost magic. As I got older and I got to see them live, I found myself throwing my hands in the air with the biggest smile I could ever create at their shows.

Leftover Salmon's original approach to making music, their unlimited creative expression, the freedom with which they played every show was a revelatory moment for many musicians when they first discovered the band.

Keith Moseley (String Cheese Incident): I was new to the whole bluegrass thing and through them was the first time I heard of Sam Bush or John Hartford or New Grass Revival. It wasn't what I thought bluegrass was supposed to be—a bunch of old guys in lawn chairs and not a lot of fun. It was a musical education seeing those guys.

Anders Beck (Greensky Bluegrass): The impression that still holds true of Salmon was my initial one. They create a vibe that allows you to do whatever you want in music. There are no rules.

Adam Greuel: Salmon unlocked a sense of musical joy in my heart and mind.

John Cowan (New Grass Revival, John Cowan Band): To me, Salmon has always been a wondrous, curious mix of serious musicianship and the revelry of vaudeville, merry pranksters, and carnival.[2]

Dave Johnston (Yonder Mountain String Band): Salmon prove you can have fun and make great music. You don't need to be overly serious. You just need to be genuine and sincere. They have always been great people. When a band is filled with great people and makes great music I have a hard time describing it, because it is not common. Usually you have a lot of great music and rude people.

Larry Keel: This band proves it is OK to be wild and crazy and be yourself, and to push the boundaries and conventional approaches to playing professional music. That example is priceless and one that made a huge impression on me when I met them around age twenty. When anyone, artist or not, is being true to their original nature, that's a success. These guys are such natural, real people, playing incredible music and making fun life moments for the world.

Ben Kaufmann (Yonder Mountain String Band): They are kind, generous, helpful people, who are so gracious with their knowledge, ability, and everything. Literally, they are the most important band and group of musicians in my life.

Keith Moseley: What they do is original and authentic with a lot of heart and soul. The songwriting, the delivery of the songs, the interaction with the audience, are all so genuine and heartfelt and delivered with an appreciation for the music and a love for what they are doing, and the people feel it. Those guys don't fake it in any way, shape, or form. They are who they are and they share that love of the music and it is infectious. Thirty years ago I felt it and I still feel it every time I see them. I hope they do it as long as they love it.

Jim Page: They are great fabulous players. They are unafraid. They are fearless. They go anywhere musically they want to go. They will play anything, in any key, at any speed. There is no ego among them.

Phil Chorney (CEO and Co-Founder Charm City Bluegrass Festival): Leftover Salmon is a band that early on made bluegrass cool, in the same way New Orleans jazz is cool. They could blend these two unique styles to create a style all their own. Their ability to engage the audience and take them on a genre-bending musical journey all within a single set of music is unparalleled and it's what makes them a special, once-in-a-generation band.

The unpredictability of Leftover Salmon shows, the anything-goes and anything-might-happen atmosphere combined with the band's never-ending search for fun, has made every one of their shows a must-see event. Over the years the band has done everything from give each other haircuts onstage, to playing while laying down, to leading huge parades, to wearing outlandish costumes, to countless other wild ideas onstage. This openness they exhibit onstage has made every one of their shows a potential life-changing event for the audience.

Adam Greuel: Salmon is a spiritual band for me. For a lot of us they carry an energy that feels spiritual. It frees some aspect of your soul and freezes time when you are at their show and it makes you want to dance and love. It frees that part of your heart that allows you to go wild and be yourself.

Eric Avey (Mountain Ride): Dance? If you don't dance at a Leftover Salmon concert, you should probably be concerned about your mental state of mind.

Billy Nershi (String Cheese Incident): Leftover Salmon showed people how to take bluegrass music, add that X factor and get everybody dancing their asses off.[3]

"Reverend" Jeff Mosier (Aquarium Rescue Unit, Blueground Undergrass): They let the audience in. They don't keep them at bay. There has never been an arena they have been in that doesn't feel like a small club.

Bill Payne (Little Feat): The pageantry of what they do is so fun and can steal your heart. They hit you on so many levels. I think for people who do not know them, what they are brought into is infectious. The relationship between their audience and what they do onstage is a participatory event.

Tim O'Brien (Hot Rize): They wanted to put on a party for their audience and keep them coming back.

Chris Castino (Big Wu): Leftover Salmon was perfectly suited for festivals. As they found a home in the festival setting, they further developed their diplomatic role therein. They played the part of festival host at many events. I remember many times seeing Vince and Drew in the back of a golf cart picking tunes while rolling through festival campsites late at night. They were the ones who seemed to behave no differently than any of the folks who saved their hard-earned dollar to be there. They were "one of us."

Tim O'Brien: They have a great infectious humor. It is a great feeling.

Larry Keel: I don't think any band before them came close to producing the energy and creativity Salmon achieves every single show. They made their mark in the music world by showing you don't have to present polished, perfectly regurgitated music to be a success and to win audiences and fellow musicians alike. They are joyously themselves. I love that. Their sense of fun and spontaneity and their ultra-open approach to adding guest musician sit-ins was off-the-charts unique at the time.

For many of the band's friends and peers, the chance to join Salmon onstage is an experience never forgotten.

John Cowan: Performing with Salmon was/is always an exercise in letting my eight-year-old self hang out with my freshman-in-college self, hang out with my present-day self. It's always nothing like you think it's going to be, but you know by their smiles they have your back, so it's okay to surrender and just go ahead and jump off the cliff with 'em. [4]

Billy Nershi: I sat in with them one night long before String Cheese. They sang "Zombie Jamboree." Vince sang, "Back to back, belly to belly, I don't give a damn 'cause I'm Billy Nershi." He has a way of making everyone feel special.

John Bell (Widespread Panic): Listening to and playing with the boys are genuine vehicles for having a good time. They are fun and funny to hang with and I've never witnessed an ego-based moment in any of them. They are a rare reminder music is best expressed with a selfless awareness. [5]

John Ginty (Dixie Chicks, Robert Randolph & the Family Band, Citizen Cope): We did quite a few shows together, the Family Band and Leftover Salmon. There were always sit-ins and any show we played in Boulder usually had Bill McKay on the bench with me. Amazing organist!

Joe Craven: I joined the boys for a set at the Hangtown Halloween Ball. We were all adorned in sartorial splendor, from Santa Claus to extraterrestrials to skeletons to pirated minstrels. The extended obnox-iousness went for some time. Seeing and feeling all in theater mode was an extra dollop of mischief that made the pickin' all the more outside the box and thus all the more memorable.

Dave Katz: We have had many sit-ins with Drew and Vince. It's always a great, high-energy experience. Drew's musicianship and versatility are amazing. We can throw anything at him and he blends in flawlessly. Vince is a monster onstage. Generally, when we have him with us, we just hand over the reins. His presence is infectious. Quite a few times we have played songs we've never heard before, let along played before. He just comes up, leads us through the tunes, and it always goes well.

Chris Castino: I remember working on a project with Jeff Austin around 2003–2004 and hearing about the shenanigans and bottle passing of the late-night picks that always seemed to follow Leftover Salmon wherever they went. I was a shitty drinker, so I knew better than to try to keep up with that road show.

The "Big Three" of Drew Emmitt, Vince Herman, and Mark Vann have been inspiring their fellow musicians since they first took the stage together.

Mark Mercier: One thing I have taken from Vince is being comfortable and relaxed with one's talent and music in general. The arts are supposed to be fun and they certainly emanated this from the very beginning.

Steve Berlin (Los Lobos): Vince generally enjoys Vince. He just seems to be happy wherever he is.

Reed Foehl: Vince is one of my all-time favorites. Such a bright light. I called him the "Pied Piper," because he could get anybody to do just about anything. Quintessential born leader.

Mark Mercier: Vince played a Camp Creek show with Rob Wasserman as a duo. They were great. After the show we spent time, until the wee hours, in a mutual friend's RV. I believe I accomplished the impossible by out-partying Vince. Difficult to do and not necessarily a moral high point in the claim-to-fame department, but fun nonetheless and we are all still here to talk about it.

Tim O'Brien: Whatever Vince can think of he will do. I remember going to a gig in Durango. He made up these stickers that said "Party," or other sayings like that you could put on your shirt. I had one I got that night that said, "Feel Better," and I still have it on my mandolin case.

Reed Foehl: Drew is sweet, kind, super talented, and has a golden voice. Always up for a jam. A bit more internal, a perfect counter partner to Vince.

Tyler Grant (Grant Farm, Drew Emmitt Band): Drew is a hell of a singer but is even more well known for his prowess on the mandolin. When he does the big, loud tremolo lick at the climax of his solos, Chris

Pandolfi and I call it the "Jet Engine Lick," it whips the hippies into a frenzy.

Jon Stickley: One time at Northwest String Summit, Drew sat politely while I sang him half the songs from *The Nashville Sessions*.

Cris Jacobs: I've had the pleasure of playing and hanging with Drew the last few years. He is such a badass. He invited me to sit in with Salmon at a festival in West Virginia in 2017, and it was such a blast. Just thinking back on being a budding musician just learning how to play and looking up to these guys and then being up there ripping it up with Drew and Vince was such a trip.

Tyler Grant: Drew is such a genuine cat who really cares about others. I became tied with his family early on when I was playing with the Drew Emmitt Band. I would fly from Nashville to Colorado for summer tour dates and stay with the Emmitts. I was kind of like Uncle Tyler cooking eggs for everyone in the morning. While in Crested Butte, Drew turned me on to mountain biking and taught me how to ski.

Greg Spatz (Farmer's Trust, John Reischman & the Jaybirds): Mark Vann was fun-loving, innovative and willing to try almost anything musically for the sheer love of playing. How that translates into a lasting impact, I don't know, but I'd imagine there's an element of jamband culture that takes it inspiration straight from the open-minded spirit of his playing.

Cris Jacobs: I caught a heavy banjo bug around 1997 and thought that's what I wanted to play exclusively. I was in awe of Mark Vann. I remember they were playing in town one night (October 17, 1997 at Pearl Street in Northampton, Massachusetts) and I showed up way early while they were sound checking with my banjo in hand. I waited quietly in the back and when they were done, I approached Mark and told him I was just getting started and loved his playing. Some guys would just dismiss this long-haired, bearded hippie and say "thanks" and be on their way, but Mark sat down with me for a good forty-five minutes and showed me some stuff and was the most gracious, sweet, humble guy.

Over their thirty-year career, Leftover Salmon has inspired count-less bands and created a template and road map for them to follow.

Jeff Coffin (Béla Fleck & the Flecktones, Dave Matthews Band): The legacy of Salmon is they loved what they did and because of that they inspired others.

Chad Staehly (Great American Taxi, Hard Working Americans): Leftover Salmon inspired me to pursue music as a profession. They made me believe anything was possible if you did the work, had fun doing it, and kept at it. They also helped me believe in real magic, when you would see the nights when it all connected, the players in the band, the crowd, the setting, the sound, the chemicals, the vibe. It was nothing short of magic, pure alchemy. They know how to open it and channel it. I've had some of the most amazing times of my life at Leftover Salmon shows and I am grateful for it to no end. They have inspired many others to believe in the magic and for that they have made the world an infinitely better place.

Keller Williams: The most visible and obvious sign of their legacy is their love of and commitment to the festivarian movement. Festival life is a bit of a community.

Joe Craven: They reinforced my conviction to cover old calypso music.

Dango Rose: They helped show me how boundaries in musical form are elusive. More than anything they showed me how to leave it all on the stage, no matter the circumstances, and to have a damn good time!

Jim Page: Their lasting influence is the fun, the experimentation, the beauty of the orchestration, the daring to do things, and the generosity. You put all that together and you have a definition of who they are. A generous, orchestral, improvisational outfit.

Rob Derhak (moe.): We saw what they were doing and it inspired us to put more energy into the live show and connect with the audience. I didn't get how important that was until I saw them.

Reed Foehl: Their lasting legacy is to just have fun with music. Work hard, but realize it is not rocket science or brain surgery. It's the eternal search for euphoria.

Jeff Austin (Jeff Austin Band): They taught multiple generations to be not only completely fearless, but to be comfortable in the weirdness and the truth that is your own fucking skin.

Jon Stickley: I find Salmon's musical evolution inspiring. To me, it seems they are all really open to everyone's musical ideas and let everyone in the band have their own personality. With each lineup change the band grows a little bit and welcomes what that person brings to the table. They also keep it real and still go straight-up Polyethnic Cajun slamgrass when they need to. One of the coolest things about the band, is everyone's personality shines through so strong to create a collective cohesive sound.

Bobby Britt (Town Mountain): I think Leftover's impact is that of bringing solid musicianship, bluegrass, and Cajun influences and creating a positive, carefree vibe, and sense of community. They made it OK to have a good time and jam, while still maintaining a level of bluegrass and roots music musical integrity.

Jon Stickley: One thing that always sticks with me about a Leftover Salmon show is everyone is making honest music and singing and playing from the heart. These guys wear their hearts on their sleeves and it makes them incredibly easy to connect with. I need to try to think more about Vince and Drew when I'm onstage with my band.

Annabel Lukins (Artist Programming at Cloud 9 Adventures): They write songs that can be your best friends.

Dave Johnston: The legacy Leftover Salmon has established and continues to establish is music is more than just being a comment on things or a self-aggrandizing version of protest. They have made music a celebration again. They do it in a way where there is nothing dishonest about it. It runs counter to what you normally see. It is not superficial. It is genuine. It is technical, but it is not soulless. There are a lot of good things they engendered in younger musicians. They have instilled a lot of great attitudes. They help foster and create that. They have this great body of music and it has helped a wonderful form of American music to change and to become relevant.

Joe Craven: Holding a richly deserved trophy in a Kodak photo moment, while occupying an honored place at the round table of jamband culture, Leftover Salmon, with all their fans in tow, proudly doth know, they have expanded and promoted jamband vitality, humanity, diversity, and unity, all the while in a joyous state of euphoric insanity.

Jeremy Garrett (Infamous Stringdusters): Leftover Salmon is an institution for how to keep a band going strong for years, but at the same time still be pushing their creativity to new dimensions.

Andrew Altman: I mean, thirty years is impressive. Having been on the road full-time for the last ten years, it can be easy to fall in a rut and some people it will just break. To hang with those guys and still see them smiling and enjoying themselves can give you hope that the road doesn't have to be the death sentence that some make it out to be.

Chad Staehly: Their legacy is the fact they are about to hit their thirtieth anniversary. It's hard to keep a band together for a year, much less thirty. That takes a lot of hard work and a lot of people responding to that work.

Their influence includes the creation of a whole new sound. One that found them melding the bluegrass music they found in the mountains of Colorado, along with a more pronounced rock sound and delivering it with an intense blast of energy that immediately found a home in the jamband scene.

Jeff Sipe (Aquarium Rescue Unit, Leftover Salmon): Salmon was among the first bands that went electric and added drums. They were influenced by everything from Bill Monroe to Jimi Hendrix and all in between. Combine that with Vince Herman's ability to hold an audience in the palm of his hand with a single phrase, Drew Emmitt's vocals and songwriting, their adventurous spirit, and love for life, and they created a brave new world.

Bob Gabing (The Blues Orphans): Seeing them plug in and put drums behind bluegrass was enormous. To see them take that into little rock 'n' roll bars was something special. They were playing bluegrass rock and no one was doing anything like that.

Pete Wernick (Hot Rize): They are the zany "explorers" out on the edge in rock-land, but still looking back over their shoulder at the bluegrass friendlies and visiting us sometimes.

Dave Katz: They melded bluegrass into a conglomeration of so many styles and really created a unique sound. Where are they today? They're still at the forefront of the jam scene getting fans of many genres to dance to their unique sound.

Annabel Lukins: They have never just been bluegrass, there is nothing standard and ordinary about them. They are the forefathers of the bluegrass jamband scene.

David Lowery (Camper Van Beethoven, Cracker): I believe they are the guys that brought bluegrass to the jam world and you see a lot of that now. It's everywhere, and they brought that in; they made that part of it. Before, it was more jazz-based and now it seems there's more roots-based stuff and clearly, they were the first ones to really do that.[6]

Sam Bush (New Grass Revival, Sam Bush Band): Their mark is their kind of newgrass, their kind of slamgrass. They are so much more than just slamgrass. If you want to slam it there is no one better at, but they can also lift the audience up when they want to do a bluegrass kind of number. I think their lasting impression will be good material, good songs they have written, and great musicianship.

Dave Watts (The Motet): Leftover Salmon is a Colorado staple and have given the Colorado music scene, especially in the genre of bluegrass and American roots music, some real credence and credibility as far as musicianship and musicality goes.

Eric Avey: Leftover Salmon assured us it was OK to party and play bluegrass. They also taught us it was OK to cross many genres with bluegrass. To me, they were the innovators of jamgrass. Although David Grisman created the acoustic version of jamgrass, Salmon took it up a few notches. Many bluegrass bands added drums but not like these guys. I am certain their music will live on long after we are all gone.

Al Goll (Left Hand String Band, Nashville String Kings): They have carved out a niche for themselves. A unique brand of music with elements of bluegrass and rock. The jam session part of it. I think it is great to have your own thing. They are at the top of the heap in their genre.

For Leftover Salmon, they have left a legacy that cannot be simply measured by ticket or album sales. Their legacy cannot be judged by normal standards; their impact, influence, and inspiration on a new generation of bands does not fit into a well-defined box that can be measured by normal metrics. Salmon's legacy is shown in the bands that have followed in their footsteps, that have played with a sense of free-

dom, with a fearlessness that they learned from watching and listening to Salmon.

Jeremy Garrett: I can't help but think about how much credit they deserve for what they have accomplished in the music industry. Not to mention the amount of influence they've had over the field through the years.

Chad Staehly: One of the most obvious signs of their legacy is how many bands have emulated them. Proof of their accomplishments is in how many of their musical heroes have joined them onstage.

Dango Rose: Leftover Salmon spreads unheralded amounts of joy at their concerts and has taught multiple generations how to enjoy life through the vehicle of music as teacher, even if it's just for a few hours at a time. That is important work in this world, and without them, I don't know if I'd be on the path I am today.

Jon Stickley: One of the most visible signs of their legacy is all the young, up-and-coming musicians they have encouraged and nurtured along the way, myself included. They have shown us the way and we are going to carry on that tradition.

Tyler Grant: Ultimately their songs, recordings, and performances stand on their own in their strength and significance, but they also drew people into their scene and showed everyone how to have a raging good time.

Jon Stickley: I think the general lack of pretentiousness, the feel-good vibes, and the spirit of love and togetherness are the main aspects of Salmon that will have a lasting influence. When I think of them and their music, I get this relaxed feeling and it makes me stop taking myself so seriously.

Jeff Austin: You cannot begin to count the impact they have had. They have taught so many people.

Jimmy Herring (Aquarium Rescue Unit, Widespread Panic): When I look at Drew and Vince I just smile every time I see them play. I just love those guys. They have carved out a special niche with what they do in this world.

Adam Aijala (Yonder Mountain String Band): From my perspective I still admire them, I still look up to them. I am so impressed by what they do.

Cris Jacobs: I have nothing but love and respect for them as a band. They just exude fun, don't take themselves too seriously and make people happy. There isn't much of a better legacy to have as a human being, let alone a band.

Chuck Morris (CEO AEG Presents - Rocky Mountain and Northwest Division): What has kept them going is a great, great live show that makes people have fun. Their live show is the heart that makes a body run. I have had more fun with that band. I love going to their shows. I love promoting them. They just make it fun. That is what has kept them vibrant and popular and everyone rooting for them.

Annabel Lukins: I'm more in love with this band now than I ever have been, and I have loved this band for twenty-two years.

Adam Greuel: I don't know if it gets any better than Leftover Salmon in terms of joy and musical exploration.

Adam Aijala: I always think, "How does everyone not know who they are, because they are so awesome."

Col. Bruce Hampton: There is nothing like them.

NOTES

PREFACE

1. Bill Frater, "Keeping the Dead Alive with Tim Lynch," *No Depression*, http://nodepression.com/article/keeping-dead-alive-tim-lynch (accessed February 14, 2017).

CHAPTER 1. DREW EMMITT

1. *Years in Your Ears* (DVD).
2. Christopher Orman, "It Felt Great to Play Bluegrass Again: An Interview with Drew Emmitt." Jambands.com, http://www.jambands.com/features/2002/05/21/it-felt-great-to-play-bluegrass-again-an-interview-with-drew-emmitt (accessed May 27, 2015).
3. Nancy Dunham, "Leftover Salmon: 20 Years Down River," jambase.com, http://www.jambase.com/article/leftover-salmon-20-years-down-river (accessed April 20, 2015).
4. Christopher Orman, "It Felt Great to Play Bluegrass Again: An Interview with Drew Emmitt." Jambands.com, http://www.jambands.com/features/2002/05/21/it-felt-great-to-play-bluegrass-again-an-interview-with-drew-emmitt (accessed May 27, 2015).
5. Audrey Dwyer, "Leftover Salmon Returns to Celebrate Ski Season," Steamboat Today, http://www.steamboattoday.com/news/2016/apr/07/leftover-salmon-back-town-celebrate-2015-2016-ski-/ (accessed August 8, 2016).
6. Benny Galloway, "Bio," Facebook.com, https://www.facebook.com/bennyburlegalloway/about/ (accessed October 21, 2016).

7. Neil Rosenberg, *Bluegrass: A History*. Urbana: University of Illinois Press. 1985, 298.

8. Left Hand String Band concert recorded at Strawberry Bluegrass Festival, Camp Mather, California, September 9, 1991.

9. Dean Budnick, "What Is a Jam Band?" jambands.com, https://web.archive.org/web/20070124191643/http://www.jambands.com/jamband.html (accessed August 12, 2016).

10. Jeremy Lach, "Interview w/ Vince Herman and Drew Emmitt of Leftover Salmon," stringcheeseradio.com, http://stringcheeseradio.com/interviews/interview-w-vince-herman-drew-emmitt-of-leftover-salmon (accessed November 2, 2016).

CHAPTER 2. VINCE HERMAN

1. McClain Johnson, "Leftover Salmon Interview," McClainJohnson.com, https://mcclainjohnson.com/leftover-salmon-interview/ (accessed June 3, 2015).

2. McClain Johnson, "Leftover Salmon Interview," McClainJohnson.com, https://mcclainjohnson.com/leftover-salmon-interview/ (accessed June 3, 2015).

3. Evan Schlansky, "Market Value: A Q & A with Leftover Salmon," *American Songwriter*, http://americansongwriter.com/2012/04/market-value-a-qa-with-leftover-salmon/ (accessed April 16, 2012).

4. "Trey Anastasio tells Bobby Weir About Life-Changing Concert," YouTube.com, https://www.youtube.com/watch?v=90ItoM-wrmc (accessed October 24, 2016).

5. Derek Halsey, "The Best Jam I Ever Heard: Vince Herman," *The Bluegrass Situation*, http://www.thebluegrasssituation.com/read/best-jam-i-ever-heard-vince-herman (accessed September 22, 2016).

6. McClain Johnson, "Leftover Salmon Interview," McClainJohnson.com, https://mcclainjohnson.com/leftover-salmon-interview/ (accessed June 3, 2015).

7. Nancy Dunham, "Leftover Salmon: 20 Years Down the River," Jambase.com, http://www.jambase.com/article/leftover-salmon-20-years-down-river (accessed September 20, 2016).

8. Nick Hutchinson, "Q &A with Vince Herman of Leftover Salmon," *Westword*, http://www.westword.com/music/qanda-with-vince-herman-of-leftover-salmon-5708191 (accessed November 8, 2016).

9. Nancy Dunham, "Leftover Salmon: 20 Years Down the River," Jambase.com, http://www.jambase.com/article/leftover-salmon-20-years-down-river (accessed September 20, 2016).

10. Jared Keller, "An Oral History of the Telluride Bluegrass Festival," *Outside Online*, https://www.outsideonline.com/1916561/oral-history-telluride-bluegrass-festival (accessed November 8, 2016).

CHAPTER 3. MARK VANN

1. Dan Maser, "Mark Vann: Playing Banjo in a Rock 'n' Roll Band!" *Banjo Newsletter*, December 2000.

2. Dan Maser, "Mark Vann: Playing Banjo in a Rock 'n' Roll Band!" *Banjo Newsletter*, December 2000.

3. Dan Maser, "Mark Vann: Playing Banjo in a Rock 'n' Roll Band!" *Banjo Newsletter*, December 2000.

4. Dan Maser, "Mark Vann: Playing Banjo in a Rock 'n' Roll Band!" *Banjo Newsletter*, December 2000.

5. Dan Maser, "Mark Vann: Playing Banjo in a Rock 'n' Roll Band!" *Banjo Newsletter*, December 2000.

6. *Years in Your Ears* (DVD).

7. Eric J. Wallace, "The Greatest, Most Original Guitar Player You've Never Heard Of," *The Piedmont Virginian*, https://piedmontvirginian.com/on-the-trail-of-larry-keel/ (accessed November 9, 2016).

8. Taco, "Jamwich exclusive interview with Larry Keel," *Appalachian Jamwich*, http://www.thejamwich.com/2012/07/10/jamwich-exclusive-interview-with-larry-keel/ (accessed September 30, 2016).

9. Taco, "Jamwich exclusive interview with Larry Keel," *Appalachian Jamwich*, http://www.appalachianjamwich.com/2012/07/10/jamwich-exclusive-interview-with-larry-keel/ (accessed September 30, 2016).

10. Scott Caffrey, "Leftover Salmon: The King of Fish," jambase.com, http://www.jambase.com/Articles/6055/LEFTOVER-SALMON-THE-KING-OF-FISH/0 (accessed August 25, 2015).

11. Scott Caffrey, "Leftover Salmon: The King of Fish," jambase.com, http://www.jambase.com/Articles/6055/LEFTOVER-SALMON-THE-KING-OF-FISH/0 (accessed August 25, 2015).

12. Jared Keller, "An Oral History of the Telluride Bluegrass Festival," *Outside Magazine*, https://www.outsideonline.com/1916561/oral-history-telluride-bluegrass-festival (accessed November 11, 2016).

13. Dan Maser, "Mark Vann: Playing Banjo in a Rock 'n' Roll Band!" *Banjo Newsletter*, December 2000.

14. Dan Maser, "Mark Vann: Playing Banjo in a Rock 'n' Roll Band!" *Banjo Newsletter*, December 2000.

15. Casey Phillips, "Q&A with Drew Emmitt of the jamgrass band Leftover Salmon," *Chattanooga Times Free Press*, April 20, 2012. http://www.timesfreepress.com/news/chattanooganow/music/story/2012/apr/20/q-drew-emmitt-jamgrass-band-leftover-salmon/75922/ (accessed November 16, 2016).

16. Nancy Dunham, "Leftover Salmon: 20 Years Down the River," Jambase.com, http://www.jambase.com/article/leftover-salmon-20-years-down-river (accessed September 20, 2016).

17. Nancy Dunham, "Leftover Salmon: 20 Years Down the River," Jambase.com, http://www.jambase.com/article/leftover-salmon-20-years-down-river (accessed September 20, 2016).

18. Scott Caffrey, "Leftover Salmon: The King of Fish," Jambase.com, http://www.jambase.com/Articles/6055/LEFTOVER-SALMON-THE-KING-OF-FISH/0, (Accessed August 25, 2015).

19. Geoffrey Himes, "The Nitty Gritty on Leftover Salmon," *Washington Post*, November 19, 1999, page 10.

20. Telluride Bluegrass Festival program guide 1990.

21. Leftover Salmon. Concert recorded in Boulder, Colorado. April 16, 1993.

CHAPTER 4. MICHAEL WOOTEN

1. Christopher Orman, "Freedom Ride—Drew Emmitt," jambands.com http://www.jambands.com/reviews/cds/2002/03/20/freedom-ride-drew-emmitt (accessed October 17, 2017).

2. *Years in Your Ears* (DVD).

3. Findlay, "Euphoric Salmon Swim to the Farm," *The Post and Courier*, Charleston, SC. August 21, 1997, 18.

4. Andy Stonehouse, "Reeling It All In: After 15 Years Leftover Salmon Takes a Breather," *Relix*, July 2004, 54–59.

5. Dan Maser, "Mark Vann: Playing Banjo in a Rock 'n' Roll Band!" *Banjo Newsletter*, December 2000.

6. Dan Maser, "Mark Vann: Playing Banjo in a Rock 'n' Roll Band!" *Banjo Newsletter*, December 2000.

7. Dan Maser, "Mark Vann: Playing Banjo in a Rock 'n' Roll Band!" *Banjo Newsletter*, December 2000.

8. Dan Maser, "Mark Vann: Playing Banjo in a Rock 'n' Roll Band!" *Banjo Newsletter*, December 2000.

9. Dan Maser, "Mark Vann: Playing Banjo in a Rock 'n' Roll Band!" *Banjo Newsletter*, December 2000.

10. Dan Maser, "Mark Vann: Playing Banjo in a Rock 'n' Roll Band!" *Banjo Newsletter*, December 2000.

11. Steve Knopper, "Boulder Band Goofy but Professional," *Daily Camera Friday Magazine*, July 17, 1992, 13D.

12. Cameron Crowe, "Carole King and Navarro Mellow Out," *Rolling Stone*, #248, September 22, 1977, 15.

13. Carole King, *A Natural Woman: A Memoir*, Grand Central Publishing, April 10, 2012, 262.

14. *Years in Your Ears* (DVD).

15. *Bridges to Bert*, Hollywood Records, 1997.

16. Margaret Hagenah, "Leftover Salmon: Bridges to Bert," *The Stanford Daily*, #49, May 4, 1995, 11.

17. *Bridges to Bert*, Hollywood Records, 1997.

18. Steve Knopper, "Boulder Band Goofy but Professional," *Daily Camera Friday Magazine*, July 17, 1992, 13D.

19. Steve Knopper, "Boulder Band Goofy but Professional," *Daily Camera Friday Magazine*, July 17, 1992, 13D.

20. Leftover Salmon, August 3, 1996, Warrenton, Virginia.

21. Allen Howie, "Bridges to Bert: Polyethnic Cajun Slamgrass," *Louisville Music News*, #78, August 1995, http://www.louisvillemusicnews.net/webmanager/index.php?WEB_CAT_ID=50&storyid=11698&headline=Leftover_Salmon_%96_Bridges_TO_Bert:_Polyethnic_Caju&issueid=78 (accessed January 3, 2017).

CHAPTER 5. TYE NORTH

1. "Tye North," *Digital Interviews* www.digitalinterviews.com/digitalinterviews/views/north.shtml (accessed June 3, 2015).

2. "Tye North," *Digital Interviews* www.digitalinterviews.com/digitalinterviews/views/north.shtml (accessed June 3, 2015).

3. Jeff Giles, "Spin Doctors: Miracle Cure," *Rolling Stone*, Issue 647, January 7, 1993.

4. Dean Budnick, "Jam Band, Jam-Band, Jamband: How We Got There and Why It Matters (Somewhat)," *Relix*, December–January 2004, 47.

5. Dan Maser, "Mark Vann: Playing Banjo in a Rock 'n' Roll Band!"

6. Dan Maser, "Mark Vann: Playing Banjo in a Rock 'n' Roll Band!"

7. Blair Jackson, *Garcia: An American Life*, 467.

8. *Basically Frightened* (DVD).

9. Elizabeth Elkins, "Pop Music—Preview—Leftover Salmon," *The Atlanta Journal-Constitution*, October 4, 1996, 3.

10. Dan Maser, "Mark Vann: Playing Banjo in a Rock 'n' Roll Band!"

11. Bill Husted, "Name's Fishy, but Leftover Salmon Doesn't Stink," *Denver Post*, July 6, 1997, A-02.

12. Michael Mehle, "Leftover Salmon Finally in the Pink," *Rocky Mountain News*, March 14, 1997, D4.

13. Dunham, Nancy. "Leftover Salmon: 20 Years Down River." jambase.com, http://www.jambase.com/article/leftover-salmon-20-years-down-river.

14. Bill Ellis, "Recordings," *The Commercial Appeal*, Memphis Tennessee, May 3, 1997, C2.

CHAPTER 6. JEFF SIPE

1. Leftover Salmon. Concert recorded in Tahoe City, California. July 9, 1997.

2. Tim Newby, "Jeff Mosier: Lessons Learned," *Honest Tune*, March 20, 2008, https://honesttune.com/jeffmosierlessonslearned/ (accessed November 12, 2017).

3. *Years in Your Ears* (DVD).

4. *Years in Your Ears* (DVD).

5. "Leftover Salmon," *Dupree's Diamond News*, Fall Winter 97, #37, 23.

6. "Jamband Extravaganza," *Guitar World*, August 1997, Vol. 17, #8, 65.

7. "Leftover Salmon," Dupree's Diamond News, Fall Winter 97, #37, 23.

8. Dave Freeman, "Leftover Salmon—From Bill Monroe to Led Zep," *Fort Worth Star-Telegram*, February 7, 1997, page 10.

9. *Years in Your Ears* (DVD).

10. Nancy Dunham, "Leftover Salmon: 20 Years Down River," jambase.com, http://www.jambase.com/article/leftover-salmon-20-years-down-river (accessed April 20, 2015).

11. Geoffrey Himes, "The Nitty Gritty on Leftover Salmon," *Washington Post*, November 19, 1999, 10.

12. Mark Brown, "Leftover Salmon Swimming with Some Big Fish," *Rocky Mountain News*, December 31, 1999, 16D.

13. Michael Mehle, "All Downstream from Here? Leftover Salmon Latest Has a Shot at Cracking Country Radio," *Rocky Mountain News*, October 1, 1999, 18D.

14. Michael Mehle, "All Downstream from Here? Leftover Salmon Latest Has a Shot at Cracking Country Radio," *Rocky Mountain News*, October 1, 1999, 18D.

15. Michael Mehle, "All Downstream from Here? Leftover Salmon Latest Has a Shot at Cracking Country Radio," *Rocky Mountain News*, October 1, 1999, 18D.

16. Dan Maser, "Mark Vann: Playing Banjo in a Rock 'n' Roll Band!"

17. Dan Maser, "Mark Vann: Playing Banjo in a Rock 'n' Roll Band!"

18. Dan Maser, "Mark Vann: Playing Banjo in a Rock 'n' Roll Band!"

19. Nancy Dunham, "Leftover Salmon: 20 Years Down River," jambase.com, http://www.jambase.com/article/leftover-salmon-20-years-down-river (accessed April 20, 2015).

20. Dean Budnick, "Breakin' Thru: Drew Emmitt & Leftover Salmon Enter New Realms," http://www.jambands.com/features/1999/12/15/breakin-thru-drew-emmitt-leftover-salmon-enter-new-realms (accessed September 22, 2017.)

21. Liner Notes, the *Nashville Session*.

22. Leftover Salmon. Concert recorded in Macon, Georgia. March 31, 1999.

23. Michael Mehle, "All Downstream from Here? Leftover Salmon Latest Has a Shot at Cracking Country Radio," *Rocky Mountain News*, October 1, 1999, 18D.

24. Keith Lawrence, "Take a Bite of Leftover Salmon," *The Ledger*, November 9, 1999, D6.

25. John Metzger, "Leftover Salmon—*The Nashville Sessions*," *The Music Box*, December 1999, Volume 6, #12, http://www.musicbox-online.com/ls-nash.html#axzz4wWVzcDcD (accessed September 22, 2017).

26. Scott Caffrey, "Leftover Salmon: The King of Fish," jambase.com, www.jambase.com/Articles/6055/LEFTOVER-SALMON-THE-KING-OF-FISH/0 (Accessed August 25, 2015).

27. Mick Skidmore, "Now, Then, and In Between," *Relix*, December 1999, 75.

28. Geoffrey Himes, "The Nitty Gritty on Leftover Salmon," *Washington Post*, November 19, 1999, 10.

CHAPTER 7. GREG GARRISON

1. Trey Anastasio Band. Concert recorded at Delfest, Cumberland, Maryland. May 24, 2013.

2. Dan Maser, "Mark Vann: Playing Banjo in a Rock 'n' Roll Band!" Banjo Newsletter, December 2000.

3. Tim Newby, "Honey Dewdrops: Heartfelt, Honest Songs," Honest Tune, January 24, 2011, http://www.honesttune.com/honey-dewdrops-heart-felt-honest-songs/ (accessed October 6, 2017).

4. Alan Lomax, "Bluegrass Background: Folk Music with Overdrive," *Esquire*, October 1959, 108.

5. Lizzy Justesen, "Interview: Leftover Salmon," jambase.com https://www.jambase.com/article/interview-leftover-salmon (accessed November 15, 2015).

6. Lizzy Justesen, "Interview: Leftover Salmon," jambase.com https://www.jambase.com/article/interview-leftover-salmon (accessed November 15, 2015).

7. Lizzy Justesen, "Interview: Leftover Salmon," jambase.com https://www.jambase.com/article/interview-leftover-salmon (accessed November 15, 2015).

8. Rick Bell, "Leftover Salmon reveals new taste," *Country Standard Time*, May 2004, http://www.countrystandardtime.com/d/article.asp?xid=565 (accessed October 18, 2017).

9. Rolling Meadows High School yearbook, 1992.

10. Nancy Dunham, "Leftover Salmon: Celebrating 20 Years, part 2," jambase.com https://www.jambase.com/article/leftover-salmon-celebrating-20-years-part-2 (accessed April , 2015).

11. Nancy Dunham, "Leftover Salmon: Celebrating 20 Years, part 2," jambase.com https://www.jambase.com/article/leftover-salmon-celebrating-20-years-part-2 (accessed April 20, 2015).

CHAPTER 8. JOHN JOY

1. Leftover Salmon. Concert recorded in Dallas, Texas. September 13, 2001.

2. Nancy Dunham, "Leftover Salmon: Celebrating 20 Years," jambase.com, https://www.jambase.com/article/leftover-salmon-20-years-downriver (accessed April 20, 2015).

3. Leftover Salmon. Concert recorded in Boulder, Colorado. November 15, 2001.

4. "Jam Bands Unite for Mark Vann," *Billboard*, November 20, 2001, https://www.billboard.com/articles/news/77679/jam-bands-unite-for-vann-benefit (accessed March 18, 2018).

5. Leftover Salmon. Concert recorded in Denver, Colorado. December 31, 2001.

6. Nancy Dunham, "Leftover Salmon: 20 Years Down River," jam-base.com, http://www.jambase.com/article/leftover-salmon-20-years-down-river (accessed April 20, 2015).

7. Bill Harriman, "Leftover Salmon," swaves.com, http://www.swaves.com/Back_Issues/Sept04/Leftover_Salmon.htm (accessed March 1, 2018.)

8. *Live*. Compass Records. 2002.

9. Scott Caffrey, "Leftover Salmon: The King of Fish," jambase.com, http://www.jambase.com/Articles/6055/LEFTOVER-SALMON-THE-KING-OF-FISH/0 (accessed August 25, 2015).

10. Scott Caffrey, "Leftover Salmon: The King of Fish," jambase.com, http:www.jambase.com/Articles/6055/LEFTOVER-SALMON-THE-KING-OF-FISH/0 (accessed August 25, 2015).

11. "Salmon Migrations; Ripsaw News interview with Leftover Salmon bassist Greg Garrison," *Ripsaw, Duluth*, MN, July 9, 2003, 8.

CHAPTER 9. NOAM PIKELNY

1. Mike Greenhaus, "Noam Pikelny Beats the Devil," jambands.com, http://www.jambands.com/features/2011/11/21/noam-pilkeny-beats-the-devil? 1, November 21, 2011 (accessed November 29, 2017).

2. Jason Verlinde, "Interview: Banjo Innovator Noam Pikelny of the Punch Brothers," *Fretboard Journal*, https://www.fretboardjournal.com/tag/noam-pikelny/, October 2011 (Accessed October 27, 2017).

3. Pat Ferris, "Leftover Salmon—Boulder, Colorado—LIV(e)—A Tribute to Mark Vann," *HotBands*, http://www.hotbands.com/reviews/20021101review.php (accessed December 8, 2016).

4. Nick Hutchinson, "Heating Up," *Westword*, October 31, 2002, http://www.westword.com/music/heating-up-5071944 (accessed April 5, 2017).

5. Mike Greenhaus, "Noam Pikelny Beats the Devil," jambands.com, http://www.jambands.com/features/2011/11/21/noam-pilkeny-beats-the-devil? 1, November 21, 2011 (accessed November 29, 2017).

6. Mike Greenhaus, "Noam Pikelny Beats the Devil," jambands.com, http://www.jambands.com/features/2011/11/21/noam-pilkeny-beats-the-devil? 1, November 21, 2011 (accessed November 29, 2017).

7. Mike Greenhaus, "Noam Pikelny Beats the Devil," jambands.com, http://www.jambands.com/features/2011/11/21/noam-pilkeny-beats-the-devil? 1, November 21, 2011 (accessed November 29, 2017).

8. Mike Greenhaus, "Noam Pikelny Beats the Devil," jambands.com, http://www.jambands.com/features/2011/11/21/noam-pilkeny-beats-the-devil? 1, November 21, 2011 (accessed November 29, 2017).

9. Nick Hutchinson, "Heating Up," *Westword*, October 31, 2002, http://www.westword.com/music/heating-up-5071944 (accessed April 5, 2017).

10. "Salmon Migrations; Ripsaw News Interview with Leftover Salmon Bassist Greg Garrison," *Ripsaw, Duluth*, MN, July 9, 2003, 8.

11. Rick Bell, "Leftover Salmon Reveals New Taste," *Country Standard Time*, www.countrystandardtime.com/d/articlex.asp?xid=565 (accessed August 14, 2017).

12. Nick Hutchinson, "Heating Up," *Westword*, October 31, 2002, http://www.westword.com/music/heating-up-5071944 (accessed April 5, 2017).

13. "On the Road with The Del McCoury Band," *Relix*, December–January 2004, volume 30, #7, 70–71.

14. Scott Caffrey, "Leftover Salmon: The King of Fish," jambase.com, http:/www.jambase.com/Articles/6055/LEFTOVER-SALMON-THE-KING-OF-FISH/0 (accessed August 25, 2015).

15. Mick Skidmore, "O Cracker? An Interview with David Lowery," jambands.com, http://www.jambands.com/features/2003/05/28/o-cracker-an-interview-with-david-lowery, May 28, 2003 (accessed December 1, 2017).

16. Mick Skidmore, "O Cracker? An Interview with David Lowery," jambands.com, http://www.jambands.com/features/2003/05/28/o-cracker-an-interview-with-david-lowery, May 28, 2003 (accessed December 1, 2017).

17. Mick Skidmore, "O Cracker? An Interview with David Lowery," jambands.com, http://www.jambands.com/features/2003/05/28/o-cracker-an-interview-with-david-lowery, May 28, 2003 (accessed December 1, 2017).

18. Nancy Dunham, "Leftover Salmon: 20 Years Down River," jambase.com, http://www.jambase.com/article/leftover-salmon-20-years-down-river (accessed April 20, 2015).

19. Laura Bond, "Backwash; Leftover Salmon's Collaboration with Cracker Goes Swimmingly," *Westword*, May 22, 2003, http://www.westword.com/content/printView/5074564 (accessed March 3, 2018).

20. "Salmon Migrations; Ripsaw News Interview with Leftover Salmon Bassist Greg Garrison," *Ripsaw, Duluth*, MN, July 9, 2003, 8.

21. Nancy Dunham, "Leftover Salmon: 20 Years Down River," jambase.com, http://www.jambase.com/article/leftover-salmon-20-years-down-river (accessed April 20, 2015).

22. Jesse Jarnow, "Leftover Salmon/ Cracker *O Cracker, Where Art Thou?*" *Relix*, June 2003, 82.

23. Mark Pantsari, "The New Face(s) of Leftover Salmon," *Post and Courier*, Charleston, South Carolina, April 22, 2004, F7.

24. Rick Bell, "Leftover Salmon Reveals New Taste," *Country Standard Time*, www.countrystandardtime.com/d/articlex.asp?xid=565 (accessed August 14, 2017).

25. Kevin McKeough, "Carrying on After a Member's Death; Bands Face Tough Question over How—and Whether—to Continue," *Chicago Tribune*, Chicago, Illinois, April 4, 2004, 14.

26. Josh Niva, "Sample a Fresh Catch of Leftover Salmon," *Anchorage Daily News*, Anchorage, Alaska, May 28, 2004, H5

27. Michael Deeds, "Quick Spins," The *Washington Post*, Washington, DC, April 4, 2004; N.10.

28. Scott Caffrey, "Leftover Salmon: The King of Fish," jambase.com, www.jambase.com/Articles/6055/LEFTOVER-SALMON-THE-KING-OF-FISH/0 (accessed August 25, 2015).

29. Scott Caffrey, "Leftover Salmon: The King of Fish," jambase.com, www.jambase.com/Articles/6055/LEFTOVER-SALMON-THE-KING-OF-FISH/0 (accessed August 25, 2015).

30. Stewart Oksenhorn, "Leftover Salmon Plays Aspen," *The Aspen Times*, February 24, 2011, http://www.aspentimes.com/news/leftover-salmon-plays-aspen/ (accessed October 16, 2017).

31. Scott Caffrey, "Leftover Salmon: The King of Fish," jambase.com, http:www.jambase.com/Articles/6055/LEFTOVER-SALMON-THE-KING-OF-FISH/0 (accessed August 25, 2015).

32. Dunham, Nancy. "Leftover Salmon: 20 Years Down River." jambase.com, http://www.jambase.com/article/leftover-salmon-20-years-down-river.

33. Scott Caffrey, "Leftover Salmon: The King of Fish," jambase.com, www.jambase.com/Articles/6055/LEFTOVER-SALMON-THE-KING-OF-FISH/0 (accessed August 25, 2015).

34. Bill Harriman, "Leftover Salmon," swaves.com, http://www.swaves.com/Back_Issues/Sept04/Leftover_Salmon.htm (accessed March 1, 2018).

CHAPTER 10. ANDY THORN

1. http://www.markvannfoundation.org.

2. Missy Votel, "A Summer Fling in the 'Grass; Broke Mountain Bluegrass Band Picks its Way into Local Music Scene." *Durango Telegraph*, Vol. 2, # 27, July 3–9, 2003, 11.

3. Leftover Salmon. Concert recorded in Telluride, Colorado. June 24, 2007.

4. Leftover Salmon. Concert recorded in Telluride, Colorado. June 24, 2007.

5. Yonder Mountain String Band. Concert recorded in Horning Hideout, Oregon. July 19, 2008.

6. Yonder Mountain String Band. Concert recorded in Horning Hideout, Oregon. July 19, 2008.

7. Justin Sachs, "Leftover Salmon: Diving Back In," *Relix*, December 21, 2011, https://www.relix.com/articles/detail/leftover-salmon-diving-back-in (accessed January 12, 2017).

8. David Accomazzo, "Different Recipe, Same Great Taste," *Boulder Weekly*, May 10–16, 2012, 18–21.

9. Wendy Kale, "Leftover Salmon's Bill McKay Arrested on Sex Charge," *Daily Camera*, January 21, 2009, http://www.dailycamera.com/ci_12954833 (accessed March 25, 2018).

10. Colorado Daily Staff, "Emmitt: McKay Not Out of Salmon," *Daily Camera*, January 22, 2009, http://www.dailycamera.com/ci_12954895 (accessed March 25, 2018).

11. Philip Booth, "Leftover Salmon: *Aquatic Hitchhiker*," *Relix*, June 18, 2012, https://www.relix.com/reviews/detail/leftover-salmon-aquatic-hitchhiker (accessed March 15, 2018).

CHAPTER 11. ALWYN ROBINSON

1. "Leftover Salmon, *Aquatic Hitchhiker*," *Bluegrass Unlimited*, September 1, 2012, http://bluegrassmusic.com/content/2012/reviews/leftover-salmon-aquatic-hitchhiker/ (accessed March 2, 2018).

2. Bill Whiting, "*Aquatic Hitchhiker* by Leftover Salmon," *Cincy Groove*, October 14, 2012, http://www.cincygroove.com/?p=10245 (accessed March 2, 2018).

3. Jedd Ferris, "Leftover Salmon: *Aquatic Hitchhiker*," *Blurt Magazine*, http://blurtonline.com/review/leftover-salmon-aquatic-hitchhiker/ (accessed March 1, 2018).

4. Dave Kirby, "Salmon Steaks, Over Easy," *Boulder Weekly*, November 28, 2013, 29.

5. Charlie Brennan, "A Year Later, Friends and Family of Boulder's Joe Cahill Ask: 'What the Hell Happened?" *Boulder News*, April 28, 2014, http://www.dailycamera.com/news/boulder/ci_25634102/joe-cahill-boulder-shooting-new-orleans-investigation (accessed February 16, 2018).

6. Charlie Brennan, "A Year Later, Friends and Family of Boulder's Joe Cahill Ask: 'What the Hell Happened?" *Boulder News*, April 28, 2014, http://

www.dailycamera.com/news/boulder/ci_25634102/joe-cahill-boulder-shooting-new-orleans-investigation (accessed February 16, 2018).

7. Charlie Brennan, "A Year Later, Friends and Family of Boulder's Joe Cahill Ask: 'What the Hell Happened?'" *Boulder News*, April 28, 2014, http://www.dailycamera.com/news/boulder/ci_25634102/joe-cahill-boulder-shooting-new-orleans-investigation (accessed February 16, 2018).

8. Charlie Brennan, "A Year Later, Friends and Family of Boulder's Joe Cahill Ask: 'What the Hell Happened?'" *Boulder News*, April 28, 2014, http://www.dailycamera.com/news/boulder/ci_25634102/joe-cahill-boulder-shooting-new-orleans-investigation (accessed February 16, 2018).

9. Dave Kirby, "Salmon Steaks, Over Easy," *Boulder Weekly*, November 28, 2013, 29.

10. Dave Kirby, "Salmon Steaks, Over Easy," *Boulder Weekly*, November 28, 2013, 29.

11. Chad Berndtson, "The Art of the Sit-in with Vince Herman," jambase.com, https://www.jambase.com/article/the-art-of-the-sit-in-vince-herman-leftover-salmon (accessed March 7, 2018).

12. Dean Budnick, "Track by Track: Leftover Salmon *High Country*," *Relix*, March 2, 2015,

13. Sam D'Arcangelo, "Leftover Salmon: *High Country*," *Relix*, December 1, 2014, https://www.relix.com/reviews/detail/leftover_salmon_high_country#ixzz5B3evj4vL (accessed March 14, 2018).

14. "Leftover Salmon: *High Country*," *Marquee Magazine*, December 1, 2014, http://marqueemag.com/2014/12/leftover-salmon-high-country/ (accessed March 28, 2018).

CHAPTER 12. ERIK DEUTSCH

1. Greensky Bluegrass. Concert recorded in Morrison, Colorado. July 23, 2016.

2. Sam Berenson, "Something Higher: An Interview with Leftover Salmon's Vince Herman," jambase.com, April 5, 2018, https://www.jambase.com/article/vince-herman-leftover-salmon-interview (accessed April 8, 2018).

3. Abby Jones, "Leftover Salmon Premiere new video for Folksy New Single, 'Southern Belle,'" Billboard, April 4, 2018, https://www.billboard.com/articles/columns/rock/8289664/leftover-salmon-video-single-southern-belle (accessed April 11, 2018).

4. "Leftover Salmon: Something Higher," *Marquee Magazine*, April 1, 2018, http://marqueemag.com/2018/04/leftover-salmon-something-higher/ (accessed April 11, 2018).

5. Jeff Tamarkin, "Leftover Salmon: Something Higher." *Relix*, https://www.relix.com/reviews/detail/leftover_salmon_something_higher, May 4, 2018 (accessed May 5, 2018).

6. Dan Maser, "Mark Vann: Playing Banjo in a Rock 'n' Roll Band!" Banjo Newsletter, December 2000.

7. Sam Berenson, "Something Higher: An Interview with Leftover Salmon's Vince Herman," jambase.com, April 5, 2018, https://www.jambase.com/article/vince-herman-leftover-salmon-interview (accessed April 8, 2018).

CHAPTER 13. LEFTOVER SALMON

1. Leftover Salmon. Concert recorded at Bonnaroo Music in Manchester, Tennessee. June 13, 2004.

2. Nancy Dunham, "Leftover Salmon: 20 Years Down the River," Jambase.com, http://www.jambase.com/article/leftover-salmon-20-years-down-river (accessed September 20, 2016).

3. Timothy Dwenger and Brian F. Johnson, "Leftover Salmon Turns 20 on New Year's: Industry Insiders Share Their Memories," *Marquee Magazine*, December 1, 2009. http://marqueemag.com/2009/12/leftover-salmon/ (accessed September 12, 2017).

4. Nancy Dunham, "Leftover Salmon: 20 Years Down the River," Jambase.com, http://www.jambase.com/article/leftover-salmon-20-years-down-river (accessed September 20, 2016).

5. Nancy Dunham, "Leftover Salmon: 20 Years Down the River," Jambase.com, http://www.jambase.com/article/leftover-salmon-20-years-down-river (accessed September 20, 2016).

6. Nancy Dunham, "Leftover Salmon: 20 Years Down the River," Jambase.com, http://www.jambase.com/article/leftover-salmon-20-years-down-river (accessed September 20, 2016).

BIBLIOGRAPHY

INTERVIEWS

Leftover Salmon:
Erik Deutsch, Drew Emmitt, Greg Garrison, Vince Herman, John Joy, Alwyn Robinson, and Andy Thorn.

Leftover Salmon past members:
Chris Engleman, Joe Jogerst, Tye North, Bill Payne, Johnny Pfarr, and Jeff Sipe.

Friends and fellow musicians:
Eric Abramson, Adam Aijala, Andrew Altman, Jeff Austin, Eric Avey, Jim Baldwin, Danny Barnes, Anders Beck, Steve Berlin, Bobby Britt, Steve Burnside, Sam Bush, Emily Cantrell, Chris Castino, Phil Chorney, Aaron Comess, Joe Craven, Rob Derhak, Vince Farsetta, Reed Foehl, Bob Gabing, Jeremy Garrett, John Ginty, Al Goll, Tyler Grant, Adam Greuel, Bruce Hampton, Jimmy Herring, Chuck Hirshberg, Dave Johnston, Dave Katz, Larry Keel, Ben Kaufmann, Annabel Lukins, Jeep MacNichol, Mark Mercier, Chuck Morris, Keith Moseley, Jeff Mosier, Chris Mrachek, Tim O'Brien, Jim Page, Lew Prichard, Dango Rose, James "Fuzz" Sangiovanni, Ed Schaeffer, Michael Slingsby, Greg Spatz, Chad Staehly, Jon Stickley, Dave Watts, and Keller Williams.

BOOKS

Brown, G. *Colorado Rocks! A Half-Century of Music in Colorado*. Portland: Westwind Press, 2004.

Budnick, Dean. *Jambands: The Complete Guide to the Players, Music, & Scene*. San Francisco: Backbeat Books, 2003.

———. *Jam Bands: North America's Hottest Live Groups*. Toronto: ECW Press, 1998.

Conners, Peter. *JAMerica: The History of the Jam Band and Festival Scene*. Philadelphia: Da Capo Press, 2013.

Fong-Torres, Ben. *Willin': The Story of Little Feat*. Philadelphia: Da Capo Press, 2013.

Jackson, Blair. *Garcia: An American Life*. New York: Penguin Press, 2000.

King, Carole. *A Natural Woman: A Memoir*. New York: Grand Central Publishing, 2012.

———. *The Phish Companion: A Guide to the Band and their Music*, 2nd edition. San Francisco: Backbeat Books 2003.

Puterbaugh, Parke. *Phish: The Biography*. Philadelphia: Da Capo Press 2009.

Rosenberg, Neil. *Bluegrass: A History*. Urbana: University of Illinois Press, 1985.

MAGAZINES, NEWSPAPERS, AND ONLINE ARTICLES

Accomazzo, David. "Different Recipe, Same Great Taste." *Boulder Weekly*, May 10–16, 2012.

Bell, Rick. "Leftover Salmon Reveals New Taste." *Country Standard Time*, May 2004, http://www.countrystandardtime.com/d/article.asp?xid=565.

Berenson, Sam. "Something Higher: An Interview with Leftover Salmon's Vince Herman." jambase.com, April 5, 2018, https://www.jambase.com/article/vince-herman-leftover-salmon-interview.

Berndtson, Chad. "The Art of the Sit-in with Vince Herman." jambase.com, https://www.jambase.com/article/the-art-of-the-sit-in-vince-herman-leftover-salmon.

Bond, Laura. "Backwash: Leftover Salmon's Collaboration with Cracker Goes Swimmingly." *Westword*, May 22, 2003, http://www.westword.com/content/printView/5074564.

Booth, Phillip. "Leftover Salmon: Aquatic Hitchhiker." *Relix*, June 18, 2012, https://www.relix.com/reviews/detail/leftover-salmon-aquatic-hitchhiker.

Brennan, Charlie. "A Year Later, Friends and Family of Boulder's Joe Cahill Ask: 'What the Hell Happened?" *Boulder News*, April 28, 2014, http://www.dailycamera.com/news/boulder/ci_25634102/joe-cahill-boulder-shooting-new-orleans-investigation.

Brown, Mark. "Leftover Salmon Swimming with Some Big Fish." *Rocky Mountain News*, December 31, 1999.

Bruce, Benjamin. "On the Road: The Buzz in Boulder, Shanti Groove." *Relix*, September–October 2004.

Budnick, Dean. "Breakin' Thru: Drew Emmitt & Leftover Salmon Enter New Realms." jambands.com, http://www.jambands.com/features/1999/12/15/breakin-thru-drew-emmitt-leftover-salmon-enter-new-realms.

———. "H.O.R.D.E. 20 Years On." *Relix*, April/May 2012.

———. "jam band, Jam-Band, Jamband: How We Got There and Why It Matters (Somewhat)." *Relix*, December–January 2004.

———. "Track by Track: Leftover Salmon *High Country*." *Relix*, March 2, 2015,

———. "What Is a Jam Band?" jambands.com, https://web.archive.org/web/20070124191643/http://www.jambands.com/jamband.html.

BurnSilver, Glenn. "How 5 Ski Bums Captured the USA." *Relix*, December 2001.

Caffrey, Scott. "Leftover Salmon: The King of Fish." jambase.com, http://www.jambase.com/Articles/6055/LEFTOVER-SALMON-THE-KING-OF-FISH/0.

Chester, Jack. "Yonder Mountain String Band & the Many Lives of Bluegrass." *Relix*, July 2003.

Colorado Daily Staff. "Emmitt: McKay Not Out of Salmon." *Daily Camera*, January 22, 2009.

Corbett, Ben. "Local Jamgrass Vets Leftover Salmon Celebrate 20 Years Together." *Boulder Weekly*, December 31, 2009.

Crowe, Cameron. "Carole King and Navarro Mellow Out." *Rolling Stone*, September 22, 1977.

D'Arcangelo, Sam. "Leftover Salmon: *High Country*." *Relix*, December 1, 2014, https://www.relix.com/reviews/detail/leftover_salmon_high_country#ixzz5B3evj4vL.

Deeds, Michael. "Quick Spins." *Washington Post*, April 4, 2004.

Dunham, Nancy. "Leftover Salmon: 20 Years Down River." jambase.com, http://www.jambase.com/article/leftover-salmon-20-years-down-river.

Dwenger, Timothy and Brian F. Johnson. "Leftover Salmon Turns 20 on New Year's: Industry Insiders Share Their Memories." *Marquee Magazine*, December 1, 2009. http://marqueemag.com/2009/12/leftover-salmon/.

Dwyer, Audrey. "Leftover Salmon Returns to Celebrate Ski Season." *Steamboat Today*, http://www.steamboattoday.com/news/2016/apr/07/leftover-salmon-back-town-celebrate-2015-2016-ski-/.

Elkins, Elizabeth. "Pop Music—Preview—Leftover Salmon." *The Atlanta Journal-Constitution*, October 4, 1996.

Ellis, Bill. "Recordings." *The Commercial Appeal*, May 3, 1997.

Findlay, Prentiss. "Euphoric Salmon Swim to the Farm." *The Post and Courier*; August 21, 1997.

Ferris, Jedd. "Leftover Salmon: *Aquatic Hitchhiker*." *Blurt Magazine*, http://blurtonline.com/review/leftover-salmon-aquatic-hitchhiker/.

Ferris, Pat. "Leftover Salmon—Boulder, Colorado—LIV(e)—A Tribute to Mark Vann." *HotBands*, http://www.hotbands.com/reviews/20021101review.php.

Frater, Bill. "Keeping the Dead Alive with Tim Lynch." *No Depression*, http://nodepression.com/article/keeping-dead-alive-tim-lynch.

Freeman, Dave. "Leftover Salmon - From Bill Monroe to Led Zep." *Fort Worth Star-Telegram*, February 7, 1997.

Giles, Jeff. "Spin Doctors: Miracle Cure." *Rolling Stone*, January 7, 1993.

Greenhaus, Mike. "Noam Pikelny Beats the Devil." jambands.com, http://www.jambands.com/features/2011/11/21/noam-pikelny-beats-the-devil?1, November 21, 2011.

Hagenah, Margaret. "Leftover Salmon: *Bridges to Bert*." *The Stanford Daily*, May 4, 1995.

Halsey, Derek. "The Best Jam I Ever Heard: Vince Herman." *The Bluegrass Situation*, http://www.thebluegrasssituation.com/read/best-jam-i-ever-heard-vince-herman.

Harriman, Bill. "Leftover Salmon." swaves.com, http://www.swaves.com/Back_Issues/Sept04/Leftover_Salmon.htm.

Himes, Geoffrey. "The Nitty Gritty on Leftover Salmon." *Washington Post*, November 19, 1999.

Hogan, Candace. "Leftover Salmon Taper's Reel." *Relix*, June 1998.

Howie, Allen. "Bridges to Bert" Polyethnic Cajun Slamgrass." *Louisville Music News*, August 1995, http://www.louisvillemusicnews.net/webmanager/index.php?WEB_CAT_ID=50&storyid=11698&headline=Leftover_Salmon_%96_Bridges_TO_Bert:_Polyethnic_Caju&issueid=78.

Husted, Bill. "Name's Fishy, But Leftover Salmon Doesn't Stink." *Denver Post*, July 6, 1997.

Hutchinson, Nick. "Heating Up." *Westword*, October 31, 2002, http://www.westword.com/music/heating-up-5071944.

———. "Q&A with Vince Herman of Leftover Salmon." *Westword*, http://www.westword.com/music/qanda-with-vince-herman-of-leftover-salmon-5708191.

———. "Jamband Extravaganza." *Guitar World*, August 1997.

———. "Jam Bands Unite for Mark Vann." *Billboard*, November 20, 2001, https://www.billboard.com/articles/news/77679/jam-bands-unite-for-vann-benefit.

Jarnow, Jesse. "Leftover Salmon/Cracker *O Cracker, Where Art Thou?*" *Relix*, June 2003.

Johnson, McClain. "Leftover Salmon Interview." McClainJohnson.com, https://mcclainjohnson.com/leftover-salmon-interview/.

Jones, Abby. "Leftover Salmon Premiere new video for Folksy New Single, 'Southern Belle.'" *Billboard*, April 4, 2018, https://www.billboard.com/articles/columns/rock/8289664/leftover-salmon-video-single-southern-belle.

Justesen, Lizzy. "Interview: Leftover Salmon." jambase.com, https://www.jambase.com/article/interview-leftover-salmon.

Kale, Wendy. "Leftover Salmon's Bill McKay Arrested on Sex Charge." *Daily Camera*, January 21, 2009.

Keller, Jared. "An Oral History of the Telluride Bluegrass Festival." *Outside Online*, https://www.outsideonline.com/1916561/oral-history-telluride-bluegrass-festival.

Kirby, Dave. "Salmon Steaks, Over Easy." *Boulder Weekly*, November 28, 2013.

———. "Strum Together: Yonder Mountain String Band and Leftover Salmon Bring Strings and Things to Red Rocks." *Boulder Weekly*, August 26, 2010.

Knopper, Steve. "Boulder Band Goofy But Professional." *Daily Camera Friday Magazine*, July 17, 1992.

Lach, Jeremy. "Interview w/ Vince Herman and Drew Emmitt of Leftover Salmon." stringcheeseradio.com, http://stringcheeseradio.com/interviews/interview-w-vince-herman-drew-emmitt-of-leftover-salmon.

Langer, Abby. "From Commune to Congress House: Mark Hallman." *Austin Chronicle*, November 8, 1996.

Lawrence, Keith. "Take a Bite of Leftover Salmon." *The Ledger*, November 9, 1999.

———. "Leftover Salmon." *Dupree's Diamond News*, Fall-Winter 97.

———. "Leftover Salmon, *Aquatic Hitchhiker*." *Bluegrass Unlimited*, September 1, 2012, http://bluegrassmusic.com/content/2012/reviews/leftover-salmon-aquatic-hitchhiker/.

———. "Leftover Salmon: *High Country*." *Marquee Magazine*, December 1, 2014, http://marqueemag.com/2014/12/leftover-salmon-high-country/.

———. "Leftover Salmon: *Something Higher*." *Marquee Magazine*, April 1, 2018, http://marqueemag.com/2018/04/leftover-salmon-something-higher/.

Lomax, Alan. "Bluegrass Background: Folk Music with Overdrive." *Esquire*, October 1959.

Mannion, Kate. "Leftover Salmon Servings Invigorate Ziggy's Crowd." *High Point University Campus Chronicle*, October 8, 1998.

Maser, Dan. "Mark Vann: Playing Banjo in a Rock 'n' Roll Band!" *Banjo Newsletter*, December 2000.

Mehle, Michael. "All Downstream from Here? Leftover Salmon Latest Has a Shot at Cracking Country Radio." *Rocky Mountain News*, October 1, 1999.

———. "Leftover Salmon Finally in the Pink." *Rocky Mountain News*, March 14, 1997.

McGill, Sarah. "The Stage Stop: Rollinsville's Neighborhood Bar Since 1868." *Westword*, March 22, 2018, http://www.westword.com/restaurants/the-stage-stop-in-rollinsville-is-one-of-colorados-oldest-bars-10104268.

McKeough, Kevin. "Carrying on After a Member's Death: Bands Face Tough Question over How—and Whether—to Continue." *Chicago Tribune*, April 4, 2004.

Metzger, John. "Leftover Salmon—*The Nashville Sessions*." *The Music Box*, December 1999, http://www.musicbox-online.com/ls-nash.html#axzz4wWVzcDcD.

Niva, Josh. "Sample a Fresh Catch of Leftover Salmon." *Anchorage Daily News*, May 28, 2004.

Newby, Tim. "Honey Dewdrops: Heartfelt, Honest Songs." *Honest Tune*, January 24, 2011, http://www.honesttune.com/honey-dewdrops-heartfelt-honest-songs/.

———. "Jeff Mosier: Lessons Learned." *Honest Tune*, March 20, 2008, https://honesttune.com/jeffmosierlessonslearned/.

———. "On the Road with The Del McCoury Band." *Relix*, December-January 2004.

Oksenhorn, Stewart. "Leftover Salmon plays Aspen." *The Aspen Times*, February 24, 2011, http://www.aspentimes.com/news/leftover-salmon-plays-aspen/.

Orman, Christopher. "Freedom Ride: Drew Emmitt." jambands.com, http://www.jambands.com/reviews/cds/2002/03/20/freedom-ride-drew-emmitt.

———. "It Felt Great to Play Bluegrass Again: An Interview with Drew Emmitt." jambands.com, http://www.jambands.com/features/2002/05/21/it-felt-great-to-play-bluegrass-again-an-interview-with-drew-emmitt.

Pantsari, Mark. "The New Face(s) of Leftover Salmon." *Post and Courier*, April 22, 2004.

Phillips, Casey. "Q&A with Drew Emmitt of the Jamgrass Band Leftover Salmon." *Chattanooga Times Free Press*, April 20, 2012. http://www.timesfreepress.com/news/chattanooganow/music/story/2012/apr/20/q-drew-emmitt-jamgrass-band-leftover-salmon/75922/.

Price, Deborah Evans. "They're Playing My Song." *Billboard Magazine*, October 30, 1999.

Sachs, Justin. "Leftover Salmon: Diving Back In." *Relix*, December 21, 2011, https://www.relix.com/articles/detail/leftover-salmon-diving-back-in.

———. "Salmon Migrations; Ripsaw News Interview with Leftover Salmon Bassist Greg Garrison." *Ripsaw*, July 9, 2003.

Schlansky, Evan. "Market Value: A Q & A with Leftover Salmon." *American Songwriter*, http://americansongwriter.com/2012/04/market-value-a-qa-with-leftover-salmon/.

Skidmore, Mick. "Now, Then, and In Between." *Relix*, December 1999.

———. "O Cracker? An Interview with David Lowery." jambands.com, http://www.jambands.com/features/2003/05/28/o-cracker-an-interview-with-david-lowery May 28, 2003.

Taco. "Jamwich Exclusive Interview with Larry Keel." *Appalachian Jamwich*, http://www.appalachianjamwich.com/2012/07/10/jamwich-exclusive-interview-with-larry-keel/.

Tamarkin, Jeff. "Leftover Salmon: Something Higher." *Relix*, https://www.relix.com/reviews/detail/leftover_salmon_something_higher, May 4, 2018.

———. "Tye North." *Digital Interviews* www.digitalinterviews.com/digitalinterviews/views/north.shtml.

Verlinde, Jason. "Interview: Banjo Innovator Noam Pikelny of the Punch Brothers." *Fretboard Journal*, https://www.fretboardjournal.com/tag/noam-pikelny/, October 2011.

Votel, Missy. "A Summer Fling in the 'Grass; Broke Mountain Bluegrass Band Picks Its Way into Local Music Scene." *Durango Telegraph*, July 3–9, 2003.

Wallace, Eric J. "The Greatest, Most Original Guitar Player You've Never Heard Of." *The Piedmont Virginian*, http://piedmontvirginian.com/2016/02/on-the-trail-of-larry-keel/.

Whiting, Bill. "*Aquatic Hitchhiker* by Leftover Salmon." *Cincy Groove*, October 14, 2012, http://www.cincygroove.com/?p=10245.

WEBSITES

Galloway, Benny "Bio," Facebook.com, https://www.facebook.com/bennyburlegalloway/about/ (accessed October 21, 2016).

Telluride Tom's Homepage, http://www.telluridetom.com/ (accessed June 3, 2016).

"Trey Anastasio tells Bobby Weir About Life-Changing Concert," YouTube.com, https://www.youtube.com/watch?v=90ItoM-wrmc (accessed October 24, 2016).

LINER NOTES

Bridges to Bert. Hollywood Records, 1997.
High Country. LoS Records, 2014.
Live. Compass Records. 2002.
Nashville Sessions. Hollywood Records, 1999.

LIVE RECORDINGS

Greensky Bluegrass. Concert recorded in Morrison, Colorado. July 23, 2016. Author's Collection.

Left Hand String Band. Concert recorded at Strawberry Bluegrass Festival, Camp Mather, California, September 9, 1991. Author's collection.

Leftover Salmon. Concert recorded in Boulder, Colorado. April 16, 1993. Author's collection.

Leftover Salmon. Concert recorded in Warrenton, Virginia, August 3, 1996. Author's collection.

Leftover Salmon. Concert recorded in Tahoe City, California. July 9, 1997. Author's Collection.

Leftover Salmon. Concert recorded in Macon, Georgia. March 31, 1999. Author's collection.

Leftover Salmon. Concert recorded in Dallas, Texas. September 13, 2001. Author's Collection.

Leftover Salmon. Concert recorded in Boulder, Colorado. November 15, 2001. Author's collection.

Leftover Salmon. Concert recorded in Denver, Colorado. December 31, 2001. Author's collection.

Leftover Salmon. Concert recorded at Bonnaroo Music in Manchester, Tennessee. June 13, 2004. Author's collection.

Leftover Salmon. Concert recorded in Telluride, Colorado. June 24, 2007. Author's collection.

Trey Anastasio Band. Concert recorded at Delfest, Cumberland, Maryland. May 24, 2013. Author's Collection.

Vince Herman. Interview with Daniel Gold, Fayetteville, Arkansas, June 5, 2001, broadcast on KXUA radio. Author's collection.

Vince Herman. Interview with Daniel Gold, Fayetteville, Arkansas, March 16, 2002, broadcast on KXUA radio. Author's collection.

Yonder Mountain String Band. Concert recorded in Horning Hideout, Oregon. July 19, 2008. Author's collection.

DVD

Basically Frightened. Directed by Michael Koepnick. 2012. Guillotine Pictures.

Leftover Salmon Live: Celebrating 20 Years. Directed by Bob and Fritz Ross. 2009. Riffactory.

Years in Your Ears . . . a Story of Leftover Salmon. Directed by Eric Abramson. 2006. Years in Your Ears.

INDEX

ABOUT THE AUTHOR

Tim Newby is the author of *Bluegrass in Baltimore: The Hard Drivin' Sound and Its Legacy* as well as a contributor to publications such as *Relix*, *Paste Magazine*, *Honest Tune*, *Glide Magazine*, *B'More Live*, and *Music Monthly*. His broad knowledge and personal experiences with the emerging jam scene and Leftover Salmon provide him with an especially deep background and skill set with which to write this book.